Fundamentals of Curriculum

PASSION AND PROFESSIONALISM

Second Edition

Decker F. Walker

Stanford University

LEA

2003

Lawrence Erlbaum Associates, Publishers

Mahwah, New Jersey   London

Senior Acquisitions Editor:	Naomi Silverman
Textbook Marketing Manager:	Marisol Kozlovski
Editorial Assistant (or Assistant Editor):	Lori Hawver
Cover Design:	Kathryn Houghtaling Lacey
Textbook Production Manager:	Paul Smolenski
Full Service Composition:	TechBooks
Text and Cover Printer:	Hamilton Printing Company

This book was typeset in 10.25/12 pt. Goudy
The heads were typeset in Optima and Goudy

Lawrence Erlbaum Associates, Inc., Publishers
10 Industrial Avenue
Mahwah, NJ 07430

Library of Congress Cataloging-in-Publication Data

Walker, Decker F.
Fundamentals of curriculum : passion and professionalism / Decker F. Walker.
—2nd ed.
        p.   cm.
Includes bibliographical references and index.
ISBN 0-8058-3502-4 (alk. paper)
1. Curriculum planning—United States. 2. Education—United States—Curricula.
    I. Title.
LB2806.15 .W35   2003
375'.001'0973—dc21   2002011441
                                                                                   CIP

Printed in the United States of America
10   9   8   7   6   5   4   3   2

Brief Table of Contents

Table of Contents

PART 2
Practice

Preface

The Curriculum Problem

What a society should teach their children is one of those nasty but wonderful problems that is impossible to solve and impossible to avoid. We can't teach everything. It's too much. On the other hand, if as a society we try to wash our hands of the problem, it just shows up elsewhere. Parents, individually and in their various groups—ethnic, religious, geographical, occupational, and so on—now face the very same problem. There's no avoiding the need to choose. Somehow, through its institutions, society must select from the unimaginably vast store of human knowledge and the immense expanse of arts, crafts, and techniques some few precious things that can be taught and learned in childhood.

From a strictly rational perspective the problem looks hopeless. What criteria should we use? If we think of the welfare of society, should we teach for military might, material well-being, political unity, religious salvation, or cultural excellence? If we think of the welfare of individual students, which virtues should we emphasize—health, courage, kindness, learning, wisdom, or happiness? What tough questions! Can there be a rational, objective way to decide such questions?

When we look at the problem socially and culturally, though, it looks trivial, at least for stable traditional societies. We teach our children what our parents taught us—our language, customs, history, religion, arts, crafts, industries, and so on. We might have to consider whether our generation should add something to the curriculum for the next generation, but this is a kind of question of customs that our traditional institutions manage easily. The conclusion of this line of thought is that social and cultural change make the curriculum problem hard. Stability makes it easy.

American society is the most dynamic society ever, so solving the curriculum problem is especially hard for us. That we are a multicultural society in which many individuals and communities follow traditional ways of life, many different traditions, makes the problem of finding a national curriculum that much harder. That we are immersed in an ever-accelerating global economy in an ever-shrinking world makes it not only harder but also more urgent.

Curriculum problems today are closer to the heartbeat of American society than they have ever been. They are central to our economic welfare, to the vitality of our democratic political institutions, to the vexing problem of the place of religion in public life, and to the character of our intellectual and cultural life. As the social fabric is stretched and ripped by change, innovators call for a new curriculum to prepare children for the New World while traditionalists call for repair and restoration. Who are we? Who do we want our children to be? What kind of world shall we prepare our children for?

The urgency and importance of curriculum problems is greater than ever before. Americans are not going to turn these problems over to professionals, but professional roles are crucial nevertheless. Professional curriculum expertise will be needed to solve these problems. The need for sound professional curriculum work is greater than ever.

Who is this Book for?

I wrote this book for readers who want to improve what teachers teach and students learn in American classrooms and schools. I imagined that some readers would be brought to the study of curriculum by passion and some by professionalism. A passion for helping high school students learn to use their minds in powerful ways brought me to it many years ago. Your passion will probably be different. Perhaps you have a passion for improving the lives of children or for social justice, community, self-expression, multiculturalism, the arts, languages, history, writing, mathematics, science, technology, religion, or similar ideals. Perhaps it is professionalism more than passion that brings you to the study of curriculum. You may be studying it to prepare to be a counselor, principal, teacher educator, state or federal education official, evaluator, researcher, or the like. Some authority may have required you to take a course in curriculum for your degree or professional certification. Both passion and professionalism are commendable motives for curriculum work. One of the themes of the book is that passion and professionalism enhance each other and that effective curriculum work requires both.

The reader I have kept primarily in mind already has some experience with curriculum matters. The more experience you have had, the better. You have at least worked with a curriculum as a classroom teacher. You may have seen an innovative curriculum being planned and may even have participated in making or implementing one. You want to make a difference. You want your curriculum work to succeed. You want the curriculums you work on to turn out as you intended rather than to backfire or morph into something you don't recognize. You want them to last, to grow, to spread, and not to be erased by the next wave of change. You want to make a difference, but you don't want to commit a blunder that disrupts your school or ignites a controversy that divides your school or community.

I think of people who do curriculum work in schools as the primary professionals in curriculum, for they are the ones whose work most directly affects what students experience. Their job titles may be teacher, lead teacher, head teacher, department chair, principal, assistant or associate principal, head, supervisor, director or coordinator of curriculum, or assistant or associate superintendent, but they do curriculum work. This book is primarily for them. It is also for other curriculum professionals whose work informs, enhances, and supports theirs—teacher educators, curriculum developers, curriculum reformers, theorists, scholars, researchers, and teachers of professional courses in curriculum.

Most readers will be teachers or former teachers, but some will have come to curriculum studies by a different path. Parents working to improve their child's school, school liaisons from community organizations, volunteers on loan from industry, and scholars or researcher interested in applying their expertise to curriculum questions have all made important contributions to curriculum. If any of these descriptions fit you, this book should help you achieve your professional goals.

Why this Book?

Graduate students and teachers of introductory graduate courses in curriculum have many textbooks to choose from, so who needs another one? During three decades of teaching graduate courses in curriculum, I have struggled to find a book that adequately introduces the subject to serious professionals at the graduate level. I found many impressive books on curriculum theory that say little or nothing about curriculum practice and many well-written books for practitioners that leave out theory and research or give them a lick and a promise. In teaching I have tried to make the best of the situation by giving in-depth attention to a few curriculum problems using original curriculum documents, then adding a few lectures about more general themes. This approach has many benefits but it sacrifices the broad, comprehensive understanding that I feel is vital for responsible curriculum practice and scholarship.

In the 10 years I spent writing the first edition of *Fundamentals of Curriculum*, published in 1990, I tried to write the book that I wanted to teach with—an introduction that is comprehensive, scholarly, and professional. I have used the first edition of the book in teaching many times since then and corresponded with colleagues who have used it. My confidence in the vision of curriculum studies that informed the first edition has grown. This revised edition has given me a welcome opportunity to clarify and extend this vision.

What's Distinctive About this Book?

Four words sum up the distinctive qualities of this book: comprehensive, rigorous, practical, and professional.

Comprehensive

This book is comprehensive in that it acquaints readers with the major schools of thought, the major value systems, the major lines of activity, and the major forms of inquiry in the field. Clearly, it is impossible to cover the field of curriculum studies in one volume. It is not even possible in one volume merely to mention all of the important types of work. A single volume can, however, be comprehensive in the sense of providing an entry into all the major forms of thought, inquiry, and practice. Readers may not find between these covers everything that will be important to them in their study of curriculum, but they should at least meet the important things and find out how they can learn more about them.

Rigorous

The book is rigorous in several ways. First, it cites and describes the most rigorous research and scholarship on curriculum questions. Every chapter presents research relevant to the topic of the chapter. Second, it uses research and scholarship to ground discussions of curriculum questions. Discussions of teaching with a curriculum are grounded in research on teaching, discussions of curriculum development by research on development, and so on. Third, in Chapter 5 on curriculum studies it introduces readers to the considerations involved in doing rigorous studies of curriculum questions.

I believe strongly that the introductory graduate level course in curriculum should introduce students to research and scholarship. Some programs leave research for advanced seminars in later years. I think that inquiry is so central to curriculum studies that it is not possible to introduce the subject adequately without it. The sooner students about to enter the field encounter research and scholarship, the sooner they can begin developing the skills and knowledge they will need to design and carry out studies that meet rigorous standards of inquiry.

Many curriculum questions are deep and difficult. Curriculum work is multivalued, complex, and varied. There are no recipes, no formulas. I have tried to acknowledge the difficulties and tried not to oversimplify. On the other hand, scholars and researchers sometimes increase the difficulties with technical terminology and unnecessary abstraction. I have done my best to minimize these and to write in a clear, straightforward style accessible to any college graduate.

Practical

This book is practical in two senses of the term. First, it is focused on curriculum practice. Theory, research, and other important facets of curriculum studies are presented as vitally important to practice, but the primary subject of the book is what teachers and others do that students experience. The book is practical also in a more philosophical sense. Philosophers since Aristotle have distinguished between theoretical questions whose object is finding the truth and practical questions whose object is deciding what to do. This book takes the fundamental questions of curriculum studies to be practical questions and the primary task of curriculum inquiry to be informing decisions about what to do.

This focus on the practical runs against prevailing trends to focus on theory in Curriculum Studies. Over the past scholarly generation, the focus on curriculum improvement that formerly characterized the field of curriculum has shifted to a focus on theory. Pinar, Reynolds, Slattery, and Taubman in *Understanding Curriculum* (1995) state that the curriculum field "is no longer preoccupied with development . . . [T]he field today is preoccupied with *understanding*. . . . It is necessary to understand the contemporary field as discourse, as text, and most simply but profoundly as words and ideas" (p. 7). The discourse that preoccupies the curriculum field today is primarily about values. Purpel and Shapiro in *Beyond Liberation and Excellence: Reconstructing the Public Discourse on Education* (1995), for instance, write about preparing teachers "who reflect on, and understand, the broader human and social purposes of what they do" and have "consciousness and conscience about the fundamental values that [they are] trying to initiate in the classroom" (pp. 109–110). Theorists such as Beyer and Apple in *The Curriculum: Problems, Politics, and Possibilities* (1998) reject technique as a focus for curriculum studies. They maintain that curriculum studies should focus on "*what* should be taught and *why* we should teach it" rather than on "problems associated with *how to* organize, build, and above all now, evaluate curriculum" (p. 3).

Discourse about ideas and values is undoubtedly an important part of curriculum studies. Advancing curriculum discourse is commendable and important. But "inveterate, unexamined, and mistaken reliance on theory," to quote Schwab's (1970) memorable indictment, ducks the central question every practitioner faces: "What should I do?" The theorist who provides a valuable new way to think about a curriculum question only leads practitioners part of the way to an answer to this practical question. As this book will show through many examples, theory does not solve curriculum problems, it only provides a resource for those who would solve them. Responsible practitioners armed with a good theory must still reason and experiment a great deal more to settle on a justified action. If curriculum studies does not help them with this necessary work, who will?

A further difficulty with so much reliance on theory is the proliferation of theories. Theorists have created so many plausible, interesting theories that the most dedicated scholar working full time could not even read them all. The field has no means to test theories and anyway a whole generation of researchers would not have time to test them all. With new theories published every month and no generally accepted way to judge their relative quality and value, practicing curriculum professionals can only shake their heads in bewilderment. To make matters worse, curriculum theorists have splintered into special interest groups that take particular perspectives—feminist, critical, postmodern, deconstructionist, Deweyan, Jungian, Lacanian, and the like—and each group speaks to its own concerns.

A practical perspective is one way to rescue curriculum studies from its current predicament. Theory's inherent shortcomings do not matter so much when we treat theory as a resource for reasoning about practical problems rather than as the answer to theoretical problems. This book treats curriculum theories with great respect. It shows readers how to critically analyze and assess curriculum theories and how to use theories of many kinds in many ways to enhance decisions and inform actions. But its focus is practical.

Professional

This book's approach to curriculum matters is professional in the narrow sense that it is designed to prepare readers for professional roles doing curriculum work. It is also professional in another sense that is moral and ethical. Professionals serve their client's interest, not their own interest and not the interest of other groups to which they may belong. In public schools, the curriculum professional's client is the local public and so the curriculum professional is obligated to serve the public interest. Throughout the book, I assume that readers will be looking for actions that they can justify as being in the public interest, whether they personally prefer those actions or not.

Finding the public interest can be difficult when the public is divided, and curriculum professionals often find themselves embroiled in controversy. Professional ideals obligate them to act fairly toward all sides, even though they may passionately favor one party. Many curriculum professionals want to lead in making curriculum improvements. Some even speak of themselves as "change agents." This causes no problems when leaders persuade the interested parties and work through established institutions to secure public approval for curriculum initiatives. But professionals overreach when they act on their own beliefs alone and undertake initiatives regardless of public support.

Questions about professional obligations and the public interest can be quite complex but some things are clear. Professionals as a rule only make curriculum decisions within the boundaries set by public policy. The public does not cede to professionals the authority to make curriculum policy. They expect professionals to follow public policy or else resign. The opinions of professionals carry extra weight beyond that of other participants in curriculum decisions only when they have greater expertise and then only to the extent that local leaders acknowledge this expertise. In short, the curriculum professional is a public servant, not a free agent. Still, as this book shows, professionals can have great power and influence in curriculum matters by virtue of their expertise and the trust they earn from other stakeholders.

Organization of the Book

This book consists of two parts, Perspectives and Practice. The five chapters of Part I, Perspectives, look at curriculum from five fundamental perspectives that every professional needs to understand: curriculum work, traditions of curriculum practice, curriculum theories, curriculum reforms, and curriculum studies. Chapter 1, Curriculum Work, answers the question "What is curriculum?" by looking at the curriculum work that teachers, school leaders, curriculum specialists, and others do. Chapter 2, Traditions of Curriculum Practice, presents an historical tour of the curriculum of American schools from colonial times to the present. Chapter 3, Curriculum Theory, focuses on the main ideas and visionary ideals that guide Americans' thinking and action on curriculum questions. Chapter 4, Curriculum Reform, takes a close look at the biggest, noisiest, most visible, and perhaps the most significant—although that's disputed—phenomenon associated with curriculum, the reform movement. Chapter 5, Curriculum Studies, introduces the most important varieties of inquiry that scholars and researchers undertake in studying curriculum questions. Together these chapters review the major ways of thinking about curriculum and doing curriculum work.

Part II, Practice, applies the ideas in Part I to important curriculum challenges that arise when people try to improve curriculums in schools and classrooms. Chapter 6, Curriculum Practice, describes what's involved in teaching with a curriculum and sustaining an existing curriculum in a school. Those who would change practice need to appreciate what it takes to maintain it. Chapter 7, Teaching with a Curriculum, treats the curriculum problems that arise for teachers in the normal life of classrooms. Chapter 8, Improving Classroom Curriculum, explores approaches to help teachers make major changes in their classroom curriculum. Chapter 9, Improving School Curriculum, explores the challenges principals and other school curriculum leaders face in making major improvements in a school's curriculum.

Each chapter includes several features. Each opens with a quotation and a set of guiding questions. I suggest that you reflect on these before you read each chapter. The main body of each chapter is written for you to read as if it were an essay. Each has an argument or story with a beginning, a middle, and an end. At the end of each chapter is a section called "Questions and Projects" that suggests inquiries you might pursue to carry the ideas in that chapter into your own professional life. Some of these suggest applying the ideas to concrete school situations you face. Others suggest ways that you could do studies that contribute to the knowledge and resources of the curriculum profession. Some can be completed in a couple of hours and others could be dissertations or even the work of a lifetime. Each chapter ends with an essay called "Further Studies" that recommends reading, Web resources, and other ways to study more about the topic.

New in the Revised Edition

This revised edition is a thorough reworking of the first edition that preserves its essential message and basic structure while changing most of the words. The number of chapters is reduced from 13 to 9 and the number of pages reduced almost as much. The text is leaner and simpler. The book is more tightly focused on the ideas, arguments, and examples that I believe are essential learning for anyone entering the study of curriculum. I have integrated the findings of many excellent studies done in the intervening decade, updating the book and at the same time strengthening it as an introduction to research and scholarship in curriculum studies. I focused the book more tightly on the concerns of primary curriculum professionals. I cut chapters on curriculum development and curriculum policy even though these are very important topics for the educational community at large because they were less central to the concerns of curriculum professionals and scholars. I clarified the practical, professional approach that is the book's main message. I also updated examples, references, and recommended reading. The revised edition is a new book that should be feel quite familiar to those who knew the first edition.

A note on terminology may be helpful. In this book the plural of curriculum is curriculums, not curricula. Both are correct, but the standard English plural sounds better to me than the Latin, and it's less pretentious and simpler. I've used a variety of terms to describe the roles of people who work with curriculum—curriculum worker, curriculum professional, curriculum leader, curriculum specialist, curriculum expert, and others. The choice I make among such terms in any particular case is usually not significant. The variety simply reflects the variety of roles occupied by people who work on curriculum matters. Similarly, I use curriculum work, curriculum practice, curriculum leadership, and a variety of related terms to describe curriculum related activities.

Suggestions for Teaching and Learning with the Book

Specifics are the things I've wished that I could put in this book but could not without writing in hypertext. Curriculum questions come to life fully only when we see specific people acting in real events in authentic settings. It's up to the readers of this book and their teachers to supply these specifics. Use the material in the book as a starting point for thinking about a specific situation. Read about traditions of curriculum practice in the book, and then use what you learn to examine traditions of practice in some situation you know well—rural schools in the Midwest, beginning reading, teacher preparation, girls' schools, New York City schools. Read about theories in the book and compare them to ideas you have heard. Do you recognize any family resemblance to progressive ideas or traditional ones, to Noddings' ideas about caring or Gardner's about multiple abilities?

Before you read, think about situations you have experienced or heard or read about that fit the content of the chapter. What did people do in those situations and how did the actions turn out? Think about educational problems you face now or anticipate facing. To what extent and in what ways do these questions apply to your present problems? Reflect on or better still write about your response to the quotation. Jot brief answers to the questions at the beginning of the chapter. This will prompt you to consider what you already know and believe about this subject.

If your schedule permits you to read a chapter at a single sitting, that would be best. A quick reading followed by re-study of those sections that seem most novel or difficult would be ideal. Read actively! As you read, apply the ideas to situations you know from personal experience and to problems you face now or anticipate facing. As you encounter key ideas, mark those that are new to you as well as those that are familiar but important. Make judgments. Disagree. Mark ideas that you think are wrong, dangerous, dubious, or worthless. If you have a chance to discuss these ideas with others, compare notes on your judgments.

After you read a chapter, note what you've learned from that chapter that may be important to you. Note, too, what questions you have now as a result of reading the chapter. Finally, keep a personal learning agenda listing things you've encountered that you'd like to learn more about later. You may not have an opportunity to learn them just then, but keeping a personal learning agenda will help you remember later what you thought was important. No single book can provide an adequate foundation for a career in curriculum. This one is only an introduction. The essay "Further Study" can guide you to sources for independent reading. I hope you find your work with *Fundamentals of Curriculum* to be personally and professionally challenging and meaningful.

Palo Alto, California
September 2001

Acknowledgments

The greatest debt I feel is to the many hundreds of curriculum scholars whose life work I have so inadequately summarized in these pages. My contributions to the subject would not fill three pages of the book and even these I was only able to do by relying on those who had gone before me. I humbly thank them one and all, living and dead. I thank my students over the years for their insightful comments and helpful suggestions. Gloria Miller was especially helpful in preparing this revised edition. I thank the librarians of Cubberley Library who have been wonderfully helpful and cheerful in guiding me through the tremendous resources of this great collection of books on education. I thank my editor at Lawrence Erlbaum Associates (LEA), Naomi Silverman. I thank the anonymous reviewers of the manuscript of the Revised Edition. I would like to thank my loved ones for their patience and support: my sons Glenn, David, and Decker, Jr. and their families.

Fundamentals of Curriculum

PASSION AND PROFESSIONALISM

PART 1

PERSPECTIVES

CHAPTER ONE

Curriculum Work

There are no rules or recipes that will guarantee successful curriculum development. Judgment is always required, and if this task is a group effort, sensitivity to one's fellow workers is always necessary.

—Elliot Eisner, American scholar of education
The Educational Imagination, Third Edition, 1994

Questions

- What is a curriculum?
- Why do people care so much about curriculum issues?
- What kinds of work do people do in connection with curriculums?
- Who does curriculum work?
- What are the challenges of curriculum work?
- What can professionals learn that will help them do better curriculum work?

People Care about Curriculum

People demand action on curriculum matters, the media report these demands, and public officials and schools respond. What better evidence could there be that people care deeply about curriculum matters? Here, for example, are several news stories that report people demanding curriculum changes. These all appeared in the *New York Times* in 1999, but the *Times* and other news media report similar stories every year.

- "Schools Taking Tougher Stance with Standards" (September 6, 1999)
  "No more fun and games: As children across the nation head back to school this fall, many are encountering a harsher atmosphere in which states set specific academic standards and impose real penalties on those who do not meet them."
  Americans often worry that children may leave school unprepared for work or higher education. As the demands of work and higher education increase, most Americans believe that public schools need to offer a more academically demanding curriculum.
- "Amid Clamor for Computer in Every Classroom, Some Dissenting Voices" (March 17, 1999)

Computers are just one example of many changes in how people work and live that provoke calls for curriculum change. Most Americans believe that schools should at least consider changing their curriculums to reflect these changes in society, although individuals may disagree about whether a particular change is a good idea.

- "Board for Kansas Deletes Evolution from Curriculum" (August 12, 1999)

    "The Kansas Board of Education voted yesterday to delete virtually any mention of evolution from the state's science curriculum...."

    "Science vs. the Bible: Debate Moves to the Cosmos" (October 10, 1999)

    "Scientific lessons about the origins of life have long been challenged in public schools, but some Bible literalists are now adding the reigning theory about the origin of the universe to their list of targets."

    Most Americans want schools to teach established truths and values that we all share. They shy away from teaching that contradicts religious convictions or that offends any racial, ethnic, or cultural group. Yet views change, and sometimes the public eventually accepts ideas that once were controversial. Conversely, views that once were accepted sometimes become offensive when sensibilities change. Most Americans believe that the school curriculum should be updated to reflect currently accepted views of what is true, just, and important, but when is it appropriate for schools to impose on dissenters views accepted by the majority?

- "A Gap in the Curriculum" (April 26, 1999)

    "The ghastly horror in Littleton, Colorado, makes all of us repeat our favorite remedies for eliminating violence...." (The article concludes that schools need to help students resolve conflicts and deal with emotionally charged issues.)

    "Earlier Work with Children Steers Them from Crime" (March 15, 1999)

    "Programs that seek to reduce violence, drug abuse, pregnancy and other dangerous or unhealthy activities among adolescents are notorious for doing too little too late and at too great a cost. But a new study has shown that by starting early...."

    Whenever many children seem to be having trouble, advocates call on schools to solve these problems. Americans often support curriculum changes intended to help children address nonacademic problems such as alcohol and drug abuse, teenage sex, reckless driving, smoking, and readiness for the world of work.

- "Serving the Less Fortunate for Credit and Just Because" (April 4, 1999)

    "For the last few years, Stacy Joseph, a senior at Half Hollow Hills West High School, has volunteered regularly at a soup kitchen...." (The article goes on to describe community service opportunities offered in schools for academic credit.)

    When a community feels itself to be in trouble, locals often demand that the schools address the community's problems. Communities expect schools to help them address poverty, crime, threats to public health, a waning sense of community, and needs for cultural enrichment. Many communities also expect schools to prepare young people for jobs in industries important to the local economy.

Curriculum Work Today

A curriculum is a particular way of ordering content and purposes for teaching and learning in schools. A common curriculum responds to a deep need that many Americans feel to offer all young people a common foundation of essential knowledge and skill. Curriculum work is important because the curriculum affects what teachers teach and thus what students learn, and in so doing it helps to shape our identity and our future. Curriculums require a lot of work—debating ideas for curriculum change, creating curriculum plans, seeking agreement from important stakeholders on those plans, bringing those plans to life in classrooms and schools, and studying curriculums and their effects.

Curriculum work succeeds when teachers and students enact a curriculum in the classroom that leads students to learn the intended content and achieve the intended purposes and that pleases teachers, school leaders, parents, and the public. Therefore, curriculum work is fundamentally work with and for teachers, but it also requires agreement and cooperation from many other stakeholders including students, parents, school officials, accrediting agencies, university admissions committees, and employers, among others. These stakeholders embrace various educational ideals, such as academic excellence, equality, and social relevance, and these ideals lead them to push for different curriculums. Many people feel strongly about curriculum matters and are willing to fight for their priorities, so curriculum work is often contentious. In schools, curriculum work is segmented by subject and by age or grade level and must often be done with very limited time and money. These conditions make curriculum work in today's schools very challenging.

While curriculum work remains the same in many ways today as it has been for a half-century or more, several strong currents of change in education are changing curriculum work and portend a transformation in the near future. Public expectations for education are rising. A movement is underway to establish a system of national standards and to develop tests that will determine whether children have achieved these standards. Educational issues, especially curriculum issues, are increasingly being fought out in the political arena, with mayors, governors, state and federal legislators, and presidential candidates playing leading roles. The public is showing greater willingness to experiment with new educational institutions such as charter schools, home schooling, and vouchers. The teaching force is changing as older teachers retire and new ones enter the profession by various routes. New forms of information technology are making computer-assisted instruction, distance learning, and other new forms of teaching and learning possible. Also, new ways of thinking about teaching and learning based on cognitive science and brain research are leading to designs for more powerful learning environments and better ways to assess learning. These developments create exciting new challenges and opportunities for curriculum specialists. Effective curriculum work in this new environment will require a mixture of old and new knowledge and skill.

What is a Curriculum?

A curriculum is a particular way of ordering content and purposes for teaching and learning in schools. *Content* is what teachers and students pay attention to when they are teaching and learning. Content can be described as a list of school subjects or, more specifically as a list of topics, themes, concepts, or works to be covered. *Purposes* are the reasons for teaching the content. Among broad reasons for teaching school subjects are to transmit the culture, to improve society, or to realize the potential of individual students. More fine-grained purposes for studying particular topics are usually stated as specific goals or objectives students should attain. Content and purposes can be *ordered* in many ways, including the tight, hierarchical ordering common in mathematics, the linear ordering by time that is often used in history, and the broad themes common in literature or social studies.

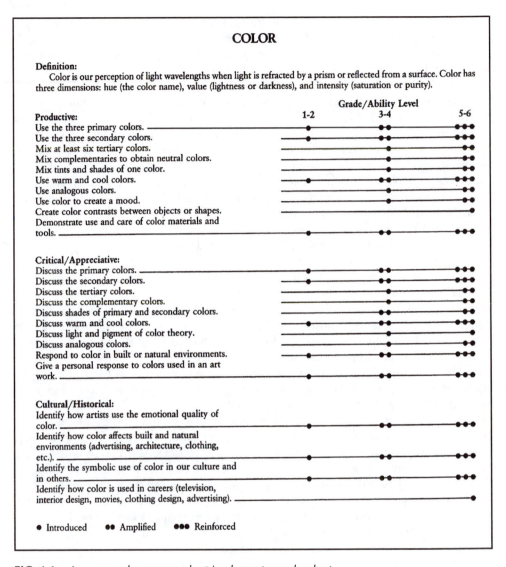

FIG. 1.1. *A scope and sequence chart in elementary school art.*
This chart lists objectives grouped in three broad domains (productive, critical/appreciative, and cultural/historical) and indicates when each is to be taught.
SOURCE: Arizona Art Education Association, 1982, Fall. Art in Elementary Education: What the Law Requires, *InPerspective, The Journal of the Arizona Art Education Association* 1:6–24.

Ask to see a school's curriculum and you may be shown any of several kinds of documents, including:

- a list of courses offered or subjects taught,
- a weekly or yearly schedule of when various subjects are taught,
- a scope and sequence chart such as the one in Fig. 1.1, which combines a list of topics with a timeline showing when each is taught,
- a collection of textbooks or teachers' guides.

Curriculum planners often represent the elements of a curriculum in more specialized ways. They may use a concept map such as the one in Fig. 1.2 to represent relationships

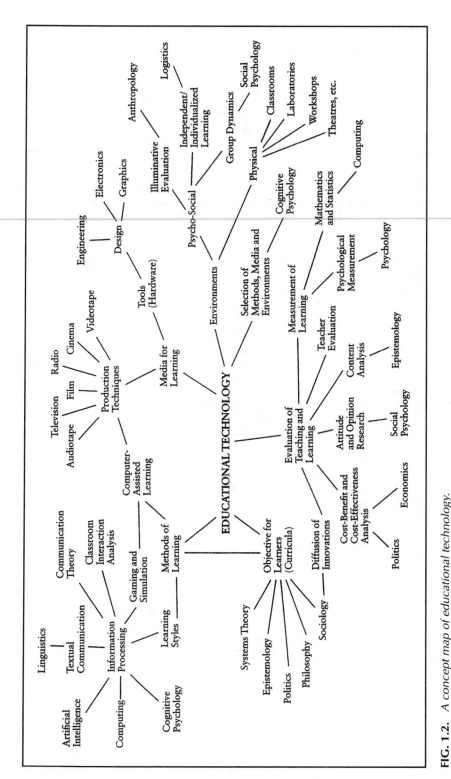

FIG. 1.2. *A concept map of educational technology.*
SOURCE: Hawridge, David, 1981. The Telesis of Educational Technology. *British Journal of Educational Technology* 12:4–18.

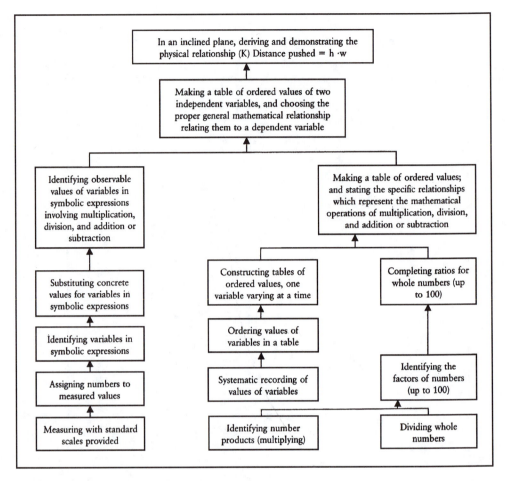

FIG. 1.3. *A hierarchy of educational purposes.*
SOURCE: Weigand, V. K. 1970. A Study of Subordinate Skills in Science Problem Solving (Robert M. Gagne, ed.) *Basic Studies of Learning Hierarchies in School Subjects.* Berkeley: University of California.

among items of content. They may use a diagram such as the one in Fig. 1.3 or a content x behavior grid such as the one in Fig. 1.4 to show relationships between content and purposes.

Such curriculum documents coordinate teaching and learning in vital ways. They help teachers keep in mind the big picture of what should be taught and learned over months and years and keep track of where they are in relation to planned progress at any given time. They remind teachers of why each topic is being taught. They help teachers coordinate their work with that of other teachers. They inform parents, school officials, and interested persons outside the school about what students are studying and when. By providing a coordinating structure, curriculum documents help to bring a degree of order and predictability into a far-flung educational system that would otherwise be more bewildering for everyone involved.

The curriculum is a quiet, almost imperceptible presence in every classroom. Experienced teachers rarely need to consult curriculum documents because they have internalized them. Curriculum documents play a vital role for new teachers, but this role remains behind the scenes, invisible to classroom visitors. Visible or not, curriculum guides, frameworks,

Illustration of the Use of a Two-Dimensional Chart in Stating
Objectives for a High School Course in Biological Science

	Behavioral Aspect of the Objectives						
	1. Understanding of important facts and principles	2. Familiarity with dependable sources of information	3. Ability to interpret data	4. Ability to apply principles	5. Ability to study and report results of study	6. Broad and mature interests	7. Social attitudes
A. Functions of Human Organisms							
1. Nutrition	X	X	X	X	X	X	X
2. Digestion	X		X	X	X	X	
3. Circulation	X		X	X	X	X	
4. Respiration	X		X	X	X	X	
5. Reproduction	X	X	X	X	X	X	X
B. Use of Plant and Animal Resources							
1. Energy relationships	X		X	X	X	X	X
2. Environmental factors conditioning plant and animal growth	X	X	X	X	X	X	X
3. Heredity and genetics	X	X	X	X	X	X	X
4. Land utilization	X	X	X	X	X	X	X
C. Evolution and Development	X	X	X	X	X	X	X

FIG. 1.4. *A content x behavior grid for high school biology.*
SOURCE: Tyler, Ralph. 1949. *Basic Principles of Curriculum and Instruction*. Chicago: University of Chicago Press.

textbooks, tests, and similar written and unwritten expectations impinge in some way on almost everything teachers do.

The following fictional story about a new teacher shows some of the ways that a curriculum works through teachers to shape what happens in classrooms. The story compresses into one occasion many experiences that would normally occur over the first few weeks of teaching when novice teachers confront directly many factors originating outside the classroom that guide and constrain what they and their students will do there.

A New Teacher Meets a School Curriculum

Terry arrives at Washington Middle School for the first official day of her first teaching job. Today is a day for teachers to get ready. Students come next week. Terry meets her department chair for a scheduled orientation to teaching in the department. Margaret greets Terry cheerfully and gets right down to business.

"Hello, Terry. Welcome!"

"I know you've already been through the district orientation. They gave you a copy of the state framework and the district curriculum guide, I assume?"

"Good. Nobody will check on whether you're following them, but they are still very important because they tell you what's going to be covered on the district and state exams at the end of the year. They've got some good teaching suggestions in them, too. If I were you, I'd use them like a bible this first year."

"And you were at the school orientation, also, right? So you've got the school calendar that tells you the dates of school holidays, final exams, and when grades are due. And you've got the personnel list that tells you who does what and how to contact them. I keep a copy of those in my grade book and another in my desk at school and a third copy at home, just in case. You'll probably be calling on the library staff and computer support staff a lot."

"You probably wonder how seriously we take those school priorities you heard about at the school orientation. Very seriously. All our in-service days for the year are focused on those priorities. We go through a fairly lengthy process of soliciting ideas from teachers, students, and parents, and then we have a series of meetings where we settle on three priorities for school improvement for the year. You'll hear a lot about these priorities this year."

"My job this morning is to orient you to the department. There are seven of us. Most of us are veterans, but we have two teachers who are in their third year and will be reviewed for tenure this year. They can give you the inside story on the tenure process in our district. You know that both the principal and I observe a class every semester for every probationary teacher. The custom at Washington is that when we visit we ask for your lesson plan. All teachers are supposed to have written daily and weekly lesson plans available for substitutes in case we're absent. Here's a sheet with the format we use for daily and weekly lesson plans in our department."

"We work together pretty closely in our department. We have department meetings every month and one of us throws a department party every semester. We make a common semester final exam for each course and that takes a lot of our time in meetings. And we deal with budget and supplies and any other issues that come up. Just send me e-mail or put a note in my box if you want to put something on the agenda. We're friendly in this department. No feuds or anything like that. You can ask anybody anything. We don't have any secrets. I've been department chair for two years now. Three of the other faculty members have been department chair before me. We all know what it takes to make a department work, and we all chip in."

"I know you've already received your teaching schedule for the year. We try to give first year teachers just two preparations, but this year we had to give you three. Our enrollment is growing and we just can't find enough qualified teachers. At least all of these courses are in your field of certification! We have two teachers in the department this year who are teaching courses they are not certified to teach. To help you with the planning I've made copies of my last year's course plan including all my weekly plans for one of your courses. And here are Lee's and Lindsay's course plans for the other two courses. As you'll see, Lee's quite an innovative teacher who uses lots of projects. I thought it would be good for you to see the range of teaching styles we have in the department."

"Here are your teacher's editions of the adopted textbooks for all three courses. As you'll see, the textbook doesn't align completely with the state framework. The district guide should help you with the topics that aren't covered in the textbook. We ordered our supplies for the year last winter. Here's a list of what we have. If you need something that's not on the list, talk to me. We have a few hundred dollars for unexpected needs. If you need something that costs more, we can apply to the Parent's Fund. The parents collect money and use it to help teachers get materials and supplies for the classroom or finance field trips and the like."

Margaret continued, talking about students, parents, and school traditions. She told many colorful stories about unusual, humorous, or otherwise noteworthy events much talked about at Washington before she concluded.

"The three most important secrets to success for a new teacher, in my opinion, are planning, planning, and planning. Make your yearly plan of units and lessons as early as you can this week. I'd be happy to go over your plan with you. And make your first weekly plan and all your daily lesson plans in preparation for seeing your students for the first time next week. Review your daily lesson plans every day. Adjust your plans for the rest of the week, make notes on improving that day's lesson, and file them for next year. Review again every week and at the end of every unit. At first it will seem like a lot of work, but believe me it will pay off."

"Well, that's all for now. Welcome once again. And call on me anytime!"

Terry just learned, if she didn't know already, that teachers are agents of an institution. Many eyes will be watching what she does in her classroom and many hands are reaching out to guide her. Some teachers welcome the guidance, others resent it. Teachers have a voice in determining the school curriculum, but most teachers find themselves disagreeing with some of their school's curriculum directives. Sometimes a teacher can ignore a directive, but it's a risky thing to do.

This picture of curriculum at Washington High may seem innocent and perfectly ordinary, but it hides the germs of many conflicts. Everything about curriculum, including its definition, is contested. Figure 1.5 shows other ways various authorities have defined curriculum.

Each definition reflects a slightly different orientation or perspective. One sees a curriculum as a plan, another as events that actually happen. One speaks of activities, another of experiences. People favor different definitions because they prefer to think and talk about curriculum in different ways. They favor definitions that make it easy for them to talk about it in the way that they prefer.

In this book we will use a middle-of-the road definition, meant as far as possible not to favor any particular stance on the ideal curriculum: *A curriculum is a particular way of ordering content and purposes for teaching and learning in schools.* This definition allows any content, any purposes, and any way of ordering them, including the most hidebound of traditions and the most radical of innovations, and does not favor any. The content of a curriculum could take the form of textbooks, films, a school garden, a public service project, or an entire school subject studied over many years. Purposes could include narrowly

- ➤ The planned learning activities sponsored by the school (Tanner & Tanner, 1977, p. 406)
- ➤ The content pupils are expected to learn (Smith & Orlovsky, 1978, p. 3)
- ➤ The contrived activity and experience—organized, focused, systematic— that life, unaided, would not provide (Musgrave, 1968, p. 6)
- ➤ A set of events, either proposed, occurring, or having occurred, which has the potential for reconstructing human experience (Duncan & Frymier, 1967, p. 181)
- ➤ Situations or activities arranged and brought into play by the teacher to effect student learning (Shaver & Berlak, 1968, p. 9)
- ➤ Things which children and youth must do and experience by way of developing abilities to do the things well that make up the affairs of adult life (Bobbitt, 1918, p. 42)
- ➤ The total effort of the school to bring about desired outcomes in school and out-of-school situations (Saylor & Alexander, 1954, p. 3)
- ➤ A sequence of potential experiences set up in school for the purpose of disciplining children and youth in group ways of thinking and acting (Smith, Stanley, & Shores, 1957, p. 3)
- ➤ A set of abstractions from actual industries, arts, professions and civic activities . . . brought into the school-box and taught (Goodman, 1963, p. 159)

FIG. 1.5. *Various definitions of curriculum.*

practical ones or extravagantly idealistic ones. It does, as any definition must, have a bias, but its bias is toward an abstract, systematic, nonpartisan analysis of curriculum matters, not toward any particular type of curriculum.

Seen in the broadest perspective, disputes about definitions are misplaced struggles over substantive curriculum questions. Those who argue promote a definition favorable to their position on some curriculum issue. People find plenty of curriculum issues to disagree about. Figures 1.6 and 1.7 list recurring issues that swirl around content and purpose, for instance. These and other fundamental disagreements about what is important permeate curriculum discussion to its very core—the meaning of the term itself.

Arguing about definitions is seldom productive. When people disagree about educational issues, they should talk about the issues, not about how to define terms. Parties who want to understand one another's views can reach tentative agreement on working definitions, or they can agree that each side will use the terms they prefer and both will "translate" what the others say. People who want to talk can find a way to discuss their differences on matters of substance. Sometimes, though, the parties to a curriculum issue believe that they stand to gain more support by campaigning for their own position than by engaging in a genuine dialogue with the opposition. Bidding for public support in open forums encourages partisan wrangling over definitions.

Curriculum specialists can seldom afford to argue about definitions. They need to work with people who hold various strong views about curriculum matters, and some of them will adamantly insist on using their own definition. A biased definition can make it more difficult to discuss curriculum issues, but not impossible. Professionals responsible for curriculum work often need to engage committed partisans in discussion of curriculum matters, and to do so they may need to learn to use biased definitions.

❑ What are the major domains of human knowledge?
❑ How can we determine which content from the whole corpus of human knowledge is most important for students to learn?
❑ What content should be presented in schools, K–12?
❑ Should the content of education be drawn entirely from academic disciplines, or should the curriculum also include content from other domains, such as the demands of everyday life or the requirements of occupations?
❑ How can the content of the school curriculum be kept up-to-date as knowledge expands?
❑ What should happen to the content of the curriculum when an item of content becomes controversial? Should schools avoid controversial topics, take sides, or present all sides?

Organization of content

❑ Should the content of school be divided into the traditional school subjects, or should the curriculum be unified, integrated, or interdisciplinary? If neither, how should content be grouped?
❑ Should all students study the same content, or should different students study different content?
❑ Which content should be presented earlier and which later?
❑ At what ages should students encounter specific bodies of content?

FIG. 1.6.   *Recurring issues: Curriculum content and organization.*

Why Curriculum Questions Matter

What children study and learn in school makes a difference in their lives. Curriculum improvement offers an opportunity to enhance the lives of many thousands of students. If we teach homemaking to girls and woodshop to boys, they learn different things than if we teach them a second language, health, art, or economics. As a result of learning different things they will develop different abilities and interests, commit to different values, pursue different careers, and live different lives. Their very identity will be shaped by what they study.

Students will be shaped by the purposes for which we teach a subject as well as by what we teach them. If we teach arithmetic in order to develop skill at calculation, students will come away with a certain set of knowledge and skills, a certain estimate of their own ability at mathematics, and a certain idea of what constitutes mathematics. If we teach arithmetic for conceptual understanding, they will come away with different knowledge and skills, a different estimate of their own abilities, and a different idea of what mathematics is.

The curriculum also shapes Americans' identity as a people. A people have a common heritage only if every new generation encounters that heritage. The curriculum of compulsory schooling helps to shape a people's national character and their political and economic values, behavior, and institutions. Every nation teaches its own native language or languages and its own version of history. It is no accident that schools in the most

❑ What should be the purposes of public education, K–12? Which should have
    the highest priority?
❑ Who should decide the purposes of schools and through what process?
    What should be the roles of students, teachers, parents, school officials, and
    others? How should controversies about the purposes of education be
    resolved?
❑ Should the purposes of education change from year to year in step with
    changes in the world outside schools? Or should they reflect more enduring
    traditions that change little over a lifetime?
❑ How can teachers and students be brought to embrace school goals and
    pursue them as their own?
❑ How do we judge progress toward attainment of the purposes of the school?

Organization of purposes

❑ Should all students pursue the same purposes, or should purposes be tailored
    to individuals?
❑ How should responsibility for achieving various purposes be allocated
    among persons and occasions within the school program?
❑ Should schools plan to attain specific purposes on particular occasions, or
    should teachers decide when the time is ripe for their students to work on a
    given purpose?
❑ Should purposes be organized in a hierarchy leading from simpler, less
    sophisticated "lower order" ones to more complex, higher-order ones?

FIG. 1.7. *Recurring issues: Purposes and their organization.*

authoritarian countries have the most rigid programs of study, while students in the most
democratic countries have the most choice in their studies. It is no accident that every
student in French schools is taught to draw or that every student in Russian schools studies
mathematics every year.

Why do we need a curriculum? Can't we just let everybody learn whatever they want?
We could. Nothing compels us to require all students to learn certain things or even to
limit their choices to certain course offerings. Parents are free to teach young children
whatever they think best and people over 18 can study anything they want or nothing.
Some radical private schools have abandoned curriculum altogether. A. S. Neill's school,
Summerhill, was an example widely admired in the 1960s. Similar proposals to let children
study whatever they and their parents and teachers want surface from time to time, but
they rarely gain widespread support and are probably best viewed as protests against the
prevailing curriculum rather than as serious proposals.

American schools have a curriculum because most of us feel that it is necessary to offer all young people a common foundation of essential knowledge and skill both for their
individual well-being and for the welfare of American society. Americans are not alone in
this. Every nation spells out what its young people should study for "nation building" and
to achieve "a common culture." Not to have a curriculum seems a species of anarchy.

Curriculums are a form of mutual obligation that people undertake as a group. Assuming
the obligation is an expression of belonging to the group and sharing in its identity. Citizens

of a country agree to educate their precious children in a certain common tradition and thus to introduce them to that tradition and enable them to live their lives within it. Willingness to assume this obligation is an indicator of the strengths of the bonds that hold the group together. In the United States, certain cultural and religious groups, notably the Amish but also many Roman Catholics, choose to educate their children in a different tradition than that represented by American public schools. In an open society, parents are free to choose among officially recognized alternative traditions, but the state retains the right to regulate and approve all schools in the interest of national welfare. In authoritarian societies, parents may have no choice about schooling their children.

In traditional societies, a curriculum reflected shared values and a shared worldview. Curriculum then functioned as a form of ritual that expressed and affirmed the tradition while also functioning as a means for transmitting it. Achieving shared worldviews can be difficult for open democratic societies. They must honor all socially acceptable worldviews, which means that the area of shared values could become quite small, perhaps vanishingly small. So they have to *negotiate* agreement on curriculum questions. In fact, the public school curriculum can be viewed as one of the ways American society faces its diversity and discovers or achieves shared values and worldviews. Viewed this way, such contentious issues as teaching about evolution, sex education, and religion in the schools become arenas for defining what it means to be an American today.

The Work Curriculums Require

Arenas of Curriculum Work

Curriculum work gets done in three major arenas: classrooms, schools or school systems, and public policy forums. The primary curriculum work done in classrooms is realizing or enacting the curriculum with students. This is sometimes called the "instructional level." Here, plans become actions that influence what students do and learn. The teacher has primary responsibility for classroom curriculum work, but as we saw with Terry, teachers receive institutional directives. Sometimes teachers receive assistance in curriculum matters from mentor teachers, department chairs, specialist teachers of particular subjects, or central office experts, and sometimes teachers work on their curriculum in grade level or subject teams. Usually, though, teachers work alone, and even when they work with others, they get the final word on the classroom curriculum when the classroom door closes.

Curriculum work in the school arena consists mainly of making and implementing official policies agreed to through established formal procedures as part of a public governmental institution. School and school system officials are responsible for work on the school curriculum, at what is often called "the institutional level." They manage the official procedures that create the curriculum documents that direct the work of all the teachers in a school or system and they must gain approval for these plans from the legally constituted local authorities. They also provide the assistance teachers need to implement the plans, and they are responsible for securing and monitoring teachers' compliance with the plans. They manage a process for selecting the textbooks and curriculum materials teachers will use. They run the process that sets requirements for students to advance from one level to the next and to graduate, and they maintain official records of students' progress. Sometimes they assess students' learning through examinations or other assessment procedures.

Curriculum work in the policy arena is a mixture of official work done within governmental institutions and work in quasi-official or unofficial agencies that influence curriculum nationwide. State governments enact legislation affecting curriculum such as course and graduation requirements. State departments of education implement legislation. In some states they develop achievement tests used to evaluate student and school performance. In some states they establish a process for selecting textbooks eligible for purchase with state funds. Federal agencies have no direct authority over schools, but they offer many grants that states and schools can use to improve curriculums.

Many other agencies act on curriculum matters in the policy arena. The National Council of Teachers of English, the Association for Supervision and Curriculum Development, the National Education Association, and dozens of similar professional societies present conferences and publish journals in which innovators present new curriculum proposals and professionals discuss their merits. Hundreds of private nonprofit organizations and lobbying groups advocate curriculum positions from time to time on behalf of their interest groups. Examples of interest groups active in curriculum matters include parents (Parent Teacher Association), religious groups (National Council of Churches), business (Chamber of Commerce), unions (AFL-CIO), and scientists (American Association for the Advancement of Science). Curriculum development organizations such as the Education Development Corporation (EDC) and Children's Television Workshop and commercial textbook publishers create curriculum materials for sale to schools or for subsidized free distribution. Theorists, researchers, and critics write articles and reports and make presentations at conferences designed to influence the prevailing view about curriculum matters among professionals and the public. News media provide forums, such as *Education Week* and the education section of the Sunday *New York Times*, for public discussion of curriculum issues.

Curriculum work at the policy level is always a form of politics. The unceasing struggle of many groups to get a common curriculum more to their liking produces an unsteady balance and a fragile prevailing view on curriculum matters that is always being challenged and contested. The resulting working consensus supports a kind of *de facto* national curriculum. However, this consensus is punctuated unpredictably by reform movements that attract enough support to challenge the *de facto* curriculum in some way.

Who Does Curriculum Work?

Teachers do the curriculum work that sustains the classroom curriculum. Some teachers follow the textbook and local curriculum guides closely. Other teachers become classroom curriculum innovators by seeking out or inventing new curriculum materials and activities, and by trying them and adapting them to work better in their classes. When teachers seek advice or assistance in curriculum matters, they first ask other teachers in their school whose skill and judgment in curriculum matters they trust. Teachers whom colleagues frequently ask for advice about curriculum become school curriculum leaders, sometimes officially designated as such, but usually not. Most schools have teacher teams of some sort, such as subject matter departments in high schools or grade level teams in elementary schools, that coordinate curriculum work among teachers. The teachers who lead these teams are also usually leaders in shaping the school curriculum.

Principals are school curriculum leaders, although in large high schools they often delegate curriculum responsibilities to department chairs or teacher curriculum leaders. In elementary and middle schools and in some smaller high schools, curriculum leadership is often a major part of the principal's job. Principals bear the responsibility for managing the educational program of the school. This includes a long list of curriculum duties:

- monitoring the quality of the curriculum through observation and reviews of student achievement,
- evaluating teacher performance,
- allocating time and money for workshops and other forms of teacher development,
- assigning teachers to courses and identifying needs for hiring new teachers,
- planning the daily, weekly, and yearly schedule
- fielding external complaints, demands, or requests about curriculum from local constituents
- interpreting curriculum to the staff and to the community
- securing teacher buy-in for school curriculum changes mandated by the central office
- long-term planning, anticipating threats to quality, recognizing opportunities for improvement, comparing the curriculum to best practices, maintaining a good balance among curriculum elements
- maintaining effective processes for making curriculum decisions
- leading school curriculum change by projecting a vision of a better curriculum, setting priorities, allocating resources, and recruiting, organizing, and deploying staff

One indication of principals' influence in curriculum matters is that they get most of the credit when local stakeholders think that a curriculum initiative is successful and most of the blame when they are not satisfied.

Most local school systems above a certain size employ central office professionals whose job is to advise and assist teachers in curriculum and teaching, among other duties. They may have titles such as supervisors, curriculum coordinators, or teaching specialists. In this text, the general term "curriculum specialists" will be used to refer to central office professionals with major curriculum advisory responsibilities. Most school systems also have a leader responsible for curriculum issues who reports to the chief administrator. Titles frequently given to the chief local curriculum leader are director of curriculum or assistant or associate superintendent for curriculum and instruction.

Working with the top curriculum leader and with principals and school curriculum leaders, the curriculum specialists on the central office staff coordinate all work on the official local curriculum. They arrange the meetings in which teachers, parents, and other constituencies consider possible changes in the school curriculum. They manage the process of producing local curriculum documents. They develop and present events for teachers and community members to prepare them for curriculum changes. They visit classrooms, review test data, and report to local curriculum leaders on the quality of the local curriculum.

Most state departments of education employ professionals to manage state curriculum policies. Typically organized by school subject, these professionals usually have doctorates or decades of successful experience in curriculum work in large local school systems or both. Their work is similar to the work of central office curriculum specialists. They arrange hearings, commission or write policy reports, work with legislators to draft legislation or regulations, and travel widely giving talks, holding meetings, and consulting with local officials. Professionals in federal agencies such as the Department of Education or the National Science Foundation Directorate for Science and Technology Education perform work similar to their state counterparts, but they also manage grant programs that award funds to school systems and curriculum developers for curriculum improvement projects.

Those who do curriculum policy work in other agencies play many different roles. Professors of curriculum in schools of education try to influence curriculum work in schools and classrooms by actions in the policy arena. They teach courses to professionals, do research, write books and articles, speak publicly, and consult with local, state, and federal agencies. Curriculum developers are often former teachers or subject experts with a talent for devising curriculum activities. Officers in professional associations work with government officials on curriculum policies in which they have a stake. An official at the AAAS or the National Science Teachers Association, for example, may meet with a member of the staff of the National Science Foundation to discuss national standards for science. They also work with local and state chapters of their society, and many publish and present an annual national conference for their members. Reformers with a mission to change curriculums in schools throughout the country organize campaigns to influence curriculum policy by working through an existing agency or founding a new agency of their own. Private foundations such as the Ford or Carnegie Foundations provide much of the funding for curriculum reform efforts.

Clearly, responsibility for curriculum work is widely shared among many agencies and individuals in many locations. The commonsense question, "Who makes the curriculum?" has no simple answer in the United States today. In some countries the national ministry of education includes an official with final legal authority for curriculum matters, but the American system has no top position of authority. The result is a shifting balance of power among many contenders. Just figuring out who is most actively influencing curriculum policy at any particular time is a challenge. Sometimes the Council of Chief State School Officers, representing the top education officials in all 50 states, seizes the initiative on a curriculum issue. At other times or on other issues, the National Governors' Association may take the lead. Some secretaries of education set the national agenda for curriculum improvement, but sometimes an independent commission whose report galvanizes reform efforts nationwide overshadows the secretary's leadership.

The Nature of Curriculum Work

Curriculums require many kinds of attention from many people in many settings, making curriculum work quite varied. Teachers who specialize in curriculum work in a particular subject can spend time studying the subject, attending conferences looking for new ideas to try in their classroom, or working with students to field test and evaluate new ideas. School curriculum leaders spend a lot of time in meetings and conferring, in reading and writing reports, and in networking and politicking. Curriculum developers design curriculum materials and apparatus. Scholars and researchers read and write research proposals and reports and give speeches. There seems to be curriculum work for any taste.

A few characteristics stand out as fundamental to all these many types of curriculum work:

- Most curriculum work involves seeking agreement.

   Responsibility for curriculum matters is widely shared, so affecting a curriculum requires seeking agreement among the various individuals and organizations who have some responsibility for shaping the curriculum. Rather than commanding curriculum change, curriculum leaders negotiate agreements among stakeholders about curriculum matters. Skill at persuasion, negotiation, consultation, collaboration, consensus-seeking, coalition-building, and similar maneuvering is therefore fundamental to most curriculum work. All that comes with a position of leadership in curriculum matters is a seat at the game of curricular influence. Curriculum leaders have to use their skills at maneuvering to parlay that into influence over what happens in schools and classrooms.

- Most curriculum professionals represent diverse interests and must try to reconcile and balance them.

    Nearly everyone has a stake in the curriculum and therefore wants a voice in shaping it. The curriculum process is open widely to participation and influence by public and professional stakeholders. Professionals who do curriculum work in public institutions cannot, either ethically or practically, put the interests they personally favor over other valid interests. The public delegates to curriculum professionals the authority to manage an open, public process of decision making, not the authority to make curriculum decisions based on the specialist's expert judgment. Because the struggle to shape curriculum is a struggle over our cultural identity, the public will never turn it over entirely to professionals. For the same reason, curriculum issues are inherently political, and so people will always fight about them. Curriculum specialists can work from a partisan stance if they work on their own behalf or if they represent a particular interest group. Most curriculum specialists in schools and school systems represent a diverse set of stakeholders, and so their work must, for both ethical and practical reasons, be done from a nonpartisan stance. This means among other things that it is very awkward and difficult for a school curriculum specialist to advocate for or against any reform that divides stakeholders.

- Curriculum specialists must be prepared for sudden shifts in the prevailing view on curriculum matters and be ever on the alert for new opportunities and new dangers.

    Curriculum work takes place in a turbulent and contentious social, cultural, and institutional environment. Most curriculum questions are contested. Both the public and the profession contain many fragmented, deeply entrenched, contrasting traditions. The public and professional media ring with controversy over hotly contested issues. Conflicting, often radical proposals spring out from right, left, and center. Generations of the best research and scholarship have led to no generally accepted foundation in philosophy or science that might resolve these issues. Curriculum policy and practice are subject to fads and fashions that change every few years, and it is impossible to know at the time which changes will last.

- Schools and school systems strive to achieve curriculum stability in this turbulent environment.

    The policy environment changes rapidly, but schools cannot change their curriculum overnight. Teachers must be involved in a major curriculum decision and then be retrained or new teachers hired. New textbooks and curriculum materials must be purchased and new curriculum guides written. Changes will be required in the budget, room assignments, school schedule, support personnel, and physical plant. Most reforms fail. If schools implement a reform that is soon reversed or forgotten, the stress and expense of change will have been wasted. Curriculum leaders must learn ways to balance institutional stability and change constructively. They must make sound judgments about which reforms will last at their school, and they must find ways to respond that keep their options open if they do not last.

- Curriculum specialists must be sensitive to the multiple values implicated in every action they consider.

    All curriculum actions favor some human values more than others. Even if a perfectly fair and neutral action were conceivable, some parties would think it was unfair. Still, actions must be taken, for even inaction is a form of action with its own value implications. Therefore, no action is perfect; every action leaves some problems unsolved and creates new problems. Most of the radical proposals that solve complex curriculum problems in one fell sweep seem attractive only if one ignores some value that is important to many stakeholders. "Let children learn what they want" solves many of the problems of trying to force children to learn things they don't want to learn, but it ignores the value of a common culture. "Set national standards for all schools and test to see how well they achieve them" may solve problems of unequal education and lead to improved achievement, but it ignores the value of local variations in what students learn. Rural stakeholders may want their children to learn agriculture, for instance. Curriculum specialists must learn to see those who fight on all sides of a curriculum issue as honorable people defending values that they hold high. Who is to say that their priorities are inferior to those of the winning side?

- Curriculum change doesn't count until teachers change the classroom curriculum.

   Among the many influences on curriculum, the teacher's influence is final. If the curriculum change is to reach students, teachers must realize the change in the classroom. Curriculum specialists at all levels must therefore become adept at working with and through teachers to help them achieve curriculum changes in their classrooms. Few curriculum reform efforts have succeeded in bringing about widespread change in what teachers do in classrooms nationwide. Some voices in the policy arena claim that this failure indicates a structural weakness in the educational system and that new institutions such as vouchers or new policies such as compensating teachers for students' test results are needed. No matter what institutions or policies, widespread curriculum change will require curriculum specialists who know how to help teachers change their classroom curriculum.

Curriculum Work in the New Millenium

The curriculum of American elementary and secondary schools needs revitalization now more than at any time in nearly a century. American society is becoming more multiethnic as immigration and differential birth rates add more South and Central Americans and Asians to the social mix. Together with large populations of Americans of African and Hispanic descent, these "minorities" are becoming a majority in the schools of many states. Together with increasing globalization of communications and business, this development opens possibilities for a more global curriculum. Should U.S. schools consider teaching more about the history of Africa, Asia, and South America? Should a new mix of foreign languages be offered? Should literature from these traditions be included in English classes?

The American economy is undergoing a far-reaching transformation from predominantly industrial production to predominantly information and services and from a world of limited competition among developed countries to a truly global economy with strong economic centers outside the West. Various forms of technology are transforming the workplace and making new demands on workers for more sophisticated knowledge and skill. School achievements that recently seemed good enough for success in work, such as arithmetic, basic literacy, and a smattering of science, now seem too limiting, and subjects that recently seemed advanced, such as algebra, chemistry, computer science, and a foreign language, now seem basic. Individual achievement is still important, but so is the ability to work in teams. Knowledge of other cultures and effectiveness in oral communication and in interpersonal interactions have greater practical value now. Should schools consider changes in their curriculums to prepare youngsters for a changed economy?

Radio, television, and opinion polls have become the primary channels of communication between citizens and government. The ability to raise money for access to these channels has become a major determinant of political power. Traditional institutions of government have become overloaded—courts overloaded with cases, legislatures overloaded with bills, the executive branch overloaded with making and implementing policies, and every agency overloaded with budget preparations and paperwork. They are all underfunded and overspent. The public's confidence in its public institutions remains low. How long can schools continue to teach civics and government as if all this had not happened? Will schools not be expected to play a role in strengthening young people's identification with their governmental institutions? What changes in the teaching of the social studies, say, or in school governance or in extracurricular activities would be helpful?

Families are changing. Increasingly both parents work. Divorce and remarriage shuffle children among families. Mobility weakens bonds between generations. As a response, more children seem to rely on their peers for emotional support. Schools are the main places where children meet with their peers. Should schools strive to change relations between students to be more cooperative, between school and family to allow more frequent parent–teacher contact, or between teacher and students to be more supportive and personal? Should students remain with one teacher for several years, for example, to provide some compensatory stability? Leisure activities have expanded and taken on more important roles in personal and family life. Television, video recording, and computers have made many households information-rich and highly entertaining. As a result, children come to school more prepared in some ways and less prepared in others. They know a great deal about endangered species, the environment, and space, and more may know their numbers and letters, but more may also lack the ability to sit quietly and concentrate or to take turns. Students' own expectations have risen. The traditional second grade unit on weather that uses weather maps cut from newspapers just does not measure up to television weather programs that show satellite photos of global cloud patterns, films of actual tornadoes, hurricanes viewed from planes flying inside the eye, and time-lapse studies of cloud formations. Schools may need to reconsider their curriculum in light of changes in what students bring with them from home.

Knowledge is still exploding. Major breakthroughs in the sciences that require us to revise what we believe about our world come almost annually. Continents now move. Protons, neutrons, and electrons are no longer the fundamental particles of physics. Newspapers describe newly deciphered protein molecules and speculate on their commercial applications. Mathematics has become the basis of our technological economy, but it is a different mathematics than we have been teaching. It is a discrete mathematics, for instance, rather than a continuous one, and a mathematics of inquiry, problem solving, discovery, and proof rather than one of numerical computation. Now anyone can buy calculators to do most of the calculations taught in the first eight grades of school. Soon anyone will be able to buy computer programs that will diagram sentences and check spelling and grammar well enough to pass high school examinations. Students can rent filmed versions of the classic novels assigned in English class complete with critical commentaries.

If the only challenge curriculum leaders faced were to adapt the curriculum to meet these new developments in society, our needs for curriculum improvement would be immense. But most opinion leaders charge that American public schools are failing to deliver today's simpler, less challenging curriculum effectively to all students. Americans have not been able to achieve system-wide curriculum improvements. The dozen or more curriculum reform movements that have attempted system-wide curriculum improvements since World War II have been costly, controversial, and generally disappointing. Not only reformers but also even mainstream politicians are declaring that the system is broken and demanding more radical measures to improve schools, such as a system of national standards tied to high stakes tests and new educational institutions (i.e., charter schools, home schooling, and vouchers). Educational issues, especially curriculum issues, are increasingly being fought out in the political arena, with mayors, governors, state and federal legislators, and presidential candidates playing leading roles.

Achieving American's rising expectations for education will require a great deal of creative curriculum work, whether for traditional schools or for new educational institutions. While much curriculum work today remains the same in many ways as it has been for a half-century or more, these strong currents of change portend a transformation of curriculum work in the coming decades. These developments create exciting new challenges and opportunities for talented, well-prepared curriculum specialists and leaders.

What Curriculum Professionals Need to Know

Curriculum specialists and leaders need to prepare for a major change in the way curriculum work is done, either a revolution or a reformation of major proportions. In either case, effective curriculum work in the new environment will require a mixture of new and traditional skills and knowledge. The core areas of expertise needed are the ability to:

- find and develop curriculums that are markedly more effective in helping students learn,
- gain working agreement among stakeholders on curriculum initiatives,
- implement curriculum initiatives in a widespread, authentic, lasting way,
- secure publicly credible evidence of learning,
- network, team, and collaborate with teachers, experts, and the public to accomplish these and other forms of curriculum work.

In my view, the well-prepared curriculum specialist and curriculum leader of the 21st century will deeply understand these four foundations of curriculum work.

1. Traditions of curriculum practice

    Every element of every curriculum has a history and that history discloses important things about it and about the values of those who made it and sustain it. Knowledge of history and traditions enables the curriculum professional to spot similarities of current or proposed practices to older ones, see how events and trends shape curriculums and curriculum work, and gain perspective on current curriculum issues.

2. Visions and values that drive judgment and action

    Ideas animate people and influence how they shape the curriculum. Curriculum professionals need to appreciate the range of beliefs and values people hold about society, students, knowledge, and education, and how these affect what they do about curriculum. They need to realize that all curriculum work favors some human values at the expense of others, that no one can take a step in any curriculum matter without standing on some value. They need to appreciate the loose consensus on broadly stated educational aims such as academic achievement and preparation for life and work that all Americans share as well as the sharp divisions between Americans on priorities between and within these broad aims and on the best curricular means to achieve them. They need to become aware of where controversy lurks.

3. Reforms and reform movements

    Every curriculum leader should know that reform movements happen and that they may bring more change than years of patient work through the usual channels.

They should know that reforms could cause damage as well as bring benefits. They should know how and why reform movements arise and how to make the most of the opportunities they bring and minimize their damage.

4. Studies that inform curriculum decisions

    Curriculum professionals should know how research and scholarship can help them do better curriculum work. They should know how to find relevant research, read it critically, and understand its implications for practice. They should know both the strengths and limitations of research and be able to integrate studies intelligently into deliberation and decision making.

Twenty-first century curriculum leaders will also have a deep understanding of the nature of curriculum work, the challenges it presents, and how others have met those challenges. Four types of curriculum work are especially important: sustaining and improving classroom curriculums and sustaining and improving school curriculums. The chapters that follow introduce these fundamental domains of curriculum knowledge and skill.

Questions and Projects

1. To understand the concept of curriculum more deeply and appreciate the subtleties involved in any definition, take turns describing a school curriculum to each other. Choose a specific school that you know well, and take 10 minutes to describe it to your partner. Your partner should take notes using the following four columns: Content, Purpose, Organization, and Other. Then switch roles so that your partner describes a curriculum and you take notes. Compare notes. How were the two curriculums similar and different? Did organizing the curriculums' features in these columns make it easier to discover similarities and differences? Did the three main categories capture nearly all of the important features of the curriculums, or did you fill up the "Other" column with characteristics that didn't fit into the three main categories? What does this experience suggest to you about defining and describing a curriculum?

2. Choose one of the definitions of curriculum in Fig. 1.5 and identify some ways it is biased. Compare it with another definition that has quite different biases. Invent a debate between two partisans on some substantive curriculum issue. Let each person favor one of the two definitions. In debate, each should try to convince observers that their position is superior. Now invent a genuine dialogue in which the two partisans try to understand their differences and, where possible, resolve them.

3. Describe a real occasion that you observed or participated in when an individual or group did significant curriculum work. Do you think that the work done was successful? Why or why not? What skills and knowledge did this work require?

4. What aspects of curriculum work as described in this chapter do you find more and less appealing?

5. In your ideal world, how would curriculum work go? Who would be involved in curriculum work and who would lead it? What would be the product or outcome of the work? Through what activities would the work get done? When and where would it be done?

6. Write your curriculum résumé. List your activities and accomplishments that you believe prepare you for curriculum work.

7. Make a personal learning agenda. List the areas where you want to learn more or become more skilled or experienced in relation to curriculum work.

Further Study

The best way to learn about any field is to study its history, biographies of its prominent members, and its seminal works. Fortunately, good examples of this kind of literature are available for the curriculum field. Biographies of prominent curriculum specialists, such as Harold Rugg's autobiography, *That Men May Understand* (1941) and original works that have influenced thinking in the field such as Ralph Tyler's *Basic Principles of Curriculum and Instruction* (1949), are an excellent way into the field of curriculum. Chapter 2 mentions many of the relevant names and titles. *The Handbook of Research on Curriculum*, and William Schubert's *Curriculum Books* (1980) are excellent companions to have at your side when you are reading.

Good journals to read about curriculum work are the *Journal of Curriculum Studies* and *Curriculum Inquiry* for research, *Educational Leadership*, *Phi Delta Kappan*, the *Elementary School Journal*, and the *High School Journal* for contemporary and emerging issues, and the various subject matter journals for developments in the subject fields.

Organizations who hold conferences where you can learn about the latest work include The Association for Supervision and Curriculum Development, Division B—Curriculum Studies—of the American Educational Research Association, and the Association for Curriculum History. Each subject matter has professional organizations where curriculum work in that subject will be discussed. Some prominent ones include the National Council of Teachers of English (http://www.ncte.org/), the National Council of Teachers of Mathematics (http://www.nctm.org/), the National Science Teachers Association (http://www.nsta.org/), and the National Council for the Social Studies (http://www.ncss.org/).

CHAPTER TWO

Traditions of Curriculum Practice

Anyone concerned with cultural progress must necessarily make use of the historical possibilities of the age in which he lives.
— Werner Heisenberg, *Physics and Beyond*, 1971

Questions

- How has the curriculum of American schools changed since Colonial times?
- How do curriculum traditions influence our thinking and practice today?
- How are these changes related to trends and events in American society?
- How can curriculum professionals use historical thinking productively?

The American School Curriculum Before 1890

Literacy and moral training were the pillars of formal schooling from the Colonial period to roughly the 1830s. Most Americans spent their six years or so of formal schooling learning how to read, write, calculate, and behave. They learned by copying from books or from the teacher and by reciting aloud in class. Teachers insisted on letter perfect memorization. Religion, nationalism, moral virtue, and strict discipline permeated the lessons. Early America's best known educator, Noah Webster, spoke for his generation when he described the purpose of his schoolbook *An American Selection of Lessons in Reading and Speaking* (1789), as "to refine and establish our language, to facilitate the acquisition of grammatical knowledge and diffuse the principles of virtue and patriotism" (preface).

Most Americans lived on farms and had to sacrifice mightily to provide schooling at all. It was not uncommon for a rural classroom to contain only a few books, and it was a rare classroom where every child had a copy of the same textbook. Therefore, most schoolwork was oral. Children copied letters from a book onto their slate. Chalkboards did not begin to be used until late in the century.

The first books children used were spellers and arithmetics. Spellers presented the alphabet and a list of syllables to be memorized followed by lists of words and, eventually, sentences. These early books do not look childish to modern eyes. They contain adult words like "heresy," "popery," "republic," and "kingdom." Arithmetics introduced whole numbers, fractions, percentages, decimals, and the basic operations of addition, subtraction, multiplication, and division using problems drawn from daily economic life. The problems in arithmetics spared students no difficulties. Children saw in their books the same problems an adult would encounter in farm, business, household, or shop. The content of American school books reflected practical life more than most European schools, but actual preparation for trades and occupations had no place in American schools.

Early Americans encountered a very basic and elementary curriculum, indeed. Children who completed it were literate and had been instilled with God-fearing and patriotic attitudes. This was enough for most Americans. Yet the curriculum was quite rigorous and demanding. Students had to memorize many words every day and make intricate arithmetic calculations, all with "letter perfect" exactness.

Local citizens made nearly all decisions about schools, including decisions about the curriculum. Nearly all schools were private. The parents whose fees supported the schools hired the schoolmaster and made curriculum decisions. Parents judged the quality of the school by listening to their children recite at home and by attending formal recitals at school. In some cases, a schoolmaster or schoolmistress attained such standing in the community that the local community accepted his or her judgment without question. In most cases, though, the schoolmaster or schoolmistress and teachers served at the pleasure of the parents and local citizenry who replaced them at will. Figure 2.1 shows a widely used beginning reading text of this period.

The small fraction of American youth who continued their schooling beyond the primary school attended private secondary schools called academies. Academies offered basic instruction in subjects required for entrance to college.

Many young men in this period studied practical subjects in preparation for careers in trades or businesses rather than prepare for college in an academy. They might study accounting, surveying, or navigation in proprietary schools or apprentice themselves to a printer,

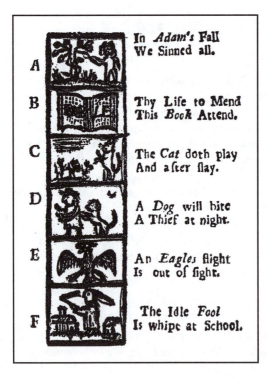

FIG. 2.1. *Selections from* The New England Primer *(1727).*

> *Notice is hereby given. That the trustees of the*
> *ACADEMY of Philadelphia, intend (God willing) to*
> *open the same on the first Monday of January next:*
> *wherein Youth will be taught the Latin, Greek,*
> *English, Writing, Arithmetic, Merchants Accounts,*
> *Geometry, Algebra, Surveying, Gauging,*
> *Navigation, Astronomy, Drawing in Perspective,*
> *and other mathematical Sciences; with natural and*
> *mechanical philosophy, &tc. agreeable to the*
> *Constitutions heretofore published, at the Rate of*
> *Four Pounds per annum, and Twenty Shillings*
> *entrance.*

FIG. 2.2. *Excerpt from Franklin's proposal for an academy (1749).*
Note. From *Source Studies in American Colonial Education. The Private School,* by Robert F. Seybolt, 1925, Urbana, IL: University of Illinois Bureau of Educational Research, Bulletin No. 28.

mechanic, or tradesman. The relative value of practical studies such as modern languages, geography, mechanical philosophy (physical science), accounting, surveying, and navigation and "ornamental" studies such as classical languages and literature became a prominent issue in discussions about secondary education in the mid-18th century. In 1749 Benjamin Franklin proposed to establish an academy that embraced both the practical and the ornamental studies. Figure 2.2 shows the studies proposed for the academy. Franklin's academy became a model for many innovative secondary schools until well into the 19th century.

After 1830 American education entered a period of far reaching change from small, local schools paid for by parents to state supported public education open to all. The extent of the change can be gauged by comparing the page from Noah Webster's speller of 1831 in Fig. 2.3 to the page from *McGuffey's Second Eclectic Reader* of 1879 in Fig. 2.4.

> (The certificate of graduation of Phillips Exeter Academy describes the
> attainment of one of its graduates . . .)
>
> *Be it therefore known that __ has been a*
> *member of the (Phillips Andover) Academy seven*
> *years, and appears on examination to have*
> *acquired the principles of the English, French,*
> *Latin and Greek languages, Geography, Arithmetic*
> *and practical Geometry; that he has made very*
> *valuable progress in the study of Rhetoric, History,*
> *Natural and Moral Philosophy, Logic, Astronomy*
> *and Natural Law; and that he has sustained a good*
> *moral character during said term . . .*

FIG. 2.3. *The program of a New England academy (1790).*
Note. From *The Phillips Exeter Academy: A History,* by Laurence M. Crosbie, 1924, Exeter, NH: The Academy.

Lessons of Easy Words, to Teach Children to Read, and to Know Their Duty

Lesson I
No man may put off the law of God:
My joy is in his law all the day.
O may I not go in the way of sin!
Let me not go in the way of ill men.

II
A bad man is a foe to the law:
It is his joy to do ill.
All men go out of the way.
Who can say he has no sin?

III
The way of man is ill.
My son, do as you are bid: But if you are
bid, do no ill.
See not my sins and let me not go to the pit.

IV
Rest in the Lord, and mind his word.
My son, hold fast the law that is good.
You must not tell a lie, nor do hurt.
We must let no man hurt us.

FIG. 2.4. *Lessons from an early American speller (1831).*
Note.   From *The American Spelling Book,* by Noah Webster, 1831, Boston: West and Richardson.

The big story of the period between 1830 and the Civil War was the success of the crusade for universal free public education. Inspired by the tireless campaigning of leaders Horace Mann and Henry Barnard, reformers established free public schools in Massachusetts (1827), Pennsylvania (1834), and later in the other states. Massachusetts enacted the first compulsory school attendance law in 1852. By 1860, a majority of the states had established public school systems, and a good half of the nation's children were receiving some formal education. In leading states such as Massachusetts, New York, and Pennsylvania, free public education expanded to include secondary schools (Cremin, 1961, p. 13).

Except for Americanizing the content of education in order to combat the influence of European ideas, curricular reforms were gradual and little noticed before 1830. After 1830, with the expansion of public schooling, several significant pedagogical reforms blossomed. Readers—books that taught children to sound out words presented in meaningful sentences—replaced spellers. Readers included material more familiar to children. Figure 2.5 shows an example from the popular *McGuffey's Second Eclectic Reader* (1879). Also, more primary schools began to teach geography and history along with the three Rs.

Many wealthy educated Americans in the cities of the northeast sent their children to universities in Europe. While in Europe they learned about innovative ideas and experiments in education underway in Europe. John Dewey, for instance, became acquainted with the radical pedagogical ideas of Rousseau and his follower, the Swiss schoolmaster Pestalozzi, when he pursued advanced studies in Europe. Pestalozzi maintained a school

---

Evening at Home

1. It is winter. The cold wind whistles through the branches of the trees.
2. Mr. Brown has done his day's work, and his children, Harry and Kate, have come home from school. They learned their lessons well to-day, and both feel happy.
3. Tea is over. Mrs. Brown has put the little sitting-room in order. The fire burns brightly. One lamp gives light enough for all. On the stool is a basket of fine apples. They seem to say, "Won't you have one?"
4. Harry and Kate read a story in a new book. The father reads his newspaper, and the mother mends Harry's stockings...."

FIG. 2.5. *A selection from* McGuffey's Second Eclectic Reader *(1879).*
Note. From *McGuffey's Second Eclectic Reader* (pp. 11–12), by William Holmes McGuffey, 1879, Cincinnati: Wilson, Hinkle.

that offered a kinder, more "natural" education. Instead of reciting memorized words and doing routine arithmetic exercises under strict discipline, Pestalozzi's pupils went on field trips, made maps and models, and studied the life around them. Other European educational reformers of the period followed German philosophers Hegel and Kant who emphasized culture and institutions as sources of human advancement. The German scholar and educator Herbart developed a model for schooling based upon systematic teaching of culturally important bodies of knowledge. Returning Americans publicized the European innovations in American journals, and some founded experimental schools using similar methods.

The German influence prevailed in post-Civil War America. Historian Lawrence Cremin identifies William Torrey Harris as the leading educator of the period. As superintendent of schools in St. Louis from 1868 to 1880, and United States Commissioner of Education from 1889 to 1906, Harris "rationalized the institution of the public school" (Cremin, 1961, p. 15). Harris believed that the curriculum should bring the child into possession of the best of civilization through orderly, systematic study of all the subjects that provided ideas about the world they lived in. Following the German philosopher Hegel, Harris saw institutions as enabling mankind to attain its highest development. In his pedagogical creed (1898), Harris attacked Rousseau's belief that children should be freed from arbitrary adult authority as "the greatest heresy in educational doctrine" (Cremin, 1961, p. 37). Civilized life, Harris wrote, was "a life of order, self-discipline, civic loyalty, and respect for private property" (Cremin, 1961, p. 17). The following passage from Harris' *Compulsory Education in Relation to Crime and Social Morals* (1885) conveys the tone and central message of his educational doctrines.

> The great object, then, of education is the preparation of the individual for a life in institutions, the preparation of each individual for social combination.... The ordinary type of school—the so-called "common school"—receives the child from the family at the age of five or six years. It receives him into a social body (for the school is a community) and educates him by "discipline" and "instruction" as they are technically called. By "discipline" is meant the training in behavior, a training of the will, moral training. It consists in imposing upon the child a set of forms of behavior rendered necessary in order to secure concert of action,—such forms as regularity, punctuality, silence, and industry. These are the four cardinal duties of the school pupil. Without them, the school cannot act as a unit, instruction cannot be given in classes, and no good result achieved.... (Harris, 1885, pp. 2–3.)

The program Harris recommended for the common or elementary school included the conventional three Rs plus geography, history, natural history, literature, and drawing.

The program for the high school included algebra, geometry, plane trigonometry, analytical geometry, natural philosophy, chemistry, physical geography, astronomy, botany, zoology, physiology, Latin, Greek, French or German, history, the Constitution of the United States, rhetoric, English literature, and mental and moral philosophy. Textbooks presented the content of these subjects to students. The teacher conducted oral recitations on assigned lessons to make certain students had read and mastered the assignments. Teachers graded pupils by achievement, regardless of age. They promoted students to the next grade only when they had passed written tests on the skills and knowledge required for that grade.

By 1890 Harris' plan came to be an accurate description of the schools in America's fast-growing cities and towns. Schooling was largely verbal and academic, permeated by strict discipline, and conducted within a rigid, highly structured institutional framework of grades, textbooks, and examinations.

By 1890 a common pattern of public school governance had emerged. The locally appointed or elected public school board, which was an arm of city, township, or county government, ran the schools. In cities, school board members were elected or appointed to represent particular wards. The school board appointed all school employees, including superintendents, principals, teachers, and janitors. Most personnel served on one-year contracts. Many superintendents, principals, and teachers lost their jobs because newly elected board members wanted their own friends or relatives in those jobs, because they had displeased one or more board members, or because another job seeker offered a bigger bribe.

Meanwhile, teaching and school administration became steadily more professional. Normal schools set up to prepare high school graduates to be elementary school teachers multiplied. Professional journals of educational theory and practice appeared. The National Education Association was founded in 1857. Increasingly, the opinion leaders in education came from the ranks of professionally trained educators. Many of these leaders went abroad to study, chiefly to Germany, where many received Ph.D.s. Significantly, the preeminent educational leader of the period, William Torrey Harris, was a professional educator, unlike earlier lay leaders such as Mann, Barnard, and Webster. By 1890 all the most influential educational leaders were professional schoolmen who saw themselves as part of a national network of professionals, trained and equipped for leadership on questions of education. This, of course, put them in direct competition with boards of education composed of laymen.

During the last quarter of the 19th century the curriculum and pedagogy advocated so ably by Harris came under increasing criticism from both lay and professional leaders. They charged that the content was irrelevant for the majority of American youth, that the emphasis on order and discipline was deadening and excessive, that schoolmasters were often cruel to children in the name of discipline, and that the system was inefficient because so many children failed and were retained in earlier grades. Many reformers thought that Pestalozzian ideas offered ways to overcome the problems of the prevailing system. Some of the more innovative American educational leaders began to experiment with more "natural" practices. The experience of one such leader, a young superintendent of schools in Oswego, New York, epitomizes the experience of many others.

Edward Sheldon had been an ardent proponent of strict order and discipline until the 1850s when he began to experiment with methods based on the work of Pestalozzi. He soon converted to the gentler, more natural Pestalozzian methods, in which instruction followed the child's interest and teachers sought to appeal to constructive motives within the child rather than to impose discipline without by force or coercion. Sheldon became an equally ardent advocate of the new methods. His success can be judged from the following report of the examining committee appointed annually by the board of education at Oswego to report on the condition of the schools.

Wherever the teachers have caught the spirit of the plan, and have made a practical application of it, the effect is very marked in the awakened and quickened faculties of the children. It was never our pleasure before to witness so much interest in any class exercise. There was no dull routine of questions and monosyllabic answers, no mere recitation of dry and stereotyped formulas, no apparent unloading of the memory, but we seemed as in the presence of so many youthful adventurers fresh from their voyages of discovery, each eager to recount the story of his successes. In their explorations, the fields, the wood, the garden, and the old house, from the cellar to the garret, will testify to their vigilance. The knowledge both of the parents and the teacher is often put to the severest test. They are continually plied with questions too difficult for them to answer. (*Annual Report of the Board of Education*, Oswego, New York, for the Year Ending March 31, 1861, quoted in Cubberley (1934), p. 344.)

Sheldon's "object teaching," together with the introduction of kindergartens and manual training, established an alternative pedagogy in some American schools that challenged the preeminence of verbal learning and strict discipline in schooling. Many merchants and industrialists of the period complained about the poor quality of the workers that came out of the schools. A rapidly expanding industrial economy needed a large supply of skilled workers, many more than were trained by apprenticeship. Industrialists wanted the schools to provide vocational training. In St. Louis in 1879, Calvin Woodward established the kind of school they wanted. His Manual Training School provided a 3-year program equally divided between mental and manual labor: mental labor consisting of practically oriented versions of the conventional academic subjects and manual labor consisting of explicit training in school workshops. This program was designed to prepare young men directly to earn a living in an industrial society. By 1890 most major cities offered private manual training schools on this model, often sponsored by businessmen. Many within industry and labor also saw a great need for "practicalizing" public schools.

Agrarian interests supported business and labor in this aim. The Grange, the principal organization representing farmers, advocated as early as 1874 the teaching of practical agriculture and domestic arts and sciences in schools (Cremin, 1961, p. 42). Cremin quotes one agricultural opinion leader of the time on the frustrations of those who sought a place for agriculture in their children's education.

... as it was 60 years ago in our boyhood, so it is today in 99 out of every 100 schools. Not a grain of progress that will help the country boy to a better understanding of the problems of agriculture (p. 45).

A new breed of social reformers criticized the educational system of the late 19th century for failing to minister to the most pressing life problems of immigrants and city slum dwellers. Socially concerned Americans in the 1890s grew increasingly concerned about the plight of the urban poor. Articles in popular magazines dramatized the sufferings of tenement dwellers. Activist reformers refused to accept the glib excuses offered for poverty—drinking and immoral living—and the Biblical conclusion that the poor would always be with us. The settlement house was the most visible expression of this awakening of conscience. Hull House, established in Chicago by Jane Addams and Ellen Gates Starr in 1889, was the most famous settlement house. Others appeared in almost every major city by 1900. From the beginning, settlement houses operated in education. They established kindergartens and nurseries, taught working men and women to read, established playgrounds and vacation centers for city children in the summer, set up drama and choral groups, and taught nutrition, English for immigrants, child care, millinery, dressmaking, and dozens of trades and crafts. The conception of socialized education that emerged from the work of the settlements stood in sharp contrast to the narrowly academic emphasis of secondary schools. Many reformers thought it set a pattern the schools should follow.

The Progressive Transformation of the School: 1890–1930

The many currents of discontent about education that ran in the post-Civil War decades became by 1890 "a nationwide torrent of criticism, innovation, and reform that soon took on all the earmarks of a social movement" (Cremin, 1961, p. 22). Changes in American society left the traditional curriculum out of step with the most vital, expanding, and influential sectors of the society. America was becoming a wealthy, powerful industrial society. To many Americans the deeds of captains of industry such as Rockefeller, Morgan, and Carnegie outshone those of the ancient heroes of Greece and Rome. The scientific discoveries of Newton and Pasteur and the inventions of Watt, Marconi, and Edison seemed to promise more progress than the classics.

The curriculum William T. Harris had championed, with its rigid discipline, reverence for ancient languages and cultures, and emphasis on verbal learning, came to seem old-fashioned, elitist, and inadequate to the demands of a modern industrial democracy. Out of these discontents arose the most far-reaching reform movement American education has yet known—progressive education.

The progressive era in American education coincided with a period of rapid educational expansion. More students came to school and stayed longer than ever before. Official government statistics report that less than 14 million students, barely 50% of the school age population, attended elementary and secondary schools (public and private) in the United States in 1889. By 1930 the same source records nearly 28 million enrolled, over 70% of the school age population. In 1890, less than 5% of American 17-year-olds were high school graduates. By 1930 nearly 30% graduated. School was becoming the place where nearly all American children spent nearly all of their childhood.

Although more radical progressive practices such as the project method and teacher–pupil planning were never widely adopted, many practices introduced in the progressive era have become established in American schools, and a progressive cast of mind still prevails among professional educators.

Broadened Elementary Curriculum

Progressives challenged most traditional school practices as unsuitable for the children of a modern industrial democracy. In place of the three Rs (readin', 'ritin', and 'rithmetic) and strict discipline (the hick'ry stick), progressives offered a much broader elementary school curriculum and a much gentler appeal to children's better nature. Going to school traditionally meant to sit quietly in neat rows of desks, to read, to memorize, to do arithmetic problems at the board and at one's desk, and to recite orally—in short, to undergo a rigorous, no-nonsense program of literacy training and discipline. Here, for contrast, is an account, published in 1900, of a visit by the mother of a prospective student to John Dewey's Progressive Laboratory School at the University of Chicago.

"None of the children seemed to have any books as they came up (to the school). I didn't see even a geography or a reader among the older children. One little girl had a live alligator in a box; a small boy was carrying a large Indian blanket in from a carriage; one child had a basket of fruit, and another a package which I had heard him tell the teacher contained "sandwiches". . . . I concluded that this must be an off day with the school; but thought that I might as well stay and see them start,—they seemed to be having such a good time. . . .

"I followed the children to the gymnasium, where seats were arranged for the morning exercises, which consisted chiefly of singing. One or two groups of children were asked to sing their 'Group Song.' Upon inquiry I was told that the charming melody and the words of the song I heard were composed by the children who sang them. . . . Upstairs I found a group of children about ten years old engaged in setting up electric bells. . . . A group of younger children had a sheepskin from which they were taking wool. . . . Everywhere the children were busy, but the morning was half gone and I had heard nothing that reminded me of a school except a class talking Latin as I passed" (Runyon, 1900, pp. 590–591).

At Lincoln School in New York City students built a play city in the first and second grades. Students studied daily life in homes, neighborhoods, shops, stores, factories, farms, towns, and cities. Progressive schools substituted social development for strict discipline. Teachers gave students practice in cooperation, leadership, and service to others. They patterned classrooms on families and made the social relationships an explicit focus of attention. Students helped to make rules and set penalties for breaking them. Students even had a say in choosing classroom activities and planning and carrying them out.

Such experiments were at first a mere drop in the bucket, but they caught the imagination of a generation of teachers and of young parents ready for a change. Gradually, elements of the new programs found their way into traditional classrooms and the curriculum of elementary schools was greatly broadened. The content subjects—history, geography, and science—were formerly considered too difficult for young children, but they became more accessible when teachers used new methods in addition to reading. Soon literacy became merely the backbone of the elementary curriculum, not its essence.

New Textbooks and Curriculum Materials

By 1930, textbooks were larger, more colorful, and easier to read and use. Primary school readers presented colorful scenes illustrating simple stories about familiar happenings in familiar surroundings. Authors controlled the vocabulary of early readers to include only the simplest, most familiar words repeated many times in the simplest possible sentences such as "See Spot run. Run, Spot, run." Textbooks included suggestions for classroom activities. Basic exercises gave all students an opportunity to practice. Textbooks gradually progressed from familiar to new and from simple to complex. And the textbooks had help from a whole battery of newly developed supplementary educational materials—workbooks, teachers' guides, standardized tests, and performance scales.

Progressives urged educators to use natural impulses to help children learn, rather than thwart natural impulses to discipline the child. Therefore, publishers made books easy and appealing rather than austere and difficult. Psychologists, notably Edward L. Thorndike of Teachers College, Columbia University, did research to determine what children found easy and difficult. He compiled the first dictionary based on actual use of words in everyday publications, and publishers used his lists of the most frequently used words to revise their textbooks. Thorndike also studied the difficulties children encountered in learning arithmetic. A new generation of educational psychologists joined Thorndike in studying and redesigning textbooks and curriculum materials. As a result of their efforts, the textbooks of 1930 were an altogether new creation, as unlike the Harris-inspired books of 1890 as these were unlike Colonial spellers and arithmetics.

The Decline and Fall of the Classics

In 1890 the classics—Latin, Greek, and ancient history—dominated the secondary school curriculum, but not without opposition. Practical Americans had long questioned the value of the classics. Benjamin Franklin's academy gave the classics a secondary place because they were more ornamental than useful. Even many university professors and college presidents opposed the tradition requiring all undergraduates to study the classics. Early in the 19th century, the classics faculty of Yale had felt so threatened by opposition from within and without that they issued a report defending the classics. The *Yale Report*, issued in 1828, made the case for the classics on the grounds that they, more than any other subjects, disciplined the mind.

The report argued that the various school subjects each contributed to mental discipline in a unique way by training a different set of mental faculties. Mathematics disciplined deductive reasoning. Physical sciences disciplined induction, probable reasoning, and the use of facts. Classics, unique among subjects, disciplined all the mental faculties: taste, memory, reasoning, ethical judgment, copiousness, and accuracy of expression—the whole lot. Thus, the classics deserved their dominant place in the undergraduate curriculum and therefore in the secondary school curriculum.

Progressive opponents of the classics attacked the doctrine of mental discipline with the tools of science. To test whether mental powers exist as independent faculties that can be strengthened with practice, psychologists conducted extensive laboratory tests. Thorndike compared the intelligence test scores of two groups of pupils, otherwise as nearly identical as could be arranged. One group had studied mathematics in school while the other had taken courses in stenography or cooking instead of mathematics. The gains in intelligence were the same for the two groups of pupils. Studying cooking led to as much improvement in intelligence as measured on these tests as studying mathematics. Subsequent studies confirmed that studying the classics did not improve intelligence scores any more than studying other subjects.

Of course, the *Yale Report* had not claimed that studying the classics improved IQ scores, and the validity of IQ scores as a measure of the educational effects of studying any subject is certainly debatable. Nevertheless, the doctrine of mental discipline lost credibility in academia, and with it fell the rationale for the classics.

Defenders had a hard time convincing students to study classics. Colleges lowered entrance requirements, sponsored preparatory schools on campus, and even instituted part-time, nondegree programs. Still, every year fewer students came to college able to read Latin and Greek. Soon many colleges dropped classics as an entrance requirement. As early as 1886, under President Charles W. Eliot's leadership, Harvard began to accept advanced mathematics and physics in place of Greek as an admission requirement. By 1903 Greek was no longer required at Yale. Historian Frederick Rudolph describes the final fall of the classics from dominance in the undergraduate curriculum this way:

> By 1915 fewer than fifteen major colleges still required four years of Latin for the B.A. degree. In 1919 Yale accepted students without admission Latin and enrolled them as candidates for the Ph.D. degree. Four years later the faculty voted to abolish Latin as a requirement for admission or for the B.A. degree, but they were overruled by the Yale Corporation, one member of which, William Howard Taft, exclaimed: "Over my dead body!" Taft died in 1930. Latin went in 1931 (Rudolph, 1977, p. 214).

High schools dropped courses in Greek once colleges ceased to require it. By 1910, in the words of historian Edward A. Krug (1964), "Greek had been surrendered as a hopeless cause" (p. 336). Government statistics for 1924–1925 showed only 11,000 students nationwide enrolled in secondary school Greek. Enrollments in Latin, however, continued to rise, although the proportions of students enrolled in Latin declined steadily from 50.6% in 1900 to 37.3% in 1915 to 27.5% in 1923–1924. Latin ceased being the pillar of the academic curriculum and became merely another elective such as art, music, or typewriting. The example of the classics shows that, in curriculum as in civilization, the mighty fall.

Reorganizing the Secondary School Studies

In 1890 college entrance requirements and secondary school course offerings varied to an extent that many found confusing and alarming. Leaders in the colleges and secondary schools cooperated in reorganizing both entrance requirements and secondary school programs, with the result that by 1930 high schools around the country offered a uniform, sequential, departmentally organized academic curriculum. Figure 2.6 contrasts typical secondary school course offerings before and after the reorganization.

Several famous national committees played pivotal roles in this reorganization of the secondary school curriculum. The first of these, The Committee of Ten, whose official name was "The Committee on Secondary School Studies," was appointed by the National Education Association in 1892 and charged to bring order into the scattered and chaotic program of studies in secondary schools. Its membership included both college and secondary school faculty, although the colleges were dominant both in numbers and influence. Charles W. Eliot, President of Harvard University, chaired the committee.

1890	1930

English
  rhetoric, logic, etymology, reading, English literature, recitation, composition, and grammar
	English
	  four years of a subject called English

Mathematics
  advanced arithmetic with logarithms, algebra, geometry, trigonometry, surveying, navigation
	Mathematics
	  general math, business math, algebra I and II, geometry, and trigonometry

Social Studies
  The Constitution of the United States, moral philosophy, mental philosophy, ancient history, European history, political economy, and American history
	Social Studies
	  American history, problems of American democracy, civics

Science
  anatomy, physiology, botany, astronomy, chemistry, navigation, and surveying, physical geography, natural philosophy, and geology
	Science
	  general science, biology, physical science, chemistry, and physics

	Other subjects home economics, consumer education, business education, agricultural education, and other vocational subjects

FIG. 2.6. *Typical secondary school course offerings in 1890 and 1930.*

The Committee's report proposed four college preparatory curriculums: classical, Latin-scientific, modern languages, and English. The committee proposed that any student who completed one of these four programs should be admitted to college. All of the subjects taken were considered as having equal value toward college preparation.

The Committee of Ten and the later Committee on College Entrance Requirements combined botany, zoology, and human physiology into a single biology course. They recommended that secondary schools offer a standard sequence of three science courses: biology, chemistry, and physics. The committees reorganized the other school subjects similarly. The NEA virtually coined the term "social studies" when it appointed a "Committee on the reorganization of the social studies" in 1917. The Committee of Ten recognized English as a subject category in 1892. The National Council of Teachers of English was founded in 1911 and its president chaired the English committee of the Committee on the Reorganization of Secondary Education in 1917.

By 1930 the academic curriculum of secondary schools in the United States attained essentially the form it has today. As high schools grew, they assumed a departmental organization along the subject matter lines laid out by the Committee of Ten. The academic curriculum that resulted has been one of the most lasting curriculum reforms in our history and one of the most substantial in its impact on all parts and phases of the educational system.

The Rise of Vocational Education

A great increase in the number and percentage of students enrolled in vocational programs took place after the enactment of the Smith–Hughes Act in 1917. The campaign for this law is one of the great political campaigns in curricular history, and set an important precedent for federal action in curriculum matters.

In 1900, advocates of vocational education could point to few successes in schools. The four high school curriculums outlined by the Committee of Ten in 1896 included no vocational courses. Proposals for separate vocational high schools encountered strong resistance from leaders of traditional schools and from those who believed that separate vocational schools would be undemocratic. Rebuffed by school leaders, advocates of industrial education began to pursue their aims in the political arena where legislators turned more sympathetic ears. In 1906 they achieved a political victory in Massachusetts that attracted national attention. The Douglas Commission, appointed by the governor to study the question of industrial and technical education in that state, called for the creation of independent industrial schools throughout the state and for the introduction of day or evening industrial courses in the regular high schools.

Also in 1906 the National Society for the Promotion of Industrial Education (NSPIE) was founded in New York "to bring to public attention the importance of industrial education," ... and "to promote the establishment of institutions for industrial training" (Constitution, *NSPIE Bulletin No. 1*, 1907, p. 10). By 1910 the NSPIE had grown from a small band of educators and educational reformers to a powerful political coalition supported by labor, business, and agriculture. This remarkable political coalition was active in campaigns in dozens of states between 1906 and 1917, ringing up many impressive political victories in the form of laws establishing publicly supported programs of industrial education.

NSPIE's early successes roused resistance in other states, though, making each battle more difficult than the last, so the NSPIE began to work toward gaining federal support for vocational education.

Seeking federal support for vocational education was a bold move. Education had always been a jealously guarded prerogative of the states, and numerous attempts to secure federal support for education initiatives had all failed, including repeated attempts over more than a century to create a national university. It took 3 long years of politicking, but in 1917 the Smith–Hughes Act passed and vocational education became the first federally financed program in American public education.

To qualify for funding authorized by Smith–Hughes, states had to prepare plans for statewide vocational education programs. State plans had to meet detailed federal criteria. Local school districts seeking funding had to establish separate arrangements for governing vocational education. The so-called dual administration scheme protected vocational education from subversion by unsympathetic local school officials. Thus, vocational education entered American high schools with federal support and with a license entitling it to an existence separate from the rest of the curriculum.

The shift from the classical and academic high school curriculum of 1890 to the comprehensive high school including vocational education is the most far-reaching transformation the American high school curriculum has yet seen.

Invention of Procedures for Planned Curriculum Change

In transforming the curriculum of American schools, the progressive reformers invented several new approaches to curriculum improvement. Early educational crusaders such as Horace Mann and Henry Barnard traveled widely, gave speeches, wrote articles, and used their personal influence with the wealthy and influential. A generation later, William T. Harris used the same strategies, speaking mainly to educational leaders. By 1930 the progressives had developed a veritable tool kit of systematic procedures for curriculum revision, including national committees, school surveys, city-wide curriculum revision, laboratory schools, scientific studies, and legislation. Each of these techniques showed great early promise of transforming the curriculum, each quickly revealed serious shortcomings, but all continue to be used for particular purposes.

National Committees

After the Committee of Ten's first great success in curriculum making in 1892, the NEA appointed a dozen new national committees over the next three decades and charged them to reconsider every aspect of precollege education. The early committees had included both school and university leaders and had tried to standardize divergent practices. They were remarkably successful in negotiating compromises that colleges, high schools, and the public accepted. Their success gave such committees an excellent reputation and quite a bit of clout, especially since they had no official standing in law and no actual authority over so much as one school or teacher. The national committees appointed after 1918 drew their members mainly from the schools and from teacher education institutions, and they advocated progressive reforms. As a result, their successes, though striking in the short term, proved less lasting.

School Surveys

School surveys began about 1910 and for a decade spread rapidly to cities throughout the country. A school survey studied the educational needs of a community, predicted future needs, and proposed changes to meet these needs. Well-known surveys were comprehensive studies by a large team of surveyors, usually headed by a university professor and funded by a foundation. They lasted several years and looked into every nook and cranny of a school system's operations. Typical sources of data included first-hand observations, interviews, existing school records, and results of standard tests. Surveys seemed scientific and objective, akin to scientific management, a prestigious movement at that time. The surveyors pioneered a number of scientific techniques including population forecasting to anticipate enrollments; studies of building design, illumination, and ventilation; and use of standardized tests to study student achievement.

Surveys soon revealed limitations as levers for change, though. Readers had such trouble drawing firm conclusions from so much data that school systems often had to appoint local committees to interpret the survey report and make recommendations. Surveys were also costly. Scholars and scientists criticized the surveys for lack of rigor, but the more rigorous they became, the more costly, complicated, and ambiguous they became. By the 1920s leading educators came to see surveys as a specialized technique with limited usefulness, not a powerful lever for reform.

Citywide Curriculum-Making Committees

Ambitious school superintendents soon began to mount their own systemwide curriculum revisions. They established committees to develop districtwide goals and philosophy. The members of these committees met after school and on weekends, donating their time in the interests of school improvement. Once the board accepted the committee's report, other committees of teachers and administrators would work out the details and put them into practice.

Citywide curriculum-making committees could stay in close touch with local teachers, students, and communities. A strong superintendent supported by a like-minded board had the authority to organize the planning and implementation of reforms, and the financial backing to put the reform into practice. On the other hand, the committees' recommendations often looked suspiciously like the superintendent's ideas. The products of committee work often lacked not only coherence but also any leading idea, reflecting instead the fashion of the moment.

Laboratory Schools

In 1896 John Dewey and his wife opened an experimental laboratory school at the University of Chicago to test new educational ideas. Well-known laboratory schools such as the Dewey's school and the Lincoln School at Teachers College, Columbia, attracted a constant stream of visitors. Educators hungry for innovation eagerly read written accounts of the work of such schools and drew inspiration from them. Scores of laboratory schools sprang up between 1900 and 1930 in cities around the country, most associated with a college or university. They produced an impressive collection of curriculum plans and materials that often found their way into the mainstream of public school practice and into commercial textbooks and curriculum materials.

Unfortunately, the experimental classrooms were not typical, because most of the students were children of college faculty and wealthy professionals. Balancing the competing goals of testing risky new ideas while offering tuition-paying parents an education that they thought first-rate proved to be nearly impossible. Also, and surprisingly, laboratory schools did little rigorous evaluation; they were more development schools than laboratory schools.

Scientific Studies

Scientific studies sought an objective basis for new practices. An early study that achieved great notoriety was a national study of spelling performance by Joseph Mayer Rice, a Boston pediatrician and muckraking journalist. Published in 1897 under the provocative title "The Futility of the Spelling Grind," Rice's study reported the results of asking children in schools throughout the country to spell a standard list of words. Rice's results showed that students in schools that allocated more time to spelling did no better on his tests than students from schools that allocated less time. The results set off a furor of controversy among educators and the public.

In the next 3 decades thousands of such studies were conducted. Researchers compared different ways of teaching and learning spelling to determine, for example, whether a small amount of practice daily produced better results than the same amount of practice concentrated on fewer days. They developed standardized achievement tests in all subjects so that educators could compare any youngster's performance with that of others of similar age and grade. Innovators then revised courses of study, textbooks, workbooks, and other curriculum materials on the basis of the findings of such studies.

Scientific studies had many early successes, but their limitations gradually became evident. They were expensive, time-consuming, and equivocal—so equivocal that they rarely resolved important educational disputes. Every study rested on assumptions that critics could attack. Extending results from the laboratory to the classroom gave critics other openings. Definitive results required a series of studies, but who could wait years?

Legislation

The NSPIE demonstrated the remarkable potential of legislation as a strategy for curricular reform. They lobbied successfully for passage of the Smith–Hughes Act of 1917, which created a nationally financed system of vocational education. The lessons of their success were learned by proponents of other educational reforms. Proponents of physical education, American history, and biology were notably successful in securing the enactment of legislation in many states mandating a place in the secondary curriculum for their subjects. Forty years were to pass before another major success was to be scored in Congress, but a pattern was set. Henceforth, any group desiring admission for their subject to the public school curriculum established local, state, and national organizations and began lobbying.

Legislation as a means of curriculum change seems a particularly effective route to quick, large-scale curriculum change. A vote, a flourish of the pen, and the matter is settled with the full force of law. Yet educators soon discovered that laws were not a royal road to curriculum improvement. Legislation did not provide teachers prepared to implement the change. Students did not necessarily elect the subjects legislators required schools to offer. Legislation proved most successful where money was appropriated to fund new programs. Even then, local officials could often thwart the intent of the legislation. In some cases legislative mandates have been successfully challenged in the courts on the grounds that they interfered with rights of free speech or religious belief. Also, the security afforded by legislation is only as great as the continuing political support; laws can always be repealed by the next legislature.

Professionalization of Curriculum-Making: 1930–1960

The three turbulent decades from 1930 to 1960 encompassed the Great Depression, World War II, the Cold War, and the Korean conflict. Throughout these years national political agenda were filled with life and death issues, and, except for the issue of funding schools, the public left educational reform to educators. School enrollments were burgeoning. Early in the period, lack of work on farms and in idle factories kept more youths in school longer. Later, the post-war baby boom accelerated enrollments. Buildings could hardly be erected fast enough to house expanded school populations, and schools were chronically short of qualified teachers. Local budgets for schools increased steadily throughout the period, especially in the post-war economic expansion, yet were barely sufficient to meet the rising costs of building and staffing new schools.

No dramatic curriculum innovations arose in this period. The main story was one of professional leaders striving to realize fully the vision of progressive education. Superintendents, principals, and teachers exposed to progressive ideas in their professional training took the lead in experimenting with a variety of basically progressive reforms emphasizing the characteristic progressive values of democracy and practicality. The culmination of these proposals was life adjustment education, which advocated preparation for the everyday realities of daily life as the primary goal of education.

Curriculum reform became bureaucratized as procedures and personnel were incorporated into the expanding administrative and governance structure of increasingly larger schools and school systems. These reforms were not without their critics, and some bruising political battles were fought over education, especially early in the period over the issue of whether schools should be agencies of social reform. But, on balance, the period was one of relative tranquility compared to the euphoria of the progressive period and the frantic reforms to follow.

Content to Meet the Needs of Youth

By 1930 many young Americans who formerly would have left school to work by age 16 stayed on, not always willingly. Some stayed because they could not find work and some because local officials began to enforce compulsory attendance laws. These new students created many problems for the schools. One of the most serious was failing marks. A 1927 survey of 300 high schools found that "30 percent of first year students failed at least one subject, with corresponding figures of 29 percent, 24 percent, and 11 percent for the second, third, and fourth years" (Krug, p. 141). In Pennsylvania high schools—probably not very different from the nation as a whole—Latin was the subject most often failed (16.9%), followed by algebra (16.1%), ancient history (11.5%), and first-year English (10.3%) (Krug, 1964, p. 141).

Another serious problem was these students' lack of interest in the curriculum offered by the schools. A 1938 report of the American Council on Education, entitled *Youth Tell Their Story* (Bell, 1938), reported that "lack of interest in school" was the second most common reason young people gave for dropping out of school (24.6%), following only "economic reasons" (54%). Teachers faced more immediate problems in the disruptions and behavior problems fomented by unhappy youths unwillingly attending school. The combination of problems spelled trouble for everyone. Many educators felt that the school curriculum must change if schools were to serve these children and to realize the dream of a truly universal and democratic educational system.

Progressive school leaders initiated efforts to ease the problems by changing the content and aims of the school program. Vocational programs already existed, of course, and enrollments in these increased faster than enrollments in academic programs. But many refused to enroll in vocational programs even though they disliked the academic program. For these students many schools developed a "general education" program that was not as academically demanding as the traditional academic curriculum, but was not narrowly focused on vocational preparation either.

Programs of general education omitted some of the more difficult subjects such as languages and abstract mathematics. They included more elementary courses on reading and practical arithmetic designed to build skills that had formerly been assigned to elementary school. Educators modified other academic courses to make them less demanding and more appealing to students. For example, they developed English courses focused on practical communication skills such as conversing, telephoning, discussing, reading to find information, reading to secure directions, and writing letters. New social studies courses dealt with "social functions" (such as production of goods and services, communication, expression of aesthetic impulses) and social problems (such as crime, poverty, war) instead of history and geography. General mathematics courses and general science courses were developed. They dealt with practical themes and everyday problems such as "how energy helps man," "using machines to change the earth," "counting helps us every day," and "using percentages." Credit toward high school graduation began to be awarded for courses in physical education, art, and music, which had not counted previously.

A 1947 report of the Education Policies Commission, the leadership of the National Education Association, expressed the rationale for these changes quite well. The report, entitled "The Imperative Needs of Youth of Secondary School Age," listed the "needs of youth" that should serve as a basis for curriculum reform:

1. "All youth need to develop saleable skills and those understandings and attitudes that make the worker an intelligent and productive participant in economic life. . . .
2. All youth need to develop and maintain good health and physical fitness
3. All youth need to understand the rights and duties of the citizens of a democratic society. . . .
4. All youth need to understand the significance of the family. . . .
5. All youth need to know how to purchase and use goods and services intelligently. . . .
6. All youth need to understand the methods of science. . . .
7. All youth need opportunities to develop their capacities to appreciate beauty. . . .
8. All youth need to be able to use their leisure time well. . . .
9. All youth need to develop respect for other persons. . . .
10. All youth need to grow in their ability to think rationally, to express their thoughts clearly, and to read and listen with understanding."

This list, an extension to secondary school of the 1918 "Cardinal Principles of Secondary Education," appealed to many educators who believed that the academic secondary school curriculum failed to serve all young people adequately. The comprehensive high school emerged from these efforts. Designed to meet the needs of all, the comprehensive school offered a smorgasbord of courses with academic content ranging from the rigor envisioned by the Committee of Ten to the relevance of life adjustment education, truly something for everybody.

Experiments with New Ways of Organizing the Curriculum

Reformers in the 1950s found the subject organization of the secondary curriculum too rigid and remote. Some secondary schools began to experiment with flexible, integrated organizational patterns similar to those of elementary schools, where a single teacher teaches all subjects to the same children all day long. Several other prominent organizational innovations were tried, including the core curriculum, unit plan, Dalton plan, contract plan, project method, and activity curriculum. Also adopted from the elementary school was the homeroom, a sort of vestigial elementary school classroom in which many of the organizational, extracurricular, and school-wide activities took place and where all students rubbed elbows in a miniature democracy.

The central idea of a core curriculum is a block of work, the core, common to all students. In some schools, half of the curriculum time was allotted for electives, the other half being taken up by required core classes. In one particularly innovative school, the core time was divided among four areas of study: health, community living, leisure, and vocation (Krug, 1964, p. 262). In other versions, the core might consist of a combined English and social studies class common to all the pupils in a given grade. Work in the core supposedly centered on the needs of youth rather than the structure of the subject.

Many innovative organizational schemes featured individually assigned units of work for each pupil. Individualized curriculums divided subject matter into small blocks and assigned blocks to individual students or to small groups with similar needs and abilities. Pupils reported regularly to a teacher, who monitored their progress but did not conduct formal group lessons. Sometimes this individual work took place in the noncore portion of a core curriculum. The Dalton Plan, organized in the high school in Dalton, Massachusetts, in 1918–19, involved fairly lengthy and complex individual contracts occupying a week or more of students' time and requiring use of the library and sometimes other outside resources. Such units culminated in written or oral reports or class discussions. Variations on the Dalton formula were legion. Some contracts were for brief tasks occupying an hour or less and requiring only the use of a textbook, little more than seatwork, really. Professor Henry Morrison of the University of Chicago developed a very popular version known as the unit plan. Each unit consisted of exploration, presentation, assimilation, organization, and recitation. Teaching involved the mastery formula: pretest, teach, test the result, adapt procedure, teach, and test again until learning is verified.

The project method became popular in progressive schools. Originally, projects meant any activity in which a group of students worked together on a task related to their coursework. William H. Kilpatrick, professor at Teachers College, Columbia, elevated projects into a general method of curriculum organization. Kilpatrick began with the belief that learning was most effective when it resulted from a purposeful act on the part of the learner. Therefore, lessons set out in advance by teacher or textbooks were less likely to lead to effective learning than lessons chosen by the student. Following this line of thought, teachers organized courses consisting of a series of student projects punctuated by brief periods of formal study of subject matter. Projects were often made the center of work in a core curriculum organization. Much less often an entire grade or school might be involved in a large common project. Projects could also be undertaken by individual pupils and thus incorporated within individualized curriculums.

Efforts to break the high school curriculum out of the subject straitjacket, as reformers saw it, were at best partially successful. The chief problems were logistical. Coordinating the work of different classes and teachers proved burdensome and time-consuming. The burden of organizing the work and monitoring progress fell fully upon the teacher, making teaching more difficult. Integrating the content of formal subjects with the material of projects was difficult. Testing was not really compatible with project methods. Students in individualized programs showed wider variations in achievement than students in conventional programs, raising questions of equity. Partly as a result, tensions developed between such reforms and college entrance requirements, reformers claiming the colleges were stifling innovation while the colleges feared the reforms neglected academics.

The Eight-Year Study

In an effort to convince the colleges of the value of innovative secondary school programs, the Progressive Education Association sponsored an extensive study, called the Eight-Year

Study, begun in 1933. In this massive study cooperating colleges agreed to admit graduates of an experimental group of progressive secondary schools solely on the basis of their high school records and recommendations. Researchers monitored the students' performance in college and compared them with matched students from similar nonexperimental schools.

The results, published in 1942, showed the students from the experimental schools to be fully comparable in academic achievement and superior in such extracurricular and cocurricular activities as class offices, student newspaper, and other voluntary student activities. Had it become the focus of public debate between progressives and traditionalists, the Eight-Year Study might have set a precedent for using evidence from careful studies to inform the discussion of controversial reforms. But by the time its results were published, World War II riveted the public's attention, and by the time the public was once again free to attend to education, other issues took priority.

Political Battles Between Progressives and Traditionalists

Prominent progressive reformers calling themselves social reconstructionists had called for schools to lead the way toward a new and better social order, less capitalist and more socialist. During the scary depths of the Depression this call found many interested listeners. Many schools revised their social studies and history curriculums to raise questions about capitalism and industrialism. Professor Harold Rugg of Teachers College worked for more than a decade to develop a social studies textbook series that enabled students to build an informed independent viewpoint on contemporary social issues. Rugg's textbooks presented data and information about social and economic questions, and invited students to consider for themselves what actions would be best for contemporary conditions.

This critical stance also found staunch opposition, mainly from two quarters: patriotic organizations and practical school people in traditional communities. After the depths of the depression, organized conservatives gained the upper hand politically. They responded to educators' challenges to the existing social order with demands for teacher loyalty oaths, and with publicity campaigns against people and practices labeled subversive and un-American.

One victim of such a campaign was Professor Harold Rugg and his social studies textbook series. The series had attained wide use and popularity by the mid-1930s when it became a specific object of attack by the Hearst chain of newspapers and self-appointed watchdogs against left-wing movements. Largely as a result of the attacks and local pressures from organizations antagonistic to Rugg's books, many local districts avoided controversy by not purchasing and adopting the books, so that sales declined rapidly and the books soon went out of print.

Opposition to the social reconstructionists also came from practical school people who argued that schools could not realistically take the lead in social change, that they had to follow the wishes of the prevailing society. Krug quotes one educator's trenchant comment:

> "Those of us who have not taken leave of our senses know that the schools and schoolmasters are not generally going to be permitted to take the lead in changing the social order, nor in conducting experiments likely to lead to a radical redefinition of the aims of that order" (Krug, 1964, p. 239).

Schools and schoolmasters *were* permitted to take the lead, however, in instilling respect for democratic ideals against the challenges of fascism and communism. With the spread of both right-wing and left-wing ideologies around the world in the late 1930s, the idea that schools should encourage criticism of American social order and its institutions began to seem disloyal. Few wanted to be seen as undermining the nation in the face of threats from enemies. Calls were made for schools to stop teaching what's wrong with America and starting teaching what's right and good about it. Debunking of cherished myths of

American history, a practice that enjoyed a heyday in the Depression, fell into disfavor. Articles appeared in professional journals outlining programs of patriotic music, celebrations of patriotic events such as flag ceremonies and speech contests on patriotic themes. Some state legislatures passed laws requiring schools to teach the superiority of democracy over other political systems. Reformers wrote about citizenship education and the development of democratic values, understandings, attitudes, and skills.

The Professionalization of Curriculum Reform

The reformers who led movements for curriculum change prior to 1900 included both professionally trained educators and members of the interested public. Joseph Mayer Rice had been a pediatrician, John Dewey, a philosopher, and Charles W. Eliot, a chemist and university president. Those earlier reformers who had been professional educators such as William T. Harris and Col. Francis Parker, for example, were individualists whose leadership flowed from their personal characteristics of energy, eloquence, and persistence. They sought to influence local education authorities, board members and superintendents. They assumed that leaders, once persuaded of the need for a reform, would realize it in schools and classrooms.

Many superintendents decided that a truly professional approach to curriculum revision required a continuing program of systematic curriculum revision with a professionally trained staff. A large city system active in curriculum revision would revise one or two subjects or grades each year. Committees of teachers and administrators would examine the city's existing curriculum in light of the present situation in the city's schools and recommend revisions to the superintendent, who would then authorize the formation of other committees to produce the plans and materials needed to implement the superintendent's recommendations. This procedure incorporated curriculum revision into the routine operations of the school system. Critics charged that this procedure bureaucratized curriculum making.

Toward a National Curriculum Policy: 1960–Present

Post-Sputnik Curriculum Projects

In October of 1957 the Soviet Union launched the first artificial Earth orbiting satellite, Sputnik I. Americans reacted with profound shock. The Soviet Union had erased the American nuclear lead in less than a decade, and now it had leaped ahead into space. Americans faced the chilling prospect of scientific and technological inferiority. In searching for a remedy, public attention soon settled on the public schools. Critics charged schools with adopting progressive reforms that sacrificed rigor and neglecting the teaching of science and mathematics. The ensuing efforts to raise the intellectual level of American education launched a new American curriculum reform.

Admiral Hyman G. Rickover, pioneer of the nuclear navy, spoke of education as "America's first line of defense." He recounted how, in his efforts to develop nuclear propulsion, he had searched vainly for experienced engineers "of independent mind and venturesome spirit" and how he was led to conclude that the schools were not producing any. "Our schools are the greatest 'cultural lag' we have today . . . I am worried about the chances which young people, so poorly equipped to deal with modern life, will have when things become more complex and difficult, as they surely will before very long" (Rickover, 1959, pp. 20–24).

The responses to such criticisms were vigorous. Scientists and mathematicians organized and led curriculum development projects to revise and modernize school textbooks. The best known of these projects were known collectively as 'the New Math,' but eventually scholars launched projects in all academic subjects. In 1959 Congress enacted the National Defense Education Act, intended to strengthen the nation's defenses by creating a greater pool of more qualified scientific talent. The Act funded projects designed to update content and curriculum materials in science, mathematics, and foreign languages, and to train teachers in the new content. It created a national agenda for curriculum reform for the first time since the Smith–Hughes act of 1919 had established a national system of vocational education. Later, in the 1960s and 1970s when other urgent national concerns arose, other large federally sponsored curriculum reforms were again mounted, but with quite different goals.

Education of the Disadvantaged

Almost as abruptly as it began, the post-Sputnik era of national curriculum reform ended. By 1965, the major post-Sputnik projects had completed curriculum materials, but teacher training was still scanty and new curriculums were implemented in only a few schools and classrooms. Suddenly, domestic social unrest turned the spotlight of national attention in a new direction.

By the late 1950s the Supreme Court decision in Brown vs. Board of Education striking down separate schools for African-American students resulted in court-ordered integration in schools all over the South. Presidents Eisenhower and Kennedy both called out the National Guard to protect children attempting to integrate schools in the South. Civil Rights demonstrations against racial discrimination erupted in the South and urban riots flared in northern ghettos. Michael Harrington's *The Other America* (1964) brought to public attention the existence of poverty in the midst of unprecedented affluence. Almost overnight, it seemed, society insisted on a new imperative for schools—equality of educational opportunity.

Again, the approach was direct. Congress enacted the Elementary and Secondary Education Act in 1965. The focus of the ESEA was equalization of educational opportunity by providing special educational programs for disadvantaged children—children of poor families and children of ethnic and racial groups who had suffered a history of discrimination. This legislation helped to fund Sesame Street, a TV program for preschoolers, and Project Head Start, a preschool curriculum designed to remedy early deficits in the education of disadvantaged children. These educational programs of the Great Society established that the power of the federal purse could be used not only for national defense, but also to implement social policies. Significantly, the Great Society programs did not challenge local and professional control over curriculum, as the post-Sputnik reforms had done, but rather provided funds and assistance for local authorities to use to implement new programs.

Before these programs had reached full maturity, the public mood had changed again. This time the stimulus was a backlash against Vietnam era protest and the social reforms of the Great Society. Opposition was most heated in the South, among those opposed to integration and among fundamentalist religionists, and strong among conservative and traditional groups in all sectors of the society. In one of the more dramatic protests, angry West Virginians bombed a schoolhouse door to show their opposition to "godless" and "sinful" textbooks. The books in question quoted prominent Afro-American spokesmen using explicit street language. But a fundamentalist minister who acted as spokesman for the dissidents also objected to the teaching of evolution, to omission of God and prayer from the schools, and in general to the teaching of godless, secular values.

Objections by religious people to the teaching of a modern scientific secular worldview have a long history in the United States. In Tennessee's famous "monkey trial" of 1921, a biology teacher, John Scopes, was charged with teaching evolution in violation of a Tennessee statute forbidding it. The trial attracted worldwide attention and is generally remembered as a victory for academic freedom, but the state won the case and the teaching of evolution was banned by state law in Tennessee for several more decades. Today, the issues are similar: banning books from school libraries, blacklisting books expressing views unacceptable to the majority, exclusion of religious worship and prayer to the public schools, and teaching religious beliefs about the creation and about man's place in the universe.

President Nixon's Commissioner of Education, Sidney P. Marland, changed course once again, setting "career education" as the top national priority. Career education was to offer something practical for the "silent majority" of youngsters who were not well served by either the college preparatory program or the vocational program. They set the goal to provide every youngster who left high school, whether or not by graduation, with a skill suitable for earning a living.

During the Nixon administration states assumed more active roles in curriculum matters. The "new federalism" of the Nixon and Ford presidencies distributed funds to states by formula and left state agencies with the responsibility for deciding how the funds should be spent. Consequently, state governments gained experience in administering statewide educational reform programs. Leaders of several populous and influential states—Illinois, New York, Florida, California, and others—used federal funds to implement such systemwide reforms as competency-based education. The idea here was to hold schools accountable for producing measurable results in the achievement of their graduates. "Back to basics" curriculum initiatives were also popular in many states in this period.

Multiculturalism and the Culture Wars

Beginning with the civil rights struggles of the 1960s, many Americans were sensitized to the ways that the mainstream American culture marginalized and excluded people on the basis of race, culture, and gender. Educators dedicated to social justice became more alert to the possibility that school curriculums reflected a bias against less favored groups. One approach to rooting out this bias favored by many educators was to develop a multicultural curriculum that celebrated the different cultural traditions that made up what they saw as the tapestry of American culture. Multicultural education took many forms. One of the most popular was to teach about the contributions of other cultures to American life, especially African-American, Hispanic, and Native American contributions. Another was to develop bilingual education programs that helped youngsters whose mother tongue was not English to maintain and develop their native language while they also learned English. In the state of New York, a review committee recommended "A curriculum of inclusion" to counter Eurocentrism and white domination of the social studies curriculum. The Portland, Oregon, school system published a series of baseline essays adopting an Afro-centric approach to the teaching of many academic subjects. Multicultural programs flourished during the Carter administration.

During the Reagan presidency, William Bennett, Secretary of Education, led an attack on multicultural and bilingual education. Aided by a number of conservative educational partisans including Diane Ravitch, Chester Finn, and E. D. Hirsch, Bennett spoke out forcefully against these programs and slashed federal funds allocated for them. Conservatives saw themselves as defending the Western intellectual tradition that had for centuries formed the backbone of the school curriculum from attack by radicals who wanted to substitute a thin, ephemeral, second-rate, and politically motivated curriculum centered on contemporary concerns of race, culture, and gender. Conservatives argued that schools neglected the teaching of the basics of our common tradition and offered instead a negative story that damned the achievements of earlier generations of Americans. They fanned fears that an emphasis on cultural differences would foment the kind of ethnic unrest found in Quebec, Northern Ireland, and so many other regions of the world. Even liberals, such as historian Arthur Schlesinger, Jr., criticized multicultural education programs for assuming "that ethnicity is the defining experience for most Americans, that ethnic ties are permanent and indelible, that the division into ethnic groups establishes the basic structure of American society and that a main objective of public education should be the protection, strengthening, celebration and perpetuation of ethnic origins and identities" (When ethnic studies are un-American, *The Wall Street Journal*, April 23, 1990). This controversy put the brakes on what had been a rapidly growing movement for cultural diversity.

Conflicts between liberals and conservatives on education and other social issues culminated in the widely discussed declaration of a "culture war" by Presidential candidate Pat Robertson at the Republican nominating convention in 1992. Robertson saw the war as one between Christian fundamentalists and secular humanists, but the conflicts seemed to mirror classic struggles between traditionalists and progressives. Whatever we call the two sides, the country seemed deeply divided along similar lines on a number of explosive social issues such as abortion, homosexuality, and euthanasia. Many of these divisive issues concerned education directly, such as religion in school, scientific versus religious accounts of creation and evolution, sex education, multicultural education, the value of facts and memorization, and the need for strict discipline. Battles over these issues continued throughout the decade in schools, courtrooms, and on the streets without a clear resolution. As often happens when a stalemate develops between equal forces, action developed around another issue: economic competitiveness.

Economic Competitiveness

While Americans remained divided on social issues, they seemed united in their concern over economic issues. Beginning with double-digit inflation, massive plant closings, and gasoline shortages in the 1970s, Americans were jolted by repeated economic shocks. One manufacturing industry after another—textiles, steel, automobiles—industries that had once been a source of pride and economic pre-eminence for Americans—went out of business in the face of cheaper foreign suppliers. The high-wage unionized factory jobs that had been a staple of the economy shriveled, replaced by low-wage service jobs, part-time jobs, and highly skilled salaried technical and managerial ones. Americans were told and came to believe that their future economic security rested on their ability to grow new, innovative industries and to respond nimbly to rapidly changing markets. This, in turn, required well-educated citizens who could do more than simply read, write, and calculate.

Beginning in the late 1950s, the International Association for the Evaluation of Educational Achievement (IEA) began work on a standardized test of educational achievement that could be administered to students in different countries. The first full-fledged use of this test was a massive study of mathematics achievement in 12 countries. Among the fascinating results, published in 1967, was the finding that students in the United States ranked last among the advanced nations in average math achievement. Critics pointed out that the United States retained a far larger proportion of children in school than practically any country, so that the comparisons were not wholly fair. Still, the results activated latent public concern about how well American children were doing in an increasingly international world. In subsequent international comparisons in other school subjects, American students consistently compared poorly to students from other nations.

From the time when standardized tests first made meaningful year-to-year comparisons possible (roughly the 1930s) the scores of American youngsters on the Scholastic Aptitude Test (SAT), the nation's main college entrance exam, had increased. It seemed that each generation of Americans was learning more than its predecessors. In 1975 the College Entrance Examination Board, the agency in charge of the SAT, announced that scores on the SAT had declined slightly but significantly over the last few years.

Many explanations were advanced, some of which could be refuted. It was argued, for example, that retention of more low income and minority children in schools during this period lowered the overall rates of achievement. But careful examination of the scores showed declines among the ablest students as well as among low scorers. Also, there were declines in regions with a very low percentage of disadvantaged racial minorities. A commission the Board established to look into the causes found many and was unable to settle on one or a few as most likely.

Whatever the reasons, it seemed definite that American students were doing worse at academic work at just the time when the country's economic competitiveness demanded that they do better. Test scores gained wide acceptance as indicators of educational quality and helped to support a movement to strengthen the academic rigor of the curriculum in the 1980s and 1990s.

Beginning in earnest in 1983 with the publication of *A Nation at Risk* (National Commission on Excellence in Education, 1983), a coalition of educational reformers led by articulate business leaders focused on economic competitiveness as the primary challenge facing the country. They made raising school achievement a national priority. How to accomplish this? The Reagan and Bush administrations and the Republican Congress in the Clinton administration were not about to pump more money into the existing school system or settle for yet one more reform movement. They wanted more vigorous actions more likely to succeed in changing a stubborn educational system. Nixon had tried the New Federalism, which redirected federal funds allocated for education to the states to spend as they saw fit. In searching for new and more powerful ways to restructure the school system, conservative reformers turned in two directions: standards and choice.

A headline in *Education Week* for September 1992, captured the mood of the moment among one group of reformers: "Fed up with tinkering, reformers now touting 'systemic' approach" (*Education Week* 12(1):1,30). Systemic reform was an approach developed in the states as a way to gain accountability from local schools. In California it worked this way. The state developed curriculum frameworks that specified what students should learn in each grade and subject. The state then developed several strategies to induce local districts to align their programs with the state frameworks. Most important among these were standardized tests the state developed to test students' learning of the content and goals included in the frameworks. States publicized the scores of each school and thereby put pressure on local officials in low-scoring schools. Some states passed laws providing for state officials to assume authority over local schools whose students consistently fell far below average in achievement on these tests. In addition to California, many of the largest and most influential states adopted systemic approaches to reform, including New York, Texas, Oregon, New Jersey, Maryland, Virginia, and North Carolina.

In the 1990s reformers began to follow a similar systemic approach at the national level. The National Science Foundation funded a Statewide Systemic Reform Initiative designed to focus the efforts of states on implementing effective reforms in science and mathematics education throughout the schools of the state. In 1989 President Bush invited the nation's governors to an "education summit" to develop a national strategy to make the nation's schools more globally competitive. They decided to develop national goals that states could voluntarily adopt. The Department of Education invested heavily in efforts to develop national goals and standards in all school subjects. The National Governor's

Association and the Education Commission of the States actively campaigned for state standards, state examinations, and tight state oversight of local schools that fail to meet state standards. The Goals 2000: Educate America Act of 1994 enacted eight broad goals for American schools. It also established a National Education Standards and Improvement Council to examine and certify state standards and assessment systems voluntarily submitted by states, but President Clinton never appointed any members and the Republican Congress abolished the Council. Nevertheless, efforts to establish national standards and to develop examinations keyed to them have continued.

Standards-based reforms point toward greater centralization of control over the curriculum at national and state levels. A competing approach sought to allow parents choose their school. Several states authorized so-called charter schools that are exempt from many regulations the states placed on public schools. Some large cities experiment with issuing vouchers to parents that could be used in any school, public or private. Numerous private ventures, most notably the Edison Project, have sprung up promising to run schools more efficiently and achieve higher test scores. Reformers such as Terry Moe and John Chubb (Moe & Chubb, 1990) and Paul Hill (1997, 1998) argue that arrangements that allow parents and students to choose their school, either within the publicly provided system or, more radically, including private schools, will result in higher achievement. They see the main barrier to more effective schools being the disorganization and lack of incentives and direction in the public school system. The remedy they favor is efficient, customer-oriented service such as that found in the private sector.

Other manifestations of economic concerns include increasing globalization of education and an emphasis on information technology. Globalization is reflected in efforts by national agencies to benchmark American students' achievement against that of other countries. Increasing demand for learning world history and foreign languages also reflect this development. Concern that American students need to be well prepared for an information economy has also spurred demands for teaching students to use computers and information technology in school.

Learning for Understanding

Seemingly independent of these larger social, political, and economic trends, scholars and educational innovators have been preoccupied with a new approach to teaching and learning based on a psychological and philosophical doctrine called constructivism or, more popularly, learning for understanding. Constructivism holds that humans are continually building mental representations that they use in their interactions with the world. Children do not receive or absorb knowledge. Rather, they construct it based on what they hear and do and experience. Reflection plays a role in learning, but active doing provides the material for reflection. So, constructivists advocate active learning and teaching methods rather than listening and reading. Constructivism echoes many of the themes of the progressive era. Indeed, Dewey is regarded as one of the main intellectual precursors of modern constructivism.

Constructivism seems to have become the major alternative for those opposed to both standards and choice. It purports to lead to deep conceptual understanding, not merely knowledge of facts that are tested on standardized tests. Its advocates claim that more students can succeed in a constructivist learning environment than in conventional dry, abstract, academic classroom. They argue that children will be more motivated to learn. They claim that learning together in teams prepares students for a work world where teamwork is also central. All this puts proponents of constructivism in conflict with a back-to-basics curriculum and with standards and testing. Constructivists favor performance assessment, an approach that judges the quality of each student's work.

Summary

During the last quarter of the 20th century, American schools were swept by a rapid succession of massive, ambitious, nationally funded and directed curriculum reforms. In each case, schools felt intense public criticism. Reformers took direct action, circumventing the established procedures for professional curriculum work in schools. Reformers from outside the schools created new curriculums, recruited new people into the ranks of teachers, administrators, and policy-makers whose views reflected those of the reforms, and made intense efforts to disseminate these programs widely. Established curriculum leaders such as teachers, principals, central office professionals, superintendents, and local school boards, as well as associations of professional educators and professors of education, found themselves bypassed by subject experts, policy analysts, interest group organizations, and politicians.

Schools that implemented these reforms found the abrupt shifts traumatic. Each reform required a major reorientation and realignment of efforts. And before a school could implement one, along came a second, and then a third. The effort exhausted many school staffs, and soured them on reform. It has become quite clear as a result of these events that large-scale curriculum change is a long, difficult, and risky proposition.

In the closing years of the century, reformers are earnestly working toward still more radical approaches to improving education. It is too soon to determine whether standards will succeed or whether choice plans will even be tried in more than a few states and cities. Although the outcome of this latest round of reform is unclear, what is clear is that the American tradition of vigorous educational innovation and experimentation is alive and well.

The Lessons of History

History does not tell us what to do, but we can learn from it, nevertheless. From this brief summary of landmark developments in the history of the American school curriculum, we can learn such lessons as the following.

- The content, purpose, and structure of American schools have changed substantially over more than 200 years.
- Actual curriculum practice has not changed as much as have ideas about what the curriculum should be.
- The school curriculum has generally reflected the prevailing views of the more educated segments of American society, and thus has seldom been either in the vanguard of change or opposed to change.
- Curriculum change, even planned change, has often come in response to pressures generated outside the educational system, including pressures from dramatic events such as wars, economic booms and panics, political upheavals, and religious awakenings, and from gradual trends, such as industrialization, immigration, population growth, economic growth, and increasing social pluralism.
- Important curriculum changes are often associated with and strongly influenced by major changes in the educational system, such as in the number and types of students enrolled, how and by whom educational institutions are governed, and the type and extent of teacher preparation.
- Excitement about ideas regarded as new and momentous usually accompanies major episodes of curriculum reform. Reforms arouse widespread optimism, excitement, and fervor among advocates and implementers.

- The methods and procedures employed in curriculum change have varied. Often they have been improvised to suit a particular situation and then subsequently the improvisation has been developed into a general method.
- Reforms rarely achieve the curriculum changes reformers promise. Many proposed changes are never realized except in a few experimental sites. Those that are realized widely never entirely displace earlier practices and seldom come to prevail, but they often find secure niches for themselves within a diverse, decentralized school system.

Lessons of history such as these give us valuable perspective on contemporary curriculum problems and help us to act wisely in attempting to resolve them. Sometimes history can also be of help in a more focused and direct way.

Using History to Make Curriculum Decisions

In addition to giving a general perspective on events, history also provides specific historical analogies and specific historical knowledge, and all three of these may play key role in current decisions. For instance, many observers today see strong similarities between the movement for academic excellence in the late 1990s and the post-Sputnik reforms. In both cases, the curriculum problem was lack of achievement in academic subjects. In both cases, advocates and the public perceived a strong external threat if our able students did not learn more in school. Here, then, is an historical analogy that educators may be able to use to guide actions in a current controversy.

Accepting the two as analogous leads us to wonder what we can learn from the earlier episode. The post-Sputnik reforms failed in their primary purpose. American science and mathematics achievement did not increase in the decade or so after these reforms. In fact, test scores declined. Many blame the failure of the earlier reforms on their use of an ineffective mechanism—the federally sponsored curriculum development project. The case against projects is that they failed to bring about change in classrooms, that teachers, having not been involved in the development of the new curriculums, were reluctant to try them. This line of reasoning has undoubtedly influenced current reformers in their decision not to press for curriculum development projects today but instead to focus on national standards and ways to support teacher change.

Historical reasoning such as this is relevant to any curriculum decision. Developing your ability to use history wisely is an important part of learning to do good curriculum decision-making. Usual practice in curriculum decision-making fits uncomfortably well with public policy decision-making generally as described by historians Neustadt and May:

> "Usual" practice, we fear, has six ingredients: a plunge toward action; overdependence on fuzzy analogies . . . ; inattention to an issue's own past; failure to think a second time . . . about key presumptions; stereotyped suppositions about persons or organizations . . . and little or no effort to see choices as part of any historical sequence (Neustadt & May, 1968, pp. 32–33).

They counsel the staffs who advise decision-makers to learn how to draw on history to frame sharper questions and examine proposed answers more critically. The first step is to describe the current situation well. "What goes on here? . . . If there is a problem to be solved (or lived with), what is it? And whose is it?" (p. 234) "Ask 'What's the story?' How did these concerns develop?" (pp. 235–236) They suggest that analysts do this by listing key elements of the immediate situation in three columns: Known, Unclear, and

Study the issue's history.

Create a timeline. Start the story as far back as it properly goes and plot the main events and trends. Ask the journalist's questions: Who, what, why, when, where, how?

Place critical organizations and key individuals on the timeline.

Try to infer what their life histories mean for how they interpret this situation.

List possibly analogous situations and for each note likenesses and differences with the present situation.

Array your options.

Try to judge feasibility in light of historical experience with similar projects.

Ask yourself if you would bet real money on an option.

What odds would you give?

Ask "What fresh data would cause you to revise or reverse your judgment?"

FIG. 2.7. *How to use history to make better decisions (based on Neustadt and May (1968)).*

Presumed. Then, historical information becomes potentially useful. Figure 2.7 summarizes their suggestions for making good use of the available historical knowledge.

Questions and Projects

1. Find out what major events and trends influenced the curriculum of schools in your region. Who were the local or regional leaders who formed your local curriculum traditions? In what ways did the curriculum in schools in your area reflect the larger national traditions described in this chapter? In what ways are your local traditions unique?

2. Study the history of curriculum in schools that served groups not defined as part of the mainstream of American life—girls, poor children in rural or urban areas, African-American children, Native American children, children of Mexican heritage, children of immigrants, for instance. How do their curriculum traditions differ from the mainstream traditions sketched in this chapter?

3. Find characteristics of contemporary American curriculum practices or initiatives that resemble practices characteristic of earlier periods. To what extent do these similarities seem to reflect actual historical relationships in which later educators learned about earlier practices from earlier ones and to what extent are they rather similar responses invented independently by later educators in response to similar problems and conditions?

4. Compare the present situation to past periods. What's similar? What's different?

5. With this context in mind, what do you see as excellent features of the curriculums of schools like yours, features that a principal should protect and enhance?

6. What lessons for influencing curriculum can you find in reading about curriculum history?

7. Briefly describe the situation of American education at the turn of the 21st century as *you* see it. Describe American society and the relation of education to society today.

8. Describe leading educational ideas and prevailing practices. Describe the key issues being contested and the groups contesting them. Describe alternative ideas and practices under discussion that challenge prevailing ideas and practices.

Further Study

Lawrence A. Cremin's *The Transformation of the School: Progressivism in American Education, 1876–1957* (1968) is both a fundamental historical account and a delightful reading experience. The three volumes of his historical trilogy on the American experience, *American Education, the Colonial Experience, 1607–1783* (1970), *American Education, the National Experience, 1783–1876* (1980), and *American Education, the Metropolitan Experience, 1876–1980* (1988) are indispensable sources. Cremin's classic histories are organized to tell the stories he finds in the historical record, rather than chronologically. The reader especially interested in curriculum issues must read actively in order to follow the continuing connections between these stories and developments in the curriculum, but the effort is well rewarded.

Edward Krug's two-volume work, *The Shaping of the American High School* (1964, 1972), is a more straightforward account of the people and events told in essentially chronological order. Krug focuses more exclusively on the schools and especially on the issues that captured the attention of the school people of the time. Readers interested in curriculum history will find it explicitly written in Krug's books. Frederick Rudolph's *The Curriculum* (1977) is the single most useful source I have found on the history of college and university curriculum. Herbert Kleibard's *The Struggle for the American Curriculum* (1986) argues that no unified Progressive Education movement existed; rather the label was given to all those who advocated alternatives to the 19th-century school program. His account is rich in anecdotes, photographs, and other details of great interest to the student of curriculum. Sol Cohen's *American Education: A Documentary History* (5 vols., New York: Random House, 1974) is a ready source of many important original documents.

In recent years younger scholars have studied the history of the education of minority populations and immigrants, finding quite a different story than the mainstream accounts of established historians of education. A good example is Joel Spring's *Deculturalization and the Struggle for Equality: A Brief History of the Education of Dominated Cultures in the United States* (2001).

CHAPTER THREE

Curriculum Theories

No scientific analysis known to man can determine the desirability or the need of anything. . . . The notion that ideals can be evolved from a process of collecting environmental facts is just another of the many delusions to which our sinful human flesh is heir.

—Boyd Bode, *Modern Educational Theories*, 1927, pp. 80–81
American philosopher and critic of progressive education

Questions

- What ideal visions do people harbor about the curriculum of American elementary and secondary schools?
- What happens when curriculum visions conflict?
- What is curriculum theory, and how is it related to the ideal visions people harbor?
- What are some representative curriculum theories?
- How can curriculum professionals benefit from knowing curriculum theories?

Introduction

When computers first appeared that were small, powerful, and affordable enough for use in classrooms, many excited educators saw the possibility of a new medium for education that would present some entirely new possibilities. Using computers, teachers could use images, sounds, animations, and video as well as spoken and printed words to reach students. Teaching materials no longer needed to be static. They could engage in a kind of conversation where computers would present a problem, students would express their understanding by entering something in the computer, and then the computer would evaluate the responses and adjust the next presentation to suit the student's understanding. Students would be able to create their own multimedia reports. Like many educators, I saw these and similar capabilities as a limitless new educational frontier and wondered what new forms of education might arise on this frontier.

The pioneers on the education frontier produced several early ways of using computers. One was computer-assisted instruction (CAI). In CAI computers tutored students, much as a human tutor might—asking questions, letting students answer, evaluating students' responses, and adjusting the next question in light of the students' responses to the previous ones. Another early pioneer developed a computer language called *Logo*, designed for easy learning by children and other novices. The philosophy behind *Logo* emphasized learning by exploration and play. Using *Logo* children gave instructions to a turtle to move on the computer screen. By telling the turtle to move in a particular way and to trace its movements with a "pen" students could draw pictures. Eventually, children could learn to draw more complex and interesting pictures using if–then statements, repeat statements, subroutines, recursion, and other basic ideas of computer science, and in so doing they learned the basic ideas of computer science. Pioneering educators also adapted many of the computer tools created for other purposes to teaching. For example, they used word processors to teach writing, graphing programs to teach algebra and data analysis, and databases of social information for studying history and social studies.

These early ways of using computers were interesting and important from many points of view, but none expressed a new educational vision. Tutoring, while not much used in schools today, is an ancient educational ideal. Educational reformers dating back to the French philosopher Jean Jacques Rousseau in the 18th century and Plato ancient Greece have advocated learning through free exploration and play. The development of educational materials and apparatus that will improve teaching and learning is also a vision that has guided educational reformers since ancient times. Ironically, innovators molded the newest technology in the image of ancient educational ideals.

This episode demonstrates dramatically how traditional educational ideals shape the thoughts and actions of innovators. Even when innovators work on curriculum problems that seem entirely new, they still work within traditions.

Curricular Ideals

Where do people get these ideas for new curriculums? There's something so inevitable about the traditional subjects—mathematics, English, history, science, and the rest. How can anyone imagine a curriculum without them? But when you start thinking about other things that we ought to teach everyone when they're young, they all seem so arbitrary. Health, nutrition, and physical fitness are important, sure. But so are emotional stability, self-defense, law, business, media, politics, love, hate, war, peace, justice, sports, fashion, and a million other things that everybody thinks about and some people study. I can see how a person might get excited about some of these other things. Investment fascinates me. I think everyone should learn to make good investments. But we're talking about forcing every young person to learn about it, and I'm not sure I'm ready to do that. For that matter, I'm not really all that sure about forcing everybody to learn parts of the traditional subjects. I don't really understand how people get so certain about what should be taught. And I don't see how they can get so worked up about it that they're ready to argue and fight over something that they want taught or not taught.

If you found yourself agreeing with the views expressed in the previous paragraph, you're in a minority. Most people, professional educators and the public alike, approach curriculum matters with conviction and passionate partisanship, not doubt and neutral objectivity. Some people assert with confidence that *Huckleberry Finn* is an American classic that every child should read. Others say with equal conviction that *Huckleberry Finn* is a racist book full of demeaning stereotypes that should not be allowed in the school library. People even feel passion and conviction about curriculum questions that don't involve controversial social issues. For instance, some people believe that children should be taught to do arithmetic calculations quickly, accurately, and automatically, while others care much more whether they know what the numbers mean. Fierce controversies have raged over this issue.

Some Traditional Ideals

People's various convictions about curriculum may seem idiosyncratic, but when you've heard or read what many people think about many curriculum questions, patterns begin to appear. Most people's beliefs about curriculum reflect a few familiar ideals, and most curriculum issues arise from clashes between these ideals. Some of the most widely held contemporary American curriculum ideals include:

- Academic excellence
- Social relevance
- Social change
- Individual well-being
- Educational equality
- Religious training.

Academic Excellence

The scholarly ideal of academic excellence appeals to many Americans who want schools to help students master the tools of thought, language, and mathematics, and acquire a foundation of knowledge about the world through literature, history, geography, and science. Many active, vocal, well-educated individuals, working through such organizations as the Council for Basic Education, strive to ensure that academic excellence is the top priority for schools today. They respond vigorously to reports of declines in test scores, needs for more remedial courses in college, or other indicators of slipping academic standards, and oppose curriculum reforms that they believe threaten academic achievement.

Social Relevance

Many Americans feel that schools should serve society by helping students learn to do whatever society needs them to do. Ancient civilizations schooled young men as warriors who could defend the kingdom against its enemies and young women as wives and mothers who could tend hearth and home. In the industrial era, many American schools taught young men skills needed in the factory and office, and young women skills needed for office work and for keeping house. In times of war, high schools have included premilitary skills. Civic education, character education, and the teaching of history for patriotic goals serve needs for social stability and national unity. Today, advocates of social relevance sponsor multicultural education and service learning.

Many socially aware and committed Americans want schools to put the highest priority on the ideal of social relevance. Whenever Americans feel a threat to their society, supporters of the ideal of social relevance can be counted on to mount vigorous campaigns to get schools to respond to the threat. The bellwether report, *A Nation at Risk* (1982), called for schools to raise academic standards in order to maintain the nation's economic competitiveness in a global marketplace, uniting the ideals of social relevance and academic excellence.

Social Change

Many view the schools as a unique opportunity to create a better society. Children have more open and flexible belief systems and values, and changing children's beliefs and values eventually changes those of society. If we could prevent children from learning prejudice or hatred of other groups, we could build a better society. Every movement for social betterment seeks in some way to influence the young, and the school is the most direct way to reach them. The desire to realize their social values brings many educators into the profession, and the same desire predisposes many of them to embrace curriculum reforms designed for social betterment.

Individual Well-Being

The ideal of child-centered education is that school should provide each child with whatever that child needs for his or her well-being. This ideal reflects a deeply held American value of individualism. Supporters of individual well-being believe that schools should help all children to meet their individual needs, to realize their own educational potential in their own way, and thus to become a unique person. The needs of an open, democratic society will best be met, in this view, by helping the individuals who make up that society to become happy, successful, and fulfilled. Academic excellence is fine for those who want that, but should not be imposed on everyone. Advocates of personal growth have campaigned for elective courses in colleges and secondary schools, student projects, independent study, high school counselors, and many forms of individualized education plans.

Educational Equity

The ideal of an equal education for all reflects American democratic ideals. It has been a potent inspiration for American curriculum reformers from the earliest days of the Republic and especially so in the 20th century. The 19th-century campaign for universal free compulsory public education and American resistance to curricular differentiation and high stakes national examinations reflect the value of equity. The notion of equal opportunity has expanded from the narrow goal of equal opportunity—providing access and an equal playing field—to the broader goal of equal results. Major curriculum reforms such as the Elementary and Secondary Education Act, compensatory education, Head Start, and Success for All have been motivated primarily by a drive for equity.

Religious Training

That the curriculum should focus on creating a religious person—a person of faith, a good Catholic, an observant Jew, or the like—is perhaps the most the ancient ideal of all. Early European settlements in North America were Christian religious communities, and religious ideals dominated the education of the time. The highest purpose of education, as of life, was salvation. Children in school were taught the Bible, the catechism, the Ten Commandments, and obedience to God, parents, and religious authority. The life of Jesus Christ was set forth as a model.

Religious ideals continue to anchor the educational judgments of many throughout the world today. The American separation of church and state, unique at its inception, has limited the role of religious ideals in public education. As a result, the ideal of spiritual development has usually played a minor role in public discussions of curriculum matters in the last century. Nevertheless, religious ideals remain a strong and living force for many parents, teachers, and children. Continuing debate about the role of religion in public education and the large number of parents who choose a private religious education for their children testify to the continuing vitality of religious ideals in American education.

The closing decades of the 20th century have seen a resurgence of religious activism in many nations, and calls are being heard for religion to play a bigger role in public education. Presently, though, the influence of religion is mainly felt on a few controversial issues, namely whether prayer or other religious observances will be allowed in public schools, whether religious accounts of creation can be taught alongside scientific ones, and whether school histories give adequate attention to the role of religion in American life. In many small communities, however, religious ideals still play a major if little noted role in the programs of local schools.

Other Views

These five traditional ideals encompass many Americans' views. By including other less prominent ideals we could describe an even wider range of views. For instance, some people hold a curricular ideal of practical efficacy—helping students to define important goals, plan, use resources wisely, be resourceful, and work with others to accomplish their goals. These are important abilities in business, politics, and other worldly pursuits.

We also find other ideals in other cultures. In India and the Far East the ideal of the great teacher (master, guru) is influential. The great teacher organizes the content and goals but also, and importantly, the teacher is a model who embodies and manifests the skills and qualities students are to learn. This ideal is not prominent in discussions of general education in the United States, but it has more support in advanced learning. In the arts, for instance, schools often form around great artists such as Balanchine in ballet or Stanislavsky in acting, and promising young scientists compete to work in labs run by Nobel Prize winners.

Commonplaces of Curriculum Thought

Curriculum specialists who must deal with people who embrace a variety of ideals need to make sense of the otherwise bewildering diversity. These traditional ideals offer one way to organize the complexity. Another framework that many curriculum specialists find useful for thinking about curriculum issues can also help us understand curricular ideals. The key idea behind this framework is that anyone who discusses any curriculum question must consider four topics or commonplaces—the student, the teacher, the subject matter, and the society (see Figure 3.1). Sometimes a curriculum ideal is clearly student-centered, teacher-centered, subject-centered, or society-centered. More usually, an ideal will have a characteristic way of thinking about students, teachers, subjects, and society and a distinctive set of relationships or priorities among the four. The mix we find in any particular ideal helps us understand the relative importance of the four crucial considerations in that ideal. Since all four commonplaces are important, a sound curriculum should have an appropriate balance among them. Historically, the actual curriculum offered by schools has reflected a fairly stable balance that gives each of the commonplaces some attention. In curricular discourse, however, we often see radical shifts rather than a static balance.

	Student	
Society		Subject
	Teacher	

FIG. 3.1. *The commonplaces of curriculum thought.*

Curriculum Theories

When people disagree about curriculum issues, they appeal to their ideals as they advo-cate their positions. Should every student be required to spend several hours each week performing a public service in the community? Some say "yes" because they believe that children need the experience of sacrificing for the good of their community. Some say "no" because they believe that academic learning should be the primary purpose of school. As they argue their case, advocates make more explicit, complete statements of their ideal, more impassioned defenses of it, and tighter, more convincing arguments to support it.

In making a case for the superiority of their ideal, advocates search for the most appealing way to state and justify it and the strongest arguments they can find. Here's what we mean by academic excellence or social relevance, and it's not what our opponents say it is. Here's why you should embrace our ideal over theirs. As they try to create an ever more convincing case, advocates write and publish statements that articulate their ideals and explain why they are worthy of support. In writing such statements they achieve a more considered, systematic, disciplined, and defensible rationale for their ideals that retains and enhances its passionate advocacy.

Writing that passionately articulates and justifies curriculum ideals is known as curricu-lum theory. A curriculum theory is different from a scientific theory. In the sciences, theories are meant to be dispassionate and as objective as possible. Scientists are supposed to accept or reject theories based on logic and evidence, regardless of their personal ideals, values, or priorities. Curriculum theories, by contrast, are about ideals, values, and priorities. They employ reason and evidence, but in the service of passion. Curriculum theories can be an-alytical as well as partisan, but unlike scientific theories, they are not curriculum theories unless they are about ideals. Curriculum theories make ideals explicit, clarify them, work out their consequences for curriculum practice, compare them to other ideals, and justify or criticize them. Consider some examples.

Examples of Classic Curriculum Thought

Early Ideas about Curriculum

More than 2,000 years ago the ancient Greek philosopher Plato (427?–347 BCE) pro-duced what is generally regarded as the first coherent theoretical treatise on government and education, the *Republic*. Plato's *Republic* sketches a complete utopian society, one in which education plays a central part. Plato's views were radical in the Athens of his day and they have remained radical for almost two millennia. Nevertheless, the ideals Plato expressed in the *Republic* have lived for two millennia and exerted a profound influence on Western education.

In Plato's ideal *Republic*, early childhood education would consist of gymnastics for the body and music for the soul. (Music at that time included reciting of literature and poetry to musical accompaniment.) This resembled the prevailing practice of education in Athens during Plato's time, so Plato's proposal was conventional, except for one feature: Plato would have the songs selected so as to instill in children desirable adult qualities. Because as adults they should be brave, children should hear stories of courage, not stories that would terrify them. Since as adults they should be reasonable, they should not hear that the gods quarreled, plotted, and fought with one another. Teach young children through play rather than compulsory tasks because play is natural to children while what adults make them learn rarely stays with them. Plato suggested that games and play could lay a foundation for later study of subjects such as arithmetic, geometry, and astronomy. Plato would forbid children to engage in the adult intellectual activity of philosophical speculation lest they develop superficial fluency, a taste for aimless contention, and disrespect for thought.

During early education adults would watch children closely for signs of excellence in health, athletics, memory, aesthetics, and moral conduct. As children grew, their teachers would expose them to stresses and temptations of various kinds—pains, pleasures, frightening sights, and challenges to their wit, skill, and character. Those who emerged from these tests whole, unspoiled, and excellent would undergo further training leading toward leadership responsibilities within the state. Those who failed these tests would be apprenticed to various trades and crafts depending on their talents and inclinations.

When they finished school the young men in the Republic would serve a compulsory 3-year basic military training. As part of their military training, young soldiers were to be taught arithmetic, geometry, and astronomy. Plato deemed these subjects to be both useful to soldiers and a stimulus toward pure thought and the search for truth. During their military service some of the soldier–students would prove to be more intelligent, courageous, enterprising, and able. The best would be selected at age 30 to undertake further study of the higher branches of arithmetic, geometry, and astronomy and also to begin study of the highest discipline of all, philosophy itself, reasoning about the good for humanity, contemplation of pure eternal truth.

During this entire period, the soldiers were to live in an austere, frugal style. They were to have no property other than a few personal possessions. They were to live communally, sharing everything with their peers. The community would supply their needs as the wages of their military service. They would not farm, trade, or engage in any way in the mundane affairs of ordinary men. After 5 years of study, they would return to active life, holding commands in war, holding public offices, and serving in other leadership capacities.

At the age of 50, those who had withstood all these tests and grown wise from study and experience would be appointed guardians of the state, empowered to make its laws and to govern it. The prohibitions on ownership of private property by the guardians would continue so as to ensure against corruption. They would oversee the affairs of the state and direct it so that it supported and encouraged the highest and best sort of life among its citizens.

Plato's plan for the Republic reflected his belief that abstract thought was the highest, noblest, most powerful, and most characteristically human of capabilities. The capacity for thought distinguished humankind from the beasts. Beasts excelled at physical feats, cunning, and the practical arts of survival, but thought alone could determine which of the many ends people sought were most worthy.

Humans could, with thought, perceive eternal truth, the forms of things, their essence. Uneducated people could only think about things as they appeared to the senses and these appearances were chaotic, changeable, and confusing. Abstract thought, by contrast, revealed the elegant, eternal truth that lay hidden behind appearances. Only thought, the light of reason, could reveal to people their true condition. Obviously, then, the training of the guardians of the state must include those studies most conducive to pure, abstract thought. As enlightened leaders, these philosopher–kings would lead the community toward ever-greater awareness of the truth and toward a life compatible with that truth.

Plato's advocacy of abstract theoretical knowledge as the highest aim of education has powerfully influenced Western education and still shines in today's ideal of academic excellence. Although Plato's elitism runs against the American democratic grain, his ideal that the best educated should govern continues to influence the views of many Americans.

Plato's ideas have greatly influenced the education of young children in America. Plato's ideas came to Americans mainly by way of the French social philosopher, Jean Jacques Rousseau (1712–1778), whose main concern was to discredit authoritarian government. Rousseau maintained, in one of several ringing phrases he bequeathed us, that "Man is born free and everywhere he is in chains." In a state of nature, according to Rousseau, a person is not subject to any government, nor to the norms of any society, and is thus free. Trouble starts when society imposes its arbitrary demands. People are naturally good; when people act badly, society is responsible. The solution is a "return to nature." This applied particularly to child rearing and education. In *Émile* Rousseau described the details of the rearing and education of a fictional child. It was an upbringing that he believed would help achieve a return to a state of nature.

Rousseau insisted that the education of a human being begins at birth. People learn most of what they know when they are very young. So, early education was fundamental. Rousseau urged well-to-do mothers to nurse their own children, rather than use wet nurses. He counseled parents to spend time with their children and develop a rich and lively domestic life, rather than living primarily for public gatherings in the highly formal society of the time. He asked adults to value childhood in its own right, as deserving of happiness in its own terms, rather than sacrificing it always to preparation for entry into adult society.

Children should not be constrained by early, artificial habits. They should eat when hungry, sleep when tired, and play freely, so that they might enjoy and appreciate their freedom from the earliest possible moment. Adults should treat children kindly, not severely, with a tender regard, indulging them in their diversions and pleasures, as befits their innocent, harmless natures. All these suggestions were at odds with the prevailing practice among the European upper classes.

When the child grew beyond infancy, Rousseau following Plato, urged that adults should coax, guide, and stimulate it to learn, not teach it directly. Parents and teachers should avoid verbal instruction. Instead, they should arrange for children to have experiences that would awaken the youngster's desire to learn. Children reason very well, Rousseau argued, when it comes to matters within their childish experience, but they fail when they try to reason abstractly about things of which they have no direct, sensory experience. Yet all the studies normally imposed on children in school concern things entirely foreign to children, such as reading, writing, and arithmetic. Rousseau portrayed Émile as learning to read because his parents sent him written invitations to dinners and parties. If he could not read, he would miss the event. Thus convinced of the value of learning to read, Émile would soon learn the skill. To Rousseau, desire to learn counted for more than refined methods of instruction.

Rousseau urged educators to cultivate children's curiosity, ask them leading questions, and respond subtly to their questions, not to quench their curiosity too readily. Follow the child's interest; don't expect the child to follow adult interests. Educators should allow children to be active. Instead of sitting quietly reading books, they should build things in the workshop and observe and experiment out in the field. Busy them with useful activities. Above all, Rousseau sought to educate Émile in a way that would leave him free and independent. He should act in ways that reflect his original nature and his own freely chosen path, not follow the dictates of society.

Rousseau's ideas influenced many American progressives in the early years of the 20th century and, through them, still influence many Americans. Plato and Rousseau are two of dozens of important pre-20th century philosophers whose ideas about the curriculum influenced later curricular ideals. Others you may want to learn more about include: Aristotle, Comenius, Pestalozzi, Herbart, and Montessori.

Progressive Curriculum Thought

American progressives around the turn of the 20th century challenged prevailing school practices as unsuitable for the children of a modern industrial democracy. The following brief passages reveal progressive and traditional positions on a number of central curriculum issues.

What knowledge is of most worth?
Progressive

- "The content of the school must be constructed out of the very materials of American life—not from academic relics of Victorian precedents. The curriculum must bring children to close grip with the roar and steely clang of industry, with the great integrated structure of American business, and must prepare them in sympathy and tolerance to confront the underlying forces of political and economic life..." (Harold Rugg, in *26th Yearbook*, 1927, p. 149).
- "We can make a child stay after school for half an hour, but we cannot make him practice kindness during that time. Nor can we assign honesty as a home lesson for to-night with any hope that one lacking it will have learned it by tomorrow.... These things can be practiced only in such life-experiences as in fact call them out. Our curriculum must, then, be the kind to include such life-experiences..." (William H. Kilpatrick, in Rugg (ed.) *26th Yearbook*, 1927, p. 122).

Traditional

- "The basic language-arts and the basic arts of computation and measurement occupy the place of major importance in universal education. This is true of the elementary schools of all civilized countries.... Beyond these basic social arts, there is in most of the civilized countries a very serious emphasis upon direct moral instruction.... As subjects of formal instruction, geography and national history apparently form the backbone of the elementary curriculum on the side of information as distinguished from skills" (W. C. Bagley, in Rugg (ed.) *26th Yearbook*, 1927, Supplementary Statement, pp. 29–30).

What should be the purpose of education?
Progressive

- "Education is not something outside of life, applied as a tool, a lever say, with which to push life forward or higher. No, education is inside of life, inherent in life, part of the very life process itself so far as life is worth while.... (E)ducation is such a process of associated living as continuously remakes life, carrying it always to higher and richer levels" (William H. Kilpatrick, in Rugg (ed.) *26th Yearbook*, 1927 pp. 130–131).
- "The main objectives of education
  1. Health
  2. Command of fundamental processes
  3. Worthy home-membership
  4. Vocation
  5. Citizenship
  6. Worthy use of leisure
  7. Ethical character"

(Cardinal Principles of Secondary Education, Washington, D.C.: U.S. Bureau of Education, *Bulletin No. 35*, 1918, pp. 10–11).
Traditional

- "The general public has a very high regard for literacy, both numerical and linguistic. This, of course, is only a highbrow method of saying that the general public desires, first of all, that the elementary school teach the three R's passing well. It may be added that the adult world apparently retains a firm faith in certain one-time virtues now generally discredited by our profession—notably 'thoroughness' and 'discipline' (both mental and moral)" (W. C. Bagley, in Rugg (ed.) *26th Yearbook*, 1927, Supplementary Statement, p. 36).

How should the curriculum reflect the nature of the student?
Progressive

- "Gradually basic articles of faith are emerging, to which all these new (child-centered) schools subscribe.... And the first of these articles of faith is freedom. 'Free the legs, the arms, the larynx of a child,' say the advocates of the new education, 'and you have taken the first step toward freeing his mind and spirit'" (Rugg and Shumaker, *The Child-Centered School*, 1928, p. 55).
- "Underlying characteristics of child growth and development...should serve as general guides to the curriculum worker and to the teacher as he designs the curriculum.... Each learner is unique.... The learner reacts as a whole.... The normal child has both capacity and appetite for learning. ... The individual learns those things which have meaning for him.... Development has a forward look..." (Stratemeyer, Forkner, & McKim, *Developing a Curriculum for Modern Living*, 1947, pp. 56–65).

Traditional

- "It is said that pupils should be adopted as the guides to the educational process because the natural unfolding of their interests and desires will lead them forward to that stage of maturity which is to be desired as the end of life. The view here defended is based on a categorical denial of the assumption that the individual unfolds because of inner impulses into a civilized being. Civilization is a social product. It requires cooperation for its maintenance exactly as it required cooperation for its evolution. Even Shakespeare did not create the English language. No child can evolve the English language. Slowly and through great effort and with the help of much patient guidance, the pupil may after long years come to the point where he can share in the social inheritance of his English-speaking environment. His nature will, it is true, unfold in the process of its adoption of the English mode of thought and expression, but this unfolding is not a spontaneous form of growth prompted from within" (Charles H. Judd, "Supplementary Statement" in Rugg (ed.) *26th Yearbook*, 1927, pp. 114–115).

What are the implications for curriculum of the nature of society?
Progressive

- "Once education could merely repeat the past. That time has gone.... Education must know that we face an unknown and shifting civilization" (Kilpatrick, in Rugg (ed.) 26th Yearbook, 1927, p. 131).
- "The mature generation is always the victim of its own past. At any moment society is so caught in the meshes of its folkways that its behavior lags behind its knowledge.... The school is an instrument for doing the difficult educational tasks, for anticipating the problems of the future, and for directing the course of social behavior" (George S. Counts, in Rugg (ed.) *26th Yearbook*, 1927, p. 85).

Traditional

- "Society in the past has established and everywhere continues to maintain schools in order to create new generations in its own likeness.... (I)t is society which determines what these interests are, and not the teachers" (I. L. Kandel, *Mobilizing the Teacher*, 1934).

- "What is the primary function of the public school system in American democracy? It is, as I see things, the training of minds and the dissemination of knowledge—knowledge useful in the good life, in the conduct of the practical arts and in the maintenance and improvement of American society. The teacher is not a physician, a nurse, a soldier, a policeman, a politician, a businessman, a farmer or an industrial worker" (Charles A. Beard. "The scholar in an age of conflicts," *School and Society* 43:278–279, February 29, 1936).

How should the curriculum be organized?
Progressive

- "The right curriculum will take account of attitudes, ideals, habits, appreciations ... Skill and facts and memorization can be made out into a regular schedule and be so taught (at least in a fashion), but these other and weightier matters must be taught differently. They can be learned only in vital experiences. ... Whether we like it or not, the old type of curriculum, with its precisely fixed-in-advance subject matter, won't bring all the needed learnings" (Kilpatrick, in Rugg (ed.) *26th Yearbook*, pp. 1927, 123–124).
- "We must invent a new synthesis of knowledge and make it the basis of the entire school curriculum. The conventional barriers between the existing subjects must be ignored in curriculum making. The *starting points* shall be the social institution, or the political and economic problem, and the capacities of children—not the subject ..." (Rugg, *26th Yearbook*, 1927, p. 155, emphasis in original).

Traditional

- "Knowledge will always have to be systematized and arranged in coherent subjects. ... The materials of instruction need to be amplified and rearranged and organized (to suit children) ... (but this) statement is not an invitation to plunge into intellectual chaos or to follow the caprice of untrained or immature minds" (Charles H. Judd, in *26th Yearbook*, pp. 116–117).
- "The effect of the mobility of the population on the continuity of education in the mobile pupil-group is a factor of prime importance in the determination of curriculum policies. ... Clearly indicated here is the need for a reasonable degree of uniformity in the grade-placement of the crucial subjects and topics of the elementary-school curriculum" (W. C. Bagley, in Rugg (ed.) *26th Yearbook*, 1927, Supplementary Statement, pp. 32–33).

Continuing Influence of Progressive/Traditional Debates

Debates between those who hold traditional and progressive ideals continue to influence Americans' judgments about curriculum matters. Their influence is so strong, in fact, that virtually all reforms seem to fall into one or the other camp, just as most political proposals seem to be either liberal or conservative, left or right.

The fundamental value difference between traditional and progressive views, as the labels imply, is the attitude each takes toward social change. Progressives view change as inevitable, pervasive, and good. They welcome it and enlist in the cause of shaping a better future. They align themselves with the young, whom they see as untrammeled by the prejudices of the past. Following Rousseau, progressives see youth as good and natural, while age and experience bring the worst evils. Progressives value freedom more than discipline, because only free exploration can discover the directions we should take toward a better future. They believe that the actual experiences of people in the present are a surer guide than the inherited "wisdom" of a past quite different from our present.

Progressives place great importance on helping individuals to learn to think for themselves. The original ideas of creative individuals help society adapt intelligently to changing conditions. Progressives seldom worry about preserving what is valuable from the past. The tremendous inertia in human affairs protects our cultural inheritance. As for the notion of "surviving the test of time," the true progressive regards every day as a new test, independent of all those that have gone before, just as likely to topple the old giant of the forest as the young seedling. In fact, the true progressive takes pleasure in the passing of the oldest traditions, because these leave room for something new to emerge, more adapted to current and future circumstances.

Traditionalists, by contrast, value continuity with the past. They view the accumulated wisdom of humanity, embodied in the culture transmitted from one generation to the next, as a supreme value, the source of nearly all that is highest and best in life. They view nature itself as favoring continuity and very gradual change. Most innovations, like most mutations, are unsuccessful. Ideas and practices that survive the test of time are more likely to be of enduring value than today's inventions, most of which have at best a temporary value. Traditionalists align themselves with the wisdom and skill of maturity and view the young as a precious human resource to be developed, but callow, unformed, and potentially barbarous if not properly initiated into civilized ways.

Two Modern Curriculum Theories in the Classic Tradition

Folk Culture, High Culture, and Industrialization: The Ideas of G. H. Bantock

According to the English author G. H. Bantock, whose ideas were especially influential in the 1970s in England, until the coming of industrialization late in the last century, Western civilization supported two cultures, a "high" culture and a "folk" culture. High cultures were confined largely to the upper classes and based on an ability to read and write, while folk cultures were based largely on traditions of oral communication. Folk cultures were not uniformly less sophisticated and were often more direct and powerful than the corresponding high cultures. The arts of high culture were often refinements of folk arts, rather than completely independent or antagonistic creations. High culture could not have maintained itself without a vital folk culture.

Bantock maintains that industrialization impoverished the everyday life of working people and undermined folk culture. Traditional agriculture and craft work had offered innumerable sensory and emotional satisfactions and had furnished the materials for folk art. Industrialization transformed work into machine-governed routines with far less aesthetic and emotional potential. Efficient, mechanical organization of work replaced organic, personal, "natural" human interchange.

The universal literacy training fostered by free, compulsory elementary schools in the late 1800s imposed on the majority of working class Europeans the rudiments of the high literary culture and ruthlessly eradicated the remnants of folk culture. School transmitted to everyone the culture of the educated minority, "the best that has been thought and said." School excluded oral folk tales and the nonliterary arts such as dancing, singing, handcrafts, popular performing arts, and the like that made up folk culture.

The results of this education for children of the working class were alienation from the only living culture open to them, along with a failure to induct them fully into the high culture. The bits and scraps of literacy conveyed in the few short years of elementary education were poor preparation for a rewarding, satisfying life in any adult community. The school stood for abstraction, for a purely mental life, whereas the authentic folk traditions from which the children came relied on direct contact and immediate participation and on the senses and the feelings. For Bantock this explains why school remains a failure for a substantial proportion of the populace.

According to Bantock, we have today a popular culture built around the mass media. It is not a folk culture because it is not created by the folk, but only consumed by them. Yet it is still largely nonliterate and appeals directly to the senses and the feelings. School still offers fragments of a high, literate culture to a population of children whose lives at home are built around a completely different popular culture. Bantock maintains that this is the chief dilemma of education in the 20th century:

> The culture of the people, then, is one which, generally speaking, appeals to the emotions. I have tried to show that, all too often, it is a cheap and tawdry culture, likely to betray one's sense of emotional reality, erecting 'images' of no substance between the individual and his attempts to grapple with the real world of relationships, inhibiting true empathy or fostering a debilitating sentimentality.
>
> Yet this too has to be said. This culture is enormously appealing, in the emotionally undereducated environment we inhabit. It clearly "gets" young people to an extent that school achieves but rarely.... (*Culture, Industrialisation and Education*, 1968, p. 71).

What sort of curriculum will enable schools to come to grips with this dilemma? First, it is important to note that no one curriculum will be satisfactory for both children of the elite literary culture and children of the popular folk culture. The traditional literary–historical curriculum does quite a good job of fitting some youngsters for later participation in the high culture into which they were born. For them, the chief problem with current schooling is the erosive effect of introducing science and technical subjects, engendering skepticism, emphasizing the material while denigrating the spiritual, the emotional, and the aesthetic concerns which lie close to the heart of literary–historical high culture. In Bantock's view, this development has gone too far and needs to be corrected.

Bantock maintains that the curriculum for children of the lower classes needs to be wholly redesigned. For them, education needs to unite thought and feeling, to use these children's natural propensities toward direct participation, toward sensing, toward feeling, but to use them to the ultimate end of induction into higher, more serious, more refined, and more encompassingly truthful and satisfying ways of dealing with reality. The central aim of elementary education, particularly, must be education of the emotions. This involves both becoming aware of one's emotions and also being able to experience emotion in new, subtler, and more articulated forms.

The methods and concerns of the arts lie at the heart of the alternative curriculum Bantock proposes. He suggests movement education as the soundest starting point. In movement education, children are involved in exploring space in a disciplined way as well as in expressing their feelings. Children are stimulated to think how they can position themselves in space and move through space in order to achieve given effects or in order to communicate their feelings. Dramatic sequences of movement and gesture can convey narrative. Gesture leads to symbol and hence to language. The path from movement to drama and the other performing arts leads in a natural way to the popular art forms of the 20th century—radio, film, and television. Through participation in and study of these forms children can develop a heightened awareness of the major media of communication they experience in their lives outside school.

In addition, schools for children who are not academically inclined should attend to home and family life and to vocational and technical education, following the principle of learning by direct contact and participation. Throughout this curriculum every effort should be made to elevate and refine emotional, aesthetic, and intellectual abilities using the materials of a culture familiar to the students, a culture in which they will live once their schooling is past.

Americans and many others who embrace democratic ideals, may find Bantock's proposal for separate curriculums for children of different social backgrounds unacceptable. But he makes his proposal in full awareness of the claims of democracy and egalitarianism. Responding in advance to the charge that he is merely trying to make the lower classes happy in their subordination, Bantock replies by asking what sort of life school presently holds out for them. He answers "repetitive work in a factory of the soul-destroying type." By contrast, the curriculum he proposes would offer, he claims, preparation for all sorts of work in the applied arts, communication, design, and so on, with at least as much promise of material reward and greater promise of personal satisfaction. "The prospect of an elite prestige job held out to youngsters presently as the reward for school completion is an illusion for all but a tiny fraction of them" (Bantock, *Dilemmas of the Curriculum*, 1980, p. 99).

A Curriculum Based on Caring, by Nel Noddings

In *The Challenge to Care in Schools* (1992) Nel Noddings asks what school would be like if its primary aim were producing caring people. She maintains that the first job of the schools is not to increase academic learning but to care for children and to help them grow into caring adults.

Noddings claims that schools have largely ignored massive social changes that have occurred in the years since World War II—two-income nuclear families, single parent families, divorce, remarriage, and families with children of mixed parentage. In the same period schools have grown larger and more impersonal. Schools have set intellectual development as their first priority and adopted impersonal ideas and methods. The result is that many students feel that no one in school cares for them.

To develop her vision of the ideal education, Noddings proposes a thought experiment. "Suppose we were raising a very large family of heterogeneous children—children with different biological parents, of mixed races, and widely different talents. How would we want them to turn out? What kind of education would we want for them?" (p. 45)

Noddings proposes caring as the organizing framework for their education. She suggests teaching children, first, to care for themselves, beginning with their physical self but also including the occupational, emotional, spiritual, and intellectual aspects of self. Children would find in school a wide range of opportunities to try their skills, develop their interests, and discover their talents. They would find opportunities to care for children, the aged, and the ill. They would learn about the stages and cycles of life.

Noddings would also have children learn about caring for intimate others. They would participate in school projects that benefit their friends and families. They would engage in dialogue with one another and with teachers around issues of acceptance and belonging that arise in their relations with one another and with their families and friends in and out of school. In this way they would come to understand human relations and the groups with which they affiliate.

Children would also learn about caring for animals, plants, and all forms of life. Caring for a pet is part of this, but so is dialogue about such questions as "Should we stop killing and eating animals?" and "Do animals have rights?" Similarly, they would learn to appreciate and care for objects, instruments, and other human creations. Finally, students would be helped to care for ideas, not just to master them, but also to appreciate them and take care in exploring and using them.

In organizing an educational system Noddings would emphasize continuity of caring. Every student would spend part of every day in studies that treat themes of care. To meet affiliative needs, teachers would spend 3 or more years with their students, forming last-ing relationships and getting to know them well. Studies would be integrated, not divided into separate disciplines. Teachers and students would build the curriculum cooperatively. Schools would get rid of competitive grading and abolish hierarchies among programs. Pro-grams for the noncollege bound would be just as rich and prestigious as academic programs. Schools would give all students opportunities to explore the great existential questions central to human life.

Noddings rejects the ideal of liberal education. She see it as designed to maintain a privileged group of college-educated professionals and leaders, not to prepare everyone for the full range of important and rewarding roles in life. It draws on only a narrow set of human abilities, primarily linguistic and logical–mathematical abilities. And it ignores "concepts, skills, attitudes, and capacities valued by and traditionally associated with women" (p. 33). Noddings maintains that "subject matter cannot carry itself." "Relation, except in very rare cases, precedes any engagement with subject matter. Caring relations can prepare children for an initial receptivity to all sorts of experiences and subject matters" (p. 36).

Conclusion

The pioneering curriculum theorists of the progressive era believed that they could reason their way to an ideal curriculum, or at least a better one. Reasoning from a variety of ideals and perspectives, they created many promising plans, but in the end scholars found all these theories to be limited if not actually faulty. As each new theory joined the others in the modest status of one interesting perspective, the faith of curriculum scholars in the power of theory to give definitive answers to curriculum problems ebbed. Today, curriculum theory of this original sort, theory that sets out to discover the best curriculum to achieve given ideals and to show that it is the best, is only one among many forms of theorizing about curriculum. Let us look at some of the other forms.

New Directions in Curriculum Theorizing

Curriculum Criticism

Criticism of curriculum theory has long been a staple of academic curriculum writing. For instance, Boyd Bode in *Modern Educational Theories* critically examined the strengths and weaknesses of progressive ideals with sympathy and yet with marvelous insight. Criticism of theory is as important as its formulation, and in recent decades criticism has established itself as an independent variety of curriculum theorizing.

Kliebard's Critique of the Tyler Rationale.   Herbert Kliebard's (1970) critique of the famous and influential Tyler rationale offers an excellent illustration of curriculum theory as criti-cism. Kliebard draws the concepts and methods he uses from many humanistic disciplines. For example, he uses historical scholarship to show that Tyler erroneously characterizes the Committee of Ten Report as recommending a program for the college bound. Kliebard notes that the Committee specifically stated that it proposed one program for all secondary school students regardless of their likely future careers. He suggests that Tyler's misunderstanding of the Committee's position reveals a bias against subjects as ends in themselves and in favor of content with social or personal relevance.

Kliebard's criticism of Tyler's use of the concept of "needs" to justify selection of objectives draws upon philosophical analyses of the concept, which show that appeal to need is a way of seeming to provide factual grounding for what is essentially and necessarily a value judgment. To claim that a survey of student reading habits, which reveals a high proportion of comic books, shows a "need" for developing broader and deeper reading interests is simply a way of cloaking a value judgment about different types of reading matter in the appearance of scientific objectivity. He also draws upon philosophy in criticizing Tyler's notion that a philosophy of education can be used as a screen for choosing among objectives generated by studies of various kinds. This amounts, Kliebard argues, to nothing more than the statement that ultimately one must choose in light of one's values, an obvious, nearly vacuous truism.

Much of Kliebard's critique relies upon his knowledge of curriculum theory and his experience with curriculum problems. For example, he asks how learning experiences can be "selected," as Tyler's rationale requires, when the student's experience is a unique and not wholly predictable interaction with the environment provided by the teacher. And Kliebard questions the wisdom of an evaluation that merely checks on the attainment of previously stated objectives. He quotes John Dewey's claim that the aim of an action is not necessarily even the most important of its consequences.

Having pointed out so many flaws, Kliebard feels a responsibility to explain how the Tyler rationale has exerted so great an influence on American curricular thought and practice. He suggests that its success is due to the moderation and wisdom Tyler has shown in applying the ideas and to the way the ideas themselves "skirt the pitfalls to which the doctrinaire are subject" and strike "compromises between warring extremes." "It is an eminently reasonable framework for developing a curriculum," but it is "not 'the' universal model of curriculum development," and a new model is "long overdue" (p. 270).

Michael Apple: A Neomarxist Critique of Modern Schooling.   Michael Apple (1979) is concerned with the role of schooling in reproducing the social order. The social order of the United States, like that of other capitalist countries, is dominated by the interests of capital, of corporations, and of business. These dominant interests exert hegemony over individuals in the society through subtle but powerful mechanisms of domination in which the school plays an important part.

Schooling functions to reproduce and maintain this unjust, inequitable, and inhumane distribution of power. It does this, in part, by purveying a selective version of history, of tradition, and of knowledge. A partial and biased set of facts is purveyed as the complete, neutral, objective truth. Also, the structure of the school as an institution acts subtly to sustain control. The work is divided up and parceled out in such a way as to discourage concerted inquiries into the fundamental forces at work. Teachers and students are busied with details, enmeshed in bureaucratic rules, and required to follow the dictates of plans and materials externally imposed upon them. Students with an inclination to question or challenge their role and status within the school are subjected to "disciplinary" action.

Apple argues that knowledge is a form of cultural capital. The school legitimizes certain kinds of knowledge by including them in the formal curriculum. By defining the knowledge everyone is expected to have schools confer special status on items of knowledge important to dominant interests while denying such status to knowledge equally or more important to other segments of the society. Thus, schools place higher value on science and technology than on the arts. In teaching history and social studies, harmony and consensus are emphasized and conflict minimized, thus conveying the impression of a society where people are basically content and happy. School thus plays a pivotal role in the preservation of the cultural capital of the dominant cultural and economic forces.

Equally or even more importantly, the school controls through a hidden curriculum. In analyzing children's first school experiences in kindergarten, Apple notes that "the four most important skills that the (kindergarten) teacher expected the children to learn during those opening weeks were to share, to listen, to put things away, and to follow the classroom routine" (p. 53), all socializing skills. He notes that children had no part in organizing the classroom activity and were unable to affect these activities.

Within weeks, children in this kindergarten class distinguished between work and play activities within the classroom. Work was compulsory, something you were told to do, supervised in doing, something on which your performance was noted and graded. Such socialization training, although not a formal part of the curriculum, functions powerfully to produce attitudes and habits that sustain the currently dominant cultural and economic order.

Apple's ideas about curriculum spring from commitment to a set of moral and political ideals having to do with social justice, collective responsibility, and "the search for a set of economic and cultural institutions that make such collective responsibility possible" (p. 162). Theory and research are tools for exposing and thus undermining the deceptive foundations of the prevailing order and for guiding the construction of a new one. "(C)urriculists must take an advocacy position on a number of critical fronts, both in and outside of education" (p. 163). He suggests that these fronts should include students' rights, teachers' rights, and the rights of oppressed minorities. He urges those in curriculum work to stand back from the prevailing ideology and institutions and to work to alter them. His work stands as an excellent example of committed, partisan scholarship.

The Reconceptualists: Curriculum Theory as Social Construction

Since the 1970s critics have taken more political, literary, and cultural approaches derived from intellectual movements such as, Marxism, feminism, gay rights, civil rights, postmodernism, poststructuralism, multiculturalism, anticolonialism, and cultural studies. Race, class, and gender are central concerns, and demands for social justice drive much of this work.

The new critics have seen the prevailing curriculum as reinforcing some of the most urgent social problems of our time, problems such as racism, sexism, homophobia, and social class, and curriculum criticism as a way of acting against these problems. They called for reconceptualizing the curriculum to make it more just and to liberate it from hierarchy, patriarchy, and the hegemony of dominant economic and social groups. The reconceptualists adopted frankly value-laden, partisan perspectives on curriculum questions, embracing values of equality, liberty, and community, and making no effort to strive for an objectivity that they saw as an unattainable ideal. The reconceptualists also valued radical ideas and proposals that offered stark alternatives to the dominant ones.

Many reconceptualists, postmodernists, and other contemporary curriculum theorists were concerned about the neglect of the personal and subjective. They focused attention on reflection, renewal, and people's subjective sense of well-being. Many are especially concerned with feelings and emotions, with the cry of the heart. They use autobiography, metaphor, literature, literary theory, and the arts of expression and interpretation to express people's personal experience of curriculum. Pinar et al. (1995) suggest thinking of the curriculum itself as a text and subjecting it to textual deconstruction. Contemporary critical theorists are concerned, too, with the failures and shortcomings of reason, the limitations of science, and with the tyranny of grand narratives.

Through criticism the reconceptualists strive to break down the intellectual foundations of those traditions and values they believe to be oppressive, dominating, and isolating. They break them down by problematizing the taken-for-granted and recasting it in the light of new perspectives. Contemporary critics urge us to question the ground we stand on when we consider curriculum questions, "to uncover the layers of meaning of the phenomena that could enrich our lives and our schooling practices" (Slattery, 1995, p. 264). Slattery in *Curriculum Development in the Postmodern Era* (1995) quotes T. S. Eliot's line approvingly: "We shall not cease from exploring, and the end of all our exploring shall be to arrive where we started, and know the place for the first time."

The "riotous array of theoretical approaches" (Janet Miller, quoted in Wright (2000)) that has sprung from critical work grounded in various disciplines of the humanities creates a jumbled, kaleidoscopic intellectual landscape. Slattery's statement about the work shows this quality in both style and substance when he writes that the reconceptualists and post-modernists offer "a vision of the postmodern curriculum that is radically eclectic, determined in the context of relatedness, recursive in its complexity, autobiographically intuitive, aesthetically inter-subjective, phenomenological, experiential, simultaneously quantum and cosmic, hopeful in its constructive dimension, radical in its deconstructive movement, liberating in its poststructural intents, empowering in its spirituality, ironic in its kaleidoscopic sensibilities, and ultimately, a hermeneutic search for greater understanding that motivates and satisfies us on the journey" (Slattery, 1995, p. 267).

Two characteristics that unite most of these disparate works are a commitment to viewing every curriculum as a social construction and a determination to analyze that construction critically to find out how it contributes to the evils of our day. Both characteristics have revolutionary implications for the enterprise of curriculum theory, but the first seems more fundamental. That all curriculum ideals and theories are social constructions created by social groups to function in a certain time and place leads to fascinating questions about the relationship of curriculums to the societies that support them.

The search for sources of social evil, on the other hand, seems a surprisingly simplistic quest for such an otherwise sophisticated endeavor. Every curriculum can be criticized from some point of view. Decision-makers must weigh the pros and cons of imperfect options. Criticism that ignores a curriculum's virtues creates a bill of indictment, not the full assessment that decision-makers need. Ironically, decision-makers who want to use contemporary curriculum theorizing must supply their own complexity, ambiguity, and recognition of the multiplicity of values, all qualities that postmodern critics claim to value.

Curriculum theorizing today is primarily the work of committed intellectuals. Their works are judged by their influence on other intellectuals rather than on the school curriculum or those who shape it. Nevertheless, contemporary curriculum theorizing offers professionals a wealth of critical perspectives on curriculum issues that they will need to hold in constructive tension with other viewpoints prominent in their communities. They need to recognize that many perspectives offer useful insights, although no perspective gives the whole truth. And they need to learn how to help people with differing perspectives, discuss curriculum issues constructively, and work together to maintain a common curriculum. Only time will tell whether today's curriculum criticism will grow to be the main branch of curriculum theory's evolutionary tree or merely a short-lived radical avant garde intellectual movement.

Marks of Quality in a Curriculum Theory

What characteristics should a good curriculum theory have? Certainly it should be clear, factually correct, and logical. It should lead to interesting and useful conclusions that are not obvious without the theory. It should be practical. And it should meet our standards of good or right conduct. Let us consider these criteria in more detail.

Validity

Validity in a theory has at least three components:

    meaningfulness: Is it clear, unambiguous, well-defined?
    logical consistency: Is it free of internal contradictions?
    factual correctness: Is it consistent with all else we know?

Meaningfulness as a Component of Validity

Meaningfulness is a question of adequacy of communication. A rough and ready standard is: If persons suitably qualified by training and experience agree on what a theory says, then it is meaningful. In short, we simply see if different readers understand the theory to mean basically the same thing. We could also watch what those who say they are using the theory do and why they say they do it. This standard is certainly fallible. Whole communities can be deceived—remember the story, "The Emperor's New Clothes."

In judging the meaningfulness of a theory, it is helpful to produce a glossary of key terms and a list of key propositions. If we have few doubts about the meaning of the terms, if they are clearly defined and used consistently throughout, then the statement of the theory is at least formally adequate. We must then look at examples and instances cited to see if they fit the definition. We should invent our own examples to see if we can find borderline cases, unclear cases, cases covered under both of a supposedly mutually exclusive set of terms, and so on. Then we look at the key propositions to verify that the terms are actually used consistently with their definitions.

Sometimes the key terms in a curriculum theory are glittering abstractions like "social adjustment," or "high-grade living," or "human dignity" that are not defined or defined so loosely that everyone can fill them with whatever they wish. When we compare notes, we find that the theory means very different things to us. The term "needs" is a good example. We all feel that a curriculum should meet students' needs, but what are they? Something lacking that hurts students in some way. Food, water, and rest are clearly physiological needs. When it comes to needs that can be satisfied through education, though, virtually anything anybody wants to teach has been claimed to meet students' needs, so that the concept is not meaningful.

Some observers have proposed to make curricular definitions more rigorous and scientific by insisting that key terms be defined in terms of observable behavior, but this goes too far. Most philosophers who have considered the question agree that the attempt to define all concepts operationally is self-defeating even in a purely scientific theory. A theory's power arises precisely because we can measure its central concepts in different ways and the theory continues to work.

Few of the terms one might want to include in a curriculum theory could, even in principle, be defined operationally. In particular, it is a puzzle how to operationally define value-laden terms—the good life, the good society, the utility of knowledge, good citizenship, and the like. Meaning in the case of curriculum is at least as much a matter of values as a matter of fact. Curriculum is not physics.

The clearer curriculum theories can be the better, but our standards must be appropriate. The appropriate standard is the clarity and meaningfulness reached by the best curriculum theories: an excellent reason to read many historically important curriculum theories.

Logical Consistency as a Component of Validity

To judge logical consistency we look at the key propositions of a theory as reasoning. The summary given later in this chapter of Gardner's theory of multiple abilities shows one way to accomplish this. List key theoretical terms and key propositions of the theory, state them as simply and baldly as possible, and show the if . . . then logical connections that lead from some of these propositions to the theory's conclusions about what curriculum we should have. Representing a theory as logical relationships among key propositions puts the reasoning in high relief and may reveal gaps or inconsistencies in the theory.

Factual Correctness as a Component of Validity

We assess the factual correctness of a theory by comparing its statements and predictions to the reality we see. The essential logic of curriculum theory is that if we take some particular curriculum action, we should get some valued student learning. We can check this kind of prediction if the theory is meaningful and if the relationship is logically coherent. The most rigorous tests are experiments in which similar students experience different curriculums in similar classroom situations. A weaker test can be made by looking at the performance of students in existing classrooms, comparing the scores of students who study one curriculum with those who study with another. Everyone wants such studies, but they are expensive and difficult to do well and critics still dispute their findings. At the very least, each of us can always test the theory's consequences against our own remembered experience.

Theoretical Power

Even if we knew that the factual claims of a curriculum theory were correct, we still might not think it was a good theory if it didn't help us much. We speak of theories as powerful when they make great contributions to our understanding or our resolution to act. Powerful curriculum theories enable us to act effectively in a wide range of situations because they give us insight about the likely consequences of acting in certain ways or the values we will uphold by acting, or both. By contrast, weak theories yield few insights, and the few that they yield do not advance us far beyond the point where common sense would have taken us anyway. Compared to scientific theories, curriculum theories and all theories about education tend to be relatively weak. None has revolutionized practice to the extent, say, that the germ theory of disease revolutionized medicine, Darwin's theories revolutionized biology, or Einstein's theories revolutionized physics. Curriculum theories offer the possibility of new perspectives, deeper understanding, and improved results, but not the prospect of scientific breakthroughs.

Serviceability

A theory both valid and powerful would still be of little use if it could not be applied under realistic conditions to help resolve the important curriculum problems people actually face. A serviceable curriculum theory helps us with the problems we actually face, and it helps under realistic conditions, in a timely, economical way. Theories can fail to be serviceable for many reasons. One of the most common, unfortunately is that the theory requires conditions not attainable in practice. It was said of progressive education, for example, that it demanded too much from teachers. Critics claimed that the progressive teacher had an "impossible role." Teachers had to plan a unique classroom program tailored to that group of students, involving individual work for each student and joint work by the class as a group, responsive to daily shifts in mood and to events in and out of the classroom.

Important aspects of serviceability include functionality (will it work?), efficiency (favorable ratio of results to resources consumed), economy (manageable cost), appeal (will people like it?), and relevance (does it apply to our situation?).

Morality

Those who use curriculum theories cannot avoid making value judgments. In fact, the influence of a valid, powerful, highly serviceable theory built upon misguided values is greatly to be feared. More likely, shallow, evanescent values will be emphasized over deeper, more enduring ones. If only there were a clear, prevailing set of moral standards, judging the morality of a curriculum theory would be no more difficult than judging its validity, power, and serviceability, but the evident diversity of moral standards found in contemporary society complicates judgments of morality. Most Americans acquire their moral standards in their family and religious groups, and these are enormously diverse. Yet public education is secular and universalistic. Our public life upholds certain political and legal standards common to all, but not common social mores and religious beliefs.

Consequently, books that some believe are classics are immoral in the eyes of others (*Huckleberry Finn*, and *The Origin of Species*). Texts sacred to any religious group may not be studied lest they offend those who belong to other groups who hold other beliefs. Subjects that some believe need extensive public discussion, such as sex, drugs, and social problems, others consider taboo. Some parents give moral reasons for preferring highly structured, authoritative classroom environments with a serious businesslike atmosphere, while others give equally moral but quite different reasons for preferring classrooms to be open, unstructured, and playful.

Under these conditions, we must content ourselves with evaluating the morality of theories by reference to moral standards appropriate to each situation. These may be a prevailing code accepted by a consensus among the relevant community, the code accepted by a dominant group or of a particular minority group, or even the code of a single individual. Naturally, the same theory may be highly laudable when judged by some of these moral standards and odious by others.

Professionals take risks when they choose among moral codes accepted by different groups of clients, but it is always appropriate for a professional to clarify the values used in any particular theory and to show how these fare when judged by some appropriate moral standards. Just how active a role professionals should play in advocacy of values within the larger community and just how conflicts between professionals and their clients over values should be resolved are matters of some controversy. Some claim that curriculum professionals have a moral responsibility to stand up for such values as justice, especially when the majority and the most powerful interests act unjustly. Others claim that curriculum professionals have no more (and no less) moral authority than any other person in such a situation. Professionals have an ethical obligation to uphold the laws and abide by codes of ethics. However, it seems clear that the professional in any field cannot claim by virtue of professional expertise any special ability to make moral judgments or any right to impose moral judgments on clients or the public.

When communities contain groups with different moral standards, curriculum leaders have two fundamental options: tolerate different moral judgments or search for common ground. To tolerate some different sets of moral standards does not necessarily imply abandonment of all morality, but to tolerate any and all moral standards does. Thus, toleration has its limits. In practice, American public school systems tend to abandon any practice that any religious or ethnic group in the local community challenges on moral grounds.

Nearly all professional writing on curriculum questions asserts or assumes a commonly accepted set of values in the form of an agreed-upon list of goals (aims, objectives). For example, Goodlad (1984) listed 62 goals for schooling under four broad headings: academic; vocational; social, civic, cultural; and personal. Goodlad's categories may include nearly all of the educational values important to any major segment of the American public, but any such inclusive list begs the crucial question of what priority should be given to each goal. Finding common moral ground among established communities who place different priorities on various values is much more difficult than producing an inclusive list of general goals.

In conflicted social contexts it is not possible to set down general rules about which values are appropriate to assessing a theory's moral acceptability. The most democratic course of action for the analyst in assessing the quality of a theory is to examine it in light of all values held by all parties to the issue. This can be complex and difficult. In many cases, the best course of action will be to use prevailing mainstream values and also one or a few of the most widely held alternative value systems. In any event, as we shall see in later chapters, the contending parties are seldom willing to leave the decision to analysts about which values to use.

Reading Curriculum Theory

Guidelines

To read curriculum theory closely and critically is a more active process than everyday reading, but the skills involved are not obscure or difficult and with a little practice anyone can learn to do it. What you must do is identify the lines of argument that are fundamental to the theory, then the fundamental ideas and values on which these lines of argument rest, and finally read between the lines by asking yourself what alternative arguments, ideas, and values might have been used instead. Once you have exposed the theory's scaffolding in this way, you will find it much easier to draw convincing conclusions about the validity, power, serviceability, and morality of the theory in comparison with plausible alternative choices open to the author. And, when you cannot reach a firm judgment, you should at least have a better idea of what further information would most help you confirm your judgment. Try the following procedure.

First, read the work straight through, just as you would any book or essay, trying to discover the author's meaning and noting for future reference any passages that make a particularly strong impression on you for any reason. Summarize the message of the work: the central concern (issue, problem) of the author, conclusions reached about this concern, and main points made in support of this conclusion. Now you have the skeleton of the argument.

Then, make a list of key terms and their defining phrases. When a term seems value-laden, try to identify the value in a word or brief phrase. Quote brief phrases that express each value most vividly. Look for the key ideas and central values on which the case rests. You can recognize these because, if you changed them, you would completely change the overall message of the work. If you have trouble sorting out relationships among the ideas, make a table that lists all the main ideas in both the rows and the columns. Then cross out all these cells where two ideas are not related and examine carefully the relationships in the other cells.

Then, check the soundness of each step in the argument. What grounds does the author give for the truth of the arguments' premises? Note strong and weak arguments as well as ones you are most uncertain about. Look for unstated assumptions; often these are more dubious than stated ones. Note the historical and intellectual origins of key terms and ideas. Often, knowing the fields of study, philosophical doctrines, or historical periods where ideas originated suggests assumptions or values that the present ideas may share with the older ones. Give special attention to turns in the argument that seem arbitrary, to places where you find yourself wondering, "Where did this come from?" Such unexpected twists in the argument may give clues about an unstated assumption or value. Look for gaps and holes in the argument.

Next, consider the theory in the context of alternative views. Try to find strong, credible alternatives to the author's key ideas, values, and assumptions. Then, ask yourself why the author chose to rely on the ones actually used instead of these alternatives. In what other ways might the issue be posed? In particular, what is the common sense view of the issue, and what are the major well-known views that run counter to the author's? Why might the author have chosen to address this issue instead of others? What may be inferred from the author's decision to pose the issue in that particular way instead of one of the others? What other positions are not considered? What other reasons could be given? What other grounds? In each case, what can we infer from the choices the author made? Is there, for instance, a pattern to the author's choices that suggests a purpose other than the stated purpose or values not explicitly embraced? Speculate about the possible significance of the author's choices. For example, which interested parties would support or oppose them? Examine the author's language for subtle cues to purpose and value. When is the tone conciliatory and when combative? How does the author use words to make something appealing or repulsive? What rhetorical or persuasive strategies does the author employ?

Finally, put together everything you have learned from studying the work into overall judgments about its strengths and limitations. Would you embrace these ideas? What changes would make you feel better about embracing them? Are other competing ideas still more acceptable? How would you judge their validity, power, serviceability, and morality? What uncertainties make it difficult for you to reach a judgment about the overall quality of this work, and what further steps would reduce these uncertainties? Make allowances for the way the author framed the work, for no work can address all problems. For example, if the work is a brief essay sketching out a direction of thought on an issue, do not expect it to provide a completely worked out solution. If the author's purpose is to develop a view that will serve as a partisan alternative for use by those, perhaps a minority who share certain values do not criticize it for ignoring prevailing values, and so on. Figure 3.2 summarizes these steps.

An Example: Critical Reading of Howard Gardner's *The Disciplined Mind*

Let us critically analyze Howard Gardner's theory supporting the multiple abilities curriculum as expressed in his book, *The Disciplined Mind* (1999). The book is a far-reaching statement of the prominent psychologist's vision of education. Gardner is well-known to educators for his books on multiple intelligences and for his advocacy for more adventurous and varied teaching methods that can motivate and teach all students, even those who dislike school and perform poorly on tests. He directed Project Zero, a 10-year effort at Harvard to develop performance-based assessments and educational methods and materials based on multiple intelligences and on related ideas from cognitive science. He has also studied and written books about the arts, creativity, and the psychological and cultural origins of some of humanity's greatest intellectual achievements in a variety of fields. This book draws on all those experiences.

The Disciplined Mind presents Gardner's educational vision both as an ideal to strive for over the long term, and also as a practical plan of action. He begins with personal observations, stressing the need to frame educational debates less parochially. He then sketches a broad account of education in the past, emphasizing the role of culture. He views the rise of the scholarly disciplines as the culmination of this history. Education in the future, he argues, must be different. Education is at a crossroads and needs a new vision. That new vision can come from scientific perspectives on mind and brain. He briefly recounts the main findings of the cognitive revolution in psychology, leaving readers with a strong impression that cognitive science has established a firm foundation of reliable knowledge on which to base new educational practices.

1. Read the work for sense noting your responses
   Summarize concerns, conclusions, and main arguments
2. Study the argumentative scaffolding
   a. main lines of argument

   What issue is addressed? What position is taken? What other positions are considered? What reasons are given for taking the chosen position? What supporting grounds are given for these reasons?
   b. key ideas
   c. central values
   d. connections and relationships
3. Check the soundness of arguments.
   a. logical validity
   b. strength of evidence
   c. hidden premises?
   d. gaps?
4. Consider the work in light of a context of alternatives
   a. other ideas
   b. other values
   c. other assumptions
   d. other language and rhetorical form
   e. origins may suggest other strengths or weaknesses
   f. what can be inferred from the author's choices?
5. Reach a summary judgment of the quality of the work
   a. validity
   b. power
   c. serviceability
   d. morality
   e. would I embrace it? with changes?
   f. judged in relation to the author's project

FIG. 3.2. *A plan for critical reading of curriculum theory.*

Having situated his vision in history, culture, and science, Gardner turns to his proposals for education. First he describes "the best preschools in the world," those of the Italian city of Reggio Emilia. He portrays them as student-centered and progressive using lengthy student projects, varied materials, lots of group work, holding high standards, carefully monitoring student progress, coaching individual students, and a culminating public exhibition of student work. Gardner also profiles several other schools that provide education consistent with his vision—Suzuki music classes; secondary schools in Germany and Singapore; Central Park East Secondary School in New York; and the Israeli Academy of Arts and Sciences, among others. Many readers will find these descriptions the most inspiring passages in the book.

In the remaining chapters he presents his proposals for realizing his vision, presenting extended suggestions for teaching three topics: Darwin's theory of evolution; Mozart's opera, *The Marriage of Figaro*; and the history of the Nazi Holocaust. The material in these chapters will be the main focus of the remarks to come.

His audience is "individuals all over the world who care about education" (p. 16). His voice is that of a literate intellectual writing for an educated lay audience. He minimizes psychoeducational jargon. He uses a few technical terms from cognitive science such as *multiple representations*, *legitimate peripheral participation*, and *model languages*, but he explains them. College educated readers should have no difficulty with the terminology.

The book is not an easy read, however. While Gardner's writing is lively and highly readable, the book ranges widely over ideas about education and cultures around the world and from prehistory to the future. The index of names contains more than 200 entries beginning with Aeschylus, ending with Virginia Woolf, and including figures as diverse as Confucius, Bill Gates, and Pol Pot. Gardner also drops many famous and obscure references to lofty works and ideas, especially ones related to Darwin and evolution, Mozart and classical music, and the Holocaust and historiography.

Throughout the book Gardner goes to great pains to emphasize that he is not offering recipes. He expects readers to draw their own conclusions from his examples and to adjust his ideas to fit different circumstances. He complains about the simplistic interpretations many have given to his ideas about multiple intelligences and asks readers to interpret his proposals with subtlety, nuance, and artfulness. He would probably be unhappy with the bald, condensed version of his proposals presented above. Still, we can't consider the whole book at once. We must isolate some key features of his proposals for intense scrutiny, just as he found it necessary to isolate certain features of Darwin, Mozart, and the Holocaust for study.

Gardner's Proposals

These five numbered principles are my best effort to identify the key elements of Gardner's proposals.

1. Schools should try to help students understand what people in their culture consider to be true, good, and beautiful (p. 186).

   Gardner acknowledges that different cultures define these ideals in different ways. Each culture must identify for itself the particular truths, beauties, and virtues that it values and teach those. Inasmuch as American society includes representatives of many cultures, he invites communities to develop schools that reflect various cultural subgroups' interpretations of the three ideals. Gardner admits that this triad of ideals is an ancient staple of the Western intellectual tradition, much criticized by cultural relativists and postmodernists, but he insists that the content of the curriculum must be drawn from them (p. 35).

2. The central goal of schooling should be deep understanding (p. 186). Deep understanding requires a curriculum that treats a few topics in depth (p. 122).

   The acid test of deep understanding for Gardner is to pose students a new problem and see how well they manage. Deep understanding means going beyond basic facts and skills to use higher cognitive functions such as problem-solving, problem-finding, creativity, taking stock of one's own thinking, and using multiple forms of representation. The antithesis of a curriculum for deep understanding is a cultural literacy curriculum in which students cover a vast number of topics and concepts deemed necessary for cultural literacy. In the inevitable choice between breadth and depth, Gardner puts all his chips on depth.

3. Mastery of the traditional academic disciplines and their ways of thinking is the best, and possibly the only, way to achieve deep understanding.

Academic disciplines provide "privileged ways into phenomena, . . . the most sophisticated means for addressing the questions that preoccupy human beings" (p. 218). "If you want to understand what it means to be alive, study biology. . . . If you want to understand your own background, study national history and immigration patterns and experiences" (p. 218). Students should undertake interdisciplinary studies only after they have mastered more than one discipline so that they can link mastered disciplines productively (p. 219).

4. To enable all students to acquire a deep understanding of the disciplines schools must use teaching methods that activate multiple intelligences.

Two "towering facts" stand in the way of achieving deep understanding of the disciplines by all students. First, attaining deep understanding is difficult for everyone. Second, individuals come to understand in various ways. Gardner maintains that the theory of multiple intelligences can help educators cope with both problems. When children use their most highly developed abilities, they make the best progress and endure the least frustration.

Attending to multiple intelligences also enables teachers to design compelling entry points to engage students in the study of important topics. Gardner describes seven types of educational entry points, each based on a form of intelligence. For instance, interpersonal entry points, such as recreating debates, reenacting historical events, and role-playing are particularly compelling for some children. Other children would find hands-on entry points, such as conducting experiments, taking field trips, and creating art, more engaging. Aesthetic, logical, numerical, narrative, or existential entry points also hold promise. Once a student's interest is engaged through such entry points, the theory of multiple intelligences suggests strategies to achieve deeper penetration into the topic, notably (1) confronting students' flawed conceptions, (2) suggesting powerful comparisons, and (3) expressing ideas using multiple representations.

5. Schools should be individualized and personalized, within limits, by allowing schools to adapt a few model national curriculums (p. 72).

Any common curriculum will favor the students blessed with strength in the abilities that this curriculum emphasizes. Yet radical individualization would not be workable because Americans insist on a degree of national unity. Therefore, Gardner suggests that several alternative national models be developed and offered to schools. As examples, Gardner suggests the canon pathway, where students read classic books and discuss them in traditional academic ways, the multicultural pathway where students study their own and other cultures and reflect on the nature and identities of America's chief racial and ethnic groups, a progressive pathway, a technological pathway, and a socially responsible pathway. He urges that national authorities officially qualify a few such pathways and require that each ensures the transmission and inculcation of basic national values.

The Disciplined Mind is a spirited defense of a broad version of traditional academic ideals taught within innovative ways similar to those advocated by progressives. Any contemporary American school system that adopted these five proposals would have to undertake some major reforms. They would need new textbooks and curriculums that cover a few topics in depth. They would need new forms of assessment to replace conventional tests. Teachers would need to use new teaching strategies that call on multiple intelligences. School leaders and communities would need to develop clear visions for each school and implement individualized programs. It would be a tall order. So let's look at the reasons Gardner believes schools should try.

Gardner's Case for His Proposals

Gardner rests the case for his proposals on a set of key ideas of which the most central are culture, understanding, disciplines, multiple intelligences, truth, beauty, and morality. Let us look in detail at how he uses these ideas in the arguments he gives to justify each of the key features of his proposals.

Why Truth, Beauty, and Goodness as the Focus of the Curriculum?   Gardner makes two main arguments to justify his proposal that the true, the good, and the beautiful should animate the curriculum.

1. These ideals are fundamental and universal considerations that lift us beyond the parochial and enlarge our universe (p. 15).
2. They have survived the test of time. For centuries millions of people throughout the world have been enriched by studying truth, beauty, and goodness (p. 40).

Gardner does little more than assert the first argument. He exalts the life of the mind, disparages the utilitarian, and expects readers to share these values. In a sense the whole book is an argument for intellectual ideals as the basis for the curriculum.

The long tradition of these three ideals is Gardner's primary justification for putting them at the center of his educational vision. As he describes the historical development of human civilization, early cultures transmitted roles and values by observation, participation, and ritual. Formal educational institutions emerged to support the learning of notational systems—writing and arithmetic—and later the mastery of formal academic disciplines. Truth, beauty, and goodness emerged as the focus of education in the earliest philosophical cultures, notably the Greek and Jewish cultures, and were later used in Europe and eventually throughout the developed world. At first, "it was relatively unproblematic to inculcate truth, beauty, and goodness through scholastic institutions . . . [but that] consensus has frayed throughout the world" (p. 35).

A strictly academic high school curriculum could be said to focus on truth only. Gardner rejects this as too narrow and incapable of motivating all students. He does not compare his ideals to others that have been proposed as the focus of a curriculum but one can guess how he would respond: self-actualization, self-realization, individual opportunity (too narrow and narcissistic); community or service to others (too parochial and utilitarian); national well-being (too parochial and utilitarian), democratic citizenship (parochial, and the disciplines are the best way to achieve it anyway); economic welfare (too utilitarian); cultural or ethnic identity (too parochial). Comparison with these alternatives highlights Gardner's choice of an idealistic basis rather than a practical, down-to-earth one. He has opted for a focus that, though broader than a strictly academic one, remains centered on the world of ideas and the perspective of scholars, academics, and intellectuals.

Gardner's triad fits squarely in the ancient Western educational tradition, the tradition of Aristotle, Jewish education, the scholastics, and the Enlightenment. Contemporary educational conservatives such as Mortimer Adler or William Bennett would support a curriculum built around truth, beauty, and goodness as represented in classic works and the academic disciplines. Gardner acknowledges this Western pedigree and defends his choice against critics of this tradition. Gardner concedes one point to the critics, however, and that is the need for various cultures to interpret truth, beauty, and goodness in light of their own values and traditions. This question will be of great concern to those committed to multicultural education.

Gardner maintains that all philosophically oriented cultures attend to some version of truth, beauty, and goodness and that they inculcate their version of what is true, beautiful, and good in each generation. He rejects both the universalist position that all cultures are fundamentally alike and the uniqueness position (cultural relativism) that every culture is one of a kind and can only be judged in its own terms. He claims that "there is a more productive way to approach cultural differences than the uniqueness or universalist perspective" (p. 100).

It's not completely clear what Gardner means by a more productive approach. He seems to mean that all cultures today are in a process of change and that part of that change should be to consider what the people of that culture think is true, beautiful, and good and to compare their interpretations to those of people in other cultures. He writes that every culture must "somehow cobble together a viable way of being" out of its resources and conditions, make an effort to appreciate other cultures' perspectives, and make its own clearer to others (p. 101).

So, even though the triad of truth, goodness, and beauty originated in the Western tradition, Gardner maintains that it is relevant to all contemporary cultures. To ask of any culture what its people consider to be true, beautiful, and good would not be to impose an alien Western perspective on them. Nor would it be cultural imperialism to ask the people of any culture to compare what they and other cultures consider to be true, beautiful, and good.

Why Deep Understanding of a Limited Number of Topics?   Gardner's rationale for seeking deep understanding of a few topics comes in two steps.

1. Deep understanding is the way the experts do it.
     But if that were the whole story, people would only need deep understanding of their field of special expertise. Secondly, then, Gardner argues that . . .
2. Deep understanding is necessary for full participation in life and culture and for productive citizenship.

For students to grow into productive citizens they need to "understand the world as it has been portrayed by those who have studied it most carefully and lived in it most thoughtfully . . . [and] become familiar with the range . . . of what other humans have achieved" (p. 20). The great works of all civilizations require deep understanding for their full appreciation, so that all people need deep understanding in order to come into full possession of their cultural inheritance.

Gardner supports the first step in this rationale by citing studies that contrast experts' understanding of important topics in their fields with ordinary people's understanding. Students come to science class bringing beliefs about motion that they use in their daily lives. Many believe that heavier objects fall faster than light ones, for example. This is not a preposterous notion—most educated people believed it until about 300 years ago and it is supported by everyday experiences such as comparing the fall of a pencil and a sheet of paper. Nevertheless, experts know that the idea is flawed, and schools try to teach the more adequate concept that all bodies fall at the same rate in the absence of air resistance.

It takes only brief exposure to this new idea to teach students to give a correct answer to the question, "Which falls faster, a heavy object or a light one?" But studies show that most students continue to use their flawed idea to think through real problems outside science class. The need for deep understanding, then, follows from what cognitive scientists have learned about how hard it is for people to achieve deep understanding.

Gardner justifies the need for citizens to have deep understanding mainly with examples, particularly three that he treats at length: Mozart's music, Darwin's theories, and the history of the Holocaust. In the way he treats these examples Gardner says, in effect, "See what a deep understanding reveals about these topics. See how much light this understanding sheds on important questions in life. Everyone needs to have this deep an understanding

of these and similar topics in order to live fully and enjoy the benefits of civilized life."
Gardner explicitly rejects the goal of making all students experts. This would mean "that
most individuals are being trained as apprentices for careers that they will never follow"
(p. 221). Rather, Gardner argues that from general education we need not experts but
citizens who can think expertly.

Why seek deep understanding of only a limited number of topics? Simple logistics. Deep
understanding takes time. The school year gives only enough time to uncover the depths
of a few major topics. The rush to cover many concepts is the chief obstacle to achieving
deep understanding.

What Alternatives are There to Deep Understanding of a Limited Number of Topics?   Gardner rejects the obvious alternative of superficial coverage of a broad range of topics, but this
means that students will remain totally ignorant of many topics that Gardner admits are as
important as the ones they've studied in depth. Students' knowledge will be spotty, their
mental landscape marred by glaring gaps. Individuals who have studied different topics may
have difficulty communicating. Those who have studied Indian ragas in depth may not
know anything about Mozart. There will be no canon. Writers will be unable to assume
that readers will understand their references. Colleges may have to offer elementary survey
courses to give students the foundations they need for true expertise.

Is a mixed strategy possible? Once students have developed a deep understanding of
a few topics in a discipline and glimpsed the world through that discipline's lenses, it
might be possible to survey quickly other important topics that yield to similar ways of
thinking. Conceivably, many students would be able to transfer their newly acquired deep
understanding to these additional topics without needing to undertake extensive study of
them, too. This could be done by reading biographical or historical essays, articles written for
lay audiences, or even encyclopedias or by watching movies like Kenneth Clark's *Civilization*
or Ken Burns' *Civil War*. Of course, time spent covering additional topics would be time not
available for further in-depth study. Gardner places all his chips on depth. Others might
want to hedge their bets.

Why a Curriculum Based in the Disciplines?   Gardner's justification for mastery of the
traditional academic disciplines as the way to achieve deep understanding is spirited but
unconvincing. He never says what he means by a discipline, yet he claims that "the ways
of thinking—the disciplines—that have developed over the centuries represent our best
approach to almost any topic" (p. 18). The terms Gardner uses in talking about disciplines—
concepts, ways of thinking, lenses, and ways of making sense of the world—are widely
accepted ways to talk about disciplines, but they emphasize the passive role of the discipline
in perception and thought and downplay its more active role in expression and creation.
Disciplines also teach us means of expression, procedures for doing things in the world,
designs, and inventions. A more active concept of discipline might have made Gardner's
proposals more dynamic and less pedantic.

How many different disciplines are there, and which of their ways of thinking should children learn? Gardner doesn't say. At one point he writes tantalizingly of "the scholarly and
practical disciplines" elsewhere without elaboration of "the several key disciplines," but he
never enumerates the disciplines he would recommend that we teach. With no clear alternative, educators are certain to see the traditional school subjects as the disciplines. At best
they'll interpret Gardner as advocating more attention to ways of thinking in those subjects.

Gardner acknowledges that any discipline includes a vast range of ways of thinking.
He waves away this difficulty with the suggestion to "give students access to the 'intellectual heart' or 'experiential soul' of a discipline" and "a sense of how the world appears to

individuals sporting quite different kinds of glasses" (p. 157). How to find the heart and soul of a discipline and the special set of lenses it affords? Gardner offers as examples his own attempts to define the heart and soul of biology, music, and history in his treatment of Darwin, Mozart, and the Holocaust. Gardner tells us that good curriculums should "expose the core ideas and approaches of the major scholarly disciplines" but not try to cover every topic needed by experts in the discipline (p. 221). I could find only examples, no principles, to guide educators in finding the core ideas and approaches.

What are the Alternatives to a Curriculum Based in the Disciplines? The criticism that has always dogged discipline-based education has been that it was lifeless, bookish, pedantic, narrow, and remote from the bright and steely clang of life. The teaching methods Gardner recommends go some way toward vitalizing the disciplines, but some will question whether the sugar coating of lively methods can interest all students in what are essentially analytical and intellectual pursuits. Others may favor a curriculum built like Dewey's around living occupations. Schools could associate with parks, museums, hospitals, day care centers, farms, factories, or offices and focus on the work of real people in those real institutions. Action research and community projects offer other bases for school programs. In light of these alternatives, Gardner's proposals seem to be relatively modest reforms, not radical, and ultimately conservative inasmuch as they suggest a way of saving the discipline-based academic tradition from its main weakness.

Why Activate Multiple Intelligences? Gardner justifies activating students' multiple intelligences on the grounds that such strategies offer the best hope for achieving deep understanding on the part of all students. Traditional schools seek deep understanding primarily through verbal and numerical means, and students with strong abilities at verbal and numerical tasks generally do well in today's schools. But a significant fraction of students in even the best conventional schools fail to develop deep understanding from conventional teaching methods. An education for all students will require teaching methods that activate multiple intelligences, so that students with all profiles of ability will have a good opportunity to learn. Gardner offers many examples of ways a multiple intelligences perspective can help educators to reach students with limited verbal and numerical abilities but with ample musical, spatial, kinesthetic, interpersonal, aesthetic, existential, or other abilities. He also offers many references to research to back up his claim.

What are the Alternatives to Teaching Methods that Activate Multiple Intelligences? Gardner disparages traditional teaching methods that rely mainly on linguistic and logical abilities. But accepting the scientific finding that multiple intelligences exist in no way obligates us to cultivate all intelligences equally.

Some would defend traditional methods on the grounds that language and logic, including mathematics, really are special among the spectrum of human abilities. If humans were deprived of music and the kinesthetic arts of expression, for instance, civilization and human lives would be much poorer, but civilization would still exist and humans would still be recognizably human. Without language and logic, civilization as we know it would be inconceivable. These abilities are what make us human. Furthermore, they play particularly important roles in economic development and in the development of the disciplines that Gardner values so highly.

By favoring methods that activate a full spectrum of intelligences, Gardner affirms values of inclusiveness and equality of opportunity. By doing so in the absence of a convincing rebuttal to the arguments supporting language and logic as uniquely valuable abilities, Gardner declares a willingness to risk the possible consequences of a relative de-emphasis on human abilities that have traditionally been exalted above others.

Why Individualize by Adapting National Options?   Gardner favors individualization because research and theory shows that people differ so markedly in their profiles of ability that no one program can possibly be ideal for everyone. His belief in individualization is also supported by his experience with innovative schools similar to the examples of outstanding schools that he profiles.

Gardner believes "that decisions about what is important are best left to a specific educational community; that all such decisions are tentative at best; and that they should be subject to constant negotiation and reconsideration" (p. 23). But he recognizes that the achievement of nationally important educational goals requires coordination of the efforts of millions of teachers in thousands of schools. So he offers his idea for multiple pathways as a way to preserve local authority yet maintain national standards. According to his multiple pathways proposal, local schools would offer curriculums adapted to their community and their students but within set patterns officially authorized by national authorities.

What are the Alternatives to Multiple Pathways?   Gardner would support national standards with local control of curriculum, but *"only* if I—or others of like mind—could play a substantial role in their creation" (p. 222). Various forms of federalism could be imagined in which federal, state, and local agencies control various levers of power over the curriculum. Gardner seems less interested in the details of power-sharing arrangements than in declaring his strong preference for some sort of middle way between national and local control.

Challenges to Gardner's Arguments

Let us consider some of the challenges that critics and skeptics might make to Gardner's positions and arguments. I have already mentioned some of these challenges, but I'll repeat them here for convenience and to facilitate reaching a summary judgment on the proposals.

Challenges to the Argument from Tradition for Truth, Beauty, Goodness, and the Disciplines. This argument will satisfy conservatives but not progressives. It assumes that because these ideals have survived the test of time, they are good and deserve to be continued, an assumption that plays well with conservatives. Progressives tend to prefer the principle that progress requires throwing off the dead hand of the past.

It is not hard to find imperfections in the Western tradition—war, social and economic inequality, racism, patriarchy, materialism, and the wanton destruction of natural environments, to name a few. Some students of the tradition would maintain that the ideals of truth, beauty, and goodness are contaminated with some of these imperfections. For instance, some contemporary intellectuals consider it more humane to seek as many interesting and productive ways to think about a thing as possible rather than seek the truth about it. In making his choice for preserving tradition in this matter, Gardner reveals a conservative leaning on the matter of the aims of education. Curriculum leaders will want to consider how this leaning suits their school community.

Gardner faces up to many serious difficulties in his attempts to define and select among disciplines, but his solutions to these difficulties are seldom completely satisfying. He doesn't define the concept of discipline except by use and by example, and this opens the doors to radically different interpretations of what is a discipline and what is the heart and soul of each discipline. Realistically, most educators will equate the school subjects with the disciplines and interpret Gardner as advocating an in-depth focus on teaching thinking skills in each subject. He acknowledges the existence of opposition to the disciplines as the basis of the curriculum, but he declines to reply to their arguments. "Some question the validity of the disciplines altogether, while others rail against the undue power of those bastions of reaction. . . . I do not agree with these critiques; yet I do not want to engage in a full-scale debate here about where the disciplines have fallen short, and where they still have value. Suffice it to say that, as an introduction to systematic thought about perennial human puzzles, virtues, and vices, I know of no reasonable alternative to the several disciplines. . . . Shorn of the disciplines, one is driven back to common sense and its inevitable undersurface, common nonsense" (p. 146).

Yes, Gardner admits, there are problems with the concept of disciplines, but we don't have any other choice. What about teaching critical thinking skills directly, as some suggest? Gardner dismisses this possibility rather lightly: "One can certainly mount specific courses in how to think, how to act, how to behave morally. Some didactic lessons are appropriate. Yet we humans are the kinds of animals who learn chiefly by observing others" (pp. 22–23). One wonders how hard Gardner looked for alternatives to the disciplines. What about the constructivist position? Constructivists maintain that individuals construct their own knowledge in a distinctive and personally meaningful form. Constructivists regard the codified disciplines as simply one authorized (and generally abridged and Bowdlerized) version of the currently dominant consensus that does not even reflect the way individual scientists, artists, or historians know their subject. Gardner does not consider this position. If, as Gardner claims, the disciplines include all forms of thought except common sense, then every curriculum qualifies as disciplinary, including the cultural literacy curriculum Gardner deplores.

Again, Gardner admits: "I have presented the disciplines as more consolidated and more schematic than they really are" (p. 158). Nevertheless, he insists "We must begin with a picture of each (discipline) and that is what I have sought to do in these pages . . ." He confesses: "I have been selective. . . . There are so many topics, concepts, and disciplines that one can fill a book of this length by just mentioning them all. . . . However, . . . I have elected to make tough choices. While I do not insist that my three selections are the only correct ones, I submit that they are serious contenders. And I go on to submit that any education geared toward understanding must eventually make similar difficult choices" (158). In effect, Gardner tells us that he can't give completely satisfying solutions to these difficulties but he claims that his solutions are as good as any and he challenges us to do better.

The problem with this argumentative strategy is that Gardner never tells us *why* the disciplines have a special capacity to foster deep understanding. He asserts that they do and he gives us examples, but he doesn't give us a principled account of how disciplines work their special magic. With no principles to rely on, we must fall back on our intuitive judgment. This opens the door to differences of judgment.

Personally, my judgment aligns roughly with Gardner's on the conclusion that the disciplines have a unique capacity to help us think about important matters, but many others disagree. Some see the disciplines as esoteric creations of a scholar caste that schools unwisely impose on all children out of a misguided idealistic belief that they have magic powers to educate. And they favor other ways to organize the curriculum—around occupations or careers, children's life problems, or society's problems, for instance. They would rather have children breed finches than study about Darwin, learn to play an instrument than study Mozart, and resolve playground disputes than study the Holocaust. I doubt that Gardner's arguments will convince them.

Challenges to the Argument from Culture Purporting to Show That These Ideals Are Relevant to All Cultures.   I feel certain that cultural relativists, including most advocates of cultural diversity, will challenge Gardner's claim that the categories of truth, beauty, and goodness are relevant to any culture and do not impose a Western value system. Cultural universalists, on the other hand, will object to Gardner's willingness to let all cultures interpret truth, beauty, and goodness in their own way. Defenders of the rights of the individual and libertarians in the American political tradition will question Gardner's claim that cultures have the right and obligation to inculcate their version of what is true, good, and beautiful on their people. Gardner's proposals allow for enough multiplicity and flexibility that none of these groups will feel seriously threatened.

Challenges to the Argument from Cognitive Science for Deep Understanding.   Any fair-minded reader would concede that experts have a deeper, richer, better understanding of their specialty than novices have and concede, too, that students would be better off with the expert's understanding. What is not yet clear is how much we should be willing to sacrifice to achieve what degree of deeper understanding on the part of how many more students.

What traditional schools do is to give students some reasonable opportunity to learn a topic. Given that opportunity, some understand it deeply, some superficially, and some not at all. If we spent more time, put more effort into planning and teaching the topic, or resorted to other measures that are more costly, time-consuming, and difficult, we would expect to get deeper understanding by more students. Gardner seems at times to imply that if we used methods based on cognitive science, all students would achieve deep understanding with little or no additional time, effort, or resources. If he does imply this, he provides no evidence to support it.

Surely there's some sort of cost/benefit assessment involved in deciding between depth and breadth. Dwelling on Darwin's theory for an entire school year of 10th grade biology would probably bring all students to a fairly deep understanding of it, given good curriculum materials and a well-prepared teacher. But surely the extra value of that deeper understanding would not be great enough to offset total ignorance of the rest of biology. Nothing Gardner presents—unless we count the three extended examples—gives us a basis for deciding how deep is deep enough or when the pursuit of depth reaches a point of diminishing returns. Clearly, a list of terms with definitions is not deep understanding. Neither is a textbook page. Between the popular article for intelligent lay readers and the expert treatise, where should we draw the line? This subject of breadth versus depth seems to require a more complex analysis than Gardner gives it. We need better means to judge depth of understanding, more empirical data about the values students actually derive from varying depths of understanding, and better analytical methods for weighing our options.

Gardner does not make a compelling case that the expert's understanding is an appropriate standard for nonexperts. Experts spend a significant fraction of a lifetime mastering families of ideas and ways of thinking. It would be nice if we could find a way to convey that understanding to nonexperts in a small fraction of the time, but what reason do we have to suppose that this is possible? If it were, why do the experts waste so much time acquiring it?

The experiments that Gardner points to in support of expert understanding show that by devoting much more time and resources, students can achieve a level of understanding that is closer to the expert's. But it is not this closeness to expert understanding that makes the deeper understanding valuable for students. Rather, the deeper understanding is valuable because it brings intrinsic satisfactions, helps students solve real problems they are likely to encounter in life, or helps them learn more about the subject later. We might speak of these as the intrinsic value, use value, and learning value of understanding. What all students need, then, is a level of understanding of key concepts that has high intrinsic value, use value, and learning value. Some parts of the expert's understanding have high value for nonspecialists; others do not.

Expert understanding is not an educational value in itself. An expert biologist may spend a year or more carrying out an experiment whose intricacies only a roomful of other people in the world can fully understand. The vast expertise the biologist uses to design this experiment is critical to the advancement of biology and, thereby, to the advancement of society. But it may not be at all important educationally because it may have little intrinsic value, use value, or learning value for nonbiologists or even for biologists outside the specialty. Those parts of the disciplines that seem to have the most value for nonspecialists are the great unifying theories and their associated ways of thinking. The other details of the discipline, vital to experts, have little value to nonspecialists. Frankly, I doubt the value for nonspecialists of some of the details Gardner includes in his treatments of the theory of evolution, *The Marriage of Figaro*, and the Holocaust.

Finally, Gardner overlooks the possibility that brief exposure to a topic may have additional value beyond that of deep understanding. Students who encounter a concept in passing will at least remember some words and facts. Then they at least know that some such idea exists. They can recognize it when they hear about it again, and maybe learn more about it later. Some may become fascinated by a glimpse of a strange idea and decide to explore it on their own. A narrow curriculum that goes into depth on a few topics may never expose students to ideas that they would find fascinating and that might have learning value for them.

In short, evidence that lavishing time on a few topics would produce deeper understanding of those topics is not sufficient. We need to know how much greater benefit we get from the greater investment of time and resources. Gardner does not show that here. In the 1960s, Jerome Bruner conjectured that deep understanding of a few topics would transfer, enabling students to learn related material more quickly and easily and thus justifying the extra time. Gardner relies on a similar argument but he does not develop it and presents no evidence for it. I think we need better reasons before we put all our chips on depth.

Challenges to Arguments from Multiple Intelligences for Certain Teaching Methods. At times Gardner seems to claim that the mere fact that children differ in their profiles of ability dictates that we individualize their education. Of course this is nonsense. Just because people differ does not mean that we should adjust schools to their individual needs. Children differ in their native language, but that does not in itself mean that every school should offer instruction in every child's native language. A multilingual society might legitimately choose a single language of instruction. The fact of difference does not in itself dictate individualization. Each individual's needs must be weighed against those of others and of the society as a whole.

The most powerful argument Gardner makes for activating multiple abilities in teaching is that the new methods are more effective in helping all students achieve a deep understanding. This seems to be an instrumental argument, but it is really about ends as well as means. If we tried to verify the claim that the new methods are more effective by comparing experimentally the results of teaching with each method, we would be unable to find criteria that both parties would support. Gardner insists on assessment procedures that allow students to use the full spectrum of their abilities, while traditional tests rely mainly on linguistic and logical abilities. To get a fair comparison we would need to develop both traditional tests and alternative assessment methods and use both to compare the learning of students who used traditional methods with those who used the new methods.

Gardner does not call for such evaluations, so it seems that Gardner wants us to make a societal bet on the new methods in the absence of evidence of their superiority. Traditional methods have survived for centuries and have shown the ability to improve the test scores of many, but not all, students. In some countries, traditional methods help an even larger fraction of students to succeed. Gardner recognizes this. "Methods of instruction that have evolved over long periods of time have much to recommend them" (p. 42). Nevertheless, he goes against tradition and sides with progressives on the issue of teaching methods.

Skeptics will question claims for the superiority of the new methods. For instance, the method of a culminating performance or exhibition raises questions about how to judge the quality and adequacy of students' various performances. "A plurality of minds begets a plurality of ways to make sense of various worlds" (p. 212). Surely then, the judges of students' performances, too, will have a plurality of minds. If all observers reach their own judgment, what happens to the disciplinary standards Gardner fights so hard to uphold?

The assessment of deep understanding is costly and difficult to administer. In order to test for understanding, we would have to present students with new projects and see how well they performed—a costly, difficult, and uncontrolled process. Ensuring fairness would be much more difficult in such a system.

Challenges to Arguments Supporting the Multiple Pathways Proposal.   Gardner sketches this proposal in such broad strokes that we have little to gain from looking at his rationale more closely. Who will officially approve pathways? What process will they use? Will appeal be possible? Can advocates of a rejected pathway reapply? How long will they have to wait? Can advocates of a pathway that the official body rejects sue in the courts? How much leeway will local schools have to adapt it to their local conditions? Who will monitor local schools' implementation of a national pathway? Gardner doesn't say. He might as well have stopped with the statement that he favors a mixed system with some national role and some local role.

Assessing the Quality of Gardner's Theory

Let us assess Gardner's proposals in light of the marks of quality in curriculum theory identified earlier: validity, power, serviceability, and morality.

Validity: Meaningfulness.   Most readers will find Gardner's ideas clear and comprehensible. The large-scale organization and development of his ideas is complex at times. He is comfortable using key terms such as truth, beauty, morality, culture, and discipline loosely, defining them implicitly through examples and repeated use.

The greatest conceptual confusion is his discussion of the disciplines. Most readers will assume that he means the academic school subjects including art and music and perhaps foreign languages. I doubt that able people of good will can easily agree on what is the heart and soul of each discipline. If Gardner's vision gains widespread support, I would expect schisms to open among his supporters based on different interpretations of the core of each discipline. Some interpretations may even lead to practices that Gardner would not approve.

Gardner's treatment of this concept would be clearer and more meaningful if he had drawn on the literature about the structure of the disciplines that flourished 3 decades ago in response to Jerome Bruner's influential book, *The Process of Education* (1960). Joseph Schwab, Philip Phenix, and various other critics and advocates of the disciplines as the basis for the school curriculum dealt with this concept more rigorously and meaningfully.

Validity: Logical Consistency.   Gardner's proposals and rationales seem to be logically consistent even though he seems not to put a high priority on logical development of his ideas. He circles back to topics again and again, sometimes repeating, sometimes elaborating, sometimes striking out in new directions. He forces readers to dig for the syllogistic skeleton of his arguments, but the logic is there.

I found no outright contradictions in the major lines of argument, but he splits some fine hairs. His arguments grounded in culture, for instance, seem to dance along a very thin edge between relativism and universalism. Truth, beauty, and goodness are not really cultural universals, he claims, but he insists that all cultures should consider them. Relativists should not worry, however, because individual cultures—indeed, individual communities—are free to interpret these ideals in their own way.

What good does it do to slap a common set of labels on ideals that may look quite different in Baton Rouge than in Peoria? Unless we establish an ongoing dialogue among cultural groups about their interpretations of these ideals and provide strong motivation to reach agreement, these ideals will not serve as an adequate basis for a common curriculum.

Gardner relies heavily on examples to persuade us of the merits of his proposals. His use of examples seems to be especially effective in justifying complex proposals that require much exercise of judgment and cannot be easily expressed abstractly. "Look here," he says, in effect, "I can't give you a principle or an algorithm for finding the heart and soul of a discipline, but I can do it for you three times and you can pick up the knack from me." Not a classic syllogism, but an effective persuasive tactic in cases that require complex judgments and delicate balancing of many considerations. I find them quite persuasive and I think many educators will also. However, the examples leave the door open for widely differing interpretations.

Validity: Factual Correctness.   Gardner presents no quantitative data. He cites research findings fairly frequently, but page numbers and dates are the only numbers in the book. Otherwise, he provides a bare minimum of factual support for his key educational proposals and arguments. All he gives us are brief sketches of the broad sweep of the history of his ideals, of the disciplines, of education, and of culture.

Gardner could strengthen his case for new methods of teaching if he provided more empirical support. Gardner repeatedly makes the claim that the new methods will enable all students to achieve deep understanding, but the only evidence he presents to support this claim are the schools he profiles. He presents no evidence of their effectiveness in helping all their students to achieve deep understanding. And, even if he had, most of these schools are special enough that a prudent educator would question whether their results could be extrapolated to every American school.

To be sure, evidence on this question may not exist. Large-scale implementations and evaluations of the new methods may not yet have happened. If so, Gardner should have tempered his claims about the new methods reaching all students, referring to this as a promising possibility rather than a firm promise, and he should have called for a program of systematic study and evaluation of the new methods.

I longed for some evidence beyond the examples for Gardner's claims for individualization, too. The problem with individualization has always been implementation. Teachers struggle to keep track of a class of students pursuing individual work, let alone provide them with guidance and coaching. Schools, potential employers, universities, and parents struggle, too, to understand what students have achieved and what they need. Skeptics need evidence that individualized schools won't collapse under the weight of these problems.

Theoretical Power.   All of Gardner's arguments are plausible but none are new and few will really compel assent from skeptics. His arguments from tradition in support of truth, beauty, goodness, and the disciplines depend on accepting the assumption that tradition is good, a weak argument at best, and totally unconvincing to those who advocate social and cultural change. His case in support of deep understanding seems solid so long as one accepts "the way experts understand a topic" as the best way for the rest of us to understand it. Who would question the value of deep understanding, anyway? The issue is "At what cost?" and here Gardner gives us only the implicit argument of his examples.

Some readers will think that the deep understanding Gardner exhibits about these three topics is well worth the time and effort necessary to bring all students to this level of understanding. Even they may wonder how many topics need to be treated in such depth and whether it might not be all right to give the rest of human knowledge at least a passing glance. Gardner's case for deep understanding will strengthen the resolve of those already inclined in this direction, but they are not powerful enough to convince skeptics.

Gardner's case for the new methods of teaching derived from theories of multiple intelligences and cognitive science is potentially the most theoretically powerful part of the book. The teaching methods themselves have theoretical rationales as rigorous and powerful as anyone has ever presented for any teaching methods. But Gardner only sketches those rationales here.

Readers, especially those who are teachers, will be excited, I think, by his descriptions of the teaching methods, both in abstract terms and in the three main examples. They seem engaging and effective. They have face validity and don't seem to need further theoretical justification. On second thought, though, I can well imagine skeptics characterizing such methods as sugar coating. Purists may object to the liberties taken with disciplines when students begin role playing a scientific meeting, for example. Gardner and his disciples will ultimately have to prove to such skeptics that the new methods will remain rigorous as well as appealing in the hands of millions of teachers.

Throughout the book Gardner, like Dewey, finds himself confronting dualisms—polarized antithetical positions. Sometimes he chooses one of the alternatives. He favors depth over breadth, for instance, and individualized over uniform education, and he rejects postmodernism, at least in its "pure" form. Occasionally he embraces both sides of a dualism, as when he resolves the question of the priority of psychology and culture by insisting that what happens inside the head is as important as what happens outside.

But sometimes he escapes from a duality in a vague and allusive way. For instance, he rejects a uniform national curriculum and he also rejects its opposite, local control. He offers instead a middle path that features a small number of officially approved national options and unspecified degrees of freedom for local communities to adapt national models to local conditions. Is this an intellectual evasion, a sleight of hand that seems to resolve the tension but really doesn't? Or is it a laudable refusal to be driven into a false dualism? Either way, it is not a very satisfying resolution, and it leaves us defending a hazy intermediate position that is difficult to articulate, let alone to defend.

Serviceability.   Gardner's proposals would seem to be quite serviceable for schools managed by well-educated leaders supported by a well-educated community. Having studied disciplines in depth in college and graduate school, the adults would know the value of in-depth study of the disciplines. They would feel confident in making judgments about the core concepts in each discipline. They would trust their own judgments of the quality of students' performance on projects. They would harbor no concerns about preparing their children for jobs after high school. Progressive communities who welcome educational innovations and place a high value on academics would be prime candidates for adoption of Gardner's proposals.

These proposals would pose severe problems for school leaders who themselves lack a strong liberal arts education, and those whose communities consist primarily of persons with a high school education or less. Conservative communities that mistrust educational innovations would probably not find enough promise in Gardner's proposals to risk the experiment.

Those communities that adopt Gardner's proposals will face many difficult judgments in the implementation process. Gardner passes over a multitude of troubles, for instance, when he writes that each culture should interpret truth, beauty, and goodness in its own terms. Multicultural communities may need a great deal of time and dialog to come to agreement on these matters. I can imagine proposals to study slavery in America, the treatment of Native Americans by the people and government of the United States, or the Holocaust that could present great difficulties for local schools. The meetings of all those committees to decide which are the core concepts in each discipline to receive intensive attention could make life interesting for local curriculum leaders.

Morality.   Gardner's proposals would reaffirm truth as a primary aim of elementary and secondary education and bring beauty and goodness back into the academic curriculum. New teaching methods based on multiple intelligences should enhance equality of educational opportunity. On the other hand, Gardner's proposals might be damaging if it turns out that teaching a few topics in depth using Gardner's new methods does not help more children learn.

The most serious moral objection to Gardner's proposals would be their failure to address the most pressing social and ethical issues of our time. Children could go through 12 years of the kind of curriculum Gardner proposes and never so much as discuss contemporary issues such as poverty, violence, abortion, or gay rights.

What To Do?

Once we have identified the proposals, examined the case for them and challenges to that case, and assessed the validity, serviceability, and morality of the theory, we have gone as far as we can with analysis. No analysis is perfect or complete. It would be good to compare and discuss two or more independent analyses. Ultimately, responsible teachers and school leaders will have to decide what to do about Gardner's theory in their situation. Analyses such as this one should help them make more informed and considered decisions, but they still must weigh the pros and cons. No analysis can decide for them.

Summary and Conclusion

Today's theoretical writing about curriculum questions belongs to a tradition of serious thought about the purpose, content, and structure of education dating back to the dawn of Western civilization. These theories are a great conversation among some of the most seminal thinkers of every era. Curriculum theories show continuous historical development in response to changing social conditions and to diverse values and perspectives. Many ideas treated as common sense today originated in one or another curriculum theory hundreds of years ago, and many of today's innovative proposals have their roots in them. We can understand today's and tomorrow's ideas and practices and their implications better if we are familiar with the originals. The brief summaries given here are of course not a substitute for reading the original works, but they offer a foretaste intended to tempt you to read them, and an overview to guide your reading. The continuing vitality of this body of work is remarkable testimony to continuing faith in the effort to employ both reason and passion in dealing with curriculum problems.

The curriculum leader who quickly recognizes when a heated curriculum debate springs from conflicting ideals and not from misunderstandings can respond more helpfully. Some precautions are in order, though. It's a mistake to assume that anyone holds some ideal in exactly the way that Plato, Rousseau, or Dewey held it. Use your knowledge of the ideas in this chapter to suggest what individuals may believe, but consider this a guess and check it out. Above all, listen carefully to what people actually say and do.

Questions and Projects

1. Which curricular ideals in this chapter most reflect your own thinking about curriculum matters? Which ideals conflict most with your own thinking about curriculum matters? Which ideals did you find most surprising, insightful, or enlightening?
2. What's your profile? Consider how strongly each of the major traditional ideals reflects your values and priorities. Rate your preference for each on a scale from +5 to −5 with 0 as neutral. Compare your numbers with those of your colleagues. Discuss the ideals on which you most differ. Try to understand your colleague's reasons and empathize with their feelings.
3. Choose one traditional ideal and examine its relationships with the others. Here's one way to do this. Think of some situation (such as an historical period or an educational program or course or activity) in which the two ideals would be compatible or mutually reinforcing and another situation in which they would conflict. Think of several such situations and then identify in more general terms how the two ideals reinforce and conflict.
4. Sketch a scenario of possible developments over the next 5 to 10 years that would result in one of these traditional ideals dominating the prevailing view about curriculum matters among educators and the public. Why might it be easier to write a plausible scenario for some traditional ideals than for others?
5. Profile another curriculum ideal. One that interests you or arouses your curiosity.
6. Comment on the following opinion of the usefulness of theory in curriculum. "The reasons why any particular society follows the educational curriculum which it does follow are always exceedingly complex. Because, in being a preparation for the future, it is inevitably a communication of what is available from past experience, only secondarily a matter of theory. The theories concerning the handling of this experience never quite compass the actuality and totality of the experience itself. They are generally rationalizations, afterthoughts, however valuable or venturesome they may be under certain of their aspects" (Walter J. Ong, American scholar, 1971).

Further Study

William Schubert's *Curriculum Books: The First Eighty Years* (1980) is an essential source of references and background information on 20th-century American curriculum thought. The works of this period which seem to me to continue to be of value for the contemporary student include most of the works on curriculum of John Dewey (Richard Archambault's collection of essays on Dewey's educational thought is also extremely valuable), Boyd Bode's *Modern Educational Theories* (1927), all of George S. Counts' works, Foshay's *Essays on Curriculum, Selected papers* (1975), and Tyler's *Basic Principles of Curriculum and Instruction* (1949). Kilpatrick, Bobbitt, and Rugg are wonderful expressions of the spirit of their time, and fun to read as memorabilia, but their ideas are dated. Taba's *Curriculum Development, Theory and Practice* (1962) is filled with nuggets of wisdom and a sound, interesting perspective, but is largely dated and takes a lot of prospecting. Robert Ulich's *Two Thousand Years of Educational Wisdom* (1947) is a valuable collection of philosophical thought on education and most of its selections treat curriculum issues. Harold Dunkel's *Whitehead on Education* (1965) is a penetrating analysis and a wonderful example of thorough, fair analysis of theory.

The best way to sharpen your skills of analysis of curriculum theory is to read more works of theory and write your own analyses of them. This also gives you wider knowledge of curriculum ideas and deepens your understanding by showing how different thinkers have approached the same issues in different ways. Dozens of references to contemporary theorists and recently published books and articles appear in this chapter. If you are using this book in a course, ask your instructor to recommend writers whose ideas are timely and important. Among contemporary American writers in the various streams of curricular thought, I find works of theory by the following authors to be generally challenging and substantial: Michael Apple, Kieran Egan, Elliot Eisner, Wells Foshay, Henry Giroux, John Goodlad, Maxine Greene, Philip Jackson, Herbert Kleibard, Nel Noddings, Linda McNeil, Janet Miller, William Pinar, Diane Ravitch, Frances Schrag, and Ian Westbury. William Pinar's edited volume, *Contemporary Curriculum Discourses* (1999) contains a diverse selection of curriculum theorizing in the contemporary style. Joseph Schwab's ideas will be dealt with in more detail in a later chapter; otherwise they would be featured here.

Some of the best contemporary writing in English on the traditionally central curriculum issues comes from authors in Great Britain, Canada, and Australia, including G. H. Bantock, Douglas Barnes, Carl Bereiter, Basil Bernstein, William A. Reid, P. W. Musgrave, R. S. Peters, P. H. Hirst, and John Wilson.

My favorite sources for current theories are journals such as *Curriculum Inquiry, Journal of Curriculum Studies, Journal of Curriculum and Supervision, Journal of Curriculum Theorizing, Educational Theory,* Teachers College Record, and *Harvard Educational Review.*

CHAPTER FOUR

Curriculum Reform

If there is a lesson to be learned from the river of ink that was spilled in the education disputes of the twentieth century, it is that anything in education that is labeled a "movement" should be avoided like the plague.

—Diane Ravitch, *Left Back*, 2000
American historian

Questions

- Where do curriculum reform movements come from? Why do we have them?
- Why are they so much more frequent in the United States than other countries?
- Do reform movements make a lasting impact on the curriculum in schools and classrooms, or do they just pass through?
- By what social processes do reforms affect schools and classrooms?
- Why do curriculum reforms get caught up in politics? Is it good or bad for curriculum issues to become politicized?

My First Experience with Curriculum Reform

When I started student teaching in the early 1960s, the public and professionals alike seemed determined to strengthen the academic quality of high school courses. Adventurous history teachers were asking students to write their own historical narratives based on original documents so that they would learn how historians think and work. I was excited by the prospect of teaching physics to high school students in a similar spirit, having them theorize, experiment, and think like physicists. I knew then that these inquiry-oriented curriculums were new, but I didn't know then that they were part of a curriculum reform movement.

I assumed then that all high school teachers would be as excited as I was by the new curriculum materials. I didn't realize that some teachers believed that academic excellence was too narrow and elitist a goal for high school students. I never dreamed that many teachers would resist these innovations, that opponents would attack them in the press, that Congress would withdraw all funding for curriculum development, and that a completely different set of issues would be making headlines in 1970.

In short, I didn't know then about curriculum reform movements, and I didn't realize that I had entered the field of education in the middle of one. Everyone who works with a curriculum should know about curriculum reform movements. They are certainly the most dramatic phenomenon the field has to offer and they can impact curriculum on a large scale and leave lasting effects. Every curriculum professional should recognize them and know how to respond constructively. Those with big ambitious should know how to foment one.

Curriculum Reform Movements

A curriculum reform movement is a hurricane of curriculum change activity. A big one sweeps through American education every decade or so, bringing great waves of enthusiasm for a new and promising curriculum. The new curriculum looks fresh and daring, in striking contrast to the standard curriculum that has become routine and a target of criticism. The new one seems to be not merely new, but shockingly new, even strange to many. As its champions explain it, though, it makes sense. They say that certain accepted ideas and practices have become outdated. They cite research showing that conditions have changed in society so much that the familiar curriculum no longer meets our needs. They offer as an alternative a vision of a radical new curriculum based on the revolutionary ideas of a visionary reformer. Whatever its details, their story explains convincingly why the familiar curriculums have failed and why the new curriculum should succeed.

A few daring innovators rethink the curriculum in light of the new ideas. Using a grant from a major foundation or government agency, they assemble a team, develop new curriculum plans and materials, and try them in a few experimental schools. The experiments seem to be working. Early stories in the education media bring the experiments to the attention of insiders. Streams of curious educators come to visit the experimental schools. Invitations come for the innovators to speak at major conferences on education. One of the innovators writes a book that sells briskly as a textbook in courses for teachers. Soon the public hears about the innovation in the mass media. A curriculum reform movement is in full swing. If it is to become truly major, it must become a hot topic in the media, prestigious schools around the country must adopt it, and sympathetic legislators must draft bills to bring its benefits to all the nation's schools.

Curriculum reform movements such as this have a long history. The crusade for the common school in the second quarter of the 19th century was such a reform movement. The 20th century opened with the progressive education movement already in progress. The many curriculum reforms related to progressive education mentioned in Chapter 3 continued into the 1940s with life adjustment education. The New Curriculum Movement brought the new math and modern science to American schools in the 1950s. The Compensatory Education Movement, also called Education of the Disadvantaged, rose to prominence in the early 1960s, focusing on early education for disadvantaged children. The 1970s brought Career Education.

In the subsequent decades, the federal government took a smaller part in fostering curriculum reform. Conservative political leaders, calling for smaller government, reduced the federal budget for education and transferred funds once used to support national reforms from the federal government to states. The reforms of the last two decades of the 20th century were therefore less intense than earlier ones. They were the work of national coalitions and state and local agencies, funded by foundations, and aided only indirectly by modest support from federal agencies.

The public rhetoric about curriculum in the 1980s was dominated by calls from conservatives for a return to the basics and to traditional academic programs. Two issues dominated public discussion of education during the 1990s—bipartisan demands for higher achievement for all students and a struggle between advocates of a voucher or choice system and defenders of public schools—and both continue. The federal Department of Education and other federal agencies have supported the movement to establish national curriculum standards and a national examination. Several states and cities have implemented experimental voucher and choice programs.

No curriculum reform achieved the status of a major movement during the last two decades of the 20th century. A series of reforms sought to reinvigorate the traditional academic curriculum while another series of reforms pushed in the direction of fostering social change. The most prominent of the reforms seeking to restore the academic curriculum was the core knowledge sequence based on the work of E. D. Hirsch, Jr. and described in his books *Cultural Literacy* (1987) and *The Schools We Need and Why We Don't Have Them* (1996). It aims to teach a common core of concepts, skills, and knowledge that characterize a "culturally literate" and educated individual.

Some other reforms, in contrast, focused on teaching thinking skills. The Higher Order Thinking Skills (HOTS) program, for instance, used computer activities, specially designed curriculum materials, and Socratic teaching strategies to enhance the thinking skills of Title I and learning disabled students in fourth through eighth grades. Curriculum reforms in mathematics and science focused on achieving deeper understanding of key ideas. The Connected Mathematics Project developed at Michigan State University is a mathematics curriculum for middle school students that is designed to foster deep understanding of key mathematical ideas. Students define and solve authentic mathematical problems themselves in mathematical investigations they do with the guidance of the teacher.

At the turn of the 21st century the major reforms focus on transforming the entire school, reforming the curriculum along with teaching, school organization, physical plant, and all. The Education Commission of the States lists on its website 26 entire-school reform models and18 skill- and content-based reform models (see Figs. 4.1 and 4.2).

One milestone of success for a curriculum reform movement is securing passage of federal legislation funding it. To get legislation passed requires a sense of national urgency and widespread bipartisan support that are difficult to achieve. Figure 4.3 lists major actions of the federal government supporting curriculum reform since 1950.

Achieving major legislative success is easier in a national crisis. The New Curriculum reforms got the government's attention when the Soviets launched the first Earth-orbiting artificial satellite in 1957, spreading panic in a nation locked in a cold war. By the mid-1960s the successes of the American space program, especially the achievement of sending the first man to the moon had eased this concern, but a new concern erupted. Civil Rights demonstrations convulsed the South and race riots devastated the inner cities of the North, precipitating what journalist Charles Silberman called in his influential book on the movement *Crisis in the Classroom* (1971). The resulting movement for Education of the Disadvantaged culminated in the Elementary and Secondary Education Act of 1965 that funded new curriculums such as Head Start and the television program Sesame Street.

Not all reform movements succeed in galvanizing the nation so completely as these two did. Many other reforms that seem to have all the basic ingredients—revolutionary ideas, a bold new plan of action, eloquent and influential champions, and the passionate support of important interest groups—fail to stir public enthusiasm. Some, such as the National Writing Project, may suffer from lack of a sense of national urgency. Others such as bilingual and multicultural education meet strong, organized opposition, become controversial, and

Accelerated Schools Project
America's Choice School Design (K–12)
ATLAS Communities (preK–12)
Audrey Cohen College: Purpose Centered Education (K–12)
Coalition of Essential Schools (formerly 9–12, now K–12)
Community for Learning (K–12)
Community Learning Centers (PreK–Adult)
Co-NECT Schools (K–12)
Core Knowledge (K–8)
Different Ways of Knowing (K–7)
Direct Instruction (K–6)
Edison Project (K–12)
Expeditionary Learning Outward Bound (K–12)
Foxfire Fund (K–12)
High Schools That Work (9–12)
High/Scope Primary Grades Approach to Education (K–3)
League of Professional Schools (K–12)
Modern Red Schoolhouse (K–12)
Montessori (PreK–8)
Onward to Excellence (K–12)
Paideia (K–12)
Roots & Wings (PreK–6)
School Development Program (K–12)
Success for All (PreK–6)
Talent Development High School with Career Academies (9–12)
Urban Learning Centers (PreK–12)

FIG. 4.1. *School reform models.*
Note. From Education Commission of the States, *Catalog of School Reform Models, First Edition,* 1998.

lose momentum. Other reforms, such as service learning and computers, have achieved much success in schools with less public fanfare and with little support from legislation. Curriculum reform movements remain mysterious and unpredictable. We know much less about their natural history and their effects on schools than we know about hurricanes.

Federal Curriculum Policy

The federal government's impact on the curriculum influence system increased greatly during these national crises, but federal control remained quite subtle and indirect by comparison with the official policy-making of most other nations. The curriculum influence system remained intact, nongovernment actors retained initiative and power over their niche, and no national curriculum was established. Nevertheless, as a result of these crisis interventions, the federal government developed a repertoire of policy tools it can use to increase its influence over the curriculums of schools throughout the nation. Figure 4.4 shows some of the tools official agencies can use to influence curriculum.

Four prominent curriculum policy tools available to the federal government are law enforcement, categorical aid programs, curriculum development projects, and prestige of office.

Reading/Language Arts Models
Breakthrough to Literacy (K–2)
Carbo Reading Styles Program (K–8)
Cooperative Integrated Reading and Composition (2–8)
First Steps (K–10)
National Writing Project (K–16)
Reading Recovery (1)
Strategic Teaching and Reading Project (K–12)

Mathematics Models
Comprehensive School Mathematics Program (K–6)
Connected Mathematics Project (6–8)
Core Plus Mathematics Project/Contemporary Mathematics in Context (9–12)
Interactive Mathematics Program (9–12)
MATH *Connections* (9–12)
University of Chicago School Mathematics Project (K–12)

Science Models
Developmental Approaches in Science, Health and Technology (K–6)
Foundational Approaches in Science Teaching (Middle School)
GALAXY Classroom Science (K–5)

Other Models
Basic Skill Builders (K–6) 195
Higher Order Thinking Skills (4–8)

FIG. 4.2.   *Skill- and content-based reform models.*
Note.   From Education Commission of the States, *Catalog of School Reform Models, First Edition,* 1998.

Law enforcement is the most potent mechanism of federal influence but also the most limited one. It can be used to enforce Constitutional rights and to apply more general federal laws about public accommodations to schools. Legislation or court rulings can, for example, require public schools to provide instruction in English or forbid them from providing religious instruction. They can authorize schools to expose students to a marketplace of ideas on political issues, require them to provide minimally adequate programs for students with special needs, and forbid them to treat such social and cultural differences as age, sex, race, or handicaps in a prejudicial or stereotypical way.

Categorical aid programs provide funds for certain specified purposes. They can be used to stimulate local schools to undertake certain curriculum reforms. When strings are attached, categorical aid can be used to coerce curriculum change in other areas. Examples include: the Elementary and Secondary Education Act of 1965, which appropriated funds for creation of bilingual education programs, programs for dropouts, and early education programs for poor and minority children; the Education for All Handicapped Children Act of 1974, which offered local districts funds and technical assistance for programs to educate children with physical, mental, and emotional handicaps. Strings attached to the latter Act encouraged an individualized curriculum structure across the school program because all teachers are required to prepare a specific written individual education plan (IEP) and to review this and the student's progress with parents periodically.

1958 National Defense Education Act (NDEA)
Authorizes funds for curriculum development, teacher training, and purchase of materials and equipment to strengthen the teaching of science, mathematics, foreign languages and other academic subjects.

1965 Elementary and Secondary Education Act (ESEA)
Aid to local schools to improve the education of the educationally disadvantaged; includes Project Head Start, Sesame Street. Title I of this act is the largest program of federal aid to education in American history.

1967 Project Follow Through
Additional aid for the educationally disadvantaged.

1968 Vocational Education Act
An extension and updating of earlier statutes continuing and expanding this program.

1969 Right to Read
Emphasis on literacy for adults and children. Done largely through libraries and other public agencies than schools.

1972 Career Education
Major initiative of Sidney P. Marland, Commissioner of Education in the Nixon administration.

1975 Education for All Handicapped Children Act
Mandates mainstreaming handicapped children into the same classrooms as other children, a major change in policy for education of the handicapped.

1978 Basic Skills replace Right to Read
Focus on improved basic reading and math skills for all students

1994 Goals 2000—Educate America Act
National standards; stronger academic content

1998 Comprehensive School Reform Demonstration Program
Helps schools implement comprehensive school reforms

FIG. 4.3. *Major federal actions on curriculum reform since 1950.*

Curriculum development projects make new curricular options available to local schools. Federal support for curriculum development also stimulates the effort of educational entrepreneurs who hope for federal funds to support their innovative projects. Commercial providers of curriculum materials may be persuaded to offer innovative materials once they see that there is a market for them. The National Science Foundation (NSF) pioneered this approach to federal curriculum policy-making in 1958 when they funded the Physical Science Study Committee to produce a textbook, laboratory apparatus, and films to improve the teaching of physics in high schools. Subsequently both the NSF and the U.S. Office of Education funded other projects in nearly every school subject at both elementary and secondary levels.

Prestige of office enables federal officials to set the terms of public discussion. Presidential commissions, congressional hearings or investigations, speeches by government officials, and

---

Incremental Policy Planning

National level:
  textbook planning (by publishers, normally)
  design of tests for nationwide use
  setting of accreditation standards
  writing regulations administering federal law
  development of curriculum plans by professional organizations
  development of curriculum plans by public interest groups
  development of curriculum plans by special interest groups
State level:
  laws governing curriculum
  (course and graduation requirements, minimal standards for school
  programs, etc.)
  administrative rules and regulations governing curriculum
  textbook adoption, in some states
  standards governing teacher education
  developing statewide curriculum plans (frameworks, syllabi, and courses of
    study)

FIG. 4.4. *Actions taken to influence school curriculums nationwide.*

sponsored research, evaluation, data gathering, or surveys all can be used to call national attention to a particular curriculum issue, idea, or proposal and lend prestige to it. Any proposal discussed approvingly in the official councils of government gains currency with the public and the profession. Pronouncements of government officials can do much to frame public and professional debate and to bring ideas into or out of currency. Because much of the funding for research and development comes from federal agencies, by selecting studies to fund, federal agencies can influence educational debate in academic and professional circles. The Federally funded Coleman Report, *Equality of Educational Opportunity*, for example, posed issues that dominated discussion of education for a decade after its publication.

Why Curriculum Reform?

People turn to reform movements when they want to make big changes in the curriculum of the nation's schools quickly. That such changes are possible seems evident from the experiences of other countries. In this century the Soviet Union, Japan, Israel, China, and India have all adopted vigorous national policies to expand and improve education in the sciences, mathematics, and languages. These policies succeeded in changing schools throughout those countries, and these changes are widely supposed to have played important roles in their economic and social development. In the 1970s, England, Sweden, and several other European countries enacted comprehensive education reforms that transformed their secondary schools from differentiated systems with academic and vocational tracks to comprehensive systems such as the United States. It is the potential power of curriculum reforms to make such sudden, far-reaching changes that makes them such an attractive idea.

The promised benefits of reform are far too tempting for activists to pass up. As challenging as it must be to rally nationwide support for a major curriculum change in a time of crisis, it much is easier than to campaign for the change through official channels. Crises bring public attention to the change, create greater demand for it, and make it easier for reformers to secure funding and to form advantageous alliances and coalitions with influential groups. These advantages make it possible for reformers to invest more to develop curriculum plans and materials of the highest quality for a national market and to offer training to teachers.

The official channels of curriculum change in America pass through 50 separate states and thousands of local school systems. Each state's process for enacting statewide curriculum change is unique and complex, involving various committees of the state legislature, various officials in the governor's office and the state department of education, and a state board of education, among other possible state agencies. Local systems are even more varied, ranging from tiny ones with only one school and a principal–superintendent through big city mammoths such as New York City, Chicago, and Los Angeles. Each system has its local politics, its unique history, its pet local curriculum programs, and its officials, board members, teacher leaders, and parent activists.

Achieving nationwide curriculum change one state or one local system at a time poses an overwhelming challenge except when a crisis galvanizes national attention. Let us look in more detail at how curriculum change happens in the decentralized American system of education.

The American Curriculum Influence System

In most of the world, national ministries of education control the curriculum of the nation's schools. The U.S. federal government, by contrast, has no legal authority over the curriculum of local schools in the United States. American schools nevertheless offer a reasonably common curriculum across a diverse continent. The American system is unique. Instead of a hierarchical system of central authority, Americans have a national curriculum influence system. This is a distributed system of decision-making loosely organized into overlapping and contending networks of authority and influence that operate in a strong national context of ideas and institutions. This national curriculum influence system is the way Americans achieve an actual national curriculum without a national authority. Reforms are an integral part of this system. It seethes constantly with reform proposals in all stages of preparation, and full-blown national reform movements are its most dramatic and powerful manifestations. To understand reform, we must understand the American curriculum influence system.

Official Agencies Responsible for Curriculum

Three very different types of agencies play major roles in the American curriculum influence system: official, quasi-official, and unofficial. The official agencies that have binding legal authority over curriculum decisions include:

- Local education agencies (LEAs) (sometimes called school districts or school corporations) managed by executive officers (usually called superintendents) and their staffs (central office staff) appointed by governing boards (school boards, boards of trustees, etc.).
- State education agencies (SEAs) are administrative units of the executive branch of state government, headed by a chief state school official (often called a state

superintendent) who may be elected or appointed by the governor and staffed by a mixture of political appointees and civil servants.

- Governors offices, including the governor, lieutenant governor, department heads, and staffs.
- State legislatures, especially committees with jurisdiction over education and influential legislators who chair and staff these committees, advised by staff members whom they appoint.
- State courts.

Quasi-official agencies derive their authority from official agencies, though they are not government agencies. Examples include:

- Accrediting associations such as NCATE and WASC
- College Entrance Examination Board
- Teacher education institutions

The work of professionals who staff quasi-official agencies is done in most other countries by staff of the national ministry of education. These agencies are typically not-for-profit corporations authorized by state law or by voluntary agreement of local agencies.

Unofficial agencies control or heavily influence particular parts of the curriculum-making process. Their actions have real, substantial consequences that local agencies cannot afford to ignore. They include:

- textbook publishers,
- the education media,
- philanthropic foundations (Ford, Carnegie, Spencer, and others who give grants for education)
- special interest groups such as the Council for Basic Education, the Business Roundtable, or the AFL-CIO.
- professional associations such as the National Education Association and the National Council of Teachers of English

Each of these agencies performs curriculum work in different arenas. Official agencies make curriculum in offices, committee rooms, and legislative chambers in various capitals and in the central offices of local school systems. Quasi-official and unofficial agencies work in their own buildings with occasional visits to schools. Each agency has its own power center. Publishers have a great deal of power over textbooks, SEAs over the writing and enforcement of regulations, and so on. The decisions that each agency controls or heavily influences give it power over the curriculum of local schools.

Occasions for making decisions about curriculum matters arise in these various agencies throughout the year uncoordinated by any common events or schedule. There is no one place where a person could find a list of all the important curriculum decisions about, say, the teaching of writing, something that is quite possible in most European countries where educational agencies coordinated by a ministry of education make all these curriculum decisions.

In the American curriculum influence system, individuals from different agencies often meet informally and at various public functions such as conferences. Those in the various agencies who work with similar curriculum issues on a given level will usually be acquainted and consider one another colleagues. For instance, reading specialists associated with a national agency headquartered in Washington, D.C., will know other reading specialists who work in other agencies in the capital, and they will probably know some prominent reading experts in certain state departments as well as prominent reading researchers in universities. Such associations create informal networks associated with particular curriculum areas. These informal networks play crucial roles in incubating and coordinating innovations.

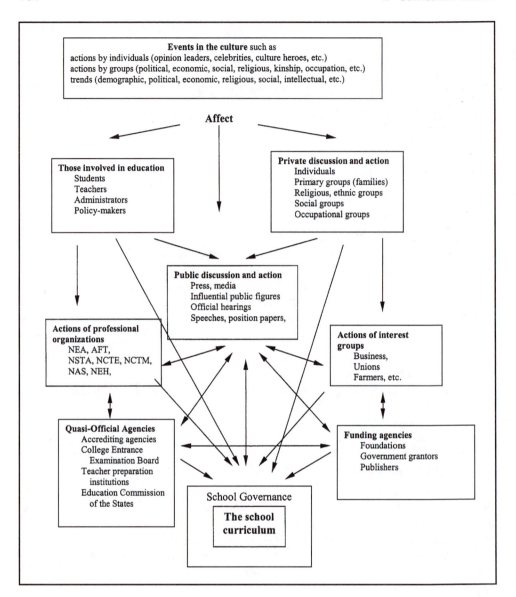

FIG. 4.5. *Major influences on curriculum policy.*

Figure 4.5 shows schematically how some of these influences affect the curriculum of local schools and classrooms. Figure 4.6 shows some of the main decisions that might be controlled at each of five levels of authority (including also school and classroom), in a hypothetical state that would not be extreme among the actual 50 states. Note the prevalence of overlapping authority.

Official Curriculum Decisions by State Governments

State governments have complete legal authority over the curriculum of public schools within their borders. States have as much authority to control education within their borders as any autonomous national government, except for a few limitations imposed by

Level	Curriculum Policy Controlled
National	national agenda for educational debate and action innovative demonstration projects monitoring quality of the nation's schools research and evaluation
State	minimum standards for high school graduation required curricular offerings mandated local minimum competency testing innovative state-sponsored programs annual statewide achievement testing selection of approved textbooks
District	selection of specific textbooks high school graduation requirements elementary school time allotments district philosophy and aims course and program approval course syllabi and curriculum guides curriculum consultants and support services minimum competencies at various grades district achievement testing in-service education of teachers
School	assignment of students, teachers to classes selection of supplementary curriculum materials elective course offerings selection of textbooks for elective courses school schedule schoolwide innovations school philosophy and aims school climate in-service education of teachers
Classroom	instructional strategies and tactics content actually covered priorities among multiple objectives testing and grading of student performance use and allocation of resources: student time, teacher time, materials classroom climate classroom activities

FIG. 4.6. *Major areas of authority for curriculum by level.*

the Constitution and the federal laws that indirectly affect education. In fact, however, few states exercise a degree of control approaching that of most other countries. States do not appoint the leaders of local school systems, educate or assign teachers, or set curriculum policy, for instance, as nearly all national ministries of education do. Instead, states delegate much of their authority to quasi-official agencies or to local school districts. The authority that remains in the capital is divided among the three branches of government and further subdivided among several executive agencies and legislative committees.

In states with more centralized traditions, curriculum specialists in the SEA will often promote curriculum innovation in schools statewide. They will launch statewide initiatives and sponsor national initiatives within the state.

In other states that hold more strictly to the tradition of local control, local districts exercise almost complete autonomy in curriculum matters except for basic regulations required for statewide coordination. State agencies in these decentralized states generally adopt a service orientation, seeing their roles as coordinating, facilitating, and assisting local districts with local initiatives. They act as conduits to transmit federal funds to local districts, but seldom intrude their own policy agenda.

SEAs are bureaucracies. A typical SEA has just under a thousand employees, though the largest employ several thousand. SEAs tripled in size between 1975 and 1990, largely due to the increased flow of federal funds for education through SEAs. Hundreds of specialists staff SEAs in many niches of expertise: finance, law, administration, certification, curriculum and instruction, buildings and grounds, and so on, serving under an appointed or elected state superintendent. Most of these specialists are busied with the meetings and paperwork required to implement state laws. Only a small fraction of SEA energy goes to development of proactive policies. SEAs do not have staff for monitoring implementation, either. Budgets for technical assistance to local schools are also limited in most states.

Education is the largest single budget item in most states, and for that reason alone is a major concern of state legislatures. Legislatures' power to control expenditures, to conduct hearings and investigations, and to authorize new programs makes them the most powerful actors on the state level when they are mobilized to legislate on education issues. Legislators listen to their constituents ("the people back home"), organized interest groups and lobbies, party leaders and members, and officials in the SEA and governor's office.

Until recently governors' main responsibilities for the public school system were to draw up the state budget and, in some states, appoint the state superintendent. In the last decade, in response to calls for reform in *A Nation at Risk*, many governors seized the initiative on a curriculum issue by proposing legislation, by executive order, or by working with the SEA and state board. Governors have been especially interested in reforms to raise standards for all students such as testing teachers, lengthening the school day, and state or national goals and standards.

State courts have tended to be overshadowed by federal courts in education issues. Curriculum issues, particularly, tend to be joined on Constitutional grounds and thus be decided in federal courts. State courts have tended to uphold most state law in curriculum matters, except when these are inconsistent with the state constitution. However, some recent exceptions are worthy of note. Beginning in the 1980s when the New Jersey state supreme court determined that the state was obligated to provide a "thorough and efficient" education to every child in the state, several state courts have mandated reform of their state's public school system.

Actions states take on curriculum matters include mandates, regulation, frameworks, curricular alignment, program support, and examinations. Mandates are orders that schools are legally bound to follow. States may regulate any of several aspects of the curriculum, including content that must be covered, course offerings, time allotments, choice of curriculum materials, entrance requirements, graduation requirements, organization or structure of the curriculum, and resource allocation among programs.

State frameworks are documents that specify the content, goals, and organization of courses or other program elements. In some states, the frameworks are only advisory to local schools while in other states they are mandatory. Some states require local districts to carry out a process of curricular alignment. Alignment involves comparing the various curriculum documents in use in the schools of a local district—goals, curriculum guides, textbooks, tests, etc.—to ensure that they are consistent. States typically require school boards to certify the alignment process.

Program support offers schools resources to be used to establish, maintain, or improve a particular type of educational program or curricular assistance such as the advice or services of experts. Local schools often need assistance with implementation of new programs, teacher in-service education, program evaluation, and with techniques demanded by new federal policies, such as the preparation of individual education plans (IEPs) for handicapped students.

Most states now have statewide minimum competency examinations. Many of the most populous and influential states have extensive statewide testing programs for all students at several points in their school careers, for all required subjects every year, and for elective subjects on a rotating basis. Examination results are front page news in many local newspapers and a major focus of discussion about education in many local communities as well as in state legislatures.

States do not require local schools to submit courses for approval and they do not police compliance with state curriculum regulations in any formal way. States do not accredit individual schools, but may require that a recognized professional accrediting association accredit public schools. Sometimes states do accredit individual programs, such as vocational education programs or early childhood programs. Guidelines for accreditation, like course syllabi, include detailed specifications of required and recommended features of the program.

Curriculum policymaking at the state level thus resembles in its basic outlines policy-making at national levels elsewhere in the world. It is carried on within a framework of official political institutions. The responsibilities of various state agencies for curriculum policymaking are established by law or tradition or both and change little from year to year. Policies adopted are put in writing in the legislation itself or in administrative rules.

State agencies are in a position to play a more active role in curriculum now than they have in recent decades. The federal role in promoting innovation has shrunk from its zenith in the 1960s. Public concern has risen and public demands for action to improve schools continue unabated. States now shoulder a greater share of funding for schools. And state officials have several decades of experience in administering the federal programs promoting curriculum change and as a result are now better able to take on the challenges themselves. It seems likely, therefore, that more states will adopt forceful, statewide policies on education in the next few years.

Official Curriculum Decisions by Local School Districts

The local school district or local education agency (LEA) is the primary agency of government for American public schools. Federal and state agencies, along with unofficial influences, converge on the LEA seeking to influence the official curriculum of the schools of the community. The highest LEA official with designated responsibility for curriculum matters is normally an assistant or associate superintendent who reports directly to the superintendent of schools. Sometimes the responsibility is lodged one level lower in a director or coordinator of curriculum. The size of the central office staff depends on the size of the district. A small district may have only a part-time teacher or two advising the other teachers. A mammoth city district such as New York, Chicago, or Los Angeles has a central office bureaucracy of more than a thousand divided among hundreds of specialties. A big city system might have specialists in elementary, middle school, and secondary; every subject taught; every category of student including gifted, handicapped, delinquent, poor, college-bound; and various special programs—funded federally, by the state or locally—operating in the district. These staff members may be called supervisors, directors, coordinators, leaders, or by other titles, and several levels of assistants and associates may be recognized.

Central office curriculum staff tends to have a broad spectrum of duties within their assigned area of responsibility. The duties of specialists in secondary English, for example, might include:

- observe and rate teachers for purposes of certification and promotion;
- offer in service education workshops for teachers;
- prepare a grant proposal seeking state or federal funding for a special project to improve the English curriculum;
- serve on committees appointed by the superintendent to investigate a possible problem with English teaching in the system;
- order books and supplies for English classes throughout the city;
- advise teacher committees doing curriculum revision and textbook selection;
- draft a policy statement on remedial reading programs in the district for consideration by superiors and the board;
- implement district plans for revising the writing curriculum;
- review test scores of students from the various high schools in the districts and confer with principals and department chairs about them; and
- carry out informal surveys and studies of conditions in English classes.

The division of responsibility between LEAs and individual schools is highly variable. Some LEAs delegate most of the authority for curriculum decisions to individual schools. Others retain central office control of curriculum matters. Adjacent districts in the same state may function in completely different ways, depending on local tradition and the views of boards and superintendents. Decentralized districts function as an oversight and coordinating agency for local schools and a buying coop for textbooks, curriculum materials, and supplies. LEAs that retain authority over curriculum matters may specify such things as (1) statements of philosophy and aims, (2) curriculum organization (entrance, promotion, and graduation criteria; school calendar, etc.), (3) courses of study, (4) curriculum materials selection, (5) special projects and programs, and (6) policies required to implement state and federal mandates. Policies in these areas nearly always require approval by the local board of education. They may also adopt systemwide examinations, textbook adoptions, and polices on grading, homework, and the like.

LEAs also take a variety of other actions that do a great deal to shape the curriculum of their schools indirectly, such as:

hiring of new teachers
assignment of teachers to schools
appointment of administrative staff of both local
    schools and the central office
pupil-teacher ratios to be maintained
construction of school facilities
in-service education of teachers
study leave, sabbatical
supervision, personnel monitoring & evaluation

When LEAs retain control of curriculum matters, the central office becomes the focus of efforts from both within and outside the community to influence the curriculum of local schools. When textbooks are selected centrally for the whole district, salespeople from textbook publishers visit the central office and make their presentations to central office staff, rather than visiting each school and speaking with the principal, department chairs, and teachers. Notices of new state policies trigger district planning, rather than being copied and forwarded to principals. Citizen complaints about the curriculum are directed to the central office rather than to individual schools, and so on.

Except in the very largest districts, face-to-face interaction is the accepted form of interaction within the LEA, between LEA and local schools officials, and among LEA and the state and federal agencies with which they interact regularly. Memos and reports are also common, of course, but tend to serve either as a formal statement of something already discussed informally or else as a stimulus for later discussion. People know one another and maintain a social relationship in addition to their formal organizational relationship. Similarly, officials in LEAs usually know their communities well and in detail. They are likely to know personally those citizens who concern themselves with school affairs. LEA officials are likely to be very familiar with such important aspects of a community as educational aspirations, expectations, and achievements of parents and students, and community traditions of support for various types and levels of education.

In recent years, LEAs find themselves increasingly stretched just to meet regulations imposed by state and federal agencies and from unofficial outside agencies such as accrediting associations, test makers, and colleges and universities. The public expects ever more sophisticated programs for dealing with special educational problems—handicapped students, poor students, students whose native language is not English, potential dropouts, potential illiterates, gifted and talented students, vocationally oriented students, and so on almost endlessly. The curriculum structures they adopt must not segregate students on racial, religious, or ethnic grounds, even unintentionally. Curriculum materials and courses of study must reflect the contributions of all such groups fairly and nonstereotypically.

Specialized programs for students who have trouble profiting from the standard school program are more costly than a single common program would be. LEAs are forced to seek additional funds to create and maintain them. Since funds are frequently available from state and local governments for these purposes, LEAs apply for grants. More and more, special projects consist of implementing generic programs some agency is subsidizing in hopes of widespread local adoption. Yet every application for funds for a special program seems to include stipulations that reduce local options. More time and energy of central office staff goes to seeking grants to support projects and to finding ways to get what they want locally while complying as much as necessary with the restrictions of the granting agency. Sometimes it seems as though it is more important for LEAs to please these outside agencies than their own clientele, but when the local community is aroused and active on an educational issue, no LEA can resist, regardless of the strength of countervailing pressures from outside.

Unofficial Curriculum Decision-Making in the American System

Much of the real action in curriculum change occurs outside the official framework of federal, state, and local policymaking. In particular, the initiative for curriculum change ordinarily originates outside the formal institutions responsible for official curriculum policy. It normally comes from advocates organized to develop, propound, and secure acceptance of the change. For officials who must represent all the citizens of their jurisdiction to act as rabid partisan advocates for a course of action opposed by some constituents exposes them to danger of political reprisal. But it is accepted that private citizens who support an idea will organize and campaign for its acceptance. Advocacy groups can maintain effort on behalf of the idea for years when it is ignored or out of favor officially, awaiting a more propitious turn of events—a Sputnik, civil unrest, or a changing of the political guard. Then they are ready with ideas and plans and reasons why their proposals are needed.

National curriculum reform movements are probably the single most important mechanism for curriculum change, and clearly the most prominent. Their ultimate origins are impossible to trace but they first surface publicly in books or articles by advocates of reform, or major news stories about them. In the case of progressive education, the series of muckraking articles by Joseph Mayer Rice, the Boston physician turned educational reformer, usually referred to by the title of one of them, "The futility of the spelling grind" (1897), brought Progressive ideas and reforms to the public eye. In the case of the post-Sputnik reforms, books such as *Educational Wastelands: The Retreat from Learning in Our Public Schools* by Arthur Bestor (1953) and *Education and Freedom* by Admiral Hyman Rickover (1959) were influential. Open education sprang upon the public scene in the form of a series of books by John Holt, Edgar Z. Friedenberg, Neil Postman, and others critical of the authoritarianism and ritualistic ineffectiveness of public school practices. The compensatory education reforms that culminated in the Elementary and Secondary Education Act of 1967 were a direct outgrowth of the civil rights struggles of the period, which dominated headlines for years and which affected schools more and sooner than any other institution of the society. In each case, the initiative for the change came from organized advocacy groups. They achieved success as reform movements when their ideas gained public acceptance and their proposals were translated into legislative programs, which received support from professional and government leaders.

In most states, a few organized groups that represent many thousands of voters vitally concerned with education have a strong influence on education legislation. These organized lobbies generally include teachers' organizations, school administrators' organizations, associations of school board members, PTA and other parent groups, good government groups, and single-issue interest groups around such issues as education of the handicapped, vocational education, or agriculture education. In most states on most issues the profession has been, until recently, united in a single lobby, which makes it the largest interest group in numbers and influence. In recent years labor–management conflicts have split teacher organizations from the other professional lobbies. Sometimes more general organizations take a special interest in an educational issue and lobby on its behalf, usually effectively. For example, during the decade before and after World War I, organized groups responded to widespread anxieties about communism, anarchism, and the perceived danger to American traditions from modern ideas and from European immigrants by lobbying for laws demanding patriotic ceremonies in schools. They also lobbied to allow Bible reading and temperance instruction and to forbid the teaching of Darwinism. In most states most of the time, though, the chief opposition to most education measures comes from taxpayer groups whose goal is to keep government expenditures as low as possible.

The Institutionalization of Reform

In recent years initiation of reform movements by unofficial partisan advocates has come to be an institutionalized feature of the American curriculum influence system. Individual advocates and organized advocacy groups have developed close personal and professional ties with the officials and agencies responsible for policy in their area of their interest. The official agency comes to regard these persons and organizations as allies in their common task of serving this particular educational need. They share information and opinions. The advocates carry out tasks indistinguishable from agency staff work—surveys, investigations of particular cases, drafting statements for inclusion in official speeches, and so on. The agency comes to depend on their services. The agency also comes to regard them as representing the interests of those they most directly serve. Thus, advocates of education for the handicapped come to represent the interests of the handicapped, and advocates of compensatory education are accepted as representing the interests of poor and minority families. In this capacity the advocates recommend people to serve on committees, react informally to early drafts of policy statements, and are generally treated as a convenient indicator of how the client group feels on any issue. Such developments have been noticed in all areas of government social service and have been aptly characterized as "the institutionalization of reform."

Thus, national curriculum reform movements are a melding of official and unofficial action, with the initiative coming primarily from unofficial sources. This melding is probably inevitable in view of the common interests of officials and advocates and the way they complement one another's strengths. The advocates have usually been around longer than the government appointees and often have considerable political clout by virtue of the numbers of votes they represent and the influential voices allied with them. They often have an inside track on foundation support for demonstration projects and may include among their number the nation's most recognized authorities on the subject. The agencies have official authority but can only exercise it with widespread political support and they cannot campaign for this support themselves. When officials and advocates hold similar views about the shortcomings of the present curriculum and the changes needed, close informal collaboration is virtually inevitable.

To be successful in drawing official agencies into a reform effort, advocacy groups must maintain a strong impression of consensus among as many interested parties as possible and the support of public opinion, as well. A savvy official being pressed to adopt a policy on, say, early education, will check around. If the official discovers that the congressman who chairs the relevant subcommittee has never heard of the policy or that the NEA and AFT are opposed to it or that organized parent groups are lukewarm to it, the official will do some more thinking and checking before acting. Organization is essential to success in efforts to influence official agencies. Coalitions must be formed and maintained if official action is to be forthcoming. Serious organized opposition or open public controversy are, in themselves, usually enough to prevent official action.

Sometimes reformers ignore the entire policy apparatus and try instead to persuade teachers, students, and parents directly through books, articles, and publicity in public and professional media. The de-schooling movement and open education followed essentially this strategy. When it succeeds, this strategy leaves the reform vulnerable to decay or reversal once it becomes old news. We do not know how many participants may continue to practice it, but new converts drop off dramatically.

Nor are full-scale reform movements the only recourse of unofficial advocacy groups. They are the heavy weapons to be called up when the time is right. Many skirmishes must first be fought with lighter weapons. Perhaps advocates can persuade a foundation to fund a study of the schools. They might fund a prominent and respected educator, such as George Conant, former president of Harvard University, or John Goodlad, Dean of the School of Education at UCLA, or a talented senior reporter such as Martin Mayer or Charles Silberman to study the schools. Advocates might form a coalition such as the Joint Council on Economic Education, which united business, labor, and professional organizations advocating the teaching of economics in the schools, or the National Task Force on Education for Economic Growth, which worked toward a consensus on ways to improve public schools to maintain the nation's economic growth. Such a coalition can keep up a constant stream of publicity, initiate curriculum development efforts, and coordinate efforts in the political arena. Perhaps demonstration projects can be mounted in a prominent school. The possibilities are limited only by the imagination of the organizers.

Quasi-Official Curriculum Regulators

Other forms of unofficial policy-making take place quietly and routinely, but not less effectively, behind the scenes. Four prominent instances include: publishers of curriculum materials; colleges and universities, through their entrance requirements, including the test makers; private, voluntary accrediting agencies; and professional organizations. These groups are at work year in and year out, usually without much publicity. Their actions influence the curriculums of nearly every school in important ways. They are normally forces for stability and for the preservation of traditional standards, but from time to time, in response to urgent, widespread dissatisfaction, they make changes—not seachanges but subtle changes of emphasis or a small addition or deletion—which then produce adjustments in schools and classrooms around the nation. Consider the following examples:

- In the late 1960s, textbook publishers, under pressure from advocacy groups, developed a voluntary industry code governing the fair and nonstereotyped depiction of females and all racial, ethnic, and religious groups in textbooks. Whatever message was subliminally conveyed by the former policy was suddenly and dramatically reversed, with who knows what effects, but undeniably reversed and throughout the land, virtually overnight.
- When colleges dropped their foreign language requirements in the 1960s, fewer high school students elected these subjects. Later, when schools faced the necessity for funding cutbacks in the 1970s, many small classes in foreign languages were dropped.
- Accrediting agencies have consistently advocated a comprehensive secondary school curriculum that includes programs and courses catering to all segments of the student population. This position doubtlessly contributed to the proliferation of elective programs and courses in high schools, which in turn shunted more and more students from the traditional academic core subjects.
- When a public demand for a return to basic skills instruction was being heard everywhere in the mid-1970s, the National Council of Teachers of Mathematics urged its members, who include most of the mathematics teachers in the country, not to relax their pursuit of problem-solving and other higher order skills in a rush to cater to the public's demands for the mathematics of checkbook-balancing and change-making.

None of these agencies is authorized to make official curriculum policy, yet each of them wields power over a vital leverage point in the curriculum determination process. So, even though these agencies have no official power over the curriculum and are not mentioned in laws or constitutions, they do exercise effective control over their own decisions, and these do influence local curriculums. They constitute a kind of quasi-official policymaking and another type of melding of unofficial and official agencies.

Reforms in the American Curriculum Influence System

In a crisis, curriculum reform movements sweep aside the ordinary procedures of state and local curriculum making. Reformers demand extraordinary actions to dispel the crisis. New actors leap onstage in new arenas. Politicians, celebrities, experts, or others who do not normally participate in curriculum decisions speak out. The mass media cover them. Highly placed government officials or even the president may call for action, request legislation,

---

National level:
   presidential commissions
   congressional study groups
   laws (National Defense Education Act, Elementary and Secondary Education
     Act, etc.)
   curriculum materials development by national projects
State level:
   governor's special commissions
   legislative study groups
   state laws
   statewide curriculum reform projects
Local level:
   special meetings of the Board of Education
   establishment of ad hoc citizen's committees

FIG. 4.7. *Crisis policy planning.*

or bring suit in court. Figure 4.7 shows the kinds of agencies and actions called into play in a crisis. Reforms take over the standard channels of curriculum work in local systems and states.

Federal Role in Curriculum Reform

Education is one of the powers the Constitution reserves to the states, so federal agencies have no legal authority over schools in the states except that Constitutional guarantees apply to the states, so that federal courts have binding authority over states and local systems in Constitutional cases. Also, Congress has powers to distribute federal funds to state and local systems with any conditions they wish to make. This power to award federal funds for targeted programs gives the federal government considerable clout in curriculum matters. And all three branches of the federal government have the power to investigate schools, hold hearings, sponsor conferences, and conduct research into them. Federal agencies active in education include:

- Department of Education, headed by the
- Secretary of Education,
- National Science Foundation, National Endowment for the Humanites, etc.

Figure 4.3 shows major actions taken by the federal government since 1950 to foster curriculum reform in the nation's schools. Since in the normal course of events, states and local governments run schools, federal actions to support curriculum reform must always be justified as responses to national emergencies. Increasingly in recent decades the quality of public education has come to be seen as important to the national welfare, and the federal government has become increasingly active in education policy. Federal activity in curriculum matters grew markedly in the period from 1958 to 1980. The budget of the U.S. Office of Education rose from $377 million in 1960 to over $8,000 million in 1981. States and local districts came to depend upon the federal government for the funds needed for new curriculum initiatives. The power of the purse and the strings attached to it gave federal agencies leverage to influence local curriculums.

Curriculum reform movements are miniature versions of the great social and political reform movements that have swept American public life from the Great Awakening in the 17th century through the pre-Civil War Abolition Movement to Women's Suffrage, Temperance, Civil Rights, and Anti-Vietnam War Movements. The public school system originated in one such movement, the 19th century Crusade for the Common School.

Strengths and Limitations of the American System

Let us briefly examine the apparent strengths and limitations of negotiated design to the extent that they can be inferred from recent history.

Strengths

First, the system deserves some compliments. The American system of curriculum determination deserves good marks for producing workable policies and for embodying American ideals of grassroots democratic government. Local schools start on time and run smoothly. When curriculum policies fail, the school still functions adequately. Credit for this achievement seems to belong to local school officials, who place the highest priority on preserving stability and avoiding disruptions. Local schools adapt external policies freely and achieve a result that, whatever its merits in other respects, fits smoothly into existing school routines.

Also, local governance of schools suits very well the American tradition of grassroots participative democracy. Interest group politics is another thoroughly American tradition, less honored but much practiced. Despite recent encroachments from state and federal agencies and unofficial influences, local school systems retain a great deal of effective control over what happens in schools and classrooms, and so we must credit these arrangements with maintaining a considerable degree of local autonomy.

We should credit the American system, too, for the remarkable extent to which the curriculum of the American public school reflects the interests of an extremely diverse population. Rural schools are not identical to urban or suburban ones. While they may not reflect rural interests perfectly, they usually do so to a greater extent than is common around the world. We find agricultural education courses and programs, Future Farmer clubs, and other curricular and extracurricular activities adapted to the local social, economic, and political situation. Similarly, we find sex education programs in schools whose communities support them, not in others. The American curriculum influence system deserves high marks for promoting diversity and choice of curriculums within the framework of a single institution.

It also deserves credit for fostering a high rate of curricular innovation. No other country in the world can boast even a fraction of the curricular experiments that have poured out of the American system with remarkable regularity for virtually this entire century. Since the 1920s, at least, the United States has been the world's foremost source of curriculum innovation. This does not mean that other countries have contributed little. Every country in Europe can boast of important curriculum innovations, but no country has produced even a small fraction of the new programs in every field, at every age, reflecting every bias and orientation that has been developed in this country almost continuously now for more than a half-century. No doubt the vigorous open competition for curricular adoptions in local school districts is responsible in part for this cornucopia.

The system does allow systemwide curriculum improvement initiatives. Figure 4.9 shows some of the factors that determine which reforms succeed in becoming policy. Clearly, success requires a convergence of factors local, state, and national, official, quasi-official, and unofficial. When these factors align behind a reform proposal, a reform movement does happen. Tremendous resources for curriculum improvement materialize and pressures for reform bear down on nearly every school.

Limitations

Some serious criticisms can be leveled at negotiated design as an approach to curriculum policy-making. Few would claim that American curriculum policies rest on fully informed consideration of their merits. The system is geared to operate politically; the substance of the matter is important mainly as a means of persuading the uncommitted. Even in the professional press, where one would normally expect to find objective, rigorous analysis, rhetoric dominates. Hessler (1977) found that articles published in educational journals on the subject of individualization of instruction were mainly persuasive appeals for this innovation. Advantages claimed for it far outnumbered mentions of possible disadvantages. Out of more than 100 articles published between 1929 and 1974, only one gave as thorough a treatment of the possible negatives as of the positives. By comparison, a sample of medical literature on heart bypass surgery was much more balanced. Virtually every medical article at least mentioned the major possible drawbacks of this operation, even when the article as a whole advocated bypass surgery.

The system rewards true believers who shape curriculum policies that embody widely held values and who then campaign to have local schools adopt them. Debate between supporters and opponents is simply irrelevant. The point is not to convince some judge, jury, or attentive audience that your policy is better than theirs, but to mobilize support for the course of action. Get enough people interested, build a credible national movement, and you win the curriculum innovation game.

The professional press in education seldom functions as a forum for discussion of the merits of potential curriculum policies. One can find thorough airings of pros and cons in research reports in obscure journals or in testimony before Congressional committees or in position papers commissioned from scholars or experts. And there is some reason to believe that this debate influences legislation, although the political clout of an interest group undoubtedly weighs more heavily with a legislature than any arguments or evidence could. Hence, the system of negotiated design earns low marks for producing informed, considered policies.

How much of the blame for the relative decline in academic achievement of American students over the past decade, as compared with students in the rest of the world, should be laid at the feet of the curriculum influence system? It is plausible to expect that the easing of standards in basic academic subjects and the proliferation of nonacademic or quasi-academic courses have had some part in creating the problem. There is not much of a local constituency for upholding high academic standards in most communities. Ambitious superintendents have not been able to make a national reputation by maintaining and upgrading a solid core of academic subjects while rejecting innovative course proposals, although this appears to be changing.

We must also weigh against the American arrangements both the necessity for the massive curriculum reform movements of the last 20 years and their failures. It is a sign of institutional pathology when a society repeatedly circumvents the institutions it has established for a given purpose and resorts to intervention by the general government. Things are out of hand when every other session of Congress is faced with a crisis in education requiring new legislation and new programs. And if these programs, created at great political and financial cost, then fail to alleviate the crises, something is dreadfully amiss. And that is exactly what has happened in the United States since 1960. It suggests that the institutions of general government are the only mechanism people believe can move American schools to respond to urgent national priorities. Whether true or not, the perception on the part of large and influential segments of the population damns the current system.

Probably the most powerful single piece of evidence that can be brought forward to support an indictment of the American system is the appalling series of defeats that have befallen every major national curriculum reform undertaken since World War II. These enormous national efforts to improve the curriculum of American schools failed to bring about substantial improvements in any aspect of the schools' performance. One of the closest students of the phenomenon wrote of "the generally melancholy picture of how little of the reform agenda of the recent past has been achieved. . . ."

> Programs were planned, curriculum was developed, teaching/learning units were packaged, teachers were trained, and the results were frustrating, uneven, unexpected, and temporary. . . Most educators realized that the amount and pace of change has fallen far short of initial expectations (Mann, 1977, p. xi).

Another writer in the same volume repeated the theme:

> An impressive number of nationally discussed and highly publicized innovations have been created to improve schools in the last half of this century. . . . Yet, despite efforts to introduce preconceived innovations into the public schools, the goal of bringing about fundamental, effective, and lasting change has not been achieved (Doyle, 1977, p. 78).

In a retrospective assessment of the impact of the federally sponsored science curriculum improvement efforts, Wayne W. Welch, an active participant in the science curriculum reforms, concluded that, on the whole, they had failed.

> What have we learned from our curricular experiences of the past 20 years? . . . The educational system is extremely stable and efforts to change it have little effect. . . . In spite of the expenditures of millions of dollars and the involvement of some of the most brilliant scientific minds, the science classroom of today is little different from one of 20 years ago . . . While there may be new books on the shelves and clever gadgets in the storage cabinets, the day-to-day operation of the class remains largely unchanged (Welch, 1979, p. 303).

Achievement test scores continued to decline over the two decades when the reforms were running at their peak. American students' tested academic achievement continued to lag behind those of students from Russia, Japan, and several European countries. Huge gaps in educational attainment remained between rich and poor children and between children of the mainstream and minority children. Most galling of all, it appeared that many schools simply never adopted the new programs, and, in those that did, many teachers continued to follow their prior practices even though nominally implementing a reform. Because of the problems encountered in implementing this federal policy, it is very hard to conclude much of anything at all about the possible success or failure of Title I projects as antipoverty strategies (McLaughlin, 1978, p. 179).

The picture with respect to the massive compensatory education reforms of the late 1960s and early 1970s is similarly bleak. In both cases, there were elements of the policy that could be shown to work when properly implemented, but the policies as a whole did not bring about substantial improvements in the nation's schools.

As for managing change well, the record of the past two decades is depressing. The prevailing pattern has been a partisan political struggle for power and influence in which the winners dismantle the programs of their predecessors and replace them with their own. Genuine achievements are thrown out along with excesses and failures and new mistakes replace the old. For example, some of the approaches to mathematics teaching developed in the post-Sputnik projects were valuable additions to the curriculum—emphasis on problem-solving, for example, and teaching about proof—while others—set theory, number bases other than 10, terminological fastidiousness—were more esoteric. Yet all were jettisoned when the "new math" fell out of favor. Math programs were developed that emphasized drill and practice on number facts, balancing checkbooks, and other everyday mathematics skills. Perversely, the ultimate beneficiaries of the millions spent on the "new math" and similar curriculum reforms may be children of other countries. Japan, the Soviet Union, China, and Israel learned from the American experience and selectively incorporated the best features of the new curriculums into their own programs.

The creators of the new curriculums are as guilty as their opponents, for they persistently ignored suggestions to incorporate more practical material into their courses and discarded previous successes in using everyday phenomena to motivate students to study basic science and math. Well-managed curriculum change would have retained the strengths of the previous program, jettisoned its weaker parts, and built the new practical math programs on that foundation. It would be difficult to make the case that curriculum change is well managed in the United States.

Conflict in this system is confined largely to a struggle for power. Each group strives to put their supporters in positions of power and influence and then use their time in office to dismantle the opposition's programs and install their own. Every curriculum reform of the past two decades has seen its period in the limelight succeeded by a period of backlash in which most of its programs are rescinded and others built on contrary assumptions put in their place. This is not constructive conflict management. Tactics of avoiding debate with the opposition work well when one party has the upper hand. And when the tables are turned the newly dominant party has no incentive for dialogue, so the original issue remains undiscussed. If it is serious, it will emerge again. Conflict avoidance works badly when conflicts are basic, enduring, and pervasive.

Summary

The American arrangements for curriculum policy formation are flexible, responsive to local concerns, and generally effective in producing workable local policies. They are free of domination by distant central authorities, yet they permit participation by official and unofficial agencies on a voluntary basis. They accommodate a wide variety of local circumstances and local customs and yet the curriculums that they produce are quite uniform nationwide, certainly enough so that high mobility seldom creates serious problems of adjustment. Wide participation tends to result in a continually shifting balance of powers among contending interest groups, thus avoiding domination by any one. Open, divisive conflict is generally avoided, in spite of serious differences in values and priorities among the population.

On the other hand, the American arrangements are of questionable effectiveness in bringing about sustained curriculum improvements on a large scale. Fads seem to come and go, but little lasting change is achieved. The baroque intricacies of the policy formation arrangements limit effective participation to those who know the ropes or who have the resources to hire those who do. Issues are seldom debated openly with a view toward finding a mutually satisfactory course of action. Rather, each side plays to its constituents and struggles for a political victory that will implement its values and priorities. Both processes and results are highly variable from state-to state and locality-to-locality. On balance, the centralized systems of other countries appear to have achieved a better record over the past quarter-century in bringing about planned permanent well-considered curriculum change. More considered policies about matters so vital as the school curriculum, better-managed curriculum changes, and more constructive resolutions of conflicts about the curriculum might give Americans better schools.

The continuing tension between two American ideologies about education that Labaree (1982) identified may explain why the American curriculum influence system takes the form that it does. One ideology "elevates liberty and promotes free markets," while the other "elevates equality and promotes participatory politics" (p. 489). Advocates of the former view want schools that prepare individual students to succeed in a competitive adult world, while advocates of the latter view want schools that enable all students to excel in their own way. The unstable compromise that Americans have negotiated between these tensions is a school system that is open to everyone but in which different students receive different curriculums.

Why the American System Works: Negotiated Design

That the American curriculum influence system can work at all seems improbable. The system is so complicated, irrational, disjointed, open, and unpredictable. Yet there is a perspective from which the American system makes sense. The argument of this section is that the entire process can be thought of as a way for the contending parties who share authority for curriculum decisions to negotiate their differences. The parties to the negotiations are the many interested individuals and agencies mentioned previously as playing official, quasi-official, or unofficial roles in the curriculum influence system. The negotiations take place in many arenas—times and places—including the meetings of various official agencies at federal, state, and local levels and the many times and places, described previously, where quasi-official and unofficial decisions are made that affect the curriculum. Each party to the negotiations may choose which decisions to try to influence. Frequent participants tend to choose certain arenas regularly, those that make decisions of most direct concern to them. The ultimate arenas are the classrooms of the nation.

The parties have their separate goals, of course, which may be generically described as follows: to control some aspect of the curriculum of local schools and classrooms throughout the country (or state or district). They succeed in this goal when their views prevail in what actually happens in classrooms. All parties share the common goal of achieving a workable curriculum. The negotiations themselves succeed when the parties agree on a policy sufficiently to provide schools and classrooms with what they need (coordination, resources, and legitimation) to sustain a curriculum. Not all of the contending parties need to cooperate actively, but their efforts to oppose the policy must not be strong enough to prevent its being carried out.

The negotiations fail when insufficient support emerges for any action. Individual schools and classrooms continue to offer their standard program without whatever support for improvements they had hoped to obtain in the negotiations (usually resources, legitimacy, and coordination). In the worst case, schools will be unable to find any curriculum that satisfies their major interest groups, even the standard one. Usually, schools faced with a negotiating stalemate will resort to some temporary expedient, such as offering options, which permit each interested party to choose what they prefer while a lasting resolution of the dispute is sought. All negotiated settlements are temporary, though, pending another round of negotiations in the same or another arena.

Figure 4.8 shows some of the major parties to curriculum negotiations, the issues with which they are usually most concerned, what they want, and what they have to offer.

Party	Controls	Needs
In classrooms:		
Teachers	Instructional planning, classroom activities, grading standards for students' work.	Time, energy, knowledge, recognition, curriculum materials, students' cooperation
Students	Cooperation, voluntary time, energy, attention	Satisfactory grades, diploma, good recommendations, preparation for success in job or further school
In schools:		
Principal	Course offerings, school schedule, teacher in-service; funds for innovation, authorization for innovations, funds for curriculum materials, access to community	Teacher compliance, funds for innovation, ideas, knowledge
In district offices:		
Superintendent	Graduation requirements, textbook selection, official curriculum guides, authority for district curriculum innovations, course offerings, overall curriculum structure	Compliance from lower levels, funds for innovation, political support, expertise
In state offices:		
Legislature	Legislative authority funds	Political support, program to sponsor, expertise
Superintendent	Rules and regulations, graduation requirements, state curriculum guides, expertise, authority of office	Compliance from lower levels, support from public
In national agencies:		
Secretary	Proposes federal budget, authority of position,	Political support, compliance from states, districts, expertise
Congress	Legislative authority, funds for innovation	Support from constituents expertise
Federal courts	Constitutionality of policies	A suit to decide compliance from executive branch

FIG. 4.8. *Some parties to curricular negotiations in various arenas: What they control and what they need.*

Level	Success Factor
National	Extensive favorable media coverage
	Complete curriculum and plan for reform available
	Convincing rationale, no strong counter-arguments
	Seriousness, urgency of the educational problem
	Seriousness, urgency of the national problem
	Support of an organized political constituency
	Support of leaders in power (President, Secretary of Education, Congressional committee chairs, etc.)
	Broad support across a wide political spectrum
	Weak, unorganized political opposition
	Broad spectrum of nation seen as benefiting
	Prestigious, able, active, organized professional leadership
	Widespread professional support
	Weak, unorganized professional opposition
State	Same factors as for nation also relevant for states
	Political and professional leadership critical
	Funding more likely to be the key issue
	Political activity more overt, standard political techniques used,
	Established interest groups
	Ability to move state department of education
	Bureaucracy critical
District	Support of superintendent, key staff
	Broad, deep support among principals, teachers
	Weak public, professional opposition
	Availability of external funding
	Urgency, importance of local problem to be solved
School	Support of principal
	Presence of able professional leadership
	Support of teaching staff involved
	Weak public, professional opposition
	Availability of external funding
	Professional status accruing to pioneers
Classroom	Understanding and support of classroom teacher
	Ability of teacher to put it into practice
	Impact on teacher time, energy, effort, rewards
	Positive student response
	Availability of curriculum plans and materials
	Consistency with preexisting routines
	Professional status accruing to pioneers

FIG. 4.9. *Factors determining which proposals become curriculum policy.*

An Example of Negotiated Design

Bidwell and Friedkin studied what happened in local school systems in Michigan when the governor demanded a 10% budget cut (Tyack, Lowe, & Hansot, 1984). When they analyzed how schools allocated staff, the investigators found that about 40% of districts had simply reassigned teachers to schools in proportion to student enrollment (an even-handed strategy). Thirty percent put proportionately more teachers in schools where students were not performing well (a compensatory strategy), and another 30% allocated teachers disproportionately to schools where students were already performing above average (a rich-get-richer strategy). Exploratory case studies of individual districts revealed why local districts responded to the same external policy event in such distinct ways. The investigators discovered that this decision followed from the distinct political cultures in the three local communities.

> The city that provided additional teachers for the neediest students had a long tradition of leaders who shared a redistributive conception of public education. The district that assigned more teachers to the high achieving schools was marked by conflict between groups in which the richest and most powerful faction won. The third case was a large suburb that lacked the "good works" ideology found in the first and the spoils system of the second (Tyack, Lowe, & Hansot, 1984, p. 224).

In this instance, the state made the decision that fell within the scope of its authority and that protected its primary interest, a 10% budget cut, while the districts made other decisions within their authority, distribution of the cuts in services among schools. No doubt each school within the three districts also adapted to the district decisions differently. The changes in educational program that eventually result from this state policy change will not have been determined by any one policy decision, but rather by an interaction of different decisions made by different agencies at different levels.

The results of negotiations may be embodied in official actions, such as laws or regulations. That they could be enacted demonstrates a sufficiency of agreement, for the time being, at least, and among the parties active in this particular round of negotiations in these particular arenas. If enough other interested groups object to the policy, other negotiations would ensue, which could overturn the policy or render it ineffective. Results of negotiations can also be embodied in the actions of quasi-official and unofficial agencies. Once again, their enactment testifies to the attainment of sufficient agreement among the parties contending in that arena, and, once again, this result can be reversed or rendered effective by later negotiations in other arenas. Generally speaking, the door is opened for unofficial policy by the deliberate insufficiency of official policy. Schools and teachers are forced to look elsewhere for the resources, legitimacy, and coordination they need. Unofficial agencies are only too happy to help in exchange for the opportunity to influence local curriculums.

Eventually, the results of negotiations must find their way to classrooms, if they are to affect the curriculum. Official actions arrive at the school and classroom door most commonly in the form of frames, as we have seen in previous chapters. Provided they stay within the frames set by higher authorities, principals and teachers are free to exercise their judgment and discretion, subject to whatever local forms of oversight may apply. Of course, a higher authority may enact mandates that leave no discretion to principals or teachers. Between levels, the main issues are securing compliance from levels below and gaining as much discretionary authority as possible from levels above.

Policy may make its way to schools and classrooms through other quasi-official and unofficial channels. For the most part these channels exist because of unmet curricular needs in school and classroom. By satisfying these, any individual or agency can attain a degree of influence over the curriculum there. Sometimes what is supplied secures the desired control directly, as when a group supplies free curriculum materials that reflect their views. Some-times, promises must be extracted from the beneficiaries, as when a foundation agrees to provide funding for an experimental curriculum only on the condition that it be evaluated using standardized achievement tests. Some common unofficial and quasi-official channels for influencing the curriculums schools and classrooms include: accreditation, testing, and conditions attached to funds or other forms of support; design or selection of plans and mater-ials; provision of human resources, especially teacher preparation, pre-service and in-service; endorsement by prestigious individuals and organizations; and publication of ed-ucational and pedagogical ideas that set the agenda and terms of discussion. The focus of official policymaking tends to be the local school district. Unofficial matters are under more or less continuous negotiation at unpredictable locations. The focus of unofficial nego-tiations tends to be the teacher/classroom and school/principal.

To achieve success in policy negotiations generally requires building a coalition, which will support the proposal at various important niches and levels. Forging a coalition that can secure favorable action on enough of these sorts of fronts to realize one's policy proposal requires great organizational skill on the part of persons in leadership positions. Such orga-nizing efforts must be sustained for years and they can be quite time-consuming. Qualified leadership, therefore, is a scarce and precious commodity in curriculum policymaking.

Schools stand the best chance of garnering resources and attention from outside agencies during times of great public concern about education, hence the predisposition toward crisis policy making. Such crises cannot be sustained for more than a few years, at most, however, and so educational reform takes place in cycles or waves, each lasting a few years and then seemingly disappearing. Reform without an injection of new outside resources requires a reallocation of resources internally. These resources are generally in high demand and are allocated in accordance with intricate face-to-face bargaining in which teachers, administrators, powerful local lay leaders, and organized groups of parents and students participate in various ways at the various levels. Although outside agencies may influence these internal negotiations indirectly, for example by establishing a climate of opinion or prevailing view through publicity or sponsorship of innovative demonstration projects, they hold a much weaker bargaining position here than in public policy arenas.

The interactions among the many actors, arenas, and decisions can become quite com-plex and produce unexpectedly powerful results. For example, a committee of teachers and parents in Detroit in the 1960s documented racial and gender bias in textbook illustra-tions and persuaded the district to threaten to boycott textbooks with biased illustrations. Other districts, emboldened by their action, soon joined in a chorus of demands for better illustrations and influenced textbook publishers to make changes that affected classrooms throughout the nation. Complex interactions can also produce surprisingly weak results. For example, for at least five decades we have seen vigorous efforts from many quarters to en-courage teachers to individualize their classroom instruction, with very little result beyond the primary grades. In spite of widespread support for the idea from teachers, public, and prestigious lay and professional leaders, it founders at several critical points. It makes more demands on teachers' time and energy. It defeats efforts at standardization of programs and outcomes. It requires more and more costly curriculum materials. And the skills teachers must acquire to make it work are more difficult to teach and are therefore not widely taught in teacher education programs.

In short, national curriculum policy for the American education system emerges from a process of negotiated design. Instead of choosing national authorities who then design the curriculum of the education system, Americans let representatives of major interest groups negotiate the design of the curriculum directly. In this way, Americans escape the threat of a curriculum czar, but they do not achieve the cherished vision of local autonomy in curriculum matters. As we have seen, the powerful interests constantly seeking to influence school curriculums do not respect local district boundaries. They resort to direct action. They turn to the organizations to which they belong, almost all of which are national in scope. A common national curriculum emerges from the struggle among these interests. Local schools, then, are subject to an impersonal, intangible, unaccountable authority. And in trying to insulate curriculum matters from partisan politics, Americans have driven those who wanted to influence their schools' curriculums to seek other avenues of influence. The results have been the emergence of the system of negotiated design, a highly political and conflicted struggle—more politics in curriculum matters rather than less.

Reforming Successfully

Standards-Based Reforms

A number of students of curriculum reform, notably Smith and O'Day (1990) and Clune (1993), have focused on policy coherence as the key to effective curriculum reform. They have outlined a strategy for school improvement that emphasizes setting national standards, coordinating action by policy makers at various levels, and setting up achievement-based accountability systems.

The key elements of policy in a standards-based alignment strategy are as follows:

- Express a unifying vision or policy goal
- Work for widespread support of the vision among the public and the profession
- Set standards consistent with this vision
- Develop guidelines for school curriculum that align it with the standards
- Identify best practices through research and use these to guide reform
- Develop a coherent strategy for instructional guidance
- Provide professional development for teachers, pre-service and in-service, consistent with the standards
- Assess achievement of standards
- Publicize assessment results by school and teacher for accountability

This standards-based alignment approach is designed to recruit the energies of all teachers, school leaders, and supporting institutions and personnel to the reform. If it is successful, nationwide reforms may finally become a reality.

While this approach to reform seems to be powerful, it also has limitations. It is a centralized approach to reform in that the directions for reform are set centrally. Forces from the center to bring educators nationwide into line with policy are strong, but means for teachers and schools to realign the central policy are absent or very weak. In fact, advocates of this policy say very little about how the central policy should be arrived at. Presumably, the process ought to allow participation from all interest groups. If so, attaining agreement on a single central curriculum policy may be difficult. Imagine some agency deciding on a national policy on the teaching of evolution, for instance, or sex education, or the contributions of different cultural groups to American society. It will not be an easy task.

Tyack and Cuban (1995) conclude from their comprehensive study of the history of school reform in 20th-century America that "reform of instruction by remote control has rarely worked well." They recommend that "reforms should be designed to be hybridized, adapted by educators" (p. 135).

Finally, national standards will undermine the tradition of local control of schools. They will leave local schools with the limited choice of how to achieve national standards. If students attending rural schools need to learn different things than students attending urban schools, then local schools will be unable to adjust. Similar problems arise if we want boys and girls to learn some different things and if we want individual students to pursue their personal talents and interests.

Porter, Archbald, and Tyree (1991) wonder if empowerment policies will replace control. They see schools as being given "a new demanding goal" to teach hard content (higher order thinking and problem solving) to all students. Control policies seek to bring this about by top down regulation. Empowerment policies seek to put more power in the hands of teachers and principals to do a better job. We need to combine them in order to get an effective system. No one knows how to do this.

Teacher Professionalism

A radically decentralized approach to curriculum reform would upgrade the professional expertise of teachers and give them a greater role in curriculum determination. Sykes (1990) argues for professionalizing teaching by collegial accountability, cooperation in curriculum, access to information, and latitude in defining work conditions. Sykes argues that doing this and then reducing outside mandates will enable teachers to restructure schools. He maintains that professional responsibility will be ultimately more successful than bureaucratic accountability (p. 84). Give teachers time to plan and opportunities for professional growth within schools. Give them power to coordinate curriculum with other teachers, and access to external sources of knowledge. Create informal leadership opportunities for teachers in connection with school and classroom improvement. Then teachers will restructure schools and reform curriculum in a lasting, substantial way.

While teacher professionalism may be an essential part of a successful curriculum reform strategy, it is difficult to see how it could be an effective reform strategy on its own. Teachers have a great deal at stake in curriculum decisions and it would be unrealistic to expect teachers to represent fairly all the other stakeholders—students, parents, business, labor, farmers, and so on. These stakeholders would not willingly cede their power in curriculum matters to teachers, no matter how professional they became. If these interests are not willing to cede control of medical policy to doctors or military policy to professional soldiers, it's hard to imagine that they would be willing to cede curriculum policy to teachers.

Explicit Curriculum Policy

Curriculum policy is a simply a settled, coherent plan or course of action with respect to curriculum matters (purpose, content, and their organization). A school district's officially adopted K–6 program for teaching reading is a clear example of curriculum policy. District high school graduation requirements are a familiar example, as are state laws that require schools to teach physical education or the history of the United States, and federal guidelines that all federally funded vocational education programs must follow. These examples are all actions of official agencies of government and therefore have the force of law, but curriculum policy may also be shaped by unofficial agencies such as accrediting associations or professional organizations, and even by individual citizens and private for-profit firms, as we shall see.

Curriculum Policymaking

"Policymaking" is a generic term for actions that shape or determine policies. It includes formulation (articulation, expression, statement) of the policy as well as consideration of the appropriateness of a policy to a particular situation. It also includes making a decision to adopt, adapt, or reject this policy for this situation.

Normally, implementation of curriculum policy, i.e., putting the policy into practice in a particular situation and evaluation of policy are spoken of as separate parts of the all-inclusive policy process.

Curriculum policy-making is sometimes a separate activity in its own right. For example, a deputy superintendent for curriculum in a state may undertake a review of the state's recommended English curriculum. In the course of this review she may chair a committee appointed by the superintendent, hold hearings, produce documents, and recommend to the superintendent that actions be taken. Usually, though, curriculum policymaking is an integral part of general educational planning and governance. For example, educational reform legislation enacted by a state may address such matters as teacher salaries, teacher recruitment and promotion, and administrative structure, as well as curriculum matters. A local school board, which increases per pupil expenditures, makes it possible to offer a greater variety of elective courses in high school. Adopting a school schedule divided into more periods gives students a wider choice among electives. The decisive act in creating or terminating a special curriculum program is often a budget authorization. Curriculum policymaking is usually part and parcel of overall school governance, administration, and leadership. The activities of designated curriculum specialists are an important part of this process, but only part. Curriculum policy deals with those aspects of curriculum that are large in scale, pervasive and important in effect, and which may be influenced by actions of policymakers. These would certainly include the factors mentioned in Fig. 4.10. Normally, implementation of curriculum policy, i.e., putting the policy into practice in a particular situation, and evaluation of policy are treated as separate parts of the all-inclusive policy process.

Curriculum policymaking is usually an integral part of general educational planning and governance. For example, educational reform legislation enacted by a state may address

- **Types of educational programs to be offered**, and the relative or absolute size permitted to each ("programs" means courses of study extending over several years, such as academic, vocational, general, classical, etc.).
- **The overall curriculum design of each program**: criteria for admission, promotion, and graduation, required components, elective components, rules for maintaining balance among components, schedule, time allocations, etc.
- **The aims, contents, and essential features of the components of each program**: syllabi, courses of study; textbooks, teaching/learning materials; course examinations; topics and time allocations; objectives; required facilities, equipment, supplies.
- **Criteria and procedures for evaluating the performance of each program**: numbers of pupils scoring above or below certain levels on external comprehensive examinations; rate of admission of students to the next stage in the education system; student or parent satisfaction; judgment of experts.

FIG. 4.10. *Major curriculum policy decisions.*

such matters as teacher salaries, teacher recruitment and promotion, and administrative structure, as well as curriculum matters. A local school board, which increases per pupil expenditures, makes it possible to offer a greater variety of elective courses in high school. Adopting a school schedule divided into more periods gives students a wider choice among electives. The decisive act in creating or terminating a special curriculum program is often a budget authorization. Curriculum policymaking is usually part and parcel of overall school governance, administration, and leadership. The activities of designated curriculum specialists are an important part of this process, but only part.

The Functions of Policy in Curriculum Matters

The most basic function of policy is to coordinate the curriculums of schools and classrooms throughout some jurisdictions. This standardization facilitates transfer of students from one school or classroom to another, simplifies school management (such as entrance and graduation requirements), makes possible uniform certification requirements for teachers, and lends a degree of common meaning to the credentials students earn upon completion of each stage of schooling. Without standard curriculum categories, each local school district would have to carry out these tasks in its own way at its own expense. Standardization makes possible economies of scale. Many millions of dollars can be invested in the production of curriculum materials for a mass market, for example.

Curriculum policy also serves a cultural function as well. It offers a people the opportunity to express shared values. A decision to teach all the children of a state about the Pilgrims and Plymouth Rock says something about what the people of the state think is important to know. A decision to leave to local schools the decision whether to teach about Spanish exploration of the southwest at about the same time says something, too. That the language of instruction in all schools is to be English, regardless of the language spoken in the students' homes affirms the society's commitment to monolingualism and to the English language, a powerful statement. A decision that all children will be taught the theory and virtues of democracy and free enterprise affirms principles upon which American society is based. Affirming such values through official policy and forbidding individual schools or teachers from omitting them or undermining them makes a strong statement about the importance placed upon them by the official agencies of government, and, so long as these are representative, by the people. Thus, policy serves to symbolize and express cultural values.

Politically, policy functions as a means of achieving concerted action on a large scale in the face of divergent interests and opinions. Political scientists speak of this process as the conversion of demands and supports into decisions and actions (Easton, 1965). In times when national well-being seems threatened and people call for action from the schools, policy provides a means of converting political demands into actions that can be debated and, if supported, implemented. Such crises have arisen repeatedly in this century. Schools developed programs to Americanize immigrants in response to the perceived threat of large numbers of immigrants from southern and eastern Europe early in this century. Schools required physical education and quasi-military training for boys to increase the supply of manpower for World War I. The Great Depression, World War II, Sputnik, the civil rights crusade, and the threat of economic competition have all produced national debate about curriculum issues, proposals for action from schools, and a variety of official, quasi-official, and unofficial policies in response. Whenever the public perceives national educational needs and insists that schools help to meet them, a political mechanism will be needed to implement these demands. Policy satisfies this need.

Policy performs the important economic function of allocating scarce educational resources among competing curricular priorities in accordance with a plan. A policy requiring every student in a state to study English for 4 years of high school, social studies for 3, and mathematics and science for 2, making all other subjects electives, effectively allocates an array of educational resources among these subjects, including teacher time and qualifications, student time, and curriculum materials.

Policy is not the only way these political, economic, cultural, and technical benefits can be realized. Traditions, which are widely accepted and followed, can perform the same functions. Voluntary organizations and networks of various kinds can also achieve these results. An elective or free market system in which students and their parents choose among classes or schools solves the economic allocation problem, sidesteps the political problem by not seeking concerted action, and lets the market set whatever standards it can. Later in this chapter we will consider the strengths and limitations of policy in comparison with other ways of performing the same functions. For now, the important point is that policy earns its role in curriculum matters by performing important functions.

High Stakes Testing as a Policy Tool

Recently state and federal policy-makers have begun to implement high stakes testing as a strategy for improving schools. New York has had its Regents' Examination for years. All high school students in New York take the Regents' Examination, which tests their mastery of basic knowledge and skill. In order to receive a Regent's Diploma students must score above the established cutoff score. Students who fail to score this well may receive a diploma from their local school system, but they will not receive a Regent's diploma.

Beginning in the 1980s, California implemented statewide tests of student achievement in basic subjects, but the results of this test were used to assess schools and school districts. Students' individual scores were not used to make any decisions that affected that student. The force of the examination came from pressures the public put on local school officials when they learned of the results for their schools and districts. Several states are making moves recently to put teeth in testing by making the stakes higher for individual students. Steps have been taken to create a national school-leaving examination, though each state would have the right to use the test or not, to determine how scores on this test were used, and what the consequences for students might be.

Such high stakes examinations seem almost certain to exert a dominant force on the curriculum of local schools throughout the nation as college entrance examinations do now. The impact on the national curriculum influence system would probably be profound.

Networks and Collaboratives

Curriculum networks are geographically dispersed sets of teachers, schools, or others who communicate regularly about curriculum matters. Collaboratives are networks in which the members work together on a common project. An early example of a collaborative is the Bay Area Writing Project, which has now become part of a National Writing Project. The Bay Area Writing Project began in the late 1970s in association with the University of California at Berkeley and has earned a favorable reputation among teachers and academics alike. Teachers must undergo a two-stage nomination process in order to be invited to participate in intensive summer institutes.

Teachers spend 5 weeks in the summer in a variety of professional development activities including working on their own writing, exchanging ideas on the teaching of writing with other teachers and University experts, and learning how to mentor and advise fellow teachers. The National Writing Project emphasizes rigorous high standards for students' writing and focuses on ways teachers can help all students to attain these standards. It features collegial interactions between secondary school English teachers and university faculty who also teach writing. (Gray & Caldwell, 1980).

A number of national school reform groups have established networks and collaboratives including the Accelerated Schools Project (*http://www.acceleratedschools.net/*), the Coalition for Essential Schools (*http://www.essentialschools.org/*), and Different Ways of Knowing (*http://www.dwoknet.galef.org/*). Education Week maintains a list of organizations on the Web at *http://www.edweek.org/context/orgs/* that lists many networks and collaboratives.

Questions and Projects

1. Write about your experiences with curriculum reform. If you have none, interview a teacher, principal, or other professional educator who has and write about their experiences. Share your findings with others and look for themes and contrasts in the stories.
2. List the curriculum reform movements that you know about. Combine your list with others' on a timeline. What do you conclude about the frequency of reform movements in American education?
3. Working with the reforms on your list, rate each one's success in producing widespread, lasting reform. Try this rating scale: 0 = almost no trace of the reform left after 10 years; 1 = reform established in some schools and school systems but not a majority; and 2 = reform has become standard practice in most schools nationwide.
4. Investigate official curriculum policymaking in a state that interests you. In what areas has the state enacted statewide policies that affect local schools? (Many states regulate pupil records, high school graduation requirements, school organization, attendance, program accreditation, and personnel certification. Some also exercise more extensive central authority over such additional curriculum matters as minimum competencies, state-approved textbooks, state syllabus, frameworks, and courses of study, and statewide examinations.)
5. Historian and partisan for academic excellence Diane Ravitch (quoted in the epigraph of this chapter) condemns reform movements. She advocates that

   > Massive changes in curriculum and pedagogy should be based on solid research and careful field-testing demonstrations before they are imposed on entire school districts and states (p. 453).

   If you agree, how do you think this change could be implemented? If you disagree, how do you think massive changes should be brought about, and why do you think your approach is better than what Ravitch proposes?
6. Are the American curriculum influence system and its process of negotiated design inconsistent with national standards? Why or why not?
7. Try to imagine a way that a compulsory national school-leaving examination could be reconciled with the American curriculum influence system.
8. Put yourself in the position of a district curriculum leader in a community that has a tradition of local curriculum development. List at least half a dozen actions your district might take to preserve this tradition if national standards and a national school-leaving examination were adopted.

9. Choose an area of the curriculum that you believe needs improvement. Use the Internet and a professional library to locate organizations and individuals who advocate this or similar reforms. Given what you've learned about curriculum reform, what do you think they would need to do in order to succeed in gaining widespread acceptance for the improvement?

10. Do a case study of a promising emerging curriculum reform. Find out what actions they are taking. Compare their actions with those of curriculum reformers and official policy-makers. Which of their actions seem more likely to be effective and which less? Can you suggest more promising actions?

Further Study

Research and scholarship on curriculum reform over the past decade have painted a discouraging picture of the prospects for achieving lasting, substantial curriculum change through reform movements. Tyack and Cuban's (1995) *Tinkering Toward Utopia*, an impressive historical interpretation of the phenomenon of curriculum reform, paints a picture of failure and argues cogently that such quick fixes from the outside are unlikely ever to work. The edited volume by Fuhrman and Malen (1991) on *The Politics of Curriculum and Testing* is the best source I've found on standards-based initiatives. A number of scholars and researchers have examined the case for teacher professional development as the central approach to reform, including Elmore and Associates (1990) in *Restructuring Schools*, Goodlad in *Educational Renewal: Better Teachers, Better Schools* (1994), McLaughlin and Talbert in *Professional Communities and the Work of High School Teaching* (2001), and McLaughlin and Oberman (1996) in *Teacher Learning*. Diane Ravitch in *Left Back* (2000) offers a literate and well-documented but partisan conservative analysis of educational reform as a misguided left-wing approach to curriculum improvement.

Unfortunately, scholars and researchers seem to have been so focused on reform that they have overlooked other approaches to curriculum improvement. As a result, older works on curriculum policymaking remain the best sources for a comprehensive picture. Specifically, Kirst and Walker's (1971) review of the research literature on curriculum policy-making and William L. Boyd's (1978) update, critique, and extension remain useful sources even though they are now badly out of date. Michael Fullan (2001) offers an excellent overview of the prevailing views among scholars on strategies for innovating in schools. The best source for understanding the political dimensions of reform movements is Wirt and Kirst's (1997) *The Political Dynamics of American Education*. The subjects of reform and curriculum are distributed widely throughout this book, but it provides priceless understanding of the politics of reform and innovation.

Even though the decade of the 1990s saw no major national curriculum reform movements (unless we count the movement for national standards as a curriculum reform movement), the American system kept producing curriculum reform initiatives. A number of sources describe reform movements underway at the time of this writing. The Education Commission of the States offers a *Catalog of School Reform Models: First Edition*, prepared by the Northwest Regional Educational Laboratory (1998) on its web site at (*http://www.ecs.org/ecs/ecsweb.nsf/*). It lists 18 "Skill- and Content-Based Reform Models" in reading, mathematics, science, and other subjects. The Education Commission of the States (1997) published *A Policymakers' Guide to Education Reform* that describes some of the most prominent reforms. The U.S. Department of Education, Office of Educational

Research and Improvement published a list of *Tested ideas for teaching and learning from the regional educational laboratories* (Levinson & Stonehill, 1997). The American Federation of Teachers (1997), Wang *et al.* (1998), and Slavin and Fashola (1998) have compiled their own lists of tested educational programs. Further information can be found at the websites of the professional associations most directly concerned with curriculum or with the specific reform such as the following:

National Education Association (*http://www.nea.org/*)
American Federation of Teachers (*http://www.aft.org/*)
National Association of Secondary School Principals (*http://www.nassp.org*)
National Association of Elementary School Principals (*http://www.naesp.org/*)
Association for Supervision and Curriculum Development (*http://www.ascd.org/*)
National Council of Teachers of Mathematics (*http://www.nctm.org/*)
National Council of Teachers of English (*http://www.ncte.org/*)
National Council for the Social Studies (*http://www.ncss.org/*)
National Science Teachers Association (*http://www.nsta.org/*)
National Art Education Association (*http://www.naea-reston.org/*)

The literature on teacher networks and collaboratives is unfortunately rather thin. The best source I've found is Alan Feldman and collaborators' (2000) interesting report of experiences in working to sustain a teacher network in science. The best way I've found to learn about networks and collaboratives is to explore their Web sites. Here are a few to start your exploration:

National Writing Project (*http://www.writingproject.org/*)
Mathematics Education Collaborative (*http://www.mec-math.org/*)
Concord Consortium (use of technology in K–12 education) (*http://www.concord.org/*)
Knowledge Network at the Center for Innovative Learning Technologies, SRI (*http://kn.cilt.org/*)

The U. S. Department of Education Web site reports on Federally funded programs supporting national standards at *http://www.ed.gov/G2K/*.

CHAPTER FIVE

Curriculum Studies

The variety of intellectual pursuits available to those who wish to contribute to an understanding of . . . curricular matters . . . is truly vast in number and therefore a bit daunting, if not downright unsettling, in its multiplicity. The boundaries of the field are diffuse, so much so that one may wonder sometimes whether it has any boundaries at all. To some, that condition is troublesome; to others, it is exhilarating; to all, it can become confusing at times.

—Philip Jackson, American curriculum scholar
Handbook of Research on Curriculum, 1992

Questions

- What kinds of studies of curriculum have researchers done?
- What sorts of questions do curriculum studies address?
- How can studies help to improve curriculums?
- What qualities make curriculum studies exemplary?

Studying Curriculum Questions

People have been pondering curriculum questions, discussing them, and trying out new practices for all of recorded history, but the kind of pointed and systematic investigation that we think of today as a study dates from the last half of the 19th century. The first curriculum studies were historical and philosophical inquiries, comparative studies of education systems in different countries, and pedagogical studies, a kind of speculative exploration of curriculum and teaching innovations. Curriculum research blossomed gloriously between 1895 and the 1930s in step with the spurt of growth in public schools and with growing public determination to modernize the education system. Under the intellectual influence of psychology, then establishing itself as an academic discipline, research in education during this period took on an empirical, quantitative, and scientific cast. Decision-makers and researchers often used scientific methods to increase the efficiency of existing practices rather than to reconsider their purposes and design. The result was a narrowing of research to extremely practical questions.

The great social, political, and economic upheavals of the period—World War I, the Great Depression, the challenge to democracy of both communism and fascism, together with the increasing triviality of research led to a period of long decline for research in education from the 1930s to the 1960s. During this period educational research was dominated by a notion of scientific rigor based on behavioral psychology that deified the experiment, measurement, and statistics. This stilted methodological ideal eventually gave way to the cognitive revolution in psychology, the emergence of other social science disciplines such as anthropology with other methods such as ethnography, and to demands from education professionals and lay leaders for research more relevant to pressing problems. Educational research received an infusion of energy, excitement, and resources from the post-Sputnik educational reforms and the programs of the Great Society, such as Head Start. Presently, studies of many kinds flourish in education, but policy-makers are also demanding greater rigor and more results from research on education.

Curriculum is a profession, not a discipline, and so research is a secondary activity, as it is in other professional fields such as business, law, medicine, and social work. Professional practice is primary, and research has value when and if it helps to improve practice. Research is vitally important in curriculum, but as a means to the end of improving curriculum practice.

Scholars and researchers in the academic field of curriculum studies, more than their counterparts in most other applied fields, apply theories and methods from both the humanities and the social sciences. Historians, philosophers, and literary and social critics as well as psychologists and sociologists take an active interest in curriculum questions and study them with the methods of their disciplines. Many respected curriculum researchers do not use ideas and methods from any academic discipline. They use the same ideas that professionals and the public use in discussing curriculum, and their methods are familiar ones used by journalists, people in business, and by all of us in everyday life—methods such as careful observation, fact collecting, interviewing, problem solving, and the like. And so curriculum studies spring from three distinct traditions of inquiry: humanistic, scientific, and practical. In this chapter, we will explore these traditions.

The practitioners, scholars, and researchers (I'll use these terms interchangeably) who study curriculum focus their efforts on many different objects of inquiry, including:

- People—the students, teachers, leaders, and others involved with curriculum matters.
- Values—beliefs about what is truly important, significant, meaningful, and therefore worthy of a place in the curriculum;
- Ideas—the concepts, terms, and notions people use to think and talk about curriculum, including images, stories, and the like;
- Practices—the repeatable events and activities associated with a curriculum that go on in schools, classrooms, and wherever curriculums are enacted;
- Settings—the environments, physical and social, in which curriculums function;
- Materials—the books, devices, and other artifacts teachers and students use, and the plans that express people's intentions about the curriculum.

Curriculum researchers ask a variety of kinds of questions, including:

- Operational questions—How do we make this curriculum work as it should?
- Outcome questions—What did students learn? How did this curriculum affect those involved?
- Design questions—What are the key features of this curriculum and how are they supposed to work? How can we modify its features to make it better?
- Value questions—What is the human significance of this curriculum? Is it good? Is it just?

They study these things using many methods, including:

- Scientific methods—both *quantitative* methods such as experiments, standardized tests, surveys, formal observations, statistical analysis, and so on, and *qualitative* methods such as ethnography, interpretive observation, think-aloud studies, and content analysis.
- Humanistic methods—historical, philosophical, literary, aesthetic, or critical methods.
- Practical methods—case studies, interviews, literature reviews, focus group discussions, shadowing, and other methods in general use but not identified with any academic discipline.

Curriculum researchers report their findings to several types of audiences in several types of forums, including:

- To clients who commission a study, through internal documents and private or public meetings
- To the general public, through hearings and the media
- To the profession through conferences and publications
- To other researchers, through scholarly and scientific meetings, circulation of preprints, publication in refereed scholarly journals, scholarly books, and increasingly on the Internet. (Communication among scholars and researchers is particularly important for setting standards for good work and guarding against error, bias, and fraud).

Figure 5.1 displays some of the variety of curriculum inquiries. In this chapter we will explore this variety in more detail.

Three Curriculum Studies

Let's look briefly at three curriculum studies that illustrate some of the many ways scholars and researchers study curriculum questions. As it happens, all three examples are related to recent proposed reforms in the mathematics curriculum, but we could in principle find similar studies on any curriculum question.

A Survey of Mathematics Reforms in Schools and Classrooms

Our first example is a large-scale study of the mathematics curriculum conducted by Andrew Porter and associates (1994) in 18 schools in six states. In two states, California and Arizona, statewide reform of the state's mathematics programs had recently been launched to make them more exploratory and constructivist. Florida and South Carolina, by contrast, had statewide curriculums that focused on teaching basic math skills. Missouri and Pennsylvania were included as states with little central curriculum push in any direction. In each state, the researchers selected two districts, one large urban and one smaller suburban or rural. In large districts they selected two high schools to study, in smaller districts only one. In each district they selected schools that served high concentrations of low-achieving students from poor families.

What do curriculum researchers study?	Practices (classroom, school, policy; development, ...) Artifacts (products, materials, documents, plans, ...) Ideas (concepts, images, language, ...) People (teachers, students, ...) Settings (contexts, milieus, environments, ...) Values (beliefs, meanings, ...)
What questions do they ask about these things?	Origins: causes, determinants Purposes: reasons, beliefs, values, motives, Description: What is it? How is it made? How does it work? ... Meaning: significance, importance Outcomes: effects, consequences Interactions with context: embeddedness, dependencies
What approaches and methods do they use to address these questions?	Humanistic Scientific Professional
What humanistic methods do they use?	Close reading and explication of texts Historiography Philosophical analysis Criticism and connoisseurship Systematic application of concepts and theories
What scientific methods do they use?	Experiments Tests and measurements: standardized tests, indicators Surveys Interviews Content analysis, expert judgment Theory, modeling
What professional methods do they use?	Watching, noticing, shadowing, Asking Trying things out Empathy Record keeping, reviewing records Reflecting, discussing, reasoning

FIG. 5.1. *Overview of curriculum studies.*

The researchers collected data from classrooms in the year 1990. To describe the curriculum in the classroom, the investigators collected daily logs from teachers that detailed coverage in two math courses taught that day. The investigators also observed some classrooms and interviewed teachers, and they interviewed school, district, and state officials about the classroom curriculums in their jurisdiction.

Several national agencies urging mathematics curriculum reform had recommended that more students take algebra, geometry, and other advanced math courses. The researchers in this study found that more students had indeed enrolled in algebra and geometry in the current school year than in previous years, just as the curriculum reformers had urged. Thinking that the content of advanced math courses might have changed as more students enrolled, they studied the content of algebra and geometry courses, and found that these courses covered standard content. The researchers also looked for evidence that increased enrollment in advanced math classes might have caused teachers to "water down" the curriculum in those classes. The teacher logs and teacher questionnaires both showed "no evidence . . . that requiring more students to take more advanced mathematics . . . resulted in compromising the curricula of the courses experiencing the increased enrollments" (Porter *et al.*, 1994, p. 6).

While the mathematics curriculum reforms seemed to succeed in increasing enrollments in advanced math courses, other reform goals were not achieved in these schools. None of the advanced math courses paid significant attention to statistics, probability, or discrete mathematics, advanced topics recommended by reformers. The researchers looked to see if teachers were having students actively engage in the construction of their own knowledge, as recommended by reformers, and found very little of this. Instead, instruction looked quite traditional. They saw "a great deal of teacher lecture and student independent seatwork" (Porter *et al.*, 1994, p. 7).

Several features of this study are noteworthy. The researchers set out to document objectively the curriculum that students actually received in their classrooms. They selected schools and classrooms to study with an explicit plan so that they would be representative of others. They collected several types of data about classrooms. They used questionnaires to collect quantitative data and teacher logs and observations to collect comparable qualitative data. They used quantitative statistical analyses of the questionnaire results. They cross-checked the quantitative survey data against data from observations and interviews. They chose their procedures carefully, using rigorous methods to enhance the credibility of their conclusions.

A Comparison of Progressive and Traditional Mathematics Programs in Two Schools

Our next example is a study comparing what students learn in classrooms with traditional mathematics curriculums to what they learn in progressive classrooms. Boaler (1997) explains the reason for her investigation this way.

> Despite the strength of allegiance demonstrated by advocates of 'traditional' and 'progressive' approaches, there has been very little evidence available to inform this debate. This has led to the position we now face whereby decisions about the raising of standards are based upon memories, anecdotes and political point-scoring, rather than data, evidence or research (p. 1).

Boaler set out to get better evidence. She studied the experiences in math classes of about 300 students over 3 years as they advanced from year 9 through year 11 in two British secondary schools. Prior to year 9, the students had received similar mathematics instruction of a fairly conventional sort in lower schools serving the same neighborhoods. Those that advanced to one school in their ninth year then received a didactic, traditional mathematics program centered on textbooks, while those who advanced to the other school received an exploratory, project-based, progressive mathematics program.

Boaler observed closely the mathematics classes in both schools. At the school with the traditional mathematics program, she saw teachers standing at the chalkboard presenting standard mathematics content. Teachers asked focused, structured questions with a single right answer. They emphasized memory of mathematical rules, and moved quickly through the content. Boaler summarized the math teaching in this school as "procedural, fast-paced, and rule-bound" (p. 39).

In this school she saw that students often based their problem-solving decisions on what they thought teachers expected of them rather than on their own judgment about what the mathematics called for. In interviews with 40 students from this school she frequently heard students say that mathematics was about learning rules for solving problems. She heard many expressions of negative feelings, especially boredom, in response to the question: "Can you describe a typical maths lesson to me?" (p. 30). She reported that the students she saw there showed a marked degree of passivity and lack of involvement.

At the school with the progressive mathematics program, Boaler saw teachers and students defining projects together in response to starting questions or themes that teachers introduced. Teachers urged students to find their own methods for solving problems. Boaler highlighted the distinctive features of this mathematics program as openness (the degree of choice given to students), concern with understanding rather than coverage, and concern with the quality of students' mathematics experiences (p. 63).

Boaler observed a fairly high rate of off-task behavior by students in progressive classes such as chatting about nonmathematical topics. When she interviewed 20 students at this school, they said that mathematics was similar to art, English, or humanities. None compared it to science. About one-third of them said they loved mathematics, another third said they enjoyed some but not all math projects, and another third consistently disliked math projects. Most of those who disliked mathematics said they disliked the open approach and not knowing what to do. They wanted more guidance from their teacher.

To study what the students from the two schools learned, Boaler looked at their performance on a variety of assessment tasks including both open-ended practical problems and standardized tests. One open-ended task called for students to decide whether the proposed plans for a new house conformed to local building codes. Codes required that the volume of the roof of a house must not exceed 70% of the volume of the main body of the house and that the two planes of a roof must not meet at an angle less than 70°. Solving this problem required students to use knowledge that students in both schools had studied, including multiplication, division, area, volume, percentages, angles, and measurement. Students from the progressive mathematics program did better on this and similar open-ended problems (p. 72).

Boaler also tested students on mathematics they had learned immediately after they studied it and then again 6 months later. Average scores did not differ on the immediate posttest, but on the delayed test students in the progressive program scored higher. Boaler compared students' performance on national tests of mathematics achievement. Overall, the two groups of students received similar grades, but when she divided the questions into conceptual ones and procedural ones, she found that students from the traditional school did slightly better on the procedural questions but worse on the conceptual ones (pp. 79–81). Boaler concluded from her study that students in the progressive program had developed more mathematical understanding that they could use in unfamiliar situations.

Note that this study compared two intact school programs covering comparable content and serving similar students. The researcher documented classroom curriculum and teaching practices in detail, using qualitative observational methods. She looked at a range of outcome indicators that cover the differing learning emphases of the two programs. She used no specialized theory or technical methods. Her methods, the things she studied—"progressive" and "traditional" curriculums, topics covered, teaching methods, tests and other forms of assessment—and her interpretations and conclusions were all in common use in schools.

A Critical Analysis of Concepts Underlying the Mathematics Curriculum

Our final introductory example is a critical analysis of mathematics programs. Davis (1995) notes that in spite of a seeming consensus among constructivist reformers, there were "profound disagreements" about the notion of constructivist mathematics curriculum (p. 325). He argues that new perspectives on the nature of mathematical knowledge challenge widely held beliefs underlying the mathematics curriculum reforms. He traces the confusion among constructivist reformers to a mode of dualistic thinking. He argues that the solution to the problem is "to turn away from the defining and definitive frames that we have constructed to contain curriculum and pedagogy and . . . to formulate a curriculum no longer founded on . . . instrumentalism" (p. 326).

He approaches his discussion of these issues by outlining an intellectual position he calls "enactivism" and then using that stance to examine current constructivist notions of the nature of mathematical knowledge, the process of learning, and the role of the teacher. No summary can do full justice to the analysis, but the summary that follows will show its flavor and direction.

Davis begins with Descartes, whose "I think, therefore I am" he sees as privileging mathematical knowledge. By viewing mathematics as pure thought, Descartes sought to make it free of the uncertainties of experience and therefore, so he thought, the most certain form of knowledge. This formalist position regards mathematical knowledge as independent of human experience. In contrast, a realist conception treats mathematics as mental constructs created by actual people to cope with certain aspects of their life experience such as measurement and construction. Davis's enactivism goes a step further, maintaining that knowledge emerges from action, from the joint actions of communities of mathematicians and users of mathematics. According to enactivism, mathematical knowledge is not something "out there" to be perceived (formalist) nor something invented (realist), but a way of interacting with the world and with each other about the world and about our ideas of it.

Traditional beliefs about learning assume that the world is objective and knowable. According to both formalist and realist conceptions of learning, individuals acquire knowledge of the objective world by thought, in the one case, and by experience in the other. In enactivism, individuals collaboratively make sense of the world through thought, dialogue, and action. Learning is not acquisition but "adequate functioning in an ongoing interactive world" (p. 332). Most of our knowledge we do not even state explicitly but enact as we use it to live. Learning mathematics is a matter of participating in dialogues with others, dialogues that focus on and use mathematical ideas.

In enactivism, teaching is not ensuring that students acquire true knowledge, but rather facilitating their construction of adequate knowledge. Teachers should ask students to strive for agreement among themselves on answers, not for right answers according to the teacher or the textbook. The only authority should be the community of those who grapple with mathematical questions. Teachers need to help students to join that community and to participate in that activity. Davis maintains that a good deal of teaching consists of listening to students as they engage in mathematical discourse and then taking advantage of opportunities to advance the discourse.

Davis' study identifies a conceptual confusion that causes a practical curriculum problem. He defines the concept and traces its intellectual roots. He compares and contrasts it with other ways of thinking about the issue and invents or adapts a conceptual framework that he believes will help people deal with the issue. He defends his proposed conception in comparison to the preexisting ones and works out the implications for practice.

How Studies Help

The major issue of curriculum practice that motivates all three of these studies is: Should schools change their mathematics curriculum from traditional to constructivist? These studies do not answer this question. But the studies do help us move toward an answer. The results of these studies suggest the following tentative conclusions.

- Current efforts to encourage teachers to add new content to advanced mathematics courses and to adopt constructivist teaching methods will not by themselves be successful.
- Constructivist and traditional mathematics courses lead to about the same results on conventional tests of mathematics achievement.
- Constructivist mathematics curriculums lead to deeper understanding of mathematics and thus enable students to use their knowledge later in a wider range of new situations.
- Constructivist curriculum proposals make sense if we think of mathematics as a social process of discussing and resolving mathematical questions.

Taken at face value, these conclusions mostly favor constructivist approaches to teaching mathematics. The Porter *et al.* (1994) study raises a question about whether it will be feasible to implement a constructivist curriculum on a large scale. At any rate, the efforts were not successful in the schools they studied. But these three studies only consider some of the many questions a prudent person would ask about the issue. What happens to those students in constructivist mathematics classes who say that they don't like them and want more direction? How well do students from constructivist mathematics programs do in further study of mathematics in college? Would schools with constructivist mathematics programs produce as many prize-winning mathematicians? Presumably other studies could address these questions, but these three studies do not resolve the issue between traditional and constructivist mathematics curriculums, although they do advance our thinking and help us to make a more informed decision.

Studies can help in many ways. They help us check the validity of claims made in debates. Recall how Joseph Mayer Rice's pioneering studies of spelling in cities across the country in the 1890s weakened the case for traditional spelling drills. They influence how we think about curriculum matters. Recall how psychological investigations of learning in the early decades of the 20th century helped to undermine confidence in the faculty theory of the mind and thus questioned the curricular value of the classics. Studies can also inspire new ways of doing curriculum work—new methods, plans, materials, strategies, and the like. Recall how research on adult reading led educators to develop the "look–say method" of reading as an alternative to phonetics.

Studies guard against self-deception. Studies can help us break out of cycles of fashion in ideas and practice and move toward a more cumulative advance of knowledge. Studies help to objectify problems, to take them out of the subjective, personal domain, and to make them publicly accessible. The demand that authorities back up their claims with studies helps to maintain a free and open dialogue that guards against demagoguery.

Studies also contribute to curriculum work in less direct ways that may be even more important than their direct contributions. For one thing, they inspire the invention of new practices. In the 1920s when researchers studied reading in great detail they discovered that good readers do not focus on letters or syllables but take in whole words at a glance. Fluent reading, they concluded, is a matter of grasping the shapes of words rather than decoding the sounds of individual letters or syllables. And so they invented the Look–Say method of teaching reading. Instead of sounding out letters and syllables, the Look–Say method teaches children to recognize whole words by shape the way fluent readers do.

Studies also help to shape a "prevailing view" about curriculum questions. Recall from Chapter 2 how the classics fell from favor when research failed to confirm claims that they disciplined the mind. Today, research on intelligence is helping to change the widely accepted idea that everyone has a definite intelligence that determines how fast and how well they can learn. Researchers such as Howard Gardner (1993) and Robert Sternberg (1997) have amassed an impressive body of evidence and strong arguments to support a new view, that everyone has multiple intelligences. Now innovators are at work designing curriculums that capitalize on visual, auditory, kinesthetic, and social intelligences as well as verbal and numerical ones.

The prevailing view among the public and policy-makers on major curriculum questions is so strong and pervasive that the lone voice of a single curriculum professional or even the massed consensus of the profession can seldom influence it, but curriculum professionals' voices can be decisive locally. A senior director of curriculum in one school district once told me that his proudest accomplishment was successfully blocking a curriculum reform in his district. The newspapers were full of stories about the need for this reform. Every professional conference featured it. All up and down the state, districts adopted it. But he thought it was unwise and he argued his case so eloquently and used his influence so effectively that his district did not adopt it. When a backlash developed a few years later and the reform fell out of favor, his district avoided the pain, cost, and demoralization that many districts suffered when they rescinded the reforms.

Three Research Traditions

People do so many different kinds of studies of curriculum questions that it would take a very large book to give even a brief description of them all. One way to begin to make sense of this variety, though, is to think of curriculum studies as belonging to three broad traditions of inquiry: humanistic, scientific, and practical. This section and the one to follow introduce these traditions.

Scientific Traditions

The movement for the scientific study of education began in earnest in the late 19th century and was well launched when the National Herbart Society for the Scientific Study of Teaching (later renamed the National Society for the Study of Education, still operating) was founded in 1895. German universities were then the acknowledged leaders in studying education scientifically, and many who would later be leaders of the movement in the United States studied in Germany, including John Dewey and William James.

At that time the public as well as intellectual leaders saw science as an engine of progress. To them it seemed natural to believe that the same scientific methods that had revolutionized engineering, agriculture, manufacturing, and medicine could also bring enormous benefits to other human endeavors. And so a generation of pioneering researchers began to apply methods that they believed were scientific to every aspect of life—management of business and industrial enterprises, selection and training of military and industrial personnel, and running schools. Franklin Bobbitt and W. W. Charters led the way in scientific curriculum-making, but even John Dewey, a philosopher, saw his work in education as an application of the scientific spirit. He called the innovative school he founded the Laboratory School to indicate his intention to do scientific work. The passion to make education scientific has waxed and waned over the intervening decades, and the methods considered scientific have changed, but the scientific tradition of research is well-established in education.

In its strongest forms the scientific tradition asks researchers to interpret curriculum problems in terms of testable theoretical principles and to use rigorous study designs and objective, quantifiable indicators to test those principles. The strictest models for scientific theories are the mathematical theories of the physical sciences. Looser theories expressed in ordinary language such as Darwin's theory of evolution by natural selection are more common in the human sciences, although some psychological and educational theories are also formulated with mathematical precision. The principles most often tested in the human sciences are expressed either as a dichotomous relationship—two variables are either related or not—or as linear mathematical relationships among several statistical variables expressed in the form of graphs or regression lines showing the joint values of two or more variables.

The strongest test of a theoretical principle is a controlled experiment in which the researcher designs the study to control other factors so that the effect of the independent variables on the dependent variables can be clearly studied. For example, experimenters control for the possibility that students in one group might have greater knowledge or ability than students in another group by randomly assigning students to groups. They control for other confounding factors by using such techniques as random sampling, pretests, and delayed posttests in their research designs. Many scientific researchers advocate controlled experiments to compare alternative curriculums.

Scientific researchers try to base their answers on objective evidence rather than opinion, authority, or merely plausible argument. To say that evidence is objective means that all qualified observers agree within some tolerable margin of error. Scientific researchers seeking an objective measure of how well children can read might have them all read the same carefully selected standard passage and answer standardized multiple choice questions about it. By contrast, ratings of a teacher who listens to children read passages that interest them and rates their performance would be a more subjective indicator of reading ability. Scientific studies often include some form of quantitative measurement of learning or performance. Close and systematic observation is also common, using checklists, rating sheets, and protocols to ensure objectivity. Reports of scientific studies are traditionally technical in content and formal in style, often using statistical analyses of numerical data.

The curriculum questions that have most attracted scientific investigators are questions about learning. Psychologists, particularly, study how students learn various things in order to plan more effective curriculums to facilitate that learning. Psychologists using new psychological theories have often played prominent roles in curriculum reforms beginning with E. L. Thorndike during the progressive era and including followers of Vygotsky today. They and their disciples in education study school learning problems and develop innovative curriculums to solve them. They study ways to detect and measure the learning of complex or subtle outcomes such as appreciation, understanding, or problem solving. Curriculum evaluation studies often use scientific measures to compare learning from innovative and traditional curriculums. Social scientists usually ask more macroscopic questions such as questions about the relationship between broad features of the curriculum and characteristics of the economy, society, or culture as a whole.

The survey of schools by Porter *et al.* (1994) described in the previous section followed many scientific research traditions. These researchers made strenuous efforts to be objective. They carefully selected schools and classrooms to study, trying to pick ones that would be

- Thorndike, E. L. (1924). Mental discipline in high school studies. *Journal of Educational Psychology, 15*, 1–22, 83–98. [Renowned psychologist studied the disciplinary value of various subjects. Also a guiding light in the study of learning in various school subjects early in the 20th century together with William S. Gray (reading), William Brownell (arithmetic), and others.]
- Bobbitt, F. (1924). *How to make a curriculum.* Boston: Houghton Mifflin. (Applied the principles of time and motion study to curriculum development.)
- Learned, W. S., & Wood, B. D. (1938). *The student and his knowledge.* New York: Carnegie Foundation. (Tested 50,000 high school and college students as high school seniors, college sophomores, and college seniors in English, math, history, and science. Tests took 8–12 hours to complete. They found great variation in achievement. Twenty-eight percent of college seniors scored lower than the average sophomore and 10% lower than the average high school senior, which led them to question the effectiveness of college curriculum.)
- Skinner, B. F. (Burrhus Frederic). (1974). *About behaviorism.* New York: A. A. Knopf. (Influenced the development of programmed instruction, computer-assisted instruction, and the behavioral objectives movement in the middle decades of the 20th century.)
- Bruner, J. *The process of education.* (Bruner and his followers led the development of the post-Sputnik curriculum reforms in the 1960s. Emphasis on learning concepts to integrate knowledge of isolated facts and skills. Famous for the claim that any child can learn any subject in some intellectually defensible way.)
- Piaget, J. (1977). *The essential Piaget.* H. E. Gruber & J. J. Voneche (Eds.). New York: Basic Books. (Inspiration for early education in the 1970s. His theories that children have thought naturally developed in distinct stages inspired disciples to develop curriculum for young children based on those stages.)
- Resnick, L. (1987). *Education and learning to think.* Washington, DC: National Academy Press. (A pioneer and leader in applying cognitive psychology to curriculum development. Suggests reforming curriculum to emphasize learning to think, using what cognitive psychology teaches about how we think.)
- Bereiter, C., & Scardamalia, M. (1993). *Surpassing ourselves: An inquiry into the nature and implications of expertise.* Chicago: Open Court. (Developed the notion of knowledge-building discourse as the key to developing an expert understanding of subjects. In their studies, children function as communities of learners in much the same way that scientists and mathematicians function as communities of researchers. Pioneers in building curriculum based on the ideas of situated cognition, treating learning as socially situated.)

FIG. 5.2. *Some learning-related scientific curriculum studies.*

typical of those they wanted to learn about. They collected several types of data, including quantitative survey data, and cross-checked them against one another. These research practices all accord well with scientific research traditions. Figure 5.2 lists some other examples of scientific studies that have influenced curriculum planning.

Curriculum evaluations are often carried out according to scientific traditions. Curriculum evaluations are a natural extension of everyone's wish to know what students really learn from their work with a curriculum. Do they learn different amounts, different things, or is their knowledge qualitatively different when they study one curriculum instead of another? Beginning in the late decades of the 19th century, researchers began to look for scientifically valid evidence of the outcomes of curriculums. Joseph Mayer Rice's trips across the country in the 1890s administering a standard list of spelling words are often cited as the earliest example of standardized testing. Following the highly publicized success of the Binet–Simon intelligence test, researchers such as the great psychologist Edward L. Thorndike designed a host of standardized tests of reading, writing, arithmetic, and other academic skills and knowledge. Researchers used these to conduct evaluation studies to determine objectively what students actually learned from studying a particular curriculum.

The initial hope, of course, was that evaluations would show that one curriculum led to more and better learning than another. Early studies comparing the outcomes of innovative and traditional curriculums in the same subject did tend to favor innovative curriculums, but the differences were disappointingly small. Worse, critics could plausibly claim that the small differences were caused by the extra excitement and care that accompanies an innovation and by a bias of the measuring instruments toward the goals of the innovative curriculum (Walker & Schaffarzick, 1972).

Over the years, researchers have devised elaborate methods for evaluating the effects of educational programs in hopes of giving definitive answers, and educational evaluation has become a field of study in its own right. Although many authorities now doubt whether we should ever expect evaluations to show a clear superiority of one well-designed curriculum over another, most believe that well-designed studies can still help us tie different practices more closely to different outcomes. By documenting what was attempted, what happened, and what traces seemed to persist, and by considering carefully why these things happened and these results ensued, we can often learn lessons that will help us improve the design of curriculums. Figure 5.3 lists some curriculum evaluation studies in a scientific tradition.

Social scientists with a scientific bent look for relationships between broad, basic features of curriculums and various characteristics of the society that maintains the curriculum. (Fields normally regarded as social sciences, such as sociology and anthropology, also include researchers who do interpretive studies of human interactions such as ethnographies and participant observations that fit better under the humanistic tradition.) Figure 5.4 lists some social scientific studies of curriculum questions.

Humanistic Traditions

Philosophy, history, and criticism are the most prevalent forms of humanistic scholarship in curriculum studies. Philosophers tackle questions of meaning and significance. They explore curricular ideals, asking why we should aspire to this or that vision of the educationally desirable, asking such questions as these: What should be the aims of education? What knowledge is of most worth? Should we design the curriculum to support the present society or to improve it? Should the demands of society take precedence over the needs of individuals or vice versa? Philosophers examine critically the answers people give to such questions and the concepts and systems of thought that they use to think and talk about them.

We already met some philosophical curriculum studies in Chapter 3. The curriculum theories of Bantock, Noddings, and Gardner are philosophical inquiries that conceptualize curriculum practices and examine curricular ideals. Bantock conceives a curriculum in "movement education" and gives meaning to this concept by explaining how this curriculum would meet the needs of lower class children. Noddings studies the concept of caring and uses it to develop a plan for a curriculum to nurture caring people. Gardner studies the

- Leonard, J. P., & Alvin C. Eurich (Eds.). 1942. *An evaluation of modern education*. New York: Appleton-Century. (A review of the large-scale studies of achievement and other variables done in cities and states prior to 1942.)
- Smith, E. R., Ralph W. Tyler, and the evaluation staff. (1942). *Appraising and recording student progress*. New York: Harper and Brothers. (A pioneering evaluation of the Eight-Year Study, a field experiment involving 30 progressive schools and 30 matched traditional schools. The evaluation team looked at an extremely broad array of outcomes, including success in college.)
- Grobman, H. (1968). *Evaluation activities of curriculum projects*. Chicago: Rand McNally. (Summarizes the evaluations of the post-Sputnik curriculum projects. These evaluations were the seed out of which the present field of educational evaluation grew.)
- Wilson, J. W., Cahen, L. S., & Begle, E. G. (1968–72). *NLSMA reports* (Vols. 1–25). Stanford University: The Board of Trustees of Leland Stanford Junior University. (The National Longitudinal Study of Mathematical Abilities compared the achievement of 112,000 students in 1,500 schools in 40 states across grades 4 through 12 over a 5-year period. The researchers created a computer database of information about the textbook used, teacher and student characteristics, and many other variables and related them all to mathematics achievement as measured on profiles of achievement on various mathematical topics. Found strong correspondence between patterns of achievement and patterns of textbook coverage.)
- Welch, W. W., & Walberg, H. J. (1972). A national experiment in curriculum evaluation. *American Educational Research Journal, 9*, 373–383. (This evaluation study of Harvard Project Physics carried out between 1965–1970 is remarkable for the variety of measures developed—cognitive, affective, and behavioral—and for studying a national random sample of physics classes and collecting extensive data on teachers and classroom environments. Found that teaching HPP changed teachers' attitudes. Students found HPP less difficult, less mathematical, and less applied than other physics, but they rated it higher on satisfaction, diversity, history, philosophy, and humanitarianism.)
- National Assessment of Educational Progress. (1999). Washington, DC: U.S. Dept. of Education, Office of Educational Research and Improvement, National Center for Education Statistics. (Results of a nationwide test of school achievement given to a large sample of all students at three grade levels. Various subjects tested in year. Reports issued in various years since 1969 cover the various subjects tested. Used to compare achievement year-to-year and to compare states and regions.)
- Pellegrino, J., Chudowsky, N., & Glaser, R. (Eds.). (2000). *Knowing what students know: The science and design of educational assessment*. Washington, DC: National Research Council. (A snapshot of the state of the art of performance assessment in education. Assessment looks at how well students can do real, meaningful tasks such as write letters persuading someone to give a talk or doing an experiment to determine which paper towels are most absorbent.)

FIG. 5.3. *Some curriculum evaluation studies.*

- De Charms, R., & Moeller, G. H. (1962). Values expressed in American children's readers, 1800–1950. *Journal of Abnormal and Social Psychology, 64*(2), 136–142. (Systematically analyzed the content of children's school readers by year of publication looking for passages encouraging children to achieve and excel. Found that such passages declined over the period, suggesting a possible cause of a decline in achievement motivation among Americans.)
- Bellack, A., Kliebard, H. M., Hyman, R. T., & Smith, Jr. F. L. (1966). *The language of the classroom*. New York: Teachers College Press. (Pioneering study using systematic observation of teachers' language and actions in the classroom.)
- Doyle, W., & Carter, K. (1984). Academic tasks in classrooms. *Curriculum Inquiry, 14*(2), 129–149. (Studies of the work of teachers and students in classrooms.)
- Stevenson, H. W., & Stigler, J. W. (1992). *The learning gap: Why our schools are failing and what we can learn from Japanese and Chinese Education*. New York: Simon & Schuster. (Summarizes cross-national research comparing mathematics teaching in Asian and American classrooms.)
- Schmidt, W. H., McKnight, C., Houang, R., Wang, H.-C., Wiley, D. E., Cogan, L., & Wolfe, R. (2001). *Why schools matter: A cross-national comparison of curriculum and learning*. San Francisco, CA: Jossey-Bass. (A comprehensive report on the relationship of achievement in math and science to curriculum variations among countries in the Third International Mathematics and Science study. Shows the state of the art in cross-cultural studies of academic achievement.)

FIG. 5.4. *Some social scientific curriculum studies.*

concept of intelligence, develops the concept of multiple intelligences, and then speculates about a curriculum that would cultivate multiple intelligences.

Philosophers have written many of the classics of curriculum thought, and references to classic philosophical works appear throughout this book. Figure 5.5 describes a few more examples. The methods philosophers use, if they can be said to follow definite methods, are about careful use of language, arguments, logic, and the like. Philosophers learn their craft mainly by example and practice rather than by studying formal methods.

History, too, has a long and distinguished tradition in curriculum studies. We already met some historical curriculum studies in Chapter 2. Historians rely on documents, mainly, to substantiate narratives about curriculum matters in former times. They study historical periods such as the progressive era, momentous events such as passage of the Elementary and Secondary Education Act in 1965 or the publication of *A Nation at Risk*, reform movements such as the post-Sputnik reforms, and the lives and works of individuals influential in curriculum matters. Some historians examine curriculum ideas and practices of the past looking for relationships among them and various characteristics of the society at that time. Some historians, for instance, look at what schools in certain times and places take to be knowledge, and why people include certain kinds of knowledge in the course of study while omitting other kinds.

If philosophers are concerned with the ideal—with what might be and should be— historians are concerned with the real—with what has been, why it happened, and therefore

- Dewey, J. *My pedagogic creed* (1897), *The child and the curriculum* (1902), *Democracy and education* (1916), *Experience and education* (1938). (No treatment of the American curriculum is complete without the work of John Dewey. These volumes show the development of Dewey's philosophical ideas about curriculum questions, beginning with his idealistic creed and ending with his sober caution and dismay at the ways his ideas had been simplified and misused by progressive reformers and their critics.)
- Ennis, R. H. (1969). *Logic in teaching.* Englewood Cliffs, NJ: Prentice-Hall. (A careful, thorough analysis of critical thinking and how we might teach children to think critically.)
- Schwab, J. (1970). *The practical: A language for curriculum.* Washington, DC: National Education Association. (A challenging philosophical analysis of the shortcomings of theory in curriculum matters and of the far-reaching implications of curriculum's practical, action-oriented nature.)
- Martin, J. R. (1994). *Changing the educational landscape: Philosophy, women, and curriculum.* New York: Routledge. (Part I of this book is a series of six thoughtful philosophical essays on issues surrounding the treatment of women in curriculum. Shows how women have been excluded "both as subjects and objects of educational thought." As a result, women who do participate are subjected to male norms, such as a verbal notion of rationality and both women and men miss the opportunity to think about what might constitute a gender fair curriculum.)
- Reagan, T. G. (2000). *Non-western educational traditions: Alternative approaches to educational thought and practice* (2nd ed.). Mahwah, NJ: Lawrence Erlbaum Associates. (Summarizes several non-Western ways of thinking about education and compares and contrasts them with prominent Western traditions.)

FIG. 5.5. *Some philosophical curriculum studies.*

how it or something similar or contrasting might happen again. Philosophers can spin glorious visions of a better life achieved through a new curriculum, but are these visions really attainable? If so, what would we need to do in order to attain them? Historical studies open for us the laboratory of the past. We can find out what others tried and what happened. Cross-cultural historical studies show us what curriculums people in other cultures have tried and how their curriculum might have reflected and affected the lives they led.

Historical and cross-cultural studies can never prove a cause–effect connection between curriculum practices and societal or individual outcomes. They can give us valuable insights, nevertheless. They can show that such-and-such a curriculum is possible by showing that these people did it or are doing it. For instance, comparisons of mathematics achievement in various Asian and European countries with achievement in the United States have convinced American policy-makers that it is possible for all students to perform as well as the very best achieving American students now perform in mathematics (Stevenson & Stigler, 1992). Historical and cross-cultural studies can also show that certain events or trends are closely associated. For instance, major changes in curriculum tend to happen soon after societies undergo major social, political, and economic changes. These curriculum changes are designed to prepare students for the changes in society and also to idealize and preserve

- Elson, R. M. (1964). *Guardians of tradition, American schoolbooks of the nineteenth century*. Lincoln: University of Nebraska Press. (Close reading of an enormous number of schoolbooks leads Elson to conclude that what schools taught trailed rather than led public opinion on contested social questions.)
- Seguel, M. L. (1966). *The curriculum field: Its formative years*. New York: Teachers College Press. (A conventional history of the pioneers of the curriculum field and their work that covers the period from 1895–1937.)
- Ong, W. (1971). *Rhetoric, romance, and technology*. Ithaca, NY: Cornell University Press. (Sweeping cross-cultural historical studies of the dominant curriculum finds it supporting the dominant modes of expression. So, when oral disquisition dominated public life, rhetoric dominated schooling. When the printed word dominated, literacy became the most important skill.)
- Schubert, W. (1980). *Curriculum books: The first eighty years*. Lanham, MD: University Press of America. (A now standard work of historical scholarship that lists curriculum by decade of publication and includes an essay for each decade describing the main currents of publications during that time.)
- Kliebard, H. (1986). *The struggle for the American curriculum: 1893–1958*. Boston: Routledge and Kegan Paul. (Interprets the events of the progressive era as a struggle among many contending movements rather than a single progressive movement.)
- Popkewitz, T. S. (Ed.). (1987). *The formation of school subjects: The struggle for creating an American institution*. New York: Falmer. (Historical essays focusing on the creation of school subjects. Sees school subjects as a way of establishing "a democratic, corporate, and Protestant nation" (p. 6).)
- Kliebard, H. (1992). Constructing a history of the American Curriculum. In P. W. Jackson, (Ed.), *Handbook of research on curriculum* (pp. 157–184). New York: Macmillan. (A comprehensive review of historical curriculum studies.)

FIG. 5.6. *Examples of historical curriculum studies.*

symbolically important elements of the formerly dominant way of life. Figure 5.6 lists some historical studies of curriculum questions.

Walter Ong's book of historical essays, *Rhetoric, Romance, and Technology* (1971) consists of what the author calls "studies in the interaction of expression and culture." Ong argues that the powerful groups in any culture use the dominant medium of expression in that culture to exercise and maintain their power. Speech was the dominant medium of expression before the spread of printing. Then schools taught rhetoric (public speaking). Students learned to memorize long passages. When students recited they were taught to use the commonplaces, lists of topics conventionally agreed to be relevant and important. (Our who–what–why–when–where–how questions are a holdover of the commonplace tradition.) "Practice of one sort or another in the use of the commonplaces . . . helped form virtually all the poetry and other literature in the Western world" (p. 264). When printing became widespread it was no longer so necessary for writers to adhere to familiar literary forms. Both authors and readers could pause to reflect on a difficult passage or read it again. "An oral culture, by and large, could recall only what was held in mnemonically serviceable formulas. In formulas thought lived and moved and had its being" (p. 275). But, "when print locked information into exactly the same place upon the page in thousands of copies of the same book in type far more legible than any handwriting, knowledge came suddenly to the fingertips" (pp. 277–278).

Schooling changed under the influence of printing. Rhetoric disappeared. Memorization declined in importance. Reading and writing skills became vital to success in the new cultural milieu. Textbooks and tests replaced the oral recitation. This story about the past that Ong (1971) tells suggests that changes in the dominant medium of communication are likely to affect school curriculums profoundly. Those who listen should be led to wonder whether the rise of electronic media may in its turn affect school curriculums profoundly and to guess what new sorts of learning may soon become basic.

In recent decades scholars specializing in criticism—literary, aesthetic, and social—have also begun to study curriculum questions. Critical scholars treat curriculum practices as performances in the case of artistic criticism or as social and political actions in the case of social criticism and study them using the methods such a critic would use. This is not criticism of ideas and theories, such as the criticism of Howard Gardner's theory of multiple intelligences in Chapter 3, but criticism of practice and of the actions of teachers, students, and others involved in curriculum practice.

Elliot Eisner has been the most active and eloquent advocate for criticism as a form of qualitative inquiry. According to Eisner (1994, p. 214), criticism is "the illumination of something's qualities so that an appraisal of its value can be made." It is not necessarily a negative judgment. Rather, it is an act of disclosing important qualities. Barone (1987, p. 460) defined criticism as "a highly disciplined reflection upon and recasting of the content of the researcher's experiences into a narrative form with a potential for reeducating the perceptions of its readers."

Critics know how to look, what to look for, and how to appreciate the qualities, meaning, and significance of what they see. Critics must render what they perceive in words, pointing to particulars that are significant and using metaphor to illuminate these qualities for the reader. Finally, critics judge the value or worth of what they criticize. Scholarly criticisms based their judgments of worth on keen observation of particulars. Critics employ ideals, visions, and ideologies as lenses through which to view what they see. Critics consider the moral and ethical dimensions of what they criticize.

Criticism of education sometimes seems to be the national sport, and Americans are not alone in playing at it. In the golden age of ancient Greece, the playwright Aristophanes in his play, *The Clouds*, wrote a hilarious comic send-up of the educational practices of Socrates and the sophists. Muck-raking journalists' criticism of traditional education spurred progressive reforms. Paul Goodman's *Compulsory Miseducation* (1964) sounded the critical note that undermined a complacent postwar America's faith in its public school system.

Humanistic scholars tend to portray people making choices and taking action, sometimes exercising free will and sometimes shaped by events and fate. The methods of humanistic research often involve close, critical readings of texts. A scholarly contribution often takes the form of a new interpretation buttressed by careful, reasoned argument. Humanistic scholars expect one another to be steeped in the relevant literature and to refer to it intelligently as they consider any particular text. Good scholarly writing is sprinkled with copious citations of primary sources as well as quotations from the work of the best authorities on the subject. Humanistic scholars interpret the meaning of their sources in relation to the source's social, cultural, and historical context. Figure 5.7 lists some notable humanistic studies of curriculum questions that use methods other than historical and philosophical.

Practical Traditions

All good curriculum research has some practical significance, but humanistic and scientific researchers look at curriculum problems in a theoretical rather than a practical way. Their questions spring from theory and they look for deep, hidden relationships that those going about the everyday business of teaching and learning might not think to look for. Practical

- Goodman, P. (1964). *Compulsory miseducation.* New York: Horizon Press. (A biting critique of mid-century education by a liberally educated writer working in an essentially literary form. Influential inspiration for the open education movement of the late 1960s.)
- Jackson, P. (1968). *Life in classrooms.* NY: Holt, Rinehart, and Winston. (One of the first scholars in education to break free of the constraints of a rigid behavioral psychology and look with fresh eyes at what happens in classrooms.)
- Apple, M. (1974). *Ideology and curriculum.* London: Routledge and Kegan Paul. (A powerful indictment of the curriculum of American schools by an early, courageous pioneer of frankly partisan scholarly criticism. Uses wide-ranging political, social, and economic speculation in a form of committed scholarship that has since become one of the dominant forms of curriculum studies.)
- Lightfoot, Sara Lawrence. (1983). *The good high school: Portraits of character and culture.* New York: Basic Books. (Paints integrated portraits of several very different schools, each good in important ways, and makes the point that a good school is more than the sum of its parts.)
- Pinar, W. (1994). *Autobiography, politics, and sexuality: Essays in curriculum theory 1972–1992.* New York: P. Lang. (Essays in a literary manner by the influential leader of the reconceptualist movement in curriculum theorizing exploring pivotal, controversial topics.)
- Eisner, E. (1994). The forms and functions of educational connoisseurship and educational criticism. In *The Educational Imagination: On the Design and Evaluation of School Programs* (3rd ed., pp. 212–249). New York: Macmillan. (Describes, demonstrates, and convincingly justifies an approach to studying curriculum based on insights and methods from the arts.)
- Greene, M. (1995). *Releasing the imagination: Essays on education, the arts, and social change.* San Francisco: Jossey-Bass Publishers. (Literary, philosophical, and critical essays urging a greater role for the arts in the school curriculum as means of expressing and cultivating imagination, including the imagining of a better world.)

FIG. 5.7. *Other humanistic curriculum studies.*

researchers, by contrast, focus directly on manifest practices and ask the same kinds of questions that concern practitioners.

Sometimes those who do practical studies hope for a quick solution to a pressing practical problem. Perhaps too many students have failed a statewide test in algebra. A study might discover which students failed and why. Studies in a practical tradition can also give timely snapshots of what is happening. How many classrooms in the state are using phonics in their reading curriculums?

Although the practical research tradition doubtlessly originated in such rough and ready responses to immediate problems, the study of practice has proven to have more lasting, general value. Curriculum practices have a sort of life of their own. Some spread like wildfire, while others struggle to gain a few adherents. Some retain their original qualities when they spread, while others take on new forms in new environments, sometimes so different that the originators no longer recognize them. So, it turns out that everyone concerned about curriculum, professional or not, needs answers to questions about practice.

How many schools and teachers have adopted a curriculum based on caring? What do these curriculums look like? Do they have some common essential qualities or at least some family resemblance to one another? Which elements of Noddings' conception appear in these various implementations and which ones fail to appear and why?

Researchers, reformers, and professionals all need a grounded understanding of both conventional practices and innovative ones in order to determine what sustains existing practices and how to sustain new and desirable ones. What are the conditions under which teachers try to realize a curriculum, and how do they respond to these conditions? What problems do teachers encounter in trying to realize particular practices, and how do they cope with them? Curriculum reformers need detailed, accurate understanding of the demands that a particular practice makes on teachers and students, and the conditions needed to sustain that practice in classrooms. Otherwise, they may find that a reform that seems promising in theory goes nowhere. Researchers of all traditions need to understand practice in order to conceptualize it clearly and accurately, in order to apply research results or theory to it, and in order to study it humanistically or scientifically.

The volume, *Interdisciplinary Curriculum: Challenges to Implementation*, edited by Wineburg and Grossman, includes nine studies that address in different ways the question: What goes on in schools in the name of interdisciplinary curriculum? The investigators talked to teachers and students, observed classrooms, and studied students' work. Their studies revealed that the practices teachers used when they implemented what they considered to be interdisciplinary curriculums posed some troubling problems.

Researchers found, for instance, that teachers defined interdisciplinary study in different ways. Some defined it as using principles from two or more established school disciplines, while others defined it as a project of any kind that doesn't fit neatly into one school subject. They found that the university scholars who advocate interdisciplinary study in schools do so because they believe that real problems require the use of principles from various disciplines. Teachers in K–12 schools, by contrast, see interdisciplinary curriculums as a solution to motivational and emotional problems of students. A K–12 teacher might have students read historical fiction to make history come alive and think of this as an interdisciplinary English/history unit. Another might teach a project on pollution as a way of combining science and social studies content in a package that would interest students more than traditional science and social studies content. The question with such projects is whether students ever learn any principles from the individual disciplines.

The investigators found that the quality of interdisciplinary units varied a great deal from one classroom to the next. One study of an interdisciplinary unit on the year 1492, vividly titled "The Photosynthesis of Columbus . . ." (Roth, in Grossman & Wineburg, 2000) found that students lacked the background for understanding the themes of diversity and interdependence that teachers chose as the unifying elements for the unit. The unit asked students who did not yet understand food chains or ecosystem cycles to learn about the diversity and interdependence of North American plants. Lacking this background, the students ended up learning little science in the interdisciplinary unit.

On the other hand, teachers in a New Mexico school succeeded in teaching students about underlying principles of mathematics, geography, and design as part of a unit on New Mexico's history through its architecture (Renyi, in Grossman & Wineburg, 2000). The teachers made sure that the students learned key disciplinary concepts as they studied architecture. What prevented this project from degenerating into making model pueblos, the investigator suggests, was that the teachers made a sustained study of the separate disciplines while planning the unit.

Practical studies like these can show us how curriculum theories and reforms work out in practice. Although they do not tell us conclusively what students actually learn, practical studies can give strong clues about what students are likely to learn. If students in many interdisciplinary projects never even encounter relevant and important science or math content, we can reasonably infer that these curriculums, even if they do motivate students, may lead to less learning of math and science. These nine studies suggest that learning disciplinary content through interdisciplinary projects poses a daunting challenge for students and teachers.

Those who design and develop innovative curriculums often do research to inform their development. Jan van den Akker et al. (1999) refer to this as developmental research. Traditional authorities on curriculum development such as Ralph Tyler (1949) have long recommended that developers conduct studies as a basis for curriculum development, including studies of the needs of students and communities and of the knowledge, beliefs, abilities, and attitudes of students and teachers. Carleton Washburne's pioneering workbooks were developed through a series of small studies that today would be termed action research that he and his faculty carried out in the schools of Winnetka, Illinois. Harold Rugg's justly famous social studies textbook series benefited from extensive but informal qualitative classroom studies in the Lincoln School and other schools. Many of the post-Sputnik projects carried out formal quantitative research as well as informal, qualitative classroom studies. Research remains an important part of the development of many innovative technology programs, including Sesame Street and computer assisted instruction (Flagg, 1990). In recent decades curriculum developers have begun to see research as an integral part of the development process and to develop and adapt research methods and strategies specifically for guiding development.

Paulo Freire, a Brazilian educator, described in *Pedagogy of the Oppressed* (New York: Herder & Herder, 1970), a method for developing a curriculum to stimulate and sustain critical consciousness among illiterate peasants that incorporates research at its core. The primary task of education according to Freire is to overcome passive attitudes and replace them with traits of active freedom and responsibility. He proposes to accomplish this through dialogue. The students and their teachers must become collaborators, coinvestigators developing together their consciousness of reality and their images of a possible better reality. This ability to perceive the world critically even in the midst of pervasive, powerful, subtle forces tending to distort and oppress is the goal of critical consciousness.

To develop such a curriculum Freire proposes that a team of educators work with the people of a given locality to develop generative themes drawn from the people's ways of life. First, the team members meet with representatives of the people to discuss their plans and to secure their permission and cooperation. Members of the team visit the locality and observe how the people live—at home, at work, at church, at play; the language used, people's actual behavior, their postures, dress, and relationships. Observers look for anything and everything that indicates how the people construe reality and their situation.

Preliminary findings of these local investigations are presented in a series of evaluation meetings held in the locality, involving members of the team and volunteers from the community. As the observers report the incidents they observed and their feelings and perceptions about them, the group discusses various ways this incident might be interpreted, ways it might be related to other aspects of people's lives. From these discussions emerge the contradictions which, if clearly perceived, would reveal to the people their oppressed state. These become the initial themes to be used in discussion and in literacy training for these people.

The investigators, having identified the themes and collected specific materials from the local community related to them, then return to the community to present them to the people to be educated in a series of "thematic investigation circles." In these meetings, the people discuss the concrete materials presented to them. The coordinator of the team elicits views and challenges speakers to reflect on the relationship of their views to those of others.

Freire uses the example of alcoholism. Instead of railing against drinking, participants are encouraged to express their views about specific incidents. In the course of discussion, comments are made that reveal dimly perceived relationships with other matters. "He's got to do something to blow off steam" leads to acknowledgement of stresses centered on work—no job security, low wages, feelings of exploitation.

When the work of the thematic investigation circles is complete, an interdisciplinary team of psychologists, sociologists, educators, as well as nonprofessional volunteers identifies the generative themes to be used in the actual instruction and develops readings, tapes, visuals, and other materials related to each theme.

Teachers present these concrete materials to the culture circles as a focus for discussion. Sometimes they act them out in informal dramas. Always they present them as problems, not as answers. Thus, the curriculum reflects people's own lives back to them, but in a way that encourages critical awareness of their situation, not passive acceptance of an oppressive interpretation. Figure 5.8 lists some other practical curriculum studies.

These Traditions are Complementary

Each of these traditions offers a helpful perspective on many curriculum questions. While they ask different questions, use different methods, and report in different styles, they are only rarely contradictory or inconsistent. Typically, studies from all three traditions contribute in different ways to our understanding of curriculum questions and our ability to deal with curriculum problems intelligently. I have contrasted them here in the interests of simplicity and clarity, but they coexist in productive tension and even borrow from one another. My personal belief is that the most productive lines of research in the future will include hybrids and mixtures of studies from all three traditions

Using Research Findings

While the number of those who do research is small, everyone who works on curriculum problems can benefit from using research. Teachers planning to adopt a challenging curriculum innovation, for instance, could benefit from reading studies of other teachers who have tried that or a similar curriculum. Curriculum leaders reviewing the quality of a school's reading program could benefit from comparing local results with regional and national averages found in published studies. All curriculum professionals should know how to locate and use studies that are directly relevant to practical problem like this.

Chapters 2 and 3 show and describe how to use historical and conceptual studies to address curriculum questions. Practical studies, by their very nature, bear directly on practical problems and so present few challenges in this regard. Applying scientific research to practical curriculum problems, however, presents some unique challenges, and we will consider these in the sections to follow.

Curriculum professionals will find it extremely valuable to be able to critically assess a body of scientific research and draw out its implications for practice. Developing this ability to a fully professional level takes years of study and practice, several graduate level courses in research and research methods, and some mentoring by professional scholars or researchers. This section sketches the basic steps involved in using research to inform practice. Consider it an overview and guide to further study.

- Collings, E. (1923). *An experiment with a project curriculum.* New York: Macmillan. (Recounts a 4-year experiment with a project-based curriculum in a rural school. Forty-three pupils aged 6 to 15 in one school used their own purposes and local resources as a starting point—no textbooks. The children made field trips to farms, formulated their own projects, carried them out, and wrote reports. Compared to 60 children in two other nearby rural schools with a traditional curriculum, students in the experimental school showed more growth in test scores and in ratings of conduct in life outside school.)
- Fawcett, H. (1938). *The nature of proof.* Thirteenth Yearbook, National Council of Teachers of Mathematics. Washington, DC: National Council of Teachers of Mathematics. (Fawcett developed a high school geometry curriculum focused on the idea of proof designed to teach critical and reflective thought. He compared an experimental group of 25 students with a control group of 25 students in the same school who studied geometry in the conventional way. The experimental group analyzed assumptions and definitions and by discussion convinced one another of the truth or falsity of geometrical propositions. They also practiced reasoning about everyday situations. They scored as high on a conventional geometry test and higher on a test of reasoning in nonmathematical situations than the control group.)
- Jackson, P. (1968). *Life in classrooms.* New York: Holt, Rinehart, and Winston. (The researcher describes his path-breaking study as "a melange. Descriptions of empirical studies are interlaced with speculative asides, tabular materials sometimes share the page with the most unquantifiable assertions" (p. vii), but he created a convincing and insightful portrait of what goes on in classrooms grounded in solid evidence.)
- Goodlad, J. I., Klein, M. F. and Associates. (1970). *Behind the classroom door.* Worthington, OH: C. A. Jones Pub. Co. (After a decade of highly publicized, well-funded early education curriculum reforms, these researchers traveled the country looking informally at what happened in actual grade 1 through 4 classrooms. They visited over 150 classrooms in 13 states and found few traces of the reforms. Just one of a long tradition of school observation studies that continues to this day.)
- Walker, D. (1971). A naturalistic model for curriculum development. *School Review, 80,* 51–65. (A study of the work of three curriculum project teams as they developed innovative curriculum materials. Found that deliberation was central to their work and that they operated with a common platform of ideas. The naturalistic model became an alternative to an objectives-based process for curriculum development.)
- Stodolsky, S. S. (1988). *The subject matters: Classroom activity in math and social studies.* Chicago: University of Chicago Press. (Observed 20 fifth-grade math and social studies classes in the Chicago area for 3 weeks running. Found that activities in all math classes looked similar. Four activities—seatwork, whole class recitations, tests, and teacher-led checking of work—occupied two-thirds of the time in math classes. By contrast, the 10 most frequent types of activities in social studies classes—activities such as answering teacher questions, oral reading, listening, working with maps, watching films, and group work—only accounted for one-third of the time. So teachers teach different subjects in different ways.)

FIG. 5.8. *(Continued on facing page)*

- Connelly, F. M., & Clandinin, J. (1988). *Teachers as curriculum planners: Narratives of experience.* New York: Teachers College Press. (The researchers look at curriculum from the standpoint of the teacher. They focus on teachers' personal practical knowledge and their experience and use teachers' own narratives to reveal these.)
- Page, R. N. (1991). *Lower-track classrooms: A curricular and cultural perspective.* New York: Teachers College Press. (An ethnographic study of tracking in two high schools. Compared the curriculum in eight lower track classes with that of regular track classes taught by the same teachers. Found that lower track classes received a stripped down, simplified version of the regular curriculum focused on bits and pieces of facts and skills using materials from daily life thought to be more relevant (magazines, newspapers). Students accept school knowledge as important but feel insecure about their ability to master it and get few rewards for the knowledge they do gain.)

FIG. 5.8.   *Some practical curriculum studies.*

Why Research is Often Hard to Understand

Research advances thinking and practice mainly because researchers use special methods more effective than simply poking around, keeping our eyes open, asking questions, and other everyday ways of looking into things.

Consider this hypothetical case. A respected public figure claims that reading skills have declined rapidly as a result of the introduction of Look–Say methods for teaching reading. Some experts agree, others disagree, so a researcher conducts a simple poll of subscribers to a journal of research on reading and finds that most subscribers don't think that Look–Say methods caused declines in reading skills. "Naturally," says the public figure, "the readers of this journal all studied under the researchers who led the movement to introduce Look–Say methods."

Another researcher looks at annual scores on standardized reading tests and finds that declines in reading scores did occur at the same time as a rise in the use of Look–Say methods. Critics of the study point out that a larger percentage of students in later age groups have been tested, raising the possibility that scores have dropped because more weak readers are now being tested, not because methods of teaching reading have changed. Further study reveals that the drop in reading scores has occurred both in states where Look–Say has been popular and in states where phonics prevails.

A chain of investigations like this informs a conversation among curriculum decision-makers by trying to nail down a disputed claim. Such conversations may continue for years or even decades. Each study adds evidence, but critics of each study always find weaknesses in the evidence. So researchers adopt more rigorous methods in order to defend against potential challenges by critics. Because more rigorous methods are often more complicated and subtle, research becomes more technical and harder to understand.

Challenges of Using Research

Using research to inform curriculum decisions poses four main challenges:

Finding the relevant research
Reading research reports critically

Combining the results of separate studies
Understanding the scope and limits of the findings.

This section treats each of these challenges briefly.

Finding Relevant Research

Your first step will be to find studies that bear on your problem. This often turns out to be surprisingly hard to do. One problem is knowing where to look. Libraries hold so many journals and books, too many to scan individually or even to sample effectively. Internet searches, too, typically return hundreds of items. You need a workable search strategy to find relevant studies in a reasonable time. Terminology is often a problem. Different investigators may use different terms for similar things. Studies on effective strategies for instituting a new curriculum may be labeled with such varied terms as *implementation of innovation, curriculum change,* or *school reform.*

The most serious obstacle to finding relevant research is often defining your problem clearly enough. Suppose your school is considering whether to use calculators in middle school mathematics classes. So you are curious about the effects of using calculators on children's mathematics learning. A computer search for "calculator" and "mathematics teaching," and "research" returns hundreds of citations. You find a study of the effects that doing drills on calculators had on scores on timed tests of basic number operations. It involved one class of fifth graders in a suburban school and followed them for one semester. Their scores on a standardized test of arithmetic did not improve significantly, but you wonder if one semester was long enough for an effect to show up. Another study looked at the effects of using calculators to explore number relationships. It was done in England 10 years ago. The students scored better on a test of number relationships that the researcher created, and they liked math better. A third study looked at the effects of a specific named curriculum designed to allow students to use calculators for solving complex practical problems.

After reading dozens of abstracts you realize that your question "What is the effect of using calculators in middle school mathematics?" is too broad. To answer it, researchers would need to study hundreds of classrooms where students used calculators in every way imaginable and compare these to an equal number of otherwise similar classrooms where teachers did not use calculators. They would have to look at various kinds of test scores and other measures in each of these classrooms. Such a massive study would be extremely costly. And the likelihood of finding a learning effect from just using calculators in any way for any length of time is quite small.

Researchers prefer to ask narrower, more focused questions about specific kinds of effects (attitude, achievement, understanding, retention, transfer, etc.) from using calculators in specific ways (drill on number facts, solving complex authentic problems, exercises or problems, alone or in pairs or larger groups, etc.). It makes more sense for you to find out how most teachers will use computers and what kinds of mathematics outcomes most interest the stakeholders in your school. Then focus your search on studies relevant to your practical situation.

A simple search strategy can help with all these challenges.

Consult Broad Sources First.

Reference works
   Encyclopedia of Educational Research
   Handbook of Research on Curriculum
   Handbook of Research on Teaching
   etc.

Textbooks
    Recently published standard texts in the field
    (e.g., mathematics education)
Reviews of Research
    Department of Education, Labs, and Centers,
    Phi Delta Kappan Fastbacks
    Review of Research in Education
    Review of Educational Research
    Major journals in the field
    Dissertations (Dissertation Abstracts)
A living expert
    Someone who follows the research on this topic,
    knows the sources, and can evaluate them.
    Conference proceedings name expert speakers

A breadth-first strategy gives you a quick overview of the body of research on the topic. The broad sources are usually authoritative, being written by established scholars who have spent a lifetime following the research and contributing to it. They strive to be comprehensive in covering all the main types of research on the topic. They should tell you the questions that have been asked and the basic kinds of studies that have been done. You will learn the specific terms most frequently used in this area of research, the names of prominent researchers, and the titles of the most often cited works.

Reading the broad sources should enable you to judge whether you need to narrow or otherwise restate your question. You may find the answer to your question. Or it may tell you that no research has yet been done on your question. If the broad sources don't mention anything relevant to your question, you're either looking in the wrong place or the research you want does not exist. In either case, you've avoided the trouble of searching through databases looking at hundreds of abstracts hoping to find relevant studies. Why should you review all these studies if an expert has already done it for you?

Look for Nuggets.   The 80–20 rule applies: A small fraction of what you read will give you most of the valuable information. Most of what you read will be of little value. Therefore, think of yourself as searching for nuggets of pure information bearing directly on your question. You'll find lots of studies that are vaguely relevant in some way. Don't waste time on them. I set up a file or folder to hold my nuggets. I begin by putting the best study I've found so far in this file—the study that speaks most clearly to my question and gives me the most direct and useful information. Then I only add studies to the file that are as good or better. From time to time I review my nuggets to confirm that all are still relevant and useful. Usually some get demoted from my "Nuggets" file to my "Useful studies" file when I look at them repeatedly.

Use your nuggets to find other nuggets. The best studies are likely to refer to the best other studies. Scan your nuggets looking for references to other studies as relevant and useful or better.

Learn to use the library. Learn to use the Internet. Cultivate an acquaintance with researchers and research librarians and seek their assistance. Work with colleagues; many pairs of eyes notice more; varied perspectives will help you see more and judge significance better.

Search print indices or computer databases only when you have learned:

some prominent issues
some key words

names of some prominent researchers
references to some prominent studies.

These will enable you to narrow your search and to evaluate the relevance of the items you turn up.

Use Theory to Find More General Studies.   The tactics of searching broad sources first and looking for nuggets should help you find studies that have addressed your specific question directly, but often studies that have asked a more general question can greatly illuminate your practical problem. By recognizing your specific problem as an instance of a more general type of problem, you can often find other studies that may be even more valuable than the nuggets you found among direct studies. For instance, studies of the implementation of technological and organizational innovations in businesses, hospitals, and other institutions may lead you to perspectives, theories, or principles that you can apply to the implementation of curriculum innovations in schools.

Use theory to point to relevant studies that ask more general questions. Here's one approach. Write a one-paragraph statement of what you have discovered about your question by reading your best studies. Write another paragraph stating the main questions or uncertainties that remain after taking into account the results of the best studies. Then rewrite these paragraphs replacing specific terms with more general ones. Statements about schools become statements about institutions or organizations. Statements about a school subject become statements about content. Statements about middle school students become statements about students or children or people. And so on. Then ask yourself what fields of study or disciplines address these broader questions. Consult one or two broad sources in those fields looking for theories that deal with these broader questions. Then search for studies that apply those theories to questions like yours.

Reading Research Critically

In using research a little knowledge can be a dangerous thing. Anyone can skim a research report and summarize its conclusion in one sentence such as "This study showed that students who used calculators did no better in arithmetic than other students who did not use them." This may be an accurate statement of the authors' conclusions, but we have no idea how much we can rely on this conclusion.

The problem is not that the study itself is likely to be wrong or deceptive. If the study was published in a refereed journal, then the editor and three other researchers read it and found no serious errors, so it is unlikely that the study contains an outright mistake of major proportions. The problem is that we do not yet know how solid and dependable the conclusion may be. All we know is that someone did a study and reached this conclusion. Was it an in-depth study? Was it well designed and carefully executed? Were the investigators unbiased and did they take pains to be impartial? Until we know the answers to such questions we cannot know how strong the evidence is in support of the conclusion.

To use the results of studies intelligently you must read study reports critically. Criticism involves appreciating a study's strengths as much as finding fault with its limitations, and still more a clear-eyed insight into what we can and cannot conclude from it. Critical reading includes a close and accurate reading of what the authors actually say, an imaginative mental reconstruction of what may have transpired in the study, and an assessment of the claims that can be supported on the basis of the study.

The first step in critical reading is simply to understand what the authors say in their report of the study.

- What did the researchers say that they intended to accomplish by carrying out this study?

  Usually researchers operating in a scientific tradition want to answer a specific research question such as "What is the effect of routine use of calculators to do text-book problems in a traditional middle school mathematics program?" They choose to collect certain kinds of data (test scores, student work samples, observations of classroom activities, etc.) about certain students and teachers at certain times and places. They hope to answer their question for the specific situations they studied and then infer from this answer an answer to the general question. It helps to keep these two steps separate in thinking critically about the study.

- Why do they say that they believe that this kind of study could accomplish this purpose?

  When they describe the research methods they intend to use, scientific researchers normally explain why and how they believe that this method—a survey, a case study, an experiment, ethnography, an analysis of existing data, etc.—will answer or partly answer their question. It is important to note the arguments that link the evidence collected in this study to the conclusion the researchers hope to reach. For instance, researchers may choose to carry out a large-scale survey of hundreds of schools that asks teachers questions about their use of calculators and collects data on mathematics achievement from publicly available statewide standardized test scores. Their argument justifying this kind of study might be that if calculators affect students' overall mastery of all the mathematical skills we want them to learn, then students who use calculators should score differently on these tests.

- Was this particular study done in a way that accomplished this purpose?

  How did researchers choose the schools and teachers to study? Exactly what questions did they ask teachers in the survey? How did they locate the achievement test scores? How did they analyze the test scores? And so on. Here you want to learn enough about exactly how the researchers conducted the study so that you can later judge whether their findings are valid for the students and schools that they studied.

- What do the researchers claim are the findings of their study?

  What conclusions do the researchers reach about the effect of using calculators on the mathematics achievement of the students and schools that they studied? What more general conclusions about the effects of calculator use on schools do they claim are warranted by the findings of their study?

With a clear understanding of what the researchers have said, the critical reader's responsibility is then to check the credibility of their claims. Credibility depends on the strength of the chain of argument and evidence that leads from the study procedures to the data and from the data to the conclusions. Lay out the steps in the argument and the evidence that each step uses. Then imagine other alternative arguments that are also consistent with the evidence. When a critic can find plausible alternative interpretations that are also consistent with the evidence collected in the study, then a critical reader cannot be certain which one of the alternative interpretations is true. Researchers speak of these alternative interpretations that are not ruled out by the evidence as threats to the study's validity.

Suppose the survey of calculator use in our hypothetical study had been returned by only 30% of the teachers to whom researchers sent it. A critical reader might wonder whether the 30% who responded were different in important ways from the 70% who did not. Perhaps the responding teachers were more likely to use calculators. Perhaps they had strong views, pro or con, about the use of calculators. Or perhaps they were simply more conscientious. If so, a positive relationship between calculator use and mathematics achievement (supposing that was the finding of the study) might be due to the special qualities of the teachers rather than to the use of calculators. How plausible do you think this alternative explanation of the study findings is?

No study can be perfect. Critics will always be able to find alternative interpretations of any study's findings. The sticking point comes in deciding the plausibility of these alternative interpretations. People of good will may differ in their standards for plausibility. When experienced researchers differ in their judgments of the validity of particular findings, the only immediate option is to hope for a majority view among researchers.

In the longer term, new studies can provide fresh evidence that may make some alternative interpretations more or less plausible. In the case of our hypothetical study, the researchers might follow up with a second mailing to the 70% who did not respond. Even if only a small fraction of them respond to the second survey, the researchers can compare their results to those of the first respondents. If the second group responds differently, then chances are greater that the original group is distinctive. If the responses of the two groups do not differ, then it is more likely that both are representative of all the teachers.

By inventing plausible alternative interpretations of the study's findings and examining their plausibility we can establish the credibility of the study's conclusions. Groups do well at inventing plausible alternative interpretations and arguing their plausibility, and everyone gets better with practice. Critiquing three or four quite different studies in a group is an excellent introduction to this important craft.

Strictly speaking, this process only establishes the credibility of the specific conclusion about the particular situations studied—the schools, teachers, and students about whom the researchers actually collected data. Whether this conclusion also applies more broadly to other schools, teachers, and students is a separate question. Researchers speak of these two as the internal and external validity of the study. A determination that the claimed interpretation is by far the strongest of the plausible alternative interpretations establishes the study's internal validity. The question of whether a similar conclusion would hold for other situations—other schools, other teachers, and other students—asks about the study's external validity.

Let's say that the calculator survey found that using calculators made no difference in mathematics achievement for the students in the schools studied and that you are satisfied that the conclusion is valid. Suppose that you are involved in a decision about whether to use calculators in another school in another district, in another state, even possibly in another country. Whether you think the findings apply to your school will depend on how similar you believe your school is to the schools in the study in relevant respects. What respects are relevant? Age or grades of students, surely. A finding valid for grades 4–6 might not apply to grades 6–8 and almost certainly would not apply to grades 1–3. Perhaps the wealth of the community is relevant. Findings from poor rural or city schools might not apply to wealthy suburban schools. And so on.

When researchers choose subjects—schools, teachers, or students in our case—at random from a certain population, they can use statistics to estimate just how likely it is that results from their sample will apply to the whole population. Random selection is therefore the "gold standard" for judging the representativeness of a sample. When random selection is not feasible, researchers can sample purposefully. Relying on what they already know about what affects their variables, researchers can design their study to compare differences explicitly. Knowing that students from wealthier communities tend to have higher mathematics scores than students in poorer communities, researchers can include equal numbers of schools serving low income and high income neighborhoods and analyze the data separately to see if they find the same conclusion in both types of schools.

Ultimately, it is up to the user of research to judge how representative the situations studied by researchers are of the situations that interest them. With experience, people who track how well research findings apply to a particular locality can develop an accurate intuition about when findings are more and less likely to apply to their situation.

These are only a few of the most central considerations to keep in mind when judging the validity of a study. A critical reader might also look at how well the researchers used previous research. All other things being equal, a study done by researchers who were familiar with previous research on the problem and had critically evaluated its relevance to their study should be better. In a humanistic study, in particular, it is vitally important for a study to place thinking on this topic in the great conversation, to show its relation to the great movements of thought through the ages. A well-developed conceptual framework that cites the best available theory relevant to the problem is another sign of quality. How well the details of the design of the study were handled, how adroitly the data were analyzed, and the extent to which the investigators showed an awareness of the limitations of their evidence are all signs of quality in a study. The cultural significance of the question or problem and its political, economic, and social importance are relevant questions.

In summary, nearly all studies have something to teach us, but they offer varying amounts of support for their conclusions and their findings are limited in various ways. The only way to know how much support and how limited is to analyze them critically. Whenever someone says, "The research shows. . . ." look for the critical analysis needed to support any such conclusion.

Combining the Results of Separate Studies

Whenever possible, important decisions should be based on a large body of research. A conclusion bolstered by many studies done by different investigators at different times and places is more credible than a conclusion supported by only one or two studies. In any large body of research, studies will reach conflicting conclusions. Some studies will find that students who used calculators did better while other studies will find that they did worse and still others that they did neither better nor worse. What conclusion should we draw when studies point to different conclusions?

The temptation in studying the results of many studies is simply to count the number of studies that favored one conclusion and compare it to the number that favored the other possibilities. In our hypothetical example of studies of calculator use in mathematics, suppose we found seven studies favoring students who used calculators, two favoring those who did not, and ten showing no differences. We could conclude that in most cases using calculators made no difference. Or we could conclude that studies favorable to calculator use outweighed studies favorable to no calculator use by more then two to one. What would be the most valid conclusion? Does this simple scorecard accurately reflect the findings of the studies? In most cases, it will not.

A better method takes into account the size of each study and the size of the difference between the groups. Researchers have developed a method called meta-analysis to do this quantitatively. Meta-analysis calls for a bit of statistical understanding and some calculations, but if you have the basic mathematical understanding you can easily learn to use meta-analysis in a couple of hours (Cooper & Hedges, 1994).

A more laborious option for quantitative studies and the only option for qualitative studies is a discursive analysis. Identify traditions, theoretical and conceptual assumptions, questions, and methods of all the studies. Cluster similar studies then compare and contrast them. Look for patterns. Are small studies finding the same results as large studies? Are test results pointing one way and teachers' judgments another? Are the studies' advocates showing favorable results while the studies' critics come out negatively? A discursive analysis calls for detective work and imagination.

When studies done with different methods lead to similar findings, their converging findings make a solid foundation for our understanding of that curriculum question. When their findings differ, they signal a failure in our understanding. Investigators trained in various traditions usually converge on such contested questions hoping to resolve the differences by achieving a deeper understanding.

Suppose the studies you find on your topic or problem are scattered among many different questions, methods, and approaches. How do you combine many studies on the same topic or problem when they ask diverse questions and use quite different methods and approaches? Such a body of research will not provide clear direction for practice. The individual studies and their range may expand your thinking. They may inspire or suggest alternative ways of thinking about the problem, for instance. But they will rarely help you converge when you are considering many possibilities, and they will never help you resolve a controversy.

Understanding the Scope and Limits of Research

While research can be of great help, it is no panacea. In particular, no one should expect research to make their decisions for them. Some people ask, "What does the research say?" naively hoping that the research will tell them what they should do. Perhaps this happened once, somewhere, but don't count on it happening for you.

Research may suggest factors that decision-makers should consider or alert them to complications they might meet with if they do this rather than that, but even the best research can never give definitive answers to practical questions. The particular situations decision-makers face never exactly match the circumstances of any study. Research can never completely disentangle the effects of a curriculum from the effects of families, the media, peer culture, and social or economic conditions. Then, too, researchers can only study what they can observe or measure, and often the outcomes we're most interested in are impossible to measure—the effect of a curriculum on children's adult personalities, career choices, or satisfaction with life, for instance. Even well-controlled experiments that compare one curriculum to another seldom lead to clear winners because the sides disagree about what outcomes are most important.

Because research on curriculum questions is never definitive, the same controversies that sent decision-makers to research looking for answers also dog research. Both sides to a controversy can always find studies that support their views. Eventually, studies may clarify what students and teachers are likely to gain and lose if decision-makers choose one side versus the other in a controversial decision, but firm conclusions take years to emerge and so confirmation often comes too late. Expect research to help you make more informed and better-considered decisions but don't expect even the best research to tell you what you should do.

The idea that research "says" anything is an oversimplification, potentially a dangerous one. It is more accurate to say that people use research in the arguments they make as they participate in deliberations and decision-making. Champions of a reform cite studies in the arguments that they give on behalf of the reform, and their opponents cite studies in the arguments that they give against it or in favor of other alternatives. Research can make arguments on both sides stronger by grounding them in documented realities and by clarifying the concepts under discussion, to cite only two of many ways.

It is not easy to marshal arguments based on research so that they build a strong case for a reform. Weaknesses in the case, even mistakes, are likely, and finding them can be difficult. The case for a reform will never be conclusive. People will always need to weigh the relative strength of the arguments on all sides, and people can differ in their judgments about this. So don't expect research to resolve controversies. At best they can clarify what truly divides the parties.

When you suspect that the case for a proposed reform may not be as strong as its champions make it sound, you should be able to examine critically the research cited in support of it. Seek the help of an expert researcher, if necessary, to understand the implications of research studies for the reform, against it, and for alternatives to it. The decision-maker who understands deeply the strengths and limitations of research will be well prepared to argue the merits of the reform in local forums and to counter ill-founded claims about "what the research says."

In view of the limitations of research, what are the alternatives? How else can we make good decisions and resolve our controversies? The judgment of the interested parties is one alternative to research. Students, teachers, and school curriculum leaders are closely involved with the school and classroom curriculum. Their close involvement gives them unique qualifications to reach informed judgments. Their judgments can be extremely well-grounded in real, first-hand experience. But their closeness also gives them strong interests that may bias their judgments. Professional judgment can be self-serving, whether by intention or not. Parents, public officials, and researchers are naturally reluctant to trust professional judgment when the professionals' interests are affected. They ask for "harder" evidence less subject to bias.

The judgment of experts can also inform decisions. Experts' judgments are informed by a wealth of experience and much study, so they often bring much skill and insight. Since outside experts usually have little or nothing at stake in the decision, they are therefore more likely to be impartial. Still, there's no guarantee of an expert's impartiality. Sometimes the same experience that leads to expertise also biases the expert's judgment. Some experts build their reputations on "selling" a particular idea or philosophy. Furthermore, the expert usually has little experience with the local situation.

Many people by virtue of their talent, training, and experience can contribute to curriculum decisions, and a strategy of participative decision-making relies on wide participation of all stakeholders to inform decisions. Such an open, democratic approach has much appeal in an open, democratic society. But participative decision-making has its limitations, too. Reconciling conflicting voices can be a challenge and is sometimes impossible. Majorities and even whole communities can be misinformed and misguided. The playwright Henrik Ibsen has Stockman, the hero of his play, *An Enemy of the People*, declare that the majority is always wrong because it always lags behind the most advanced understanding.

In short, the other alternatives have limitations, too. So, in spite of its limitations, research has a vital role to play in helping us make informed, considered curriculum decisions. And curriculum professionals have the privilege and the responsibility to bring it to bear productively and constructively.

Doing Curriculum Studies

Scholars and researchers spend several years in graduate school studying and working alongside experienced mentors to develop the skills and knowledge they need. This entire book is an introduction to these studies. This section focuses on learning how to do curriculum studies. It offers a brief overview of a learning process that takes years to master. Researchers have personal styles, like writers or filmmakers, and learning to become a researcher is a unique journey for each individual. The advice given here is necessarily generic. As I tell the graduate students I work with, take a look at this advice and tailor it to your talents, inclinations, and situation. Each researcher must find a niche where they can make a contribution and gain personal satisfaction.

Steep Yourself in a Research Tradition

Your ultimate goal should be to become a participating member of a community of curriculum scholars and researchers. To belong, you need to know the language and lore. Who are the founders and heroes? What are the best known and most respected works? What issues have been most talked about and written about? What methods have been most used and most praised? Who are the prominent figures today? Where do you find the best work being published today? What issues are talked about and written about now? What methods are most used and most admired today?

You must choose early which tradition of inquiry to steep yourself in. You can learn about other traditions, too, but your want deep understanding and fluent mastery of one tradition. The humanities offer many research traditions in addition to those indigenous to education, including philosophy, history, cultural anthropology, the literary, visual, and performing arts, and criticism, for example. Each of these fields of study has its own traditions of inquiry. The sciences offer many traditions, too, including anthropological science, communication, linguistics, psychology, and sociology. Those interested in practical research can also draw from traditions outside education, including research in fields such as business, engineering, law, medicine, and social work.

You can learn much of the lore of your research tradition by reading. Summaries, overviews, reviews and histories of research in your tradition are particularly valuable. Books on research methods are also gold mines of information. Buy a handbook of research methods and use it regularly. Barzun and Graff; Richard Jaeger; . . . Nothing can substitute for reading individual studies. Read many, read them critically, and discuss them with your peers and mentors. Take notes as you read and be sure to note the names of prominent figures, schools of thought, and the titles of prominent works, both contemporary and historical.

Find ways to associate with researchers who belong to your tradition. If you are in graduate school, your professors and fellow students are convenient associates. Volunteer to assist with ongoing research. Faculty and advanced graduate students always have research in various stages and most will welcome help from volunteers. Attend lectures of visiting scholars.

Professional conferences are wonderful occasions to see and meet members of the curriculum studies community. At annual meetings of the American Educational Research Association, for instance, you are likely to hear prominent figures in curriculum studies as well as new entrants giving talks and responding to questions. Division B of the Association is devoted specifically to curriculum studies. Division B regularly holds seminars for graduate students with prominent figures in the field. Meeting someone in person whose research reports you have read and realizing their humanity can make the tradition real to you and have a powerful impact on how you see their work and the field as a whole. The Association for Supervision and Curriculum Development also holds conferences of interest to scholars and researchers in curriculum. And there are dozens of organizations devoted to specific subjects, types of schools, and categories of student whose conferences are of great interest to specialists in those areas. Even when you can't attend a conference, scan the agenda on the Internet and read relevant contributions in the proceedings. Conferences are the most accessible face of your tradition.

Focus on a Problem Area

As a scholar and researcher you will need expert knowledge of the problem you study. So choose a curriculum problem or topic to focus on right from the start. You can change it later if you want or need to. Choose something that fascinates you and is important to many others, too. A school subject or an age group of students is a place to start, but you want to narrow your focus further than that. Or, you may be interested in issues that cross subjects and grades, such as curriculum for self-esteem, motivation for learning as an outcome, cultural diversity, or the potential of computers and information technology. Again, you want to narrow your focus to a more specific problem within these broad areas.

Immerse yourself in the problem. Keep a journal of your notes and thoughts. Read about the problem. Read everything you can find on the topic—news, theory, practice, research. If it's a conceptual problem, find out where people talk or write about it and listen, read, and study what they say. If it's a problem of practice you're interested in, find settings where it happens. Talk with informants. Observe. Participate. Take notes.

Review your notes. Identify the problems you see people having that you think are most important. Articulate and document the problems you discover. Try to understand how each problem arises and why it persists in spite of people's efforts to get rid of it. Argue the case for each problem's significance. Study how people cope with these problems. What do people do to avoid, solve, or manage these problems? How do people think and talk about these problems?

Theorize about the problem. Generate as many different interpretations of the problem as you can. Apply existing theories. Compare their implications to one another and to what people actually do and say. Compare what you find about this problem to what others have found about other problems, similar and different. As you go, identify research questions and imagine studies that would be useful.

Develop Your Technique

The reading, observing, interviewing, and note taking that you do as you become expert on the problem you've chosen to focus on are a kind of research, but a very rudimentary kind. To plan more powerful and penetrating studies that can advance our understanding more, you will need to use more powerful research methods. This means studying research methods and learning techniques for planning and carrying out each method rigorously. You need a basic understanding of all the methods in common use, but you will need to focus on mastering one or a few methods at first.

Figure 5.9 lists some of the methods commonly used in curriculum studies. Your choice of a method or two to master should be informed by your studies of your research tradition and the curriculum problem you've chosen to focus on. Choose a method that seems to you to give a great deal of insight into important aspects of your problem. Choose methods that you can use alone or with the collaboration of a few peers, methods that require a budget you can afford, and that can be completed in a few weeks or months. Later, if necessary, you can master more elaborate, expensive, and time-consuming methods.

Read what the appropriate handbooks of research say about your method. Study any books that have been published about your method. If you can, take courses in it. Understand the challenges critics mount to conclusions from research that uses your method and the measures experts recommend for guarding against these challenges. Learn to recognize studies that are strong and rigorous by the standards of your tradition. Read reports of studies that use your method and compare the procedures they use with those recommended in the

Humanistic	Scientific	Practical
Autobiography	Achievement testing	Action research
Biography	Assessment instruments	Case studies
Ethnographic case studies	and procedures	Retrospective case
Connoisseurship and	Attitude measurement	studies, esp. of
criticism	Correlational studies	successes and
Content analysis	Data analysis, large-scale	failures
Critical methods (literary,	evaluation research	Focus groups
social)	methods	Informal interviews
Dialogue, deliberation	Field experiments	Journals, diaries
Diaries, journals	Laboratory experiments	Teacher judgments
Ethnographic methods	Longitudinal methods,	Expert judgments
Etymology of words used	(life consequences	Participant
Historical methods	of learning)	observation
Language studies (coined	Mathematical models,	Testing and
terms, idioms, . . .)	simulations	assessment
Metaphors, analysis of	Meta-analysis, best-	Tryouts of new
Participant observation	evidence synthesis	practices
Philosophical (conceptual)	Policy-capturing study	Analyses of
analysis	Policy research methods	curriculum
Role-playing	Projective testing	Materials and plans
	Rating scales	Studies of student
	Simulation, mathematical	work: errors,
	models	misunderstandings,
	Stimulated recall	difficulties.
	Structured observation	Comparison of
	Survey research methods	successful and
	Synthesis of best evidence,	unsuccessful
	meta-analysis	cases
	Teaching experiments	Studies of school
	Think-aloud protocols	records
	Thought experiments	Journalistic reports

FIG. 5.9. *Research methods in common use in curriculum studies.*

research methods books. Where you find weaknesses, note techniques the researcher could have used to make the study more rigorous.

Participate in Research

Doing research is a practical art, and learning the art takes practice, lots of practice, in many and varied situations. Studies typically take weeks, months, or years to plan, carry out, and report, so learning to do research purely by experience is especially slow. Beginners are much better off when they can build on others' research experience. Those who find a team of researchers collaborating on several studies have even more opportunity to watch and learn.

Volunteer to work on studies alongside more experienced researchers. Advanced graduate students planning or conducting dissertations usually welcome help. Even if your job is only clerical, you can still watch and see what the experienced researchers do. If you enter a project already in progress, ask to see the proposal and any work already completed so that you have a picture of the research process from beginning to end.

You will also want to do studies of your own that focus on the questions that interest you. In the beginning, do small studies or partial studies. Study a single student or teacher. Observe for just a few days. Review the literature on a problem and treat that as a study in its own right. Replicate studies you read on a small scale or local population. Extend or improve studies you have critically analyzed and found wanting. Do preliminary studies for a study your mentor or a more advanced student is planning. Use standard and classic studies in your chosen tradition as models.

Treat these small or partial studies seriously. Your research question in a literature review is something like "What does the research literature say about <your problem>? Describe your methods rigorously enough that someone else could replicate your search. Keep your notes as if they were data. Conduct your analysis systematically and report it completely. Draw your conclusions carefully and note the limitations of your findings. Write it all up in a style suitable for publication in the premier journals of your field. Show it to your peers and mentors and ask for suggestions for improving it. Often you can use such miniature studies in lieu of other assigned work to meet course requirements.

Look for solicitations from government agencies or foundations that give grants to researchers in your area. Write brief prospectuses responding to these solicitations or even whole research proposals, just for practice. Discuss them with your peers and get reviews from your mentors.

In all this work, keep a research journal. Record in it all the details of every study you do. Also put down your own thoughts. Paste in clippings that you find inspiring or want to recall. Review it weekly. Record your reflections. Reflect on your progress, and note things you want to learn.

Doing Better Curriculum Studies

What is Good Curriculum Research?

In *The Conduct of Inquiry* (1964) the eminent philosopher Abraham Kaplan argued that research done in and for a context of discovery should use different methods and be judged by different standards than research done in a context of verification. Studies designed to settle much-disputed questions need to use the most rigorous and widely accepted procedures if all sides are to accept their results. On the other hand, when the purpose is exploration and discovery in a new area, quite informal studies may make important contributions.

The challenges of improving curriculum practice create contexts of both kinds. Curriculum innovations and reforms usually run ahead of existing knowledge. Their champions propose novel practices that no one knows much about and so create an ideal context for discovery-oriented research. Controversies, when advocates of various curriculum proposals contest one another's claims, form ideal contexts for verification.

The rich diversity of curriculum studies have provoked thought and generated ideas, but they have not delivered either exciting and surprising discoveries or telling and convincing verifications of disputed claims. How might researchers improve curriculum studies so that they perform these basic functions of inquiry better?

One way to try to improve curriculum studies would be to insist on more rigor in research methods. This is the most common response of researchers who try to improve research in their field of study.

Some elementary standards apply broadly to studies of any kind. For instance, researchers of all traditions must:

- clearly state their problem
- build on previous research and theory
- plan their study carefully
- follow established methods meticulously
- report their methods accurately and in detail
- analyze data correctly and without bias
- report results clearly and completely.

Closer adherence to stricter standards in performing these basic functions might improve curriculum studies.

Adopting methods and standards from other disciplines in the scientific, humanistic, and practical traditions is another way to make curriculum studies more rigorous. All traditions of inquiry include discussions about methods and standards. As beginning researchers study a particular research tradition they learn what counts as a good study in that tradition. Those who study scientific traditions discover that experiments command respect among scientists, and they will learn the standards for good experiments. As they study research in curriculum, they will see how experiments are used in curriculum studies. Those who steep themselves in humanistic and practical traditions will learn corresponding methods and standards in those traditions. If they used these methods and standards in curriculum studies, then perhaps studies would deliver more discoveries and better verification.

Many of the most respected curriculum studies have used methods and standards imported from other disciplines, and their contributions to curriculum studies is beyond question. Nevertheless, efforts to make curriculum studies more rigorous according to the standards of other fields have at best a mixed record. In particular, a curriculum study that adheres too closely to inappropriate standards of rigor imported uncritically from an academic discipline may distort the curriculum question. For instance, many researchers operating in a scientific tradition have imported the technique of multiple-choice standardized tests from educational psychology, judging them to be more rigorous measures of academic achievement. As a result, research on curriculum outcomes has been distorted to favor verbal or mathematical learning, much of it factual in nature, recalled quickly, with little need to use it, relate it to other knowledge, or reflect on its meaning.

A study that is good by the standards of philosophy, history, or psychology may still not be a good curriculum study. To judge whether methods imported from other fields will contribute constructively to curriculum studies, researchers need standards for good research on curriculum. Can we develop standards that are particularly appropriate for judging the quality of curriculum studies, regardless of tradition?

Ideally, we would like standards that everyone could agree on, but this may be too much to expect in a field split by radical differences in value and perspective. The seeker after objectivity can more reasonably aspire to develop standards that all the interested parties agree are relevant, and then let them debate the application of those criteria to particular studies. In the discussion that follows, the pronoun "we" acts as a kind of variable to allow for differences in value and perspective. Treat "we" as meaning "all interested parties" and the standard becomes a universal one. Treat "we" as meaning some particular interest group such as "progressives," "traditionalists," "advocates for a constructivist curriculum," or the like, and the standard functions as a limited agreement among like-minded persons.

With this reservation noted, most curriculum researchers would consider the following questions particularly important in judging the quality of a curriculum study.

1. How much do we learn?

    From a good study we learn something important about some important curriculum question. One indication that we learn from a study is that its findings surprise us. What we learn may be something more than factual knowledge, such as a change in how we think about something, a change in the questions we ask, or the methods we use. We are the ones who judge what we learn, and we are the ones who judge whether the question is important.

2. Are the indicators or measures of curriculum matters used in the study credible and authentic?

    A good study well and credibly documents the characteristics of the curriculum and its antecedents and outcomes. Informed curriculum professionals should be satisfied that the researchers have really captured what is of most interest about the curriculum matters they studied, not just something indirectly and possibly related to what's really of interest.

3. Does the study consider the subjective experiences of the people involved?

    A good curriculum study looks not only at objective matters such as performance and behavior, but also at humanly important subjective matters such as meanings, perceptions, and feelings. A curriculum is for the public benefit but also for the benefit of the individual students and teachers who enact and experience it. Their felt experiences are always relevant to curriculum questions.

4. Does the study consider multiple perspectives?

    A good study acknowledges in appropriate ways the different perspectives held by the most important stakeholders in the curriculum issues being studied. Researchers should recognize that every curriculum issue has multiple important stakeholders, that these stakeholders typically hold different values and perspectives, and that a good study should consider these different perspectives in some appropriate and fair way. A study that ignores some of the competing perspectives or shows a bias toward some is not as good as a study that acknowledges the existence of competing perspectives and treats all fairly.

    Partisan studies may usefully advance one side of a contested issue by frankly adopting one perspective and rejecting others. Researchers should clearly label such studies as partisan. A partisan study may or may not address the concerns of those who hold other perspectives, but they should acknowledge them so that readers know of their existence and know that the researchers know, and they should treat them fairly if they treat them at all.

5. Does the study explicitly state and defend its value judgments?

    All curriculum questions involve value judgments, and curriculum scholars and researchers have an obligation to state and defend the value judgments they necessarily make in their study. In some studies the value judgments will be so simple and straightforward that a brief allusion to them will suffice, but in most studies, particularly studies that bear on contested issues, the stating and defending of value judgments will be a major part of the study report.

6. Does the study consider a range of relevant settings and situations?

    The same curriculum plays out differently in different situations. A good study takes into account in an appropriate way the diversity of settings, people, occasions, motivations, ideas, etc., that might affect the outcome. Some studies may focus on a narrow range of situations for a good reason, but all other things equal, studies that give information about a range of situations are better.

7. Are the study's contributions timely?

A good study comes in time to help with pressing issues. The value of findings about curriculum questions decays with time as curriculums, schools, and society change. Premature or tardy findings are less valuable than timely ones.

8. Are the study's benefits high in relation to its costs?

A good study makes such excellent use of the resources needed to carry it out that we can't imagine another study that would help us as much for the same price or less. Costs may include intangibles such as inconvenience, time diverted from other tasks, and loss of good will, political consensus, or effective organization.

9. How well does the study balance the sometimes competing considerations implicit in the previous standards?

Rarely if ever can a single study meet all these standards simultaneously, including those specific to curriculum studies as well as those from other research traditions and standards applicable to all studies. Usually researchers must make sacrifices on one standard to satisfy another better. In some situations some standards are more crucial than others are. A good study sacrifices standards that are less important in the situation being studied to better satisfy a standard that is more important in this situation.

Viewed in the light of this broader set of standards, rigor in curriculum studies takes on a new look. Experiments without control groups, unstructured interviews, case studies, and a host of other methods generally considered not to be rigorous may make very valuable contributions if they use credible and authentic indicators that capture what's important, address the subjective experiences of students and teachers, and consider multiple perspectives. A series of small, quick, cheap studies may contribute more than a single formal controlled study that takes longer and costs more. Simple studies, relatively uncontrolled and therefore vulnerable to many challenges, may be good enough for an urgent but uncontroversial decision when decisionmakers have little prior knowledge to fall back on. In many cases curriculum researchers may be well advised to do a series of quick, simple studies rather than a single more elaborate and controlled ones.

Beyond Rigor

Enforcing higher standards of rigor, even by these extended standards, may not lead to more discoveries or better verification. As we have seen, rigor is often costly and time-consuming. The quest for rigor may distort the questions asked and introduce new complications into the research enterprise. Striving for greater rigor is one way of improving curriculum studies, but not the only way.

Good research is not a matter of method alone, and good methods do not ensure good research. We must also ask good questions, be alert to emerging events, and exercise imagination and insight. Too much effort to create a definitive study immune to any challenge often results in studies that are narrow, mechanical, and not very informative. There are other ways to garner convincing evidence.

One alternative is to carry out several simple studies. When many studies done by many investigators using a variety of methods converge on a result, the evidence can be quite compelling even if the evidence from any one study is vulnerable to criticism. Firm conviction then comes from a review of many studies rather than from any single one.

Another path to improved curriculum studies is to rely more on judgments and strive to make them more objective. Video and audio recording and digitized samples of students' work make the primary materials on which judgments are based publicly available. With primary materials subject to public review, anyone can check on anyone else's judgments.

Staging debates and dialogues among contending parties on controversial issues can be a productive strategy for generating more valuable studies. Such discussions should clarify disputed points and indicate questions where studies might have the most impact in resolving or reformulating the disputes. It would be interesting to see the effect on curriculum research of establishing annual meetings of interested parties to a controversial curriculum issue for a period of years and inviting partisans from all sides to contribute studies to the ongoing discussions.

Case studies of attempts at curriculum innovation deserve to be a staple form of curriculum study. These interventions are authentic and meaningful in their own right. They concern matters of vital interest to curriculum stakeholders. The deliberations and debates surrounding them suggest processes and outcomes to look for, and qualitative methods, such as unstructured observation and analysis of student work, provide rich and convincing evidence.

The simple observational case study is a staple of curriculum studies for good reason: curriculum situations are so complex and involve so many intertwining strands of action meaningful on so many levels that sorting out the simple facts of the case is a necessary preliminary to any deeper inquiry. W. A. Reid (1973) puts this point very well when he writes, "Even where the case study is not the answer to a particular problem, some kind of limited case work is almost certainly desirable before wider enquiries are attempted."

Conclusion

I agree with Reid (1999) that "the constraints put upon curriculum research by the nature of the data it has to handle and the kinds of decision–processes to which its results relate, both seem at the present moment to tend in the same direction—towards a naturalistic, humanistic, impressionistic mode of research, with an emphasis on description, on case study, and on a stance which recognizes the political nature of much curriculum activity" (pp. 97–98).

Looking at the history of curriculum studies, I believe that the main challenge today is to carry out simpler but still powerful studies that bear directly on important questions. Any inquiry that advances some stakeholders' understanding, is clearly described, well justified, and reasonably free of bias makes a contribution to curriculum studies and will be accepted regardless of methods employed and regardless of whether the study conforms to academically accepted methodological canons. Our need is not for more sophisticated studies but for more basic ones that speak more directly and powerfully to our most important issues. I hope that this book may inspire some readers to carry out such studies.

Questions and Projects

1. Consider the three studies of the mathematics curriculum summarized in this chapter. How would you decide whether to believe their findings? Assuming the findings are all valid, which study do you think would be of most value to a teacher struggling to

decide whether to adopt constructivist reforms? Why? Think up situations for which the other two studies would be more useful than this one.

2. In which of these situations would you think it would be worthwhile to spend several days locating and summarizing relevant research?

   A. A school board is considering adopting a very new and radical curriculum reform that few teachers want. Teachers have expressed their opposition, but the board is not persuaded. A vote is scheduled for next month.

   B. A teacher believes that the textbook series many fellow teachers favor for adoption by the district is inferior to the series they have been using.

   C. A well-organized group of teachers and parents have proposed a new curriculum to the superintendent and board and backed up their proposal with research findings showing much higher achievement with the new program than with conventional ones.

3. Read an article in a professional journal about a contemporary curriculum issue, such as how to use technology in classrooms or how to make the curriculum more inclusive of all cultures' contributions. Locate all references to research findings in the article. Write out in a single sentence each argument that cites research. Can you find convincing counterarguments? What kind of research might confirm or disconfirm either the argument in the article or your counter arguments? Compare notes with your colleagues. What does this experience tell you about the use of research to ground curriculum arguments?

4. Spend an hour in the library searching for research related to some contemporary curriculum issue. How many studies were you able to find? Were you able to find a review of research? Compare notes with your classmates or colleagues? What does this experience teach you about the ease or difficulty of finding research on curriculum issues?

5. Find an impressive study on a topic that interests you. Read it critically and discuss its merits. How convincing did you find it? What changes to the study would make it more convincing?

6. Identify a researcher who has made important contributions to a curriculum question that interests you. Use the Internet and library to trace the researcher's career. Consider writing to the researcher to ask for a copy of their *curriculum vitae* if you can't find it on the Internet. What sort of development do you see in the person's work over their career. Has the researcher worked alone or collaborated? Is the researcher asking different questions or using different methods now than earlier? How many research methods has this researcher used?

7. What kinds of studies do you find of most value to you in your curriculum work? Why? What's involved in learning to do this kind of study? What skills would you have to develop? How long might it take?

8. Christina Hoff Sommers argues in the Summer 2001 issue of *The Women's Quarterly* (*http://www.iwf.org/pubs/twq/Summer2001b.shtml*, accessed August 27, 2001), that schools should teach penmanship. Read the brief article and critically assess the use of research to ground the arguments. Among the claims: Boys suffer more than girls do from poor handwriting. Teachers give students with better handwriting higher grades. Children who have trouble with the mechanics of writing are distracted when trying to put their ideas on paper, and this accounts in substantial part for the gap in writing scores between boys and girls. Evaluate the strength of the research support cited in the article for these and similar claims.

9. Critically analyze the three studies of mathematics curriculums summarized in this chapter. How strong is the support that they provide for their conclusions? What would you suppose are the most plausible alternative interpretations? In your

judgment, how valid is each study internally and externally? What limits would you place on their findings?

10. In a study of literacy at home and school (Betty, Shockley, Barbara Michalove, and JoBeth Allen. (1995). *Engaging Families: Connecting Home and School Literacy Communities*. Portsmouth, NH: Heinemann) the investigators reported carefully categorizing the data from many interviews and observations. After reflecting on this formal analysis they concluded that it was distancing them from the reality that they were studying. So they discarded the categorization and instead had a writer's retreat, complete with food, walks on the beach, and long conversations, as a result of which they felt they understood their data better. How would you defend this method of data analysis? What are its strengths? Its limitations? Should curriculum professionals be encouraged to employ this and similar methods for analyzing data?

Further Study

The single most important step on the way to becoming a scholar or researcher is to read, critically analyze, and discuss studies on curriculum questions. The various chapters of this book cite the best studies that I know of. Reading the original reports of those studies that pertain to the questions that most interest you would be a good way to start. You can find other studies in research journals. Two of the best research journals in curriculum are the *Journal of Curriculum Studies* and *Curriculum Inquiry*. The *Journal of Curriculum Theorizing* publishes challenging theoretical works on curriculum questions. Subject matter journals and journals focusing on other specialized curriculum topics make excellent sources of reports of original research and scholarship. Set aside time specifically to read original research and scholarship. Keep notes on your reading and plan to write a review of research summarizing what you learn. You can also find the latest studies reported at conferences, especially the American Educational Research Association (AERA) annual meeting. Division B, Curriculum Studies, annually presents exciting new studies as well as discussions on methodology and other topics of interest to curriculum researchers. The annual meeting of the Association for Supervision and Curriculum Development (ASCD) focuses more on curriculum innovation, reform, and improvement, but it also presents research. Form a study group with others who are preparing to become researchers and scholars on curriculum. If you can't find any collaborators locally, send out a call to nearby universities or over the Internet.

The second most important step is to do studies. Choose a mainstay research method and learn to design and carry out studies using this method. If you can, find a mentor who does the kinds of studies you want to do and work with this mentor on whatever studies are underway at the time. If you can find a team doing research on curriculum, that is even better. Plan small, pilot studies on your own initiative, get your mentor to review your plans, carry them out, write them up, and submit them for publication. If your submission is rejected, you will still receive the reviewers' comments and these should be very helpful in planning better studies next time. If you are enrolled in a doctoral program, your dissertation should not be the first study you do but the third or fourth, at least.

The indispensable resource for any scholar or researcher who wants to study curriculum questions is the *Handbook of Research on Curriculum* (1992) edited by Philip Jackson. The chapters on "Curriculum studies and the traditions of inquiry: The scientific tradition" by Darling-Hammond and Jon Snyder, "Curriculum studies and the traditions of inquiry:

The humanistic tradition" by Lincoln, and "Methodological issues in curriculum research" by Walker are relevant to all curriculum researchers. Other chapters focus on particular categories of studies, such as Herbert Kliebard's chapter, "Constructing a history of the American Curriculum," which is a crucial resource for historians of the curriculum or Elmore and Sykes' chapter "Curriculum policy," which is an excellent review of research on that topic. My advice to all beginning scholars and researchers is to own a copy, read it carefully, and consult it often.

Any of the many handbooks of research on the teaching of specific school subjects such as mathematics or art would be indispensable to students of those specialties. A valuable resource for those curriculum researchers whose work is enhanced by a psychological perspective will find the *Handbook of Educational Psychology* (Berliner & Calfee, 1996) to be useful. Part III on "School curriculum and psychology" and Part IV on "Teaching and instruction" have relevant material. A valuable general resource on becoming a scholar or researcher is Goldsmith, Komlos, and Gold's *The Chicago Guide to Your Academic Career* (2001).

On scientific research methods of research on curriculum I recommend David Krathwohl's *Methods of Educational & Social Science Research: An integrated approach* (1998). His broad, thoughtful revisionist interpretation of the traditional hypothetico-deductive model of social and behavioral science research will appeal to many who are repelled by a narrow, dogmatic scientism. Krathwohl argues that good scientific research studies try to optimize several criteria, including information yield, credibility with the audience, and resource allocation. Also, researchers must balance concern for internal validity with concern for external validity, a process that inevitably involves complex and subtle judgments of several important issues. I also admire Donna Mertens' *Research Methods in Education and Psychology: Integrating diversity with quantitative & qualitative approaches* (1998). On synthesizing the findings of many studies Cooper and Hedges' *Handbook of Research Synthesis* (1994) is a sound and accessible source.

On humanistic research methods there are so many outstanding sources representing so many different stances that any recommendations are inevitably highly personal. I have always admired Barzun and Graff's *The Modern Researcher* (5th edition, 1992) for basic methods of documentary research. In education, I admire Carr and Kemmis's bold defense of action research in *Becoming Critical: Education, Knowledge and Action Research* (1986), Glaser and Strauss's innovative and influential defense of exploratory studies in *The Discovery of Grounded Theory* (1967) and Schein's defense of clinical studies in *The Clinical Perspective in Field Work* (1986). Mary Aswell Dodd in *Like Letters in Running Water* (2000) has written thoughtful essays about ways that literature can help us to capture the lived experience of a curriculum.

On practical research methods the literature is not so extensive. The last section of my chapter, "Methodological issues in curriculum research," in the *Handbook of Research on Curriculum* makes the case for a distinctive methodology for practical inquiry. Cooley and Bickel in *Decision-Oriented Educational Research* (1986) describe and give thoroughly annotated examples of what they call decision-oriented educational research, adopting Cronbach and Suppes' (1969) distinction between conclusion-oriented and decision-oriented inquiries. Cooley and Bickel advocate eclectic use of methods and strategies best suited to the problem, designing research to suit the needs of decision-makers, monitoring important indicators of educational outcomes rather than doing discrete studies of particular programs, adjusting practices to improve results, documenting practices in detail, and using computer-based information systems to reduce and interpret massive amounts of data. Argyris in *Knowledge for Action* (1993) describes an approach to action research that theorizes about changes, makes them, and observes the results closely and rigorously, on the theory that one of the best ways to understand the world is to try to change it.

Much of the literature on curriculum evaluation can be generalized to other types of practical research. Cronbach's *Designing evaluations of educational and social programs* (1982) and Cronbach et al.'s *Toward reform of program evaluation* (1980) have thoughtful treatments of issues of rigor in evaluation studies. Bloom, Hastings, and Madaus's *Handbook of Formative and Summative Evaluation of Student Learning* (1971), now sadly out of print, is a wonderful compendium of tips and techniques for assessing student learning.

Notice the books about methods that your favorite scholars and researchers cite and check them out.

PART 2

PRACTICE

CHAPTER SIX

Curriculum Practice

Life is brief, art long, opportunity fleeting, experiment perilous, judgment difficult.
—**Hippocrates, Greek physician, fourth century, B.C.E.**

Questions

- What is curriculum practice?
- What are the main types of curriculum practice?
- What kinds of challenges does curriculum practice pose?
- How do teachers and curriculum professionals cope with them?
- What skills does school curriculum leadership demand?

Curriculum Practice

Teachers do curriculum work, so do principals, school board members, textbook authors and publishers, testing agencies, scholars and researchers, state and federal educational officials, and many, many others. Ultimately parents, elected representatives, many interest groups, and the public participate in some way in curriculum work. But not everyone who participates in some way practices curriculum professionally, just as not everyone who gives an aspirin practices medicine. Those who practice curriculum deal with curriculum matters frequently and focally, not occasionally and incidentally.

The most important groups of curriculum practitioners include:

- Teachers, who practice curriculum when they enact the classroom activities that bring a curriculum plan to life.
- School leaders, those who share in curriculum decisions in schools and in the institutions that govern schools.
- Developers, those who develop curriculum plans and materials for teachers and students to use.
- Influences, those who strive to bring about curriculum improvements from afar by influencing other practitioners.

Teachers are the primary practitioners, since their curriculum work impacts students directly, while the others' work is mediated through teachers. We will begin by examining what's involved in teaching with a curriculum.

Teaching a Curriculum

Teaching varies tremendously depending on the students' age, the subject, and the teacher's style, and how the teacher works with the curriculum depends on how they teach. To take just one example, curriculum will have different meaning for a teacher who acts as a "sage on the stage," dispensing information and directing classroom activities, than for a teacher who acts as a "guide on the side," launching student-directed activities and coaching from the sidelines. The implicit model of teaching used in this section reflects conventional practice as documented, for instance by Cuban in *How Teachers Taught* (1993). It's mainly teacher-centered teaching spiced with occasional student-centered elements. Readers with a passion for a particular style of teaching can reflect on how well the points in this section apply to that style.

Teachers Bring the Classroom Curriculum to Life

This section explores the challenges that teachers face in doing the basic work of realizing a curriculum. Teachers practice curriculum in several ways but the most basic is by realizing it or bringing it to life in the classroom. Beginning with some sort of curriculum plan or guide, teachers do whatever it takes to make learning activities happen in their classroom that fulfill the curriculum plan. All teachers do this as an integral part of their teaching. Realizing a curriculum in a classroom can be complex and difficult even when the school provides teachers with a detailed curriculum plan. A brief summary of this part of a teacher's job description would look like this.

- Select and plan daily classroom activities.
- Schedule and pace the activities throughout the year.
- Present the activities to students in a way that enables them to comprehend and follow them.
- Motivate students to participate in the activities.
- Evaluate students' performance on the activities.

Let us look in more detail at each of these challenges of realizing a curriculum.

Select and Plan Classroom Activities

Teachers typically make some sort of plans for their classes prior to the start of each academic year and then make more detailed plans for units and lessons throughout the year. Teachers' plans have to satisfy various outside authorities including the local district, state agencies, and colleges who set entrance requirements. The general name for all these constraints is "curriculum frames." Frames are conditions imposed by institutional actions outside the classroom that define and limit what teachers may do inside the classroom. Early in the year teachers discover what frames will govern their work in the year ahead and factor these frames into their planning. What courses or grades will I be teaching? How many students will be enrolled in each? What are their academic backgrounds? What do local parents, teachers, and officials expect students to learn in these courses? What textbooks and other curriculum materials will I be able to use? What external examinations will my students be taking?

Frames set the major purposes and content for the teacher. Still, teachers face much more work to build a course plan that covers the subject, conforms to all the frames, and works for their students. Studies of teachers as they plan show that most teachers start with the textbook or district curriculum guide as a course outline and adapt it to their specific classroom situation. Their first step in adaptation is usually to consider the content authorities expect them to cover in the class. They rely heavily on textbooks for this (Zahorik, 1975; Peterson, Marx, & Clark, 1978; Clark & Yinger, 1987; Yinger, 1977). Various studies (Komoski, 1976; McCutcheon, 1980) have revealed that a great deal of what happens in classrooms (estimates range from one-half to over ninety percent) involves published instructional materials like textbooks. When students take external examinations, they also become important curriculum frames for teachers.

Early in the planning process teachers start to think about what classroom activities they could use. Teachers believe that classroom activities lead to student learning, and so they devote much planning time to selecting good classroom activities. Experienced teachers have well-stocked memories and files of many hundreds of activities that they have tried or heard about. Teachers' editions of textbooks commonly suggest activities, as do the courses of study and curriculum guides provided by the school district. Teachers are free to select other activities instead of these if, in their judgment, students would learn better from them than from the suggested activities in official sources.

How do teachers judge one activity to be better than others for a given purpose? Studies of teacher planning show that teachers usually select activities for practical reasons. The activity fits the teacher's personal teaching philosophy and style. The teacher has previous successful experience with the activity. A respected colleague recommends it. It's convenient. Apparently teachers rely on such practical considerations rather than on the proven effectiveness of an activity as demonstrated by research and evaluation, even when relevant studies exist (Yinger, 1977; Clark & Yinger, 1987). This emphasis on practicality dismays researchers and reformers, who wish teachers would think more deeply about their classroom activities and consider more radical alternatives.

Schedule and Pace Activities

Time limits constrain teachers at every turn. In planning, teachers need to estimate the time students will need for each part of the curriculum and reconcile that with the time they have available. A schedule of class activities is the primary curriculum planning document most teachers use. Keeping up with the schedule despite unexpected delays is a major concern throughout the year.

Teachers must make complex judgments when considering their schedule of classroom activities. How long would it take for students to learn the scheduled material thoroughly? Would they stand a better chance of learning it if they revisited it after studying other material for awhile? Will they suffer later if they fail to learn it thoroughly? To make these judgments teachers need an intimate and extensive knowledge of the students, the subject matter, and their own capabilities.

The best laid plans for a curriculum often go awry in the classroom and need to be adjusted to adapt to unforeseen circumstances. Students may enter the class not knowing everything assumed in the plan or they may have already learned some of the things the plan called for teaching them. An activity included for its motivating value may turn out not to be interesting to this group, or the subject itself may prove so intrinsically interesting that a motivating activity is superfluous. Good, timely adjustments to curriculum plans can make an immense difference in what students learn from the class.

Davis and McKnight (1976) give a hypothetical example that illustrates the intricate connections between teaching adjustments and curriculum.

Change time allocations
Change sequence
Add or delete topics or activities
Modify topics or activities
Change grading criteria
Raise or lower achievement standards

FIG. 6.1. *Ways teachers adjust topics or activities.*

One can attempt to restrict a mathematics curriculum to a sequence of undemanding tasks, done individually in workbooks. This leads to a quiet and orderly classroom, but, we suspect, implies limitations on the mathematical content that will be learned.... As the problems in a workbook are made more challenging, students will need more help from the teacher. This, at the least, will lead to many students wanting to see the teacher for help, which, in turn, means a need to wait, with attendant impatience and temptations to disorder. If the subject is genuinely profound, most students may be unable to learn it from independent reading, and class discussion may be necessary—but this means, in many cases, large group instruction (pp. 216–217).

Teachers adjust their curriculum plans in light of students' responses to it. Learning to interpret students' responses to a curriculum accurately is one of the great arts of teaching, but unfortunately little studied. Able, experienced teachers can often predict when students will have problems. They come alert at the first signs that students are struggling. They recognize the misconceptions students most frequently form about a subject, and they know what to do about them. They can tell constructive struggles from futile ones, and have a large repertoire of contingency plans. Figure 6.1 shows some of the adjustments teachers make.

Present the Curriculum to Students

In the first days of the school year teachers introduce themselves, their classroom, and their curriculum to a new group of students. They tell students what the class will be like, what kind of performance will be rewarded, and which of their abilities to employ when, for how long, and in what way. If they do not, students will make their own assumptions. Some may assume that they should memorize as much as possible and repeat it verbatim, while others may assume that they should improvise and be creative with what they learn. Portraying the subject vividly and accurately to students is an important purpose of general education, too. It helps them decide whether to continue studying the subject, for instance.

The ground rules and standard operating procedures teachers lay down in the first few days of school also affect the direction and extent of students' engagement with the classroom curriculum. Teachers of traditional mathematics might establish such ground rules as "Each person works alone," "Grades are based on tests," "There is only one right answer," and "Every answer is either right or wrong." In art classes, on the other hand, teachers generally make it clear early in the course that there are many good solutions to an art problem, that grades are based on the product but also on effort, and that students are encouraged to help one another to improve their art. Such ground rules define for students what art and mathematics are like and define what it takes to be a good student of that subject.

- Describe the purpose, content, and structure of the course in a lecture in the first few days of class.
- Have students speak or write their own thoughts about the course and subject; discuss their ideas; correct any misconceptions about the curriculum.
- Show students some questions or problems that they will be able to answer when they have completed the class; explain what they will need to do in order to master this material.
- Involve students in an opening activity that is prototypical of the subject and then help them to reflect on what they must do to become able to do such things themselves. For example, in a chemistry class students might view reports of chemical analyses of water samples taken from their own community. Then they might discuss how the findings were obtained, to what extent the results can be relied upon, and what the findings may mean for them and their community and then follow up with a discussion of how they can learn to do such chemistry as this.
- Read and discuss a biography of a great contributor to the subject; point out what that person did that made this person a good learner of that subject.

FIG. 6.2.   *Ways to introduce students to a curriculum.*

We know surprisingly little about how teachers actually introduce children to the classroom curriculum in any subject. Figure 6.2 lists some options that seem plausible, but no one seems to have studied either the tactics that are most effective or the tactics teachers actually employ. Figure 6.3 shows some of the types of procedural ground rules that communicate strong messages about the classroom curriculum to students.

In order to introduce students to a curriculum, teachers need to know a great deal about the students. What do they already know about the subject? What preconceived ideas do they have about it? What do they expect their experience in the class to be like? What do they hope might happen? What do they fear might happen? What sorts of school experiences do they find rewarding and what sorts punishing? Teachers need to know such things about their students in order to find good ways to introduce the curriculum to them.

Motivate Students to Follow the Curriculum

A curriculum comes to nothing if students do not follow it. By fostering students' engagement with classroom activities teachers connect students with the curriculum and make it effective for them. Others can make plans. Books and videos can present content to students and even test what they have learned, but only a teacher who knows the students personally and has established a personal relationship with them can motivate them to engage their hearts and minds in the activities.

A teacher who can work with students to create a classroom where study and learning are central, spontaneous, intrinsically rewarding, and self-sustaining can realize any curriculum. When teachers appraise other teachers, they value most their ability to motivate students. Researcher Lortie found in extensive interviews with teachers that they were "impressed by teachers who establish and sustain cordial, disciplined, and work-eliciting relationships with students" (Lortie, 1975, p. 133). The teacher's challenge is to persuade students to

- Grading
  What really counts? Test results? Homework? Participation? Effort? To what
    extent does the teacher base grading on subjective judgment versus objective
    performance?
- Norms for pupil conduct
  How hard should students work in class?
  How much homework is expected? How difficult?
  Are students' expected to interpret assignments in original ways or to follow
    instructions to the letter?
- Norms for classroom interactions and relationships
  Is helping forbidden or encouraged?
  Do students work alone or in groups?
  Do students cooperate or compete?
  Are students' work and teachers' evaluations of it shared in public or kept
    private between student and teacher?
- Expectations about the outside world
  Will what is studied in this class have a close relationship with life outside
    school?

FIG. 6.3. *Ground rules and procedures that shape students' perceptions of a classroom's curriculum.*

adopt the curriculum's goals as their own and then to help them keep their attention focused on the curriculum despite distractions. One important way teachers do this is by helping students to make sense of class activities. Students who understand why they are doing these activities can appreciate how they might contribute to their personal goals.

Modeling sends a powerful message. Students naturally assume that the way their teacher thinks and acts reflects the way other specialists in this subject think and act. The more they admire the teacher, the more they will want to learn what the teacher says is important and to become like the teacher. Teachers who motivate students to learn a subject may do them a great service if they then reveal the intrinsic character of the subject in an appealing way. But if students confuse their attitude toward the teacher with their attitude toward the subject, they may make decisions they will regret later.

Evaluate Students' Performance on Activities

Participating in an activity does not always guarantee that a student learns what the activity is designed to teach, and so teachers need to find ways to assess what students have learned. Teachers evaluate students' learning informally by examining the work they do during the activity in class and as homework. Tests are the most common formal method that teachers use to evaluate students' learning. Teachers may select test questions from the textbook, teachers' guide, or other curriculum materials provided by the school, they may look in other sources, or they may make their own test items. Occasionally a teacher may ask students to evaluate one another's work or use expert judges from outside the classroom to evaluate student work.

Devising an appropriate evaluation of an activity is an art in itself, and many books have been published to help teachers evaluate student learning better. The most fundamental considerations in designing evaluations are coverage of the activity's content and goals, difficulty, reliability, and validity. Ideally, the evaluation instruments teachers use should cover all of the important goals and content of the activity in proportion to their importance. The tasks selected for the evaluation should measure all the important goals, easy ones as well as more difficult ones. Reliable evaluation instruments give consistent results every time they are used. Making sure that instructions are clear and the items well crafted and ensuring that the instrument includes several items measuring the same learning are good ways to ensure reliability. Validity means that the specific items or tasks in the evaluation instrument should faithfully reflect the learning teachers are looking for.

For best results, teachers should deliver the results of evaluations to students as soon as possible and encourage students to review their performance and identify ways to improve.

Students Influence the Classroom Curriculum

Ultimately, formal education is a compact between children and adult society. Adults provide schools that give children a good opportunity to learn things that adults believe will be important for them throughout their lives and they expect students to make a good effort to learn. Students must accept on faith that what adults tell them to learn in school will eventually be worthwhile, even when they cannot appreciate its value and find it unappealing, betting their lives, literally, that adults know better. In many American subcultures, children pay adults this much respect and are even grateful that adults care enough to provide for them in this way. More commonly, though, children receive mixed messages from adults and choose to learn different things than their parents, local community, or school recommend.

No one, certainly not children, can know in advance what learning something new may mean to them. If I learn American history, I may discover something that challenges my patriotic ideals. A science course might undermine my religious faith. If I learn algebra, I may discover that I'm not good at advanced math and that my dreams of becoming a scientist are unrealistic. I may be bored, scared, or excited by what I learn. It may influence me to choose an occupation I never before imagined, decide to undertake years of further study, make new friends, and become a significantly different person.

If students avoid the risks of learning something new, they may never learn what they are capable of and what life has to offer them. The price of finding out is an investment of themselves—of time, energy, effort, attention, and courage, the courage to risk failure. When youngsters try to learn mathematics, for example, and their efforts meet with success, their investment of time and effort is repaid, and their faith in the institution that told them to study mathematics is justified. If failure comes too often and if benefits are rare and meager, faith in either self or others, or both, may falter.

As they mature, children should move gradually from complete dependence on adults to determine what they study toward the ability to make independent choices. Indeed, enabling students to make better decisions about their future learning is a major goal general education. The art lies in sustaining progress toward independence as a learner while maintaining high goals and standards. And this is a collaborative art. Students, teachers, curriculum-makers, and school and community leaders all contribute.

The Curriculum and Students' Actions

Regardless of how much direction, help, and influence a teacher may give, students must muster their personal abilities in active efforts to learn. The most fundamental thing students do that affects what they learn in school is simply to expose themselves to the classroom environment—to attend, to listen, to participate. To attend and participate presumes voluntary control of attention, willingness to exercise that control, and willingness to follow the direction of the teacher and the curriculum materials. Teachers' emphasis on such rules as "listen well," "follow instructions," and "do your best" testifies to the importance of attention and participation and also to students' tendency to need reminding. Students' main challenge in learning to control attention is to manage their emotions. They must block out other impulses that can arouse strong feelings, such as fear of failure, desire for adult approval, and desire for the attention of peers.

Beyond paying attention, students must manage a range of poorly understood personal learning processes in order to achieve the goals of a curriculum. Students process sensory input, recall it, relate it to their other knowledge, and think about it, or in psychological terms, students do cognitive processing. They also monitor their own state of knowledge or ignorance and make judgments about how well they are learning, what psychologists call metacognition. But not even psychologists know the details of the cognitive and metacognitive processes students must use on any specific classroom task. Both students and teachers are, for the most part, flying in the dark, guessing and speculating.

Conventional curriculums do not make assumptions about the details of each student's learning process. They simply give students an opportunity to learn something, assuming that most of them, most of the time, will learn it. Curriculums provide an opportunity to learn through very rough, crude, but powerful cognitive and social means. They set aside time and space for learning certain things. They provide an adult teacher who knows those things. They provide a group of peers to learn with. For securing children's engagement they rely on children's socialization to obey adult authorities and abide by adult rules and their desire to belong to social groups and participate in social activities. For presenting material to be learned, they rely on teachers' gestures and acting, pictures, and spoken language at first, and later on reading and writing.

From reason and experience, teachers determine what kinds of activities students can manage, and students for the most part respond to the activities in roughly the intended way and learn more or less what they are expected to learn. As Philip Jackson concluded from his review of a half century of research on children's attention to classroom activities:

> Although the amount of attention may vary considerably from class to class and even from minute to minute within a class, it would seem that most of the time most students are attending to the content of the lesson (Jackson, 1968, p. 101).

For the most part, when it comes to academic learning, students generally learn what they are taught in school and seldom learn what they are not taught (Walker & Schaffarzick, 1972). Cognitive science and computer technology may make it possible to monitor and control students' learning processes with a precision and power never before attainable. If so, new types of curriculum may be possible that offer precision learning opportunities tailored more precisely to each student's learning needs and preferences. Even then, curriculums that offer coarse, general opportunities to learn will remain the basis for most learning because they will be so cheap and easy to produce and use.

Students' Difficulties with Curriculums

Real curriculums do not always function as smoothly and powerfully as their designers hope. If they did, we would not hear so many calls for reform. For a variety of reasons, students often struggle and fail to learn everything that our curriculums supposedly give them an opportunity to learn. Whatever the ultimate causes of such failures, their immediate causes must lie in the students' interactions with the classroom curriculum.

Students may struggle to:

Maintain engagement with classroom activities
Comprehend classroom communication
Perform classroom activities
Advance on curriculum goals

Challenges of Realizing a Classroom Curriculum

Teachers know that realizing a curriculum in a classroom is not easy. As we have already seen, realizing even a familiar curriculum, let alone a new and innovative one, requires a great deal of skilled work from teachers. As we will now see, realizing a curriculum also poses many challenges to a teacher's knowledge and skill.

Teaching successfully requires teachers to juggle several important goals. Westbury (1978) lists four crucial goals that teachers must accomplish simultaneously:

1. Coverage—presenting certain topics, content, or material to students
2. Mastery—acquiring certain levels of achievement, demonstrating certain qualities of performance
3. Affect—maintaining positive feelings and attitudes in the classroom
4. Order—maintaining good conduct, discipline, and order in the classroom

Losing sight of any one of these four goals can cause a lesson or unit or entire school year to fail for a teacher.

By emphasizing one goal a teacher may make teaching easier day to day, but eventually students will fail to achieve important long-term goals. For instance, covering more topics in a superficial way (emphasizing content but sacrificing mastery) is likely to lead to lower scores on achievement tests and difficulties in learning later material that depends on mastery of the current content. Making satisfactory progress on all four in a reasonably balanced way is a challenge for teachers.

The following sections cover some other important challenges that teachers often face in realizing a curriculum and some ways teachers cope with them.

When Students Fail to Learn from Activities

When an activity "doesn't work" for whatever reason, teachers face a crucial decision: spend more time on the activity, try another activity, or move on to another topic, perhaps to return later. If they spend more time on the activity or try another, they take time that they had previously allocated for other learning. Will spending more time on the activity enable students to learn adequately, or would they stand a better chance with another activity? Would it be better to give up on this learning, at least for now, and move on? The cumulative result of a year's worth of such decisions can make the difference between a successful and an unsuccessful realization of the curriculum, between students who learn most of what the curriculum envisions and are prepared for their next step and those who do not and are not.

In order to respond appropriately teachers first need to recognize signs that students are not learning what they expected from an activity. Sometimes there are early signs: students ask many questions, seem puzzled, complain, misbehave, and avoid participating. The work they produce in class and as homework falls short of expectations. Even when teachers spot early signs that students are struggling, the best course of action may not be clear. Sometimes students learn important lessons by struggling to learn something that they find difficult.

A teacher who gives up too quickly deprives them of an opportunity to learn how to marshal their own resources to overcome this kind of difficulty. A teacher who lets students struggle too long, on the other hand, wastes time and risks discouraging them. It's not easy to judge when and how to intervene.

Experienced teachers probably weigh many competing factors to decide what to do when students fail to learn from an activity. How important is this material? Will students be hindered in learning later material if they fail to learn this? How much time would it take to learn this thoroughly, and what other learning would students forego if they spent more time on this? Would students stand a better chance of learning it if they revisited it after studying other material for awhile? To make these judgments teachers need an intimate and extensive knowledge of the students, the subject matter, and their own capabilities. Able, experienced teachers can often predict when students will have problems and have prepared contingency plans. Discovering how experienced teachers make these judgments is a wonderful problem for research.

The easy, natural, and seemingly humane response when students are having difficulty is to ease expectations in some way—allow more time, accept lower standards of performance, or delete difficult topics. This tactic is generally successful in lowering students' anxiety, maintaining their effort, and achieving scaled-back short-term results, but at the expense of long-range achievement and high expectations of students as learners of the subject. In extreme cases, students can graduate from high school virtually illiterate and only dimly aware of their disability because teachers consistently lowered their expectations, inflated grades, and passed the student along to the next grade.

When teachers consistently sacrifice curricular plans whenever students encounter difficulties, they communicate that mastery of the content and goals of the course is not really important. On the other hand, rigid adherence to a planned curriculum regardless of students' responses to it communicates a lack of concern for students. No one benefits when students are forced to keep up a pace they cannot sustain (or a pace they could easily increase) or to learn material that is too difficult (or too easy) for them.

Teachers can explore several options when their students have difficulties: increase motivation, employ more effective teaching methods, study in detail the difficulties students are having, and devise ways to overcome them. Dropping a topic or lowering expectations because students have difficulty with it should be a last resort and is always something of an admission of failure by the teacher, failure to realize the curriculum expected by the institution and the community.

Teachers can respond to failure more aggressively response by pushing the mastery/coverage/affect tradeoff even harder. Actively seek ways of helping students to succeed at difficult learning tasks. Vary the intensity and pace of the course to accustom students gradually to higher levels of performance. Seek out different types of activities that call upon different student aptitudes and abilities. Arrange for students to help one another to overcome difficulties. Try to find ways to help students learn to enjoy working hard and achieving success in spite of difficulties. Refuse to let them fail; insist on persistence and eventual success. Establish the attitude that everyone is expected to learn everything thoroughly and permanently, and let your tests and grading reflect this attitude. At all costs, avoid debasing and watering down the curriculum and lowering your expectations. At all costs, avoid putting students in situations where they will fail no matter what they do.

Teachers can forestall some problems by making sure that students understand what's expected of them and know how to do their best to meet those expectations. Early in the year, unless teachers make the expectations explicit, students can only guess what the year will be like. Will we be reading a lot? Will the reading be more difficult than we've done before? Will we be writing? How will you grade my writing? Will we be solving problems?

What kind? How many? How hard? What will I have to do to get an A? To pass? Will what I learn this year help me in other classes next year? Will it help me realize my dreams for my education, career, and life? Students will put out more or less effort depending on what they guess may be the answers to such questions. Their effort (or lack of it) will affect how they perform in the critical first few weeks of the year.

Activities are more likely to succeed when students know what kind of effort to make. Should they accept what the textbook says or question it? Should they take pains to write good prose or is it acceptable to produce lists of phrases and sentence fragments that show an understanding of the content? Should they memorize the solution to important types of problems or try to solve them on their own? Should they use their intuition or ignore it in favor of applying the principles they are learning?

When Students Resist the Curriculum

To realize a curriculum fully students need to give it their best effort. When teachers suspect that students are not doing their best, they need to find out why and find ways to engage students fully. Able, experienced teachers constantly probe and push to discover the best that students can do. They compare students' performances in various situations, looking for maximum effort and maximum success so that they can gauge effort and success better on a daily basis. They notice what motivates particular students and whole classes to intensify their effort and also what causes them to slack off.

Many factors may cause students to refuse to pay attention or participate or to put forth half-hearted efforts. The topic does not interest them. They don't believe that they will benefit from making the effort to learn it. They find it offensive or distasteful for some reason. They fear that they can't learn it no matter how hard they try. They are saving their energies for other things that are more important to them. They are distracted by other events in the classroom, the school, or their lives outside school. Teachers need to find the cause or causes and respond appropriately.

Students play active, overt roles in shaping their classroom curriculums, even when the authorities do not offer them any explicit choices. Students influence the pacing, the standards of mastery, the emphasis, and even the coverage of all their courses. By giving or withholding their cooperation, students can, in effect, bargain with teachers over the terms of their work in the classroom. Becker (1961), studying medical schools, coined the term "grade-performance exchange" for this negotiated agreement between teachers and students on the terms of their trade. The deal is that teachers award grades in exchange for specified levels of performance from students. When teachers make it more difficult for students to achieve high grades, students counter by making classroom life more difficult for teachers. They may complain or misbehave or withhold responses they know the teacher wants, such as friendliness, enthusiasm, timely delivery of assigned work, or even class attendance and attentiveness, in an effort to induce the teacher to adopt more favorable terms of exchange.

A class where students hold the teacher's performance demands to a minimum may cover less content and realize less lofty goals than another in which students and teacher negotiate a grade-performance exchange that calls for higher performance standards. Speaking informally with students in a high-income, academically oriented Bay Area high school, I found that some of them made quite intricate calculations of the time and effort they needed to allocate to different activities in order to achieve the grades and honors they wanted. When a teacher made extra demands that upset students' plans, the students said that they would tell the teacher that the assignment interfered with their other work and ask the teacher to cut back their demands. Teachers in this school reported feeling pressures from students and from parents anxious about their children's academic success.

Some teachers reported that such pressures led them to organize their courses more fully in advance, to make the terms of their grade-performance exchange explicit, and to limit or drop open-ended assignments, surprise quizzes, and anything else that added to the uncertainty of the grade-performance exchange. The phenomenon noted by Doyle (1977), that students work to reduce the ambiguity and risk they bear in the grade performance exchange, seems widespread, perhaps universal. And it can play a major role in shaping the classroom curriculum.

Sometimes students actively oppose the established curriculum as an act of rebellion against authority. In a passage in his novel, *The Ogre* (1972), the French writer Michel Tournier shows the protagonist as a student rejecting the school curriculum.

> I had crossed out the teachers, and the world of the mind into which they were supposed to initiate us. I had got to the point—but have I ever been at any other?—of considering every author, historical personage or book, any educational subject whatever, as automatically null and void as soon as it was annexed by adults and dished out to us as spiritual nourishment (Tournier, 1972, p. 10).

Rejection of the official curriculum by rebellious students is commonplace in classroom life and poses a challenge to a teacher's authority as well as expertise.

Curriculum studies offer little guidance for teachers on how to win over such rebels to constructive engagement or, indeed, when to consider changing the curriculum so that it deserves their engagement. Some teachers and schools treat rebels firmly, refusing to discuss their objections and insisting that they conform to authority. Others believe in a genuine dialogue with rebels that leaves open the possibility of changing the curriculum to accommodate their objections. By far the most thoughtful treatment of this issue is Joseph Schwab's *College Curriculum and Student Protest* (1969). Teachers of young children will find little they can use here, though.

When many students are chronically disengaged from curriculum activities, teachers face a career-threatening crisis. Possible causes are numerous: students discouraged by a history of school failure; inadequate teaching skills; inadequate knowledge of the subject; an inappropriate curriculum; distractions from outside activities such as sports, dating, jobs, or violence; negative attitudes toward school in the community; and so on.

In most cases where students chronically do not engage with school curriculum a combination of deep causes is probably at work. Anthropologist John Ogbu studied low achieving students in a California high school and found that many were happy with grades of C or even D. They felt satisfied that they passed. The students Ogbu interviewed also believed that they knew something simply because they had been exposed to it, whether they had mastered it or not. Their attitude was "I've had that already." The curriculum materials provided enough easy material to give all students the impression that they were succeeding, no matter how little effort they expended or how meager the results. Teachers failed to make it clear to these students and their parents that their performance would not qualify them for further schooling and employment (Ogbu, 1974). Somehow, nothing students encountered in school conveyed to them a realistic appraisal of their performance. It is not easy to convince young people to raise their sights when they think their progress is satisfactory.

Many times students enter a subject with strong prejudices that interfere with their learning. An adolescent female may dislike science and avoid studying it because she thinks it is not feminine. A teacher can accept such prejudices and excuse the youngster from all science that is not strictly required of all students. Alternatively, a teacher can introduce that student to science in ways that might overcome her prejudice, perhaps by including in early classes some science content more likely to appeal to females or by showcasing the work of a scientist who happens to be female.

Students would be better able to manage their own learning efforts if they were more involved in decisions about purpose, content, and structure of their classes. At the very least teachers should share with students the plans for their courses and their rationales for them. If the material is required, students should understand why those responsible for their education consider this material important enough to require them to learn it. When students have curricular choices, they should receive information about the consequences of their choices. What other topics or subjects will they be enabled to study if they succeed in learning this one, and what kinds of careers will be open to them?

Students also shape the curriculum. If their influence is so often negative, it is surely at least in part because they are unaware of the eventual costs they bear when they use strategies that reduce the expectations placed on them. Our aim should surely be to encourage students to think of the curriculum as an opportunity and of meeting curricular standards as both a valuable accomplishment and a matter of personal pride. If curriculum professionals cannot wholeheartedly recommend the curriculum to students in such terms, they should devote their energies to improving the curriculum until they can.

When Some Students Succeed and Others Fail

More than any other kind of curriculum work, realizing curriculum plans brings teachers face to face with individual and group differences and confronts them with hard choices about equity. Sometimes teachers make curriculum adjustments that are favorable for some students but unfavorable for others. For instance a pace that most students find comfortable may be too fast for some and too slow for others. What pace is fair?

It is wonderful when a curriculum decision happens to be best for all students, but the hard question is what to do when every choice serves some students better than others.

- Favor the high achievers. They deserve it, they've achieved what the curriculum asked of them, they are likely to benefit most and to make the greatest contribution to society, and they can be an inspiration to others by setting high standards of excellence.
- Favor the low achievers. They have the greatest need, they will suffer more if they fail, they will be a greater burden on society if they are not adequately educated.
- Treat all students equally. If one decision favors high achievers, let another decision favor those at the low end of achievement.
- Insist on activities that work best for all. Use multiple representations and multiple abilities. Let students work together in collaborative teams. Make teams responsible for all members' learning. Clearly the best solution when you can do it, and a wonderful vision to strive for, but is it practical? Can we find such activities for the whole curriculum? Does this approach really work or does it still hold back the ablest and short-change the least competent?

Individualization is not necessarily a solution, because some students may do less well in an individualized program than they would have done in a common program.

This is probably one of those so-called "wicked" problems that have no completely satisfactory solution. Every curriculum is a compromise that leaves some students with a curriculum that is not optimal for them. And so every curriculum leaves sensitive teachers feeling dissatisfied and searching for something better. Slogans such as "education for all," "meeting every student's needs," or "equal educational opportunity for all" inspire us and signify our intention to treat all students fairly, but they do not help teachers make difficult choices. Some teachers accept the dilemma and endure a bittersweet situation. Idealists, perfectionists, and passionate advocates find it impossible to accept curriculums that disadvantage some students. The struggle to distribute these inevitable injustices in a generally acceptable way is the source of much recurrent curricular conflict.

When Activities Drift and Lack Focus

Sometimes teachers select wonderful daily activities that students participate in with gusto and learn as the teacher hoped they would, and yet somehow the learning doesn't add up to a deep understanding of anything important. Each individual activity succeeded, but the whole curriculum failed to cumulate to deeper understanding.

The problem here is an unprincipled choice of activities. Instead of selecting activities to fulfill a larger long-term purpose, the teacher or the outside curriculum maker whom the teacher follows adopted a shortsighted policy. Usually this happens when teachers overemphasize narrow practicality in choosing activities. Doyle and Ponder (1977) suggest that teachers' emphasis on practicality probably arises from the overwhelming demands that more principled choices would place on teachers' time and expertise. Teachers look for ways to economize and an ethic of practicality results.

Teachers' guides should suggest activities that cumulate. If they do, and if teachers follow them, this problem should not arise. But it does. Teachers' guides may suggest many optional activities in an effort to appeal to teachers' varied interests, leaving teachers with the responsibility for ensuring continuity and cumulation. Also, teachers' guides may only roughly sketch activities or give many options, again hoping to accommodate diversity of teaching styles, but leaving teachers with the responsibility for ensuring continuity and cumulation.

Sometimes districts provide detailed scripts that link activities to district and state goals and examinations. The public schools in Chicago, for example, supply every teacher with what amounts to a script for every lesson, "a detailed, day-by-day outline of what he or she should be teaching—and when—in the language arts, mathematics, science and social studies" (*New York Times*, November 26, 1999). These lesson plans also identify the section of the district-approved standardized test to which that lesson contributes. Under what conditions regimenting teaching in this way may lead to better results than allowing teachers more freedom in planning their own activities is a fascinating and controversial question.

When Teachers Object to Curriculum Frames and Mandates

When teachers believe that the frames that govern their classroom curriculum are limiting, harmful, or otherwise unacceptable, they face an ethical dilemma. If they follow the mandated curriculum, they betray their professional obligation to offer students the best possible education. If they violate the governing frames established by the appropriate authorities, they betray their professional obligations to the school system, to the community, and to the state.

Teachers should try to resolve such dilemmas by working to change the frame or by securing official exemption from it. When teachers deviate from the prescribed materials without the blessing of school authorities, they assume full ethical and legal responsibility, whereas the authority of the institution protects them if they use the materials provided. On the other hand, school systems incur serious costs if they try to force teachers to comply with frames they object to.

Sustaining a School Curriculum

Officials in schools and school districts make curriculum decisions that guide and constrain what teachers and students do in the classroom in direct and powerful ways. The school leaders and representatives of the local community who participate in these decisions affect the curriculum in hundreds or thousands of classrooms. To understand their work and the challenges they face in making curriculum decisions we need to understand schools. Schools vary enormously depending on their tradition, organization, budget, and the communities they serve. The image of school used in this section is a composite intended to reflect the mainstream of American public schools. It is essentially bureaucratic with occasional unconventional elements. Readers with a passion for a particular unconventional type of school can reflect on how well the points in this section apply to the schools that interest them.

The main features of the school curriculum are deeply ingrained in the operations of school and school system. One can no more separate a real curriculum from its school than one can separate a skeleton from the body it supports. The school system organizes its personnel, schedule, and facilities by curriculum categories, i.e., school subjects. Many teachers' professional identities are tied to the subjects they teach. Courses, textbooks, tests, and other teaching/learning materials are organized by curricular area. To understand the school curriculum, we must understand schools.

American Public Schools

Here are nine propositions about schools that help to explain what's involved in sustaining a school curriculum.

1. Schools are like communities.
   They include people with diverse purposes who "live" there. They are not single-purpose organizations with a bottom line of profit or loss where people only work.
2. Schools allocate significant life opportunities.
   Success in school entitles students to more challenging educational opportunities and marks them as candidates for desirable occupations and for leadership roles in society. This close tie between economic and social advancement and schools shows up most strikingly in the awarding of grades, tracking or selective admission to courses or activities, and the awarding of honors and credentials, but it also affects most other aspects of schools' operation.
3. Most schools maintain diversified educational programs.
   Beyond the elementary grades nearly all schools offer electives and many offer a choice among several different tracks, multiyear programs of education, such as an arts program, a science program, or a vocational or academic track.
4. Schools are formal institutions.
   They are established by the authority of the state and run by government, in the case of public schools, or regulated by government, in the case of private schools.
5. Schools are workplaces.
   Teachers, principals, secretaries, janitors, and other employees work there. Many teachers love schools but have serious problems with them as workplaces. One investigator (Corcoran, 1988, p. 156) listed 16 working conditions that teachers identified as problems including low salaries, large class size, heavy workload, inadequate

preparation time, lack of opportunities for professional growth, and undesirable student behavior and attitudes.

6. School–community ties are close and strong.

As one student of the subject puts it, "Almost nothing happens in a school that is not or cannot become the community's business" (Saxe, 1975, p. 9). School activities, such as athletics, arts performances, and school-affiliated clubs, are often a vital part of community life. Many local employers fill their entry-level positions with graduates from the local school system. In small communities the school are a major employer. Schools will seldom stray far from a course approved by the local community. Also, any community problem that concerns school-age children will probably be confronted at school, including dangerous driving, delinquency, drug abuse, or teenage pregnancy.

7. Schools support a rich informal social life.

Schools are a collection of social niches with distinctive goals. In order to exercise authority over the local curriculum formal leaders must cultivate influence over those who control the various social niches.

8. Teachers are nearly autonomous in their classroom.

Teachers do not work in truly interdependent teams like the cast of a play or a team of surgeons. The typical school more nearly resembles a building full of dentists' offices that offer professional services independently. Teachers are monitored lightly in most school systems once their initial probationary period has passed, and the sanctions available to those who evaluate teachers are few and weak.

9. Schools are organizations.

They have a formal administrative and governance structure. The principal is responsible for assignment and evaluation of all personnel, for preparing and administering the school budget, for establishing and enforcing schoolwide policies, and so on. In secondary schools, teachers are assigned to departments, in elementary schools to grade level teams. Channels of authority lead from student to teacher up to the principal and then to the superintendent and board of education. Figure 6.4 lists some additional organizational characteristics that apply to most schools.

School Curriculum Leaders

The school principal has potentially a more important voice in curriculum decisions than any other person in the school, but few principals choose to exercise that voice. Most prefer to delegate it to other school curriculum leaders, leaders that principals often appoint. Other positions that school curriculum leaders often hold include vice-principal for curriculum and instruction, department chair, team leader, or mentor teacher. Unofficially, respected senior teachers, counselors, school psychologists, or librarians may lead in certain school curriculum matters.

Principals control the purse strings. Each school will normally have its own budget drawn up by the principal and approved by the superintendent's chief financial officer. Teachers who need funds to implement a curriculum change request them from the principal. Principals also must approve grant proposals required to obtain outside funding.

Principals hold power over teachers that they can transform into curriculum influence if they wish. Principals select new teachers. They evaluate teachers' work performance, with such consequences as pay increases (in school districts with merit pay), desirable classes, assignment to special committees and projects, and promotion. They appoint persons to leadership positions as department chair, team leader, counselor, vice-principal, and so on.

Schools are traditional organizations.
People judge them by how well they sustain certain valued activities more than by their results.

Schools are custodial institutions.
One group (adult citizens) maintains them to serve another group (students), who are compelled to attend and not allowed to determine how the institution is to be run. Custodial institutions have trouble enlisting enthusiastic participation from their charges. Also, schools are caught in the middle when these two groups conflict.

Schools are organizations of professionals.
Professionals claim expertise and corresponding discretion in their practice. Professionals demand a greater voice in the operation of their organizations, and nonprofessionals are excluded from judging the quality of work done by professionals. Work is lightly supervised.

Schools and school systems are aggregates rather than true hierarchies.
Schools are collections of classrooms; districts are collections of schools; state systems are collections of districts; the organization grows by adding new units, which are treated organizationally like the existing ones.

Units of school systems are loosely coupled.
The various units aggregated in a school organization are only loosely coupled with one another.
   They are loosely tied by authority, exchange few resources, and seldom communicate about vital matters and are therefore poorly equipped for coordinated action. State departments of education are loosely coupled to school districts, districts to schools, and schools to classrooms.

Work in schools is not very interdependent.
Division of labor is infrequent and unimportant; the work of one teacher depends little on that of another.

Schools have only weak organizational incentives.
Securing conformity to the school's purposes is therefore more difficult.

Schools are labor intensive.
They make very little use of capital goods to increase productivity.

FIG. 6.4. *Some organizational characteristics of schools.*

The principal can set schoolwide policies and regulations that affect curriculum; policies on record-keeping by teachers, on assignment of homework, on grading, and on field trips, and similar matters that affect what an individual teacher can and cannot do in the classroom. Principals have closer contact with parents than teachers do and can mediate between parents and teachers on curriculum matters. Some schools have a school–community council whose community members may be chosen by election but whose professional members are usually appointed by the principal. In some cases principals work closely with the council while in other cases principals try to isolate and ignore them. Principals are the official contact with the local school system and through them with state and federal agencies.

Perhaps the principal's greatest power is the power to organize curriculum work. The principal has broad authority to call teachers' meetings, appoint committees, schedule workshops, establish teacher teams, and generally to determine how all the work of the school gets done.

The greatest limitations on the principal's leadership in curriculum matters are laws and regulations, the press of other responsibilities, the need to secure cooperation from teachers, and the impossibility of being sufficiently expert in all curriculum areas. The job of school curriculum leadership is too big for any individual. Principals usually lead in curriculum matters with a team approach. They keep in touch with leaders of all constituencies and create a vision that represents their own priorities as well as those of other key stakeholders. They select and cultivate teacher–leaders who can help them realize this vision and appoint them to open positions of formal leadership when an opportunity arises. Some choose to work with others who hold different visions and priorities while others try to win them over or to defeat them.

The Central Office

The central office of the school district usually includes a number of curriculum leaders who work with the schools in the district. Most districts have a chief curriculum officer in charge of curriculum matters for the district. This leader may be an assistant or associate superintendent for curriculum and instruction, a curriculum coordinator, a director of curriculum, or hold another similar title. In some districts most curriculum policies and guidelines are established districtwide, while in others most decisions about curriculum are left to individual schools. In many districts supervisors are assigned to coordinate the programs of, say, English and language arts throughout the schools in the district. Districts may also administer standardized tests to the students in every school and use the results as an indicator of the quality of the school and of the work of its staff. Textbooks and curriculum materials are usually selected on a districtwide basis, both because unit costs are lower in larger orders and because it helps to coordinate the curriculums of the various schools within the district.

Let us look in more detail at the local school system.

Governance of Public Schools

Local school systems are staffed, managed, and operated by professional educators answerable to a public governing board representing the local community. The board is legally responsible for the operation of the school system and approves all major actions. The school board contracts with a superintendent of schools to administer the local system according to their policies. The superintendent chooses professionals to operate the school system, subject to board approval. Most superintendents delegate responsibility for curriculum to a deputy or assistant superintendent or a director of curriculum or curriculum coordinator.

The line of authority for operating individual schools usually runs directly from the superintendent to the principal of an individual school. Officers in intervening positions, referred to here as central office staff, may be delegated certain of the superintendent's powers in relation to principals, but principals do not normally report to them. The principal is usually responsible for all aspects of the operation of the local school, though in some districts central office directives closely circumscribe the principal's authority, especially over curriculum. Many schools have school–community councils with equal representation of parents and teachers who must approve all major curriculum actions.

While in theory this board has complete legal authority over the affairs of the district, in practice they must depend upon the superintendent and the professional staff to make most decisions and confine themselves to setting goals, making policy, and resolving serious issues. This makes school administrators the crucial link between school and community.

Local school districts' control of their schools is not complete and seems to be gradually eroding. They are subject to a wide variety of pressures and influences from many organizations, official and unofficial, national, state and local. State and national constitutions and laws may, for example, require schools to offer certain courses, set high school graduation requirements, specify in detail the health and safety requirements of all school buildings, establish procedures for hiring, awarding tenure, and dismissing teachers, and even set limits to the amount of money local districts may collect in taxes, despite the wishes of taxpayers.

Boards and top administrators spend a substantial part of their time on meetings and paperwork required by external authorities. Collective bargaining agreements with teachers' organizations limit local school boards' control. State, national, and even international influences on local public schools are increasing. Some board members, superintendents, and observers consider that such encroachments on local authority have become so extensive as to threaten the principle of local control. Nevertheless, local school boards retain considerable authority and can, with determination, when supported by the local community, be decisive on any issue not directly governed by state or federal law.

Local School Politics Are Distinctive

Political scientists assure us that "a governmental unit with an elected governing board making policies cannot exist in a democracy without politics" (Iannaccone & Lutz, 1970, p. 16). Yet "getting the schools out of politics" was a major goal of American educational reformers for more than half a century. The result of these efforts was to create a unique form of low profile, decorous but unrepresentative local politics of education that can often be surprisingly unresponsive to the wishes of the local populace.

In most communities, a relatively small in-group of laypeople involve themselves in local school affairs. Like school board members, they tend to be better educated than their communities, more prosperous, older, and economically and politically more conservative. These are the "supporters of the public schools." Iannaccone and Lutz (1970) speak of "a politics of insiders," "invisible politics," and "a closed system."

> A civic cocoon of advisory groups, lay committees, parent–teacher organizations, grade mothers, Girl Scout Brownies, and athletic boosters surround, politically protect, and nurture the local educational leaders in school district matters. . . . Here the discussions and debate of proposed solutions for school district problems takes place before these solutions are put before the school board (Iannaccone & Lutz, 1970, p. 15).

The insiders discourage open public conflict on school issues. Tucker and Zeigler (1980) found that found that the 11 boards they studied voted unanimously 85% of the time. "Of greatest importance (to boards) is unanimity in decision-making, especially voting decisions. Dissent should be minimized and should not be articulated once a majority position has been established" (Tucker & Zeigler, 1980, p. 133). They quote a manual for school board members as stating: "Nothing is more damaging to a board—to its internal relations or its prestige with the public—than for a board member to quarrel publicly with a decision a board has made" (p. 133).

The effect of conflict avoidance is to dampen debate and forestall direct confrontation of contending parties. The politics that results is the "low-pressure, invisible politics of the initiated rather than the high pressure, colorful politics of the marketplace" (Iannacone &

Lutz, 1970), a politics that seeks consensus by polite, informal means rather than by facing conflict directly and seeking to negotiate a resolution. Since a certain amount of difference of opinion is inevitable in any community, even among the elite, avoiding controversy implies that differences must be worked out quietly behind the scenes before the matter is raised officially in public. This behind-the-scenes preliminary discussion takes place in a variety of school–community forums populated largely by influential laypeople and professional leaders.

Once an issue emerges from the murky world of informal school politics and becomes a formal proposal put before the board by the superintendent, the board's options are limited. The board is faced with the extreme alternatives of accepting or rejecting staff recommendations *in toto*. The voters' choices are even more limited. Voters must often choose between moderate candidates who support the local establishment and extremists adamantly opposed to some policy but with no constructive alternative vision.

Thus, while the formal governance mechanism of public schools appears to be democratic, even populist, the effect of keeping schools out of politics has been anti-democratic. It has created a behind-the-scenes informal local school politics dominated by community elites and professional leaders. In many communities this type of politics insulates schools from the voting public most of the time and deprives most voters and taxpayers of any direct say in the running of local schools.

School Administrators Link Communities and Their Schools

School administrators link schools to the formal social, economic, and political institutions of the community. Administrators mediate all of the community's contacts with the school. This linking role puts administrators in a pivotal position that is both powerful and risky: powerful because only the link knows about and deals with the total situation, risky because the parties to be linked have different interests and tend to have different views on educational questions. Community members, for instance, tend to favor more traditional teaching practices and procedures for grading, promotion, and the like, than the teachers who staff their schools (Gross, 1958).

Administrators insulate teachers and community members from potential occasions for conflict and, as if in return, administrators gain greater influence over school operations. Where the community elite and top school administrators share stable educational priorities, the schools will reflect them, even when teachers or the majority of the community do not share them. In theory, an alliance between teachers and a grass-roots community majority could overcome the combined power of top administrators and the community elite, but such an alliance is improbable because of the extreme differences in educational views and values that typically separate these two groups.

School–community interaction centers on relations between the school board and the school administration. Tucker and Zeigler (1980) studied the operations of local school boards in 11 school systems in the Northwest "to explore the extent to which school district officials are responsive to their lay publics" (p. 6). The title of their report, "Professionals Versus the Public: Attitudes, Communication, and Response in School Districts" reveals their conclusion. They found that school administrators dominated school board meetings. Administrators set the agenda and put forward nearly all the proposals the board considers. They provide the board's only source of professional advice and expertise. Administrators regularly make their policy preferences known, and boards accept nearly all administrator recommendations.

One of the first generation of strong superintendents, Carleton Washburne, describes his relationship with the Winnetka, Illinois, Board of Education this way:

Legally, the Board of Education has all power, the superintendent none. But the Board, if it is wise, delegates most of its power on all professional matters to the superintendent.... It was ... my responsibility and that of my successors to see that the board did not step out of its role and interfere with the detailed administration of the schools, or try to substitute lay judgment for the professional decisions of the teaching and supervisory staff of the schools (Washburne & Marland, 1963, p. 149).

Administrative dominance is particularly great on issues of curriculum and instruction. Tucker and Zeigler assert that "virtually all studies which classify issues coming to the attention of the board find that the educational program receives scant school board attention" (p. 11). They note that "In most districts, the school board agenda is devoted largely to housekeeping matters. Conspicuously absent from these agendas are topics of educational governance.... Also curious is the small proportion of discussion devoted to curriculum matters" (pp. 113–114).

In relations with other community groups, the superintendent attracts attempts to influence the schools like a lightning rod. When influence attempts conflict with one another or with district plans or procedures, the superintendent becomes the focus of conflict. Many superintendents find that they must assume an overtly political role if they are to manage this conflict. Blumberg (1985) quotes a superintendent he interviewed as saying: "Being political means having a real sense of the workings of groups—power groups, pressure groups, decision-making processes. You're dealing with different constituencies, with people interacting with each other with their own special interests. And you really have to have that all sorted out so that you can anticipate their reactions. You have to be political!" (p. 54).

Principals must manage conflict between teachers and parents. Teachers feel vulnerable when they confront parents or community members who challenge their professional authority. McPherson (1972) in *Small Town Teacher* entitles her remarks on this subject "Natural Enemies: Teachers and Parents." She quotes one experienced teacher in her school:

Whatever you do is wrong with the parents. You have to be so careful what you say. I won't give any more F's. It's not worth the struggle with them (p. 124).

Parents feel equally helpless. McPherson quotes one parent as saying:

What can a parent do? You bring up your child as well as you can and then you send him off to school. He has all kinds of teachers—cruel ones and ones without any experience—and when you try to object to something, they give you the runaround. It is frightening (p. 125).

Parents expect principals, as public officials, to defend their interests. After all, they are taxpayers, clients, and members of the community that governs the school. Teachers, on the other hand, expect principals, as professionals, to defend their interests. Saxe puts the matter in these terms:

Teachers ... look to administrators to protect them from parents. And, because teaching is so far from being a science, the teacher expects precisely that the administrator will back him in all situations, whether he has acted wisely or unwisely, rightly or wrongly. The belief among teachers is that a united front must be presented to outsiders and that any criticism of the teacher that the administrator might have must be delayed until the confrontation is over and then given in strictest confidence (Saxe, 1975, p. 27).

Their monopoly of the school–community linkage gives local school administrators a great deal of power in dealing with those curriculum issues in which the community takes an active interest. It should come as no surprise that the fate of any proposal to change the local school curriculum depends most upon the attitudes, talents, and actions of the principal and the superintendent. But even they cannot override determined opposition from community leadership.

Concluding Note: Why Are Schools Bureaucratic?

Probably the most frequent criticism made of schools is the prevalence of rigid and deadly routine. Much of the rule-bound quality of school can be explained as an adaptation to a few basic characteristics all schools share. First, they are crowded. Compared to homes, offices, stores, and factories, schools have more people per square foot of floor space than virtually any other setting. When we consider that the people involved are immature and therefore not fully socialized, we can appreciate that rules are needed simply to avoid bedlam. Second, schools are compulsory. This places a heavy custodial burden on them. Schools are legally obligated to know where students are all the time and to provide adult supervision for them wherever they may be. Third, schools are heavily regulated. This means that records are required to substantiate everything. Fourth, the expectations various publics hold for what should be accomplished by the school are, taken altogether, many times greater than the schools could possibly meet. Following official policy enables teachers and school leaders protect themselves from charges that they failed to meet these expectations.

Schools adapt to these conditions by instituting routines or standard operating procedures. Establishing and enforcing such routines as fixed class periods, daily schedules, hall passes, and written excuses for tardiness and absences inconveniences everybody, but the chaos that would result without them would be even more inconvenient and unmanageable besides.

Even though schools are service organizations doing "people work," they must establish routines, and this creates a tension that can be troublesome. Idealistic beginning teachers, attracted to teaching as an opportunity to help young people, may be upset to find that they must play the role of rule-enforcer. Others are temperamentally attracted to the enforcer role to such an extent that the rules become an end in themselves rather than a necessary evil. Different schools resolve this tension differently. A curriculum that works fine under one set of routines may sputter under another. For example, a biology program that calls for frequent field work on school grounds or in nearby parks may work fine in a school that tolerates hall traffic, but be unworkable in a school where doors must be locked and halls patrolled by guards. Making a curriculum work within a particular school's routines is one of the important skills of local curriculum work.

The School Curriculum

Schools Set the Main Features of the Curriculum

Decisions made at the school level set the major frames for work at the classroom level. School decisions determine how the students' time in the school will be divided up, what classes or subjects will be offered, requirements for entrance and for graduation, what teachers will be hired, and what books will be used.

The school curriculum is shaped by many school level decisions, among which three stand out as fundamental.

1. What learning opportunities (conventionally bundled as courses) the school will offer.
2. How to coordinate those opportunities over the years of a student's school career.
3. Conditions of access to the school's learning opportunities.

Considered together, these three decisions about the school have a greater impact on what teachers teach and students learn than any others. Compared to them, such decisions as textbook selection, course of study development, and selection of tests are mere details.

Schools typically represent their curriculum in documents that can be reviewed, approved, and disseminated as official school policy. Figures 1.2 and 1.4 in Chapter 1 show samples of two often-used types of curriculum documents, a scope and sequence chart and a content × behavior grid. Some schools also produce teachers' guides.

To understand the school curriculum more deeply, we must recall that the curriculum is a pattern in the operations of a school, not a specific set of activities. In order to track the school curriculum through the jungle of school operations, we need a concept that focuses our attention on the abstract pattern. Opportunity to learn is the concept we need.

School Curriculum as Learning Opportunities

A school can be thought of as giving students opportunities to learn. The following are some of the components of opportunity to learn.

1. A source that presents what is to be learned in a form comprehensible to the student, such as a textbook or teacher.
2. Time and space, free of distractions, for students to comprehend the message and incorporate it with their previous learning.
3. Signs singling out this particular information as more important to learn than other information present in the environment.
4. A procedure for determining whether the item has been learned well enough.
5. A person who has mastered the information and can guide students in their efforts to comprehend it and help them overcome difficulties.
6. Incentives for students to apply themselves to this learning task until they succeed.
7. Equipment or facilities needed to learn.

We may think of these seven items as facets of a learning opportunity. In contemporary schools these are provided by:

Qualified teachers (1, 3, 4, 5, 6)
Suitably equipped classrooms (2, 7)
Textbooks (1, 4)
Tests (4, 6)
Curriculum materials and apparatus (7).

If students' learning is to be cumulative then the learning opportunities they encounter must be coordinated with one another over an entire school career. Schools accomplish this coordination by such means as:

Designations of requirements and electives
Time allotments
School schedules
Entrance requirements and standards
Graduation requirements and standards.

We can speak of the school curriculum, then, as the learning opportunities provided in and by the school, together with the conditions and constraints schools attach to them.

Stability and Change in School Curriculums

The school curriculum is sturdy, built to last. Course offerings continue from year to year unless something happens to cause a change. The one who makes the school schedule starts with last year's schedule then makes only necessary changes. Adding a new offering is difficult; dropping one is only slightly easier. Textbooks have a useful life of 7 to 10 years. Tests do not change greatly from year to year. Teachers have tenure and in most communities the turnover rate among teachers is low. Only enough funds are budgeted for curriculum revision to permit a small fraction of the total offerings to be officially reconsidered each year.

Yet change does come. This year's students choose different electives than last year's students. Some teachers leave and new ones are hired and the qualifications of the incoming teacher never exactly match those of the departing one, so adjustments in teaching assignments or even course offerings may be needed. When new principals, superintendents, or central office staff members assume their posts, they often sponsor curriculum changes. Textbooks wear out and become obsolete. Tests and test norms do change from year to year and in a few years can drift noticeably.

Most important, the preferences and expectations of teachers, parents, and school leaders can change, leading to calls for curriculum reform. Curriculum reform movements often inspire changes in local course offerings—the addition of advanced placement courses or, in earlier years, courses on black literature. And offerings change simply because teachers get bored teaching the same course, lose enthusiasm, and need refreshment.

These forces for change chip away at the neatly planned school curriculum and, unless someone pays careful attention, a strong, coherent, well-focused curriculum can become a miscellaneous collection of courses in a year or two. In some schools, the disruptions are so great that even the best efforts of everyone involved are not enough to maintain the quality of the school curriculum. It does not take much to disrupt a school curriculum. Two or three of the following happenings in one year could be enough to threaten the quality of a good school curriculum:

- resignation of a few key teachers,
- appointment of a new principal or superintendent,
- curriculum controversy in the community,
- a teacher strike,
- a hotly contested school issue on the ballot,
- enrollment increases or declines, or
- changes in the demographic composition of the community.

When too much change happens school leaders must give up all hope of achieving improvements and do their best to hold the line. In fact, during good times and bad, most of the energy and resources devoted to curriculum work in schools goes simply to maintain a desired level of service and quality.

Maintaining the Quality of the School Curriculum

Maintaining the quality of a school's curriculum, even when nobody's complaining and no improvement projects are under way, can be a struggle. The work needed to keep the curriculum going is seldom conspicuous. For the most part, it is folded into the routines of running a school. For example, ordering textbooks is an essential part of maintaining a school's curriculum, but it is often treated as a routine part of the requisitioning of supplies. Securing teachers qualified to teach what is offered in the curriculum is clearly an essential part of maintaining a good curriculum, yet this function is typically assigned to a personnel department that operates independently of the curriculum planning process. Assigning teachers and pupils to classes is an essential part of maintaining a curriculum, yet scheduling is generally treated as a routine administrative chore. Thus, the small fraction of the effort of running a school that is devoted specifically to curriculum work is mostly accomplished as part of general administrative tasks, and distributed widely among different branches of the school and district organization. Let us call this work, these low-profile, routine but important tasks, curriculum management.

Nearly all of the resources and time devoted to curriculum goes to curriculum management. One of the foremost students of educational innovation, Matthew B. Miles, laments this fact:

> The major portion of available energy goes to carrying out routine operations and maintenance of existing relationships within the system. Thus the fraction of energy left over for matters of diagnosis, planning, innovation, deliberate change and growth is ordinarily very small (Miles, 1964, p. 437).

When we consider the small amount of energy available, it is no cause for wonder that most of it is consumed in curriculum management. The paramount concern in day-to-day management of a school curriculum must therefore be conserving resources, time, and energy. The work of maintaining the quality of the school curriculum must be reduced to routines to minimize the demands on these limited resources. Like washing dishes, brushing teeth, and servicing the car, curriculum management is essential maintenance.

School Routines

Smooth school routines are the most common indicator people use to define good school administration, just as smooth classroom routines are the most common criterion of success for teachers, and for the same reason: to make such complex social systems function at all requires an exacting discipline. The school routines that do the most to structure curriculum management activities in contemporary schools are:

scheduling
the organization of professional staff
ordering curriculum materials
provisions for in-service education
teacher performance assessment procedures
arrangements for monitoring and advising students

The School Schedule

The schedule is the master school routine. It brings together teachers, students, curriculum materials, and facilities and provides a framework for assigning purposes to occasions. It defines the curriculum offerings of the school on a yearly time scale. Teachers adjust their activities to fit the length of school periods, the rhythm of the school week, and the scope of the school year. All other school officials match their schedules to the school schedule. For example, textbook adoption must be completed so that books arrive on time for the start of classes, and new teachers must be hired so that they arrive then. Because so much else depends upon it, the construction of the school schedule is perhaps the single most powerful tool school leadership has for shaping the school curriculum.

The dictates of the schedule are most consequential for the more peripheral elements of the curriculum. The academic core of elementary education—reading, writing, and arithmetic—and secondary education—English, math, and required science, social studies, and physical education courses—can be expected to appear on every master schedule as a matter of routine. But more peripheral subjects must struggle for a place in the schedule every year in life or death competition with other subjects for students' elective choices. The school schedule may substantially affect the nature and quality, if not the existence, of offerings even in core academic subjects. The number of semesters or sections of an established subject may be increased or reduced. Optional elective course offerings in a required subject may be expanded or reduced. Students of varying abilities may be distributed in various ways across the courses in a core academic subject.

School Staff Organization

How the teachers and school administrators employed by the school are deployed, the roles they are asked to play, how responsibilities are allocated, and how individuals in various roles interact with one another determines how curriculum work will get done. In some schools, individual teachers have virtually complete autonomy over the curriculum in their classrooms; subject only to the implicit requirement to follow official guidelines; in many cases compliance with this requirement is not even monitored. In other schools, the principal exercises close control over the curriculum, sometimes to the point of insisting that teachers make and submit weekly lesson plans. Some schools have more differentiated staffing arrangements in which teachers and school staff are organized into teams or departments with some autonomy and authority, often including a budget, for completing their assignment.

Depending on how the school staff is organized, curriculum work may be collaborative or individualistic, integrated or compartmentalized, centralized or widely distributed. Patterns of staff organization also influence the priority put on curriculum work within the larger set of tasks required to run the school, as well as the expertise of the persons who make curriculums decisions. Still, differentiating by curriculum area brings its own set of problems, such as how to coordinate the work within the separate subjects. Specialization erects barriers to reallocation of staff. More differentiated organizations foster wider participation but they also take more time and make interpersonal conflict more likely than well-run hierarchical organizations, for example. So, though the specific work required to maintain a good curriculum would differ substantially depending on the staffing arrangements, it is not clear that one type of organization is always superior from a curriculum standpoint.

Provision of Curriculum Materials

The availability of curriculum materials limits what teachers can realistically hope to cover in their classrooms, and hence is an important frame for the classroom curriculum. Textbook series coordinate the content presented over years of study in a subject, often from kindergarten through grade 6 and sometimes through grade 12. Decisions about adoption of a textbook series come only every 5 to 10 years, the useful life of the books. But selection of workbooks, supplementary books, films, laboratory apparatus, computer software, art supplies, posters, and other equipment and supplies happens annually. The timely delivery of curriculum materials is critical to supporting teaching and learning in the classroom. The cost of these materials, together with the implicit cost of the time involved in selecting, ordering, budgeting, and processing them, is the major part of a school's budget for curriculum. Changes in the budget for materials can trigger substantive changes in the curriculum. In one school, an English program built around the reading of novels in paperback was eliminated when school budgets were reduced, and the department reverted to a program based on a cheaper anthology. Costs of apparatus have been a significant factor hindering widespread adoption of hands-on science programs in elementary schools.

In-Service Education

In most schools the only way for teachers to do curriculum work on school time is to call it in-service education. Except for an hour or two a month set aside for faculty meetings run by the principal, in-service education for teachers is the only time most schools provide for teachers to interact with one another over professional matters. Teacher meetings are barely adequate for disseminating essential information about curriculum policy such as changes in entrance or graduation requirements, testing, or the logistics of providing curriculum materials. If, say, a consultant is needed to help a school consider how to improve students' writing, the work must be called in-service education. As a result, curriculum work competes with improvement of teaching skills, dealing with students' problems, and handling school organizational and interpersonal issues, among many other matters, for a few days' of teachers' time each year. If teachers did not spend a good deal of unpaid time and time allocated to other matters, such as computing grades and ordering supplies, on curriculum work, much curriculum management simply would not get done. In fact, a main obstacle to teachers' playing a more substantial and responsible role in curriculum work is simply the lack of time for this work in their schedules.

A school with a generous in-service education budget can afford to provide substitutes for teachers in order to release them for curriculum work. Such a school can attend to weaknesses in its program better than a school with a more constrained budget for in-service education. It can also respond better to unanticipated disruptions and can contemplate more considered, more ambitious, and more thoroughly implemented innovations. The number and scope of innovations that a school can support at any time sets a firm limit on the rate at which curriculum improvements can be made. If, as experts on implementation of innovations argue (Fullan, 2000), social interaction among teachers is crucial in bringing about changes in their classroom behavior, then lack of time for interaction may well be a major cause of implementation failures of curriculum reforms from the 1950s to the present. Schools that must rely exclusively on textbooks, teacher's guides, and other printed materials to support teachers in improving their classroom curriculum may well be attempting the impossible. Accomplishing even minor adjustments needed to preserve curriculum quality becomes difficult when only a few hours per year are available for teachers to work on school curriculum matters. The prominence given to curriculum issues in in-service education is an important determinant of the quality of curriculum management in a school.

Teacher Performance Assessment

Principals and central office staff are supposed to monitor and evaluate the performance of every teacher every year. What we know about teacher assessment (see Bridges, 1986, for example) indicates that most of this effort is devoted to evaluating probationary teachers and that the major concerns of evaluation are classroom management and relationships with students. School leaders also bear a responsibility to monitor the quality of the classroom curriculum both for conformity to law and policy and to foster quality by the standards of the school and the profession. This may involve reviewing course outlines and lesson plans, observing classrooms, analyzing test results of a teachers' students, and conferring with teachers about curriculum matters. It may involve requesting advice from others—subject matter specialists, other experienced teachers—if the principal is not competent in the teacher's subject. Whatever the procedures, if principals convey a clear message that the quality of the curriculum a teacher maintains in the classroom is a major sign of good teacher performance, then teacher assessment can be a powerful process for maintaining curriculum quality.

Monitoring and Advising Students

The quality of a school's curriculum depends upon how well its offerings are assimilated by the students that want and need them, as well as upon the quality of the list of offerings. The first step in getting the offerings to students is placement in appropriate classes. Decisions about placement of students in the school program are made on the basis of records, formal and informal assessment of students by teachers and (occasionally) other professionals, and the preferences of students and parents. These data find their way sooner or later into the student's "cumulative record file," the master file of records the school keeps on each pupil. Every student's cumulative file contains lists of every school and course enrolled in, Carnegie units completed, grades received, daily attendance records, teachers' comments, and test scores, among other items. Teachers, counselors, and, ultimately, the principal decide on placement of students, based upon data included in that file and their professional judgment.

Ideally, placement decisions should maximize the rate and extent of the student's educational progress. Officially, students' progress through school is defined in curriculum terms—courses completed, grades earned, promotions achieved. A key issue the school faces for every student in every course or program every year is the readiness of the student to undertake the work in the curriculum units that follow the present one. Decisions about readiness are complex, important, and difficult to justify to the complete satisfaction of professionals, let alone parents and students. When the school offers several alternative tracks or levels of study, the decision about placement of students in various tracks becomes even more difficult and complex. Evidence strongly suggests that in tracked programs early placement decisions tend to become self-fulfilling as students in more advanced tracks receive more and better instruction and are held to higher standards and so pull further away year after year.

How well the school makes its thousands of placement decisions each year is a crucial determinant of the quality of the school program. Stories of honor students who graduated from high school unable to read signal blatant failures of monitoring and advisement. Less dramatic instances can be equally damaging. Primary school students with limited English speaking ability may be diagnosed as having low academic ability. High school students, especially girls, may not learn that high school algebra is required for entry into business as well as technical fields in college. Students may be allowed to miss a course required for college entrance.

Given the universally acknowledged difficulty of these decisions, it seems prudent to build in as many safeguards and monitoring points as feasible. Some possibilities include:

- special reviews by qualified outside experts of the files of students in the top and bottom quartiles of assignments to tracked classes
- conferences with students and parents beginning years in advance of crucial placement decisions, to ensure that they know the criteria that will be applied
- special summer and after school classes to boost top students from one level or track to another or to solidify a student's readiness to remain in the present track the coming year
- checking criteria used in making placement decisions periodically against actual student performance to make certain that the criteria and decision-rules are working out as hoped.

In general, nothing beats giving students a chance to perform at a higher level and seeing if they are able to capitalize on it. This can be done in brief units within the regular curriculum in such an unobtrusive way that students will not be under any special evaluation stress.

Maintaining Priorities in the Face of the Unexpected

When everything has been reduced to routine that can be, the events that remain fill the days of school people. Every study of what school administrators do on the job shows that they are in virtually constant communication with others, that they control the time, place, and subject of only a tiny fraction of these encounters, and that most of the problems they deal with are unscheduled and unanticipated (Kimbrough & Burkett, 1990). In short, school leaders spend most of their time coping with the unexpected. From a curriculum point of view, the chief challenge of this fact of school life is to maintain goals and priorities in the face of this random activity.

The cumulative effect of hundreds of small daily compromises can be a school program that is far different, and more probably than not, far worse, than the one planned. In extreme cases, perfectly sound plans and adequate resources to implement them nevertheless result in programs that are truncated, worn away, and trivialized by compromises. Good programs can be ruined by scheduling many events that preempt classes, accepting unqualified substitutes for absent teachers, cutting corners on curriculum materials purchases, or using teachers' in-service education time for doing routine administrative business.

Disruptions of the daily operation of the school program should be minimized, of course, but unplanned events will probably always be frequent in schools. Children are not fully socialized and cannot be expected to conform as readily to routines; schools are crowded places where people pursue many different institutional goals in close proximity; the school population is diverse, and their participation is not always voluntary. Draconian measures designed to eliminate disruptions will establish an authoritarian school climate. The challenge for curriculum management is to maintain consistency of purpose and priorities in the midst of all this randomness. To do so will require that all those involved be continually reminded of the importance of the school's major goals and priorities and urged to be diligent in pursuing them. School leaders must reflect this attitude in their behavior as well as in their statements. By enunciating and projecting a vision and repeatedly making split-second decisions on the basis of this vision, school leaders can guard against the erosion of program quality by the inevitable randomness of their daily work.

Qualities Needed for School Curriculum Leadership

The duties of school curriculum leadership are so many and varied that it's hard to imagine one person being able to do it all. A curriculum leadership team should have among its members highly developed skills in the following areas.

- Maintain good working relationships
  All members of the team should be adept at establishing and maintaining trust, good will, and constructive relationships among all stakeholders and interested parties and their representatives so that they can work together productively on curriculum matters. Individuals who are polite, cheerful, and willing to listen closely and carefully to opinions that bore them or offend them make good candidates for a curriculum leadership team.
- Sponsor productive interactions
  Getting the right people together in the right environment with the right direction and enough time and resources is essential to good school curriculum work.

Good candidates for school curriculum leaders are adept at organizing and running meetings, guest speakers, workshops, visits to innovative schools, coffees and other informal get-togethers, and many other formal and informal occasions for social interaction around curriculum matters. They know what can and cannot be accomplished in each kind of occasion, and exercise good judgment in choosing the right occasion for accomplishing the right task.

• Initiate and sustain dialogue

Dialogue is two-way communication. The give-and-take of dialogue is crucial in enabling all the coordination and shared decision-making necessary for making school curriculum decisions. It prepares the way for hard decisions by enabling all the interested parties to understand and appreciate one another's perspectives. Curriculum leaders need to enable deliberation to happen by bringing the appropriate people together in suitable forums and setting appropriate ground rules.

• Conduct effective deliberation

Deliberation is the discussion that accompanies decision-making. Groups empowered to make decisions or recommend consider various proposals, argue their merits, balance the pros and cons, and reach decisions that they can justify. Curriculum leaders need to encourage and support deliberation. They need to insist on decisions and recommendations supported by strong rationales, not simply votes or consensus.

• Conduct effective negotiations

When facing a decision that important stakeholders have discussed thoroughly and still disagree about, curriculum leaders need to help those with decision-making power to negotiate a satisfactory working agreement. The minimum goal of a working agreement is a policy that most interested parties will support and whose opponents will go along with and not disrupt or refuse to cooperate, at least temporarily while working within the system to change the decision to one that they can wholeheartedly support. Negotiations may take many forms from formal negotiations that may be mediated or arbitrated to informal meetings. Curriculum leaders need to remain calm in the face of conflict, analyze the parties' positions on the issue in detail to isolate points of agreement and disagreement, invent ingenious bargains that the parties will accept, and persuade reluctant parties to go along.

• Communicate and coordinate

School curriculum leaders need to keep in touch with the sources of curriculum change and funnel important information to locals who would benefit from knowing it. They need to stay in touch with district officials, state officials, professional associations, parent and community groups, and others who represent the views of important stakeholders. They also need to communicate about the school with outside agencies, letting them know the status of the school curriculum, innovations underway, needs, and the like. Curriculum practitioners must coordinate far-flung activities. They must somehow communicate with teachers in different schools, even in different states. They must work in concert with other practitioners moving in similar directions and adjust to others acting independently so that teachers do not face total chaos.

• Provision of resources

School curriculum leaders need to secure resources to support the ongoing curriculum and curriculum initiatives in the school. Textbooks and other curriculum materials as well as consumable supplies such as paper, pencils, and equipment such as computers or overhead projectors need to be ordered and supplied in time for the start of school. Substitutes must be arranged and paid for when teachers are released from classroom assignment to work on curriculum innovations. Workshops, demonstrations, visits to other schools, guest speakers, and the like must be arranged and paid for. Requests always exceed resources, so curriculum leaders must often say "no."

Sometimes teachers engaged in worthy projects fail to request resources they should have. Curriculum leaders need to recognize this and coach them.

- Design

  School curriculum leaders will participate in choosing and developing curriculum documents, materials, equipment, and facilities. They need to be able to create documents for teachers, other professionals, and the public that communicate clearly and simply. They need to be good judges of teaching materials such as textbooks, workbooks, tests, and laboratory apparatus. They need to be able to develop effective teachers' guides and local curriculum materials.

- Inspiring excellence

  Curriculum leaders who merely assist others in doing curriculum work are not leading at all, only supporting. Leaders must project a vision of excellence in curriculum and stand up for this vision in their daily work. They must throw their weight on the side of excellence as they and the leadership team see it. They must display a positive, can do attitude and encourage the same in teachers. They must be committed to excellence and lifelong professional development and support teachers and colleagues in their development.

Curriculum Practice in School and Classroom

It is important for anyone who hopes to improve the curriculum of any school or classroom to understand the work teachers and school leaders do just to maintain the existing curriculum. Any curriculum, innovative or traditional, is a form of practice, created and sustained by the active efforts of many people and agencies. Any curriculum requires coordination. Teachers and other curriculum practitioners must reach working agreement on what's to be done. They must coordinate their actions to achieve continuity and sequence. Documents and face-to-face communication express agreements and coordinate actions. Practitioners and the public disagree, sometimes radically, about curriculum questions, but some degree of agreement is essential for there to be a school or a curriculum at all. Agreement need not be total. Any curriculum varies from teacher to teacher, from school to school, and from time to time.

Some misconceptions and half-truths are widespread. Anyone who hopes to influence the curriculum must work through teachers. Teachers and students realize the curriculum that students experience. For reforms to succeed, teachers must make them work under real conditions with all the constraints of time, resources, and environment that they and their students actually face. As we will see in the next chapter, realizing an innovative curriculum poses some immense challenges for teachers. To have a reasonable chance of success, reformers need to provide teachers with a great deal of support and assistance.

Questions and Projects

1. Interview an experienced teacher and discuss how the teacher works to bring the curriculum in their classroom to life. What do they find especially satisfying about this work? What challenges do they find especially daunting? Ask them how what they do now is different than what they did in their first year as a teacher. How did they learn to do the things they do now?

2. Have an informal discussion with students of an age you plan to work with professionally. Get them to talk about things they have seen students do that affect what gets taught and learned in their classes. If necessary, probe with questions like these: "Have you ever seen a student introduce something new into the class that everyone went on to study?" "Have you ever seen a student cause a teacher to drop some topic or goal that they were planning to cover?" How would you summarize their answers? For instance, do the students seem to feel powerful or powerless? Do they feel that it is legitimate for them to intervene in curriculum matters?

3. Interview an experienced curriculum professional about how they learned their work. "What work do you do?" "How did you get to be a <job title>?" "What are the most important lessons you have learned about curriculum work over the years and how did you learn them?"

4. Interview an experienced curriculum professional about the most notable experiences they have had in doing curriculum work. "Tell me about some of the highlights of your career." "What are some of the most important events that you have seen that have shaped the curriculum, for good or ill?" Probe for detail about the situation and who did what, why, and how. Write down the stories they tell you. Compare with fellow students. What does this tell you about the highs and lows of curriculum work?

5. Interview an experienced curriculum professional about the capabilities they think a person in their position needs to have in order to be effective. Combine your results with others' to develop a competency list for that position.

6. Compare how progressive classroom practices and traditional practices satisfy or fail to satisfy the demands of order, affect, coverage, and mastery. What does your analysis suggest about the challenges that face a school intending to adopt progressive classroom practices whose teachers now use traditional ones?

7. The conventional classroom takes on significantly different forms in different grades and subjects. Choose a subject and grade you know well and describe as exactly as you can the conventional pattern of teaching in those classes. Compare your description with others' descriptions of other subjects and grades. Speculate on reasons why these differences might arise. (Consult Stodolsky (1988) to discover findings of research on these questions.)

8. Seatwork is a common pattern found in classrooms. In seatwork, students complete paperwork independently at their seats. Compare and contrast seatwork with the conventional classroom interaction pattern as described in this chapter. Does seatwork help teachers to cope with the demands and limitations of the classroom setting? Under what conditions would you expect that seatwork might be better suited to the demands and limitations of classrooms than the conventional pattern? What difficulties would you predict an accomplished conventional classroom teacher might face in attempting to use seatwork?

9. Compare and contrast individualized instruction with the conventional classroom interaction pattern. What are the advantages of individualization for teachers? For students? What are the costs and risks for teachers of switching from a conventional pattern to an individualized one? On balance, how strong do you think the incentives (or disincentives) to switch would be for an experienced classroom teacher? What actions on the part of a principal might contribute most to improving the incentives for such a teacher to switch to individualized instruction from conventional classroom teaching?

10. Expand or enlarge one of the frames to which classrooms are now subject and see whether teachers would have more options for ways to satisfy the demands of coverage, mastery, affect, and order in their classroom. Which frame do you think puts

the most severe limitations on teachers' options? Why? Why do you think this frame remains as confining as it is?

11. If students generally go along with the curriculum provided in the classroom and if they usually learn what they are taught, then why wouldn't issuing more demanding curriculum plans and textbooks improve students' achievement?

12. Study your own tacit, internal learning activities during a classroom lesson. Reserve at least 2 hours immediately after a class that you are taking. Tape-record the class session. Immediately afterward, play back the tape and record the thoughts you had at the time as well as you can recall them. Note places where your attention wandered and why, places where you were puzzled and how you coped with your puzzlement, places where you questioned the ideas presented, and so on. Would you describe your role in this lesson as especially active? If you can, play the first few minutes of the tape for a friend who has never studied the material, and compare your thoughts with your friend's. Chances are that you did some things while listening that made you a more effective learner in this lesson than your friend. Describe them.

13. Try to write out the implicit curriculum of a classroom you know well. Do this by listing the norms and expectations that are generally followed there. What do you think would happen if these were written out and presented to students at the beginning of the school year in every class? If you think doing so would be a good idea, explain why the practice has not caught on. If you think it would be a bad idea, describe and explain its bad effects.

Further Study

Walter Doyle in "Curriculum and Pedagogy" (1992) reviews the research on the relation of curriculum to teaching practices. Larry Cuban's *How Teachers Taught* (1993) offers an excellent summary of the evidence for the stability of the conventional pattern of teaching and alternative explanations of its stability. Most scholars and researchers now take it for granted that conventional or traditional teaching is highly robust and have turned to related questions such as what variations occur around or within this pattern, teachers' experiences within this pattern, and ways to change this pattern. Susan Stodolsky in *The Subject Matters* (1988) presents strong evidence that the activities in social studies classes differ from those in mathematics classes in elementary schools even when the same teacher teaches both subjects. This shows that the conventional pattern is not caused entirely by teachers' lack of ability to teach in other ways or by the teacher's personal preferences. Hillocks (1999) studied English teachers and concluded that their beliefs about teaching and learning were crucial in holding them to the conventional pattern.

Other investigators have begun to study adventurous teaching in great detail in order to discover what makes it particularly challenging for teachers. Edited volumes by Cobb, Yackel, and McClain (2000) and Lampert and Blunk (1998) describe the challenges teachers face in trying new approaches to mathematics teaching in which students and teachers use mathematics as a symbol system for communication. Lengthy, intensive teaching experiments in which investigators work with the teacher to implement adventurous mathematics programs and then monitor teaching and study the difficulties teachers faced in teaching in this new way appear to be emerging as a standard research strategy. If teaching mathematics in this more adventurous way requires as much from teachers as it seems to—much deeper understanding of mathematics and more complex teaching decisions—then widespread adoption of more adventurous teaching practices may require expanding some of the frames of the conventional classroom.

Philip Jackson's *Life in Classrooms* (1968, reissued in 1990) remains an insightful treatment of students' experience of the curriculum. The chapter in the *Handbook of Research on Curriculum* (1992) by Erickson and Shultz on "Students' experience of the curriculum" is a welcome summary of research to that point. They note that "questions about students' inner attention go unasked" (p. 467). Barbara Morgan-Fleming et al.'s "Children's interpretations of curriculum events" (1997) is an insightful addition to the literature on this neglected topic. I feel strongly that a deeper understanding of what students do and experience in connection with curriculum has great potential for improving curriculum practice. For instance, Erickson and Shultz (1992) point out the importance for students of the "the risk of embarrassment and loss of face" (470). Some students will refuse to try to learn rather than risk the loss of face by trying and failing. Being asked to give an answer in public may frighten students raised in some kinds of families. In view of the apparent importance of the topic, I'm puzzled by how little close study is being done of what happens in classrooms between students, teachers, and curriculum materials.

The studies of teacher planning that emerged in the 1970s gave us a solid basis for thinking about how teachers plan their classroom curriculums. They verified, for instance, that teachers usually began their planning with the content to be presented and that they relied heavily on plans found in textbooks and curriculum materials (Peterson, Marx, & Clark, 1978; Yinger, 1977; Zahorik, 1975). In the subsequent decades investigators asked more penetrating questions. What role do textbooks and curriculum plans play in teachers' planning (Komoski, 1976; McCutcheon, 1980)? How do teachers cope with curriculum policies made outside the classroom (Schwille et al., 1983)? What is the significance of teachers' emphasis on practicality in planning (Doyle & Ponder, 1977; Elbaz, 1983)? How do teachers respond when they confront curriculum materials that are in some way incompatible with their beliefs and preferences (Floden et al., 1981)? How do teachers think about curriculum matters in their planning (Ben-Peretz, 1975; Elbaz, 1983; Kremer & Ben-Peretz, 1980; Ben-Peretz, Bromme, & Halkes, 1986)? Investigators have recently begun to look at how the curriculum enters into interactions between teachers and students in the classroom (Barr & Dreeben, 1977; Carlsen, 1988). How do subject matter and teachers' conceptions of subject matter influence classroom interactions (Barr, 1986; Carlsen, 1988; Davis & McKnight, 1976; Stodolsky, 1988)? We have also learned a great deal about teachers' experiences of the curriculum from studies by Connelly and Clandinin (1988) and others. Our understanding seems much more complete and now we see what teachers' difficulties are, and so researchers are turning more to the question of how to enable or empower teachers to try other, more adventurous curriculums in their classrooms. This is the subject of Chapter 8.

We understand how the curriculum of schools is sustained much less than we understand how the classroom curriculum is sustained. We lack detailed studies of parent and public interactions with principals, teachers, and curriculum leaders. I find Alan Peshkin's (1978, 1982, 1986, 1997, 2001) ethnographic studies of schools to be particularly enlightening but their combination of specifics from one case and an overall narrative account says nothing about the relative frequency of various kinds of events. John Ogbu's (1974) *The Next Generation* and *Minority Education and Caste: The American System in Cross-cultural Perspective* (1978) provide an especially insightful perspective on minority communities and their relationships with schools, but it suffers from the same limitation. Saxe (1975) *School-Community Interaction*, though hopelessly dated, still provides the best overview I have found of the various aspects of the relationship between schools and communities. Similarly, Salisbury's (1980) *Citizen Participation in the Public Schools* is still the best summary of ways citizens participate formally in public schools. Tucker and Zeigler's (1980)

Professionals Versus the Public: Attitudes, Communication, and Response in School Districts views the relationship as predominantly antagonistic and supplies considerable evidence to support their conclusion. Fortunately, Wirt and Kirst's *The Political Dynamics of American Education* (1997) provides a current treatment of political aspects of school–community relationships.

Schools have received more critical than analytic attention over the last couple of decades. Among the critical works I find most informative are Diane Ravitch's *The Schools We Deserve* (1985), Phillip Cusick's *The Egalitarian Ideal and the American High School* (1983) and *Inside High School* (1973), and Oakes and Sorotnik's (1986) *Critical Perspectives on the Organization and Improvement of Schooling*. In a more analytic vein, I think Barker and Gump's *Big School, Small School* (1964) is an enlightening and powerful application of the concept of behavior settings to schools with enduring value. Seymour Sarason's *The Culture of the School and the Problem of Change* (1982) is full of brilliant insights about the realities of schools. Good and Brophy (1986) have reviewed the research done over the past decade to identify characteristics of effective schools, i.e., schools whose students score better than expected on standardized tests. Other works on schools worthy of attention include Goodlad's *A Place Called School* (1984), Sara Lawrence-Lightfoot's *The Good High School* (1983), Ernest Boyer's *High School: A Report on Secondary Education in America* (1983), Powell, Farrar, and Cohen's (1985) *The Shopping Mall High School* and Theodore Sizer's *Horace's Compromise* (1984, 1992).

Curriculum researchers have seriously neglected the school curriculum as a subject of study in its own right. The bureaucratic and organizational structures and their decision processes are surely not as attractive to many curriculum scholars as the dynamic flesh-and-blood interaction of students and teachers, but the effects of school-level curriculum work powerfully affect students' and teachers' lives. We need more detailed understanding of such vital issues as the assignment of teachers and students to courses and programs, the achievement of a working relationship between school-level and classroom-level authority, the coordination of purpose, content, and standards within the school and over time, and the interaction of curriculum with school climate, culture, and values. We barely even know what courses are offered and how students' time is allocated among subjects. Serious longitudinal studies of schoolwide patterns of course offerings and enrollments are badly needed. Jeannie Oakes' (1985) *Keeping Track: How Schools Structure Inequality* begins to reveal some of the subtleties hidden behind routinely reported national statistics on course offerings and enrollments. Linda McNeil's studies of the impact of school reform on Texas schools in *Contradictions of School Reform* (2000) also begin to move in the needed direction. As with the study of classrooms, researchers' attention has already turned to how to reform and restructure schools for improved achievement for all students, a topic for Chapter 9.

CHAPTER SEVEN

Improving Curriculum Practice

The spirit of liberty is the spirit which is not too sure that it is right; the spirit of liberty is the spirit which seeks to understand the minds of other men and women; the spirit of liberty is the spirit which weighs their interests alongside its own without bias.

—Judge Learned Hand, in comments to newly naturalized Americans

Questions

- What are the most important things to keep in mind in trying to improve the curriculum of a classroom or school?
- How would you determine whether a proposed curriculum improvement is sound and better than competing alternatives?
- What is practical reasoning and what does it have to do with curriculum improvement?
- What skills are needed to lead curriculum improvement efforts?

Approaches to Curriculum Improvement

The commonsense approach to curriculum improvement is to get the interested parties to agree on what needs to be done and just do it. Find out what teachers, school leaders, parents, and other interested parties dislike about the present curriculum and what new possibilities excite them. Pick a curriculum improvement focus that has broad support and little opposition. Appoint a committee of able teachers and charge them to develop curriculum plans and materials to bring about the targeted improvements. Have the committee's work reviewed widely by all interested parties, revised if necessary, and submit it for approval by the proper authorities. Finally, enlist the cooperation of teachers and school leaders to implement the newly adopted curriculum in schools and classrooms. This common sense approach is not necessarily easy to carry out, but it is direct, straightforward and not at all mysterious. It is doubtlessly the most commonly used approach to improving the curriculum of schools and classrooms.

Those who see education as a way to make the world a better place often turn to curriculum improvement as a means to achieve their vision, whether they want to build a brave new world, sustain the world they have, or return to a former golden age. Often reformers' visions of better worlds include visions of new curriculums. Plato's plan for his ideal state featured a plan for educating its rulers, and many later visionaries have followed Plato's example. To articulate a social and educational vision and then work out its implications for curriculum is the approach of curriculum theory. We saw several examples in Chapter 3. And, as we saw there, curriculum theorizing continues to be a popular approach to curriculum improvement.

A theoretical approach has one major advantage over common sense approaches—it makes the grounds for its curriculum choices explicit. Curriculums derived from theories give principled reasons for including particular content, purposes, or forms of organization. Noddings' ideas about caring give principled reasons for advocating a broader curriculum than a strictly academic one. Gardner's ideas about multiple abilities give principled reasons for emphasizing visual/spatial and musical skills on a more equal footing with word and number skills.

Instead of principled justifications for curriculum decisions based on a theory, common sense approaches offer intuition and judgment. Those involved feel upset about some things in the curriculum and excited by some new possibilities, but they may not say or even know why. If they do justify their intuitions, their reasons may be unrelated to one another or to any underlying themes or ideas. For common sense approaches it is enough that the parties agree. If they disagree initially, any compromise that yields a working agreement is satisfactory. Curriculums built with common sense approaches therefore often seem miscellaneous, lack coherence and organization, and may be idiosyncratic or even eccentric. Sometimes it seems that the committee members threw all their pet ideas into the pot and stirred.

Curriculums built on theories generally are more coherent, but they have some fundamental shortcomings of their own. First, curriculum issues are too many-sided for any single theory to cover. No single theory can unite ideas about students (their previous knowledge, needs, abilities, interests), teachers (their beliefs, knowledge, skill, experience), the subject (key ideas, structure) and the society (its needs,) into one all-encompassing set of ideas. Theories usually deal with one of these commonplaces and leave the rest out, something curriculum decision-makers cannot responsibly do.

Second, theories never completely capture all the relevant features of the individual case that we must consider when we make wise curriculum decisions. Curriculum problems happen to specific, unique, living people, institutions, and communities, and a good curriculum decision must be right for a particular case. Third, theories that deal with curriculum are always contested. As one of the most articulate advocates of practical reasoning in curriculum noted "There is not one theory of groups, but several. There is not one theory of learning but half a dozen. All the social and behavioral sciences are marked by 'schools'" (Schwab, 1970, p. 28). This is certainly true of curriculum theories.

When people use theoretical approaches, the curriculums they make often seem narrow, artificial, and doctrinaire. All too often theories offer simple solutions to complex problems. Schwab wrote of "the dispatch, the sweeping appearance of success, the vast simplicity which grounds [a] purported [theoretical] solution to the problem of curriculum" (Schwab, 1970, p. 21).

There is another principled approach to curriculum improvement that uses ideas to inform curriculum improvement—practical reason. In practical reasoning decision–makers consider what action, if any, is best for this situation all things considered. Those who work to improve curriculums can find help with the many quandaries they face by treating them as practical problems. In this chapter we will explore practical approaches to curriculum improvement.

The Realm of the Practical

Practical Reason

The idea of practical reason can be traced to Aristotle's distinction between the realms of the theoretical, the practical, and the productive. Aristotle argued that theoretical knowledge was appropriate for solving problems in the realm of ideas where problems and solutions are timeless and universal. Philosophy and mathematics are the quintessential theoretical disciplines, and formal logic is the pattern for theoretical reasoning. Practical problems arise when people need to take action or make decisions in the real world. Aristotle thought that politics was the quintessential practical activity because it requires people to make collective decisions and take concerted action in public affairs. Productive problems involve making things, something that also required the powers of reason but in a way different from both the theoretical and the practical.

Theoretical problems are solved once and for all time by an idea or invention of the mind, and productive problems are solved by skilled performance in manipulating material objects with one's body, but practical problems are resolved, not solved, and not by an idea but by a decision. When the person or group confronted with it decides what to do, that particular practical problem is resolved. The conclusion that a certain action is best for this situation is called a *practical judgment* (Gauthier, 1963). Strictly speaking, a practical problem can be considered fully resolved, as distinct from resolved in principle, only after the fact, when action has been taken and found to eliminate the problem. With theoretical problems we can sometimes find ideas that completely satisfy all the conditions of the original problem, whereas with practical problems the actions that resolve them usually lead to a new set of conditions only somewhat less problematic than the original ones.

In searching for actions to solve practical problems, decision-makers should strive for the best informed, most thoroughly considered decision. This means that they should consider the pros and cons of all the most promising alternative actions in light of the best available knowledge. This consideration of possible actions, called deliberation, is the core of practical reasoning.

Schwab described deliberation in these terms:

> (Deliberation) treats both ends and means and must treat them as mutually determining one another. It must try to identify, with respect to both, what facts may be relevant. It must try to ascertain the relevant facts in the concrete case. It must try to identify the desiderata in the case. It must generate alternative solutions. It must take every effort to trace the branching pathways of consequences which may flow from each alternative and affect desiderata. It must then weigh alternatives and their costs and consequences against one another, and choose, not the right alternative, for there *is* no such thing, but the best one (Schwab, 1969, pp. 20–21).

As an example, consider a school facing the curriculum problem of whether to differentiate the school curriculum or to maintain a common curriculum for all students. This problem calls for the leaders of the school to decide on a course of action for the school. A committee would typically be appointed to consider the question and make a recommendation to the Superintendent and school board. The committee would probably be charged to consider fully the pros and cons of each alternative. In the process the committee might well consider various ideas and theories, including some framed in abstract terms such as democracy and equity and others framed in down to earth terms such as cost and appeal to parents, teachers, administrators and students. Having given the matter due consideration, the committee would reach a judgment that either a common or a differentiated curriculum was preferable for their school at this time.

Let us suppose that they recommended a common curriculum. Their recommendation to this effect might signal the end of the deliberation, but more likely it would mark the beginning of another round of public discussion as the Superintendent and school board make an official decision. The official decision by the institutional authorities resolves the curriculum problem in principle.

After the schools implement a common curriculum, it may happen that the curriculum leads to serious, widespread difficulties. Parents of gifted or handicapped children may complain that the common curriculum is unsuitable for their children. Or teachers may be unable to agree on what should be included in the common curriculum. Such difficulties might lead the Superintendent or the Board to reconsider the issue. On the other hand, those involved may consider the matter settled and regard these new difficulties as new problems to be resolved within the framework of a common curriculum, in which case the original problem will now be fully resolved. Clearly this case can be construed as a practical problem. Equally clearly, it is not a theoretical problem.

Questions of curriculum policy or practice, such as the following clearly qualify as practical problems.

- What curriculum should we offer for these students in this school or classroom?
- What actions should we take in order to maintain and improve the quality of this curriculum?

Those who take the basic questions of curriculum to be theoretical questions such as the following naturally look to theory for answers.

- What should be the aims of education?
- What is the nature of the good and how can education enable humanity to achieve it?
- What knowledge is of most worth?
- What is the proper role for education in society?

Adopting a practical perspective on curriculum matters refocuses our attention on decisions and actions in concrete situations rather than abstract notions.

Both ways of treating curriculum problems use ideas, but in quite different ways. Curriculum theory begins with ideas and applies them to particular cases, whereas the practical begins with the case and asks what ideas may be helpful in dealing with it. A theoretical approach insists that curriculum problems be grounded in ideas that form a coherent and systematic body, a curriculum theory, whereas the practical permits grounding in an eclectic variety of ideas. Theory strives for the greatest possible degree of abstraction and generality, whereas the practical is content with principles at any level of abstraction that help to resolve the problem. Theory looks for better answers to deep questions, whereas the practical looks for better decisions.

I believe that a practical approach to curriculum improvement is the only way to bridge the gap between theory and practice. It allows us to bring ideas to bear on curriculum in a way that common sense approaches do not. It is a principled approach, yet it frees us from the dictates of a single theory and gives room for the play of intuition in choosing among theories and in balancing theoretical considerations with rules of thumb based on experience. I will follow a practical approach in this chapter and the ones to follow.

A Curriculum Problem Considered and Resolved

Let us consider an example of a practical approach to a real curriculum problem. The following example of curriculum deliberation is taken from tape recordings of actual discussions among a team of curriculum developers. The team included scientists, teachers, and science education specialists, about a dozen people altogether. The team was collaborating on a curriculum development project at the University of California at Berkeley. The project, called the Science Curriculum Improvement Study (SCIS), was funded by the National Science Foundation in the late 1960s to develop inquiry-oriented, hands-on curriculum materials for elementary science. The quotations are verbatim except for minor editing to enhance intelligibility.

The meeting that will concern us here began with one member of the team demonstrating some apparatus that had been designed for use in elementary school science classes. He first demonstrated to the assembled team of curriculum planners a simple pendulum made of a piece of nylon fishline with a lead sinker tied on its end. The pendulum was clamped to the back of the child's desk in a way that made it possible for the sinker to swing freely. As he demonstrated the apparatus he commented:

> The general object of the exercise as I saw it was to have the children investigate, in the first place, how you describe the system, and in the second place, how you describe the motion, and in the third place what properties of the system are important in determining what kind of motion takes place. . . .

Those present were encouraged to examine the apparatus and its motions.

Other pieces of apparatus being considered for use in this same lesson were similarly demonstrated, including various simple setups with balls rolling in curved tracks, and various arrangements for comparing the motions of different swinging or oscillating objects. The presenter noted that two balls of different size (radius) can be placed side by side in curved tracks and, when released together, will roll back-and-forth in unison for a considerable time. He noted that they stay in step longer if the apparatus is larger and commented that "It's more convincing that way." He noted that if you use tracks with different curvature, the balls do not stay in step at all, commenting that "it's very easy for students to see that the shape of the track is important and that the motion is nearly independent of the radius of the ball." He pointed out that once these phenomena have been demonstrated to the children, they can be led to ask similar questions about the pendulum and the factors that determine its back-and-forth motion.

He then demonstrated how the children were supposed to use the pendulum to answer these questions:

> One way we've tried that worked well for some children, at least, was to use the clock's second hand and ask them to count the number of swings in half a minute, ... And they very quickly come to the conclusion that, yes, the length of the pendulum does indeed make a difference—the longer the pendulum, the fewer swings you have.

> Then we can ask another question. Does the size of the weight on the end make any difference? And there we have to be careful because some of us already know the answer, and that's a disadvantage. The answer is, no, it doesn't make a difference. But you ask the children to try this out and they will almost invariably come to the conclusion that, yes, it does make a difference. And then you have to go into the business of, well, how big a difference and is it an important difference or not.

He then described several approaches that they had considered for dealing with the problem, concluding with the one that his subgroup believed resolved the problem most satisfactorily:

So we thought we'd approach it rather obliquely in this way. Make two pendulums side by side. Don't say anything at all about the length of the two pendulums (which have different weights) but ask the children to take one pendulum set it in motion, . . . and then ask what length does the other pendulum's string have to be to swing exactly in step with the first pendulum. We tried this out just yesterday . . . and they did in fact discover that in order to synchronize the two pendulums the lengths must be less than one half inch different. It is interesting that they were able to adjust the pendulum precisely enough to synchronize the motion of the two pendulums quite precisely so that they'll stay in phase for several swings.

Someone then asked whether all the weights were the same size. No, they were different both in size and weight. Someone remarked and all agreed that, ideally, they would have weights that were the same size, but different weight. The presenter continued:

That'll involve some bother, making those. Make one out of wood, one out of lead. But that will eliminate the uncertainty that I think accounts for the half-inch, because that half-inch is pretty surely the result (of the fact) that they don't know whether they should measure to the center of the weight or the point where the thing is attached to the string. We haven't gone into this question. In fact, that's too subtle a question to settle anyway, but that whole question will be circumvented if we use two objects of the same size.

The presenter then went on to indicate that the next question for the children to take up was whether the amplitude of the swing (the range of its back and forth motion) makes a difference in the time taken for each swing. He pointed out that it does make a slight difference especially at larger amplitudes, but that he doubted whether the children would be able to detect the difference with their method of timing. He pointed out that the effect might be detected by comparing two identical pendulums set in motion with different amplitude, but they had not yet had a chance to try this in their experimental classrooms.

He then demonstrated a different oscillating system, a flat saw blade clamped to a table at one end so that it could be bent and released to vibrate freely. He showed how clamping weights and moving them back and forth along the length of the saw blade could slow the vibration down. This contrasted with the pendulum where weight made no difference.

A question then came from the floor: "How are kids going to understand that notion that you just suggested to us?"

I'm not sure that they will understand. I'd hope they will understand it. In fact, they understand that gravity is an essential ingredient for this pendulum because we described this system (in an earlier unit). . . . But I think we have to make it clear that for the pendulum the earth is an essential part of the system, . . . (whereas) for this system (the spring) the earth is not really essential. . . .

There were then several interchanges among those present on this question, pointing up the complexity of the situation in the case of the saw blade and the difficulty of making the comparison they wanted the children to make. As he returned to his demonstration of the saw blade and how children would use it to answer the same sorts of question as they had answered for the pendulum, he mentioned, as an aside, a difficulty they had encountered in using the materials.

The guiding principle in all this has been to try to get the children to think about what things are really of primary importance in deciding how the system operates, what things are not very important, and along with that trying to get them interested in making some reasonably precise measurements. So that we try to encourage them . . . to actually measure the length of the pendulum and to actually tell us the number of swings in a given interval of time. We try to underline the importance of making quantitative observations, which they are very reluctant to do. This is a real stumbling block. . . .

This question of how to stimulate children to make accurate measurement, how to show them the value of precise measurement, how to give them a reason for it, dominated the rest of the two-hour meeting, although it had not been on the agenda.

In the subsequent course of the deliberations of this meeting, several possible courses of action were proposed and considered for stimulating the children to take careful measurements of the swing of the pendulum:

- Simply telling the children that measurement is important, that qualitative description is not enough;
- Setting a problem that would lead children to feel the need for accurate measurement;
- Relating measurement to overcoming problems commonly encountered in children's daily lives;
- Giving children data and having them infer the existence of something hidden, in order to illustrate the power of quantitative data;
- Giving children a table of data on pendulum lengths and times and having them construct a pendulum the data applies to; and
- Having children take additional measurements to extend a table of data they would be given in the curriculum materials.

As the team considered the merits of each these alternatives, they advanced a wide range of desiderata, matters to consider in making their decision.

- Would it interest the children?
- Would it be too difficult for them?
- Was it good science?
- Would it serve as a sound basis for later work in measurement?
- Would the lesson fit well in this place in the course?
- Would it encourage the proper balance between doubt and commitment in the budding scientist?
- Could schools afford it?

The strategy that met with most favor and emerged as their resolution was to have the children discover how much longer a heavy pendulum had to be to swing in time with a light one. They outlined an activity in which children began with two identical pendulums, and showed that they took equal times to swing. Then children were to add weight (or amplitude) to one until they found out, as exactly as possible, how much longer or shorter the second pendulum must be made to compensate for its heavier weight or larger amplitude. The request for a quantitative answer (How much longer?) and for explicit comparison rewarded attempts at precise measurement and revealed its value in scientific work. The children would then follow a parallel procedure in studying the vibrating saw blade. Their measurements would be accurate enough to show that the weight attached to the saw blade made a definite difference in its swing-times, in contrast to the case of the pendulum. Thus, children would see the value of taking careful measurements.

At this point, the group turned to other questions, evidently satisfied with their resolution of the problem at least for the time being.

This episode is a good illustration of deliberation as it occurs in curriculum development. Episodes of deliberation about other kinds of curriculum problems such as those encountered in school or school district curriculum planning would be similar in form. Note the following general features of curriculum deliberation apparent in this example:

1. The deliberating body's purpose is to agree on a course of action they will take on a curricular problem.
2. Discussion centers on particular courses of action, not general principles, ideas, or theories.
3. The group insists on principled reasons for choosing one course of action over another. "It feels right to me" is not an acceptable reason.
4. In evaluating a possible course of action the group weighs competing considerations of very different orders drawn from different realms of discourse. This group considered the nature of science, what should count as evidence, what kinds of evidence children would find convincing, whether children could understand something, and cost, for example.
5. The group considers the issue resolved when they find a course of action that will resolve their problem better than other actions that they have considered. Notice that someone applying theory would not meet any of these criteria except the third.

Skills of Practical Reasoning

Practical reason can contribute to curriculum improvement in many ways. We will consider some of these under two main headings: posing the problem and reaching a satisfactory resolution.

Posing the Problem

From a Sense of the Problem to a Statement of It.   Practical problems originate in feelings of unease, discomfort, dissatisfaction, and the like, or in a sense of challenge, opportunity, a feeling that something better is possible. We call these feelings a *sense of the problem*. Sometimes our sense of the problem seems quite clear, even though we might have difficulty expressing it in words. At other times, our sense of the problem presents itself to us in the form of a vague uneasiness or dissatisfaction, a feeling that something is not right, a longing for something more, an intuition that something better is possible.

We may even experience difficulties of which we are not consciously aware, becoming aware of them only when someone else describes them in ways that we recognize. Life is filled with discomforts that we learn to live with and never identify as problems. To *pose* (or *articulate*) a problem is to transform this inarticulate sense of the problem into an explicit statement of the problem that we can communicate to others.

Posing Problems Well.   To pose a problem is to begin with an inarticulate sense of something being amiss and use that to develop an explicit statement of what's wrong. This is surprisingly difficult. Many times what passes for a posing of the problem is really a solution in disguise. "We are not using computers in all academic classes" may be a fact but it is not yet a problem. To find the problem we need to ask who is suffering what hardships or missing what opportunities from not using computers.

Problems can be posed in different ways and how you pose them makes a difference in how you look for solutions. Some people see the Commission report, *A Nation At Risk* (1983), as posing the problem of low academic achievement. Others see the problem as having a curriculum that is not challenging enough. Those who pose it in the latter way will naturally look for ways to make the curriculum more challenging, while those who pose it in the former way will probably consider a wider range of possible causes of and responses to low achievement. It is also possible to pose a problem both too narrowly and too broadly. "How to raise test scores" is a very narrow way of posing the problem. "How to improve education" is certainly too broad.

The ideal in posing problems is to describe the problematic situation concretely and in such a way that relevant and important features and values are highlighted. Just describing the distress students or society experience in a way that says nothing about their causes is an important step. Who is unhappy? What do they say that they are unhappy about? What do they say is wrong with things as they are? How would they like things to be? Such a low-level description is a very good start, but it does not give enough guidance about where to begin looking for solutions. For this you need some ideas about possible origins and causes of these symptoms.

A good posing of the problem would describe the origins and causes of distress and its ramifications and consequences. It sees the distress as a symptom of an underlying condition. It explains how the condition gives rise to these symptoms and what the consequences and ultimate course of the condition will be. Posing the problem also tells us why the distress is significant and not just one of life's many annoyances.

An adequate posing of a practical problem is an intellectual achievement in itself. Sir Geoffrey Vickers in *Value Systems and Social Process* (1968) calls it "an appreciation of the situation" and maintains that reaching agreement on a shared appreciation of the situation that is adequate to the demands of the problem is the heart of practical problem-solving. In most instances, posing a curriculum problem well is an important part of discovering a resolution for it, often the most difficult part. As the saying goes, "A problem understood is half solved."

Unfortunately, people seem to have a strong tendency when they sense a problem to begin looking for solutions immediately. Anyone who has tried to persuade a group to define the problem first before they look for solutions has felt the strength of this tendency to leap directly to solutions. An important role for curriculum leaders is to make sure groups take the time to pose the problem well before they start looking for the solution. In addressing curriculum problems, time spent understanding and posing the problem is usually well spent.

The deliberations of the science curriculum development team presented earlier in this chapter show the importance of the way the problem is posed. The team began by trying to help students describe a physical system that exhibited regular repeated motion so that they could investigate the factors that affected the motion of that system. Acting on this understanding of their problem, they developed some apparatus and activities. When they tried these activities, they discovered that students were too easily satisfied with their own rough estimates and saw no need for careful measurement. As a result, many students "confirmed" their misconceptions about the pendulum's motion. The lesson therefore did not succeed in resolving the original problem—enabling students to explore the factors that affect motion.

In discussing these field trials the deliberating group reached a better understanding of the students' learning difficulties. They redefined their problem as one of making students aware of the need for careful measurement in studying this system. In this new formulation, they were eventually able to resolve the problem.

Exploring Potential Courses of Action

Groups will not choose the best option if they never consider it, and most curriculum improvement teams only consider a narrow range of options, usually variations on practices they have already seen. By looking further afield, people may find new models that will suggest original courses of action.

Visits to pioneering schools, to teachers in other communities or to other educational settings such as museums or training facilities may suggest new ideas. Reading about new ideas and innovations or consulting with an outside expert may extend the group's thinking. If someone has produced a thorough analysis of the problem that describes the factors that produce and sustain the it, you can use that to develop courses of action that, if the model is correct, should mitigate the problem. For example, the science education development team shared a sophisticated conception of science as the study of systems in interaction, and they used this repeatedly in designing classroom activities.

Martin Hughes in *Children and Number* (1986) expresses ideas about teaching early arithmetic that could easily guide the improvement of an early mathematics curriculum. Hughes and his colleagues noticed that preschool children could do simple arithmetic in informal contexts. They can, for example, count on their fingers, judge which of two sets of objects contains the greater number, and remove objects from the larger set until the two sets are equal. They can, as Hughes verifies experimentally, solve problems with objects that they cannot solve with numerals, problems such as $3 + 7 = 10$ or $10 - 7 = 3$.

Hughes concludes that what's hard about arithmetic for children is linking their understanding of number in concrete objects to the formal notation. He proposes to help them by building on the strategies they naturally use to solve number problems concretely. He would encourage children to invent their own formalisms and discuss them with teachers. He suggests that teachers help children compare the merits of various representations, including the accepted adult representation as well as those of other children. He suggests teaching the history of the conventional representation. He proposes using games, such as those based on dice, spinners, or playing cards, and computers to provide practice in using basic number skills in a variety of concrete situations.

Seymour Itzkoff, in *How We Learn to Read* (1986), provides ideas that offer a starting point for improving the reading curriculum. Itzkoff deplores the polarization of the debate about beginning reading instruction between advocates of phonics and advocates of the Look–Say method. He believes that advocates of phonics have an important part of the truth: children need to catch on that the letters stand for words and that sound is the key to the correspondence. On the other hand, sounding out words is much too slow and cumbersome to allow the fluency good readers need.

Studies of mature readers show that they process huge chunks of material phrases, sentences, paragraphs, even pages—in single gulps. They use the shapes of the letters and words as cues for a guessing game in which they constantly guess what the text will say and scan mostly to confirm their guesses and to guide the formation of further predictions. Itzkoff calls this "predicting one's way" through the text. To keep children fixated on letter–sound correspondences inhibits the development of predicting abilities.

He recommends teaching reading in three steps. The first, training children's sensory system to recognize letters in context, is normally accomplished by preschool or kindergarten. The second, training children to integrate letters into words that they can pronounce, is essentially phonics. Here the student slowly learns to extract spoken equivalents from written language. With much experience the process gradually becomes automatic and the child's attention shifts from sound to a direct association of letter and word shapes with meaning. At this point, about grade 3, the child should be able to read with enough fluency to do school work and to experience continuing satisfaction with reading. From then on the role of the school should be to assist in the development of fluency. "The key is steady day-by-day . . . instruction that will expose the child to a variety of challenges and thus expand horizons and fluency with the thinking demands of the written word" (p. 113). Students may need help with specific skills, such as keeping the eyes moving—a finger works well for this purpose. Students can also be taught reading strategies, such as quick scanning followed by selective study of the more difficult passages.

The various branches of educational theory and research and the various behavioral and social sciences offer a wealth of ideas that can guide curriculum improvement. Ideas from the learning sciences seem to hold particular promise of leading to new and powerful learning materials and activities. The volume, *How People Learn: Brain, Mind, Experience, and School*, published by the National Academy of Sciences (Bransford et al., 2000), explains many of these ideas clearly for educators and the public.

Choosing the Best Course of Action

To resolve a practical problem is quite different from solving a theoretical problem. A solution to a theoretical problem solves the problem for all time as any qualified person can verify by checking the proof or repeating the experiment. A practical problem, by contrast, is resolved in principle when those addressing the problem find a course of action that they judge to be better than any others known to them. It is resolved in fact, i.e., fully resolved, when the course of action has been completed and the results found to be satisfactory.

Solution of theoretical problems and resolution of practical problems both depend ultimately on human judgment, but the form and process of judgment differ radically in the two cases.

When experts exercise judgment in determining whether a proposed solution does or does not solve a theoretical problem, they exercise a limited, circumscribed form of judgment, one they are extensively trained to make, and one that is hedged about with checks to ensure agreement among experts. If mathematicians agree that a certain proof demonstrates that the ratio of the circumference of a circle to its diameter is not a rational number, the likelihood that a lawyer, business proprietor, or psychologist can add anything useful to their collective judgment on this professional matter is essentially zero. The considerations relevant to the judgment are limited and the community of mathematicians has accumulated generations of experience in making this kind of specialized judgment. Specialists' judgments on theoretical questions are limited judgments.

By contrast, the resolution of most curriculum problems requires open-ended judgments. Open-ended judgments are ones in which we cannot limit the relevant considerations in advance. Most life decisions are open-ended. We cannot produce a checklist of all the important things to consider in choosing a friend, deciding to have a child, or taking a job. Nor can anyone tell in advance what considerations will be important in establishing the major aims, content, and structure of an educational program. These judgments are open-ended. Once some open-ended judgments have been made, later judgments, for example, of particular objectives and details of content and structure, are then limited by the earlier open-ended choices, but still much more open than is typical of theoretical issues.

Open-ended judgments involve bringing many values to bear on each alternative. In resolving practical problems incommensurable criteria of merit must somehow be weighed on a common scale of value. In comparing two curricula, we may find that one leads to better achievement among academically able students while the other leads to better achievement among low achievers. How do we weigh these competing merits in a common scale in order to decide upon a curriculum? On what rationally defensible grounds can we choose between adding economics, music, or sex education to an already full elementary curriculum, assuming we have sound proposals and strong support for each? These are examples of multivalued choices

Because the alternatives in a multivalued choice do not claim to offer the identical benefits to the same recipients, no straightforward calculation of overall merit is possible. Instead, we must ask what trade-offs people are willing to make among competing but incommensurable values.

All resolutions of curriculum problems involve trade-offs among competing values. When those involved in the decision disagree on values or priorities, the process of reaching a common judgment is further complicated. How different this is from solving theoretical problems!

Solutions of theoretical problems are eternal and absolute, but resolutions of practical problems may apply only to the particulars of local circumstances. When even one person has found a solution to a theoretical problem, it remains a solution for all persons and all circumstances, so long as the terms of the problem and the standards of the discipline remain the same. By contrast, resolutions of practical problems are relative to all the particularities and realities of life. Actions taken too late will not resolve the practical problem, nor will actions that are too expensive, too complicated, or lack political support. Resolutions of practical problems must also be adapted to realities of limited time, resources, knowledge, and skill. Theorists may take generations to settle a dispute, but those faced with a practical problem do not have the luxury of suspending judgment. For them, not to act is to act. To judge the adequacy of a proposed resolution of a practical problem, therefore, one must be acquainted with the particularities and realities of the situation where the problem exists.

The process by which either individuals or groups decide what to do about a practical problem is complex and mysterious. It involves subconscious components, subjective meanings, and the operation of all sorts of psychosocial needs such as those for power and prestige. For now we will neglect these mysteries and pretend that the process is fully rational in the broad sense of the term. That is, we will assume that people have reasons for their judgments and that they can express these reasons publicly. Their reasons may hold only private, personal significance, and they may be complex, inconsistent or incorrect, but we will assume that they have reasons and that they can express them if they wish. We will not assume that people's reasons will always seem good to others or even make sense, only that they have them and can express them if they wish.

Given this assumption, the essential logic of the process of reaching a shared judgment on a public course of action is straightforward. We imagine a course of action that might possibly resolve the problem and ask ourselves, "Would this course of action eliminate the problem?" Using our knowledge and experience, or by reasoning or guesswork, we reach a judgment: yes, no, or not sure. We compare our answers with others' and, when we differ, we ask for and give our reasons for our judgment. We continue in this way, eventually choosing the one of our imagined actions that seems best, all things considered. The process is a form of mental trial-and-error, in which we substitute some form of judgment for the trial itself. "Suppose we did this," we say. "What would happen, and how would we like it?"

When a course of action is proposed and a deliberating body has debated its merits, it often happens that the group can generate an even more promising course of action by modifying this one to accentuate its strong points and overcome its weak points. Thus, the proposal gets shaped in the course of deliberation. We may then speak of the problem as having been resolved by design.

Often when a curriculum problem is resolved by design the resolution is not expressed in words or symbols, but in curriculum plans or materials that embody the design. Resolutions achieved by design may be more subtle and intricate than resolutions achieved verbally. Resolution by design is therefore particularly appropriate when the success of a course of action depends crucially on many details. In such cases broad principles are insufficient guides to action, and the deliberating body must find a way to specify in detail the configuration of factors they believe to be crucial to the success of the broadly described course of action.

To express such subtleties in words is usually impractical. A live demonstration with opportunity for questions would be ideal—recall that the science curriculum deliberations presented earlier centered on just such a presentation. Often the best way to communicate resolutions of curriculum problems to many distant strangers is to design objects that embody the desired relationships (curriculum materials) or to design plans or procedures that others can use to make such materials. By examining, using, and even building the materials, others should understand the developers' intentions better than by reading any description of them.

The quality of any resolution that emerges from such a process depends critically on the basis we have for our practical judgments. A basis is a reason given to support a judgment, and the basis for a judgment is the complete set of reasons given to support it. If all you can say to justify your judgment is "It seems to me that a common curriculum would be better for our school," then your intuition is the only basis for your judgment. Your judgment is then completely subjective, since no one else knows why it seems so to you. This does not mean that the judgment is necessarily bad: some people have very good intuition about some things. But the best that others can do to judge the likelihood that your judgment will be good is to check your record in past decisions of a similar kind.

When you provide a more objective basis, others can check them to validate your judgment. For example, you might point to other schools that have adopted a common curriculum and argue that they, their students, staffs, and communities are better off than comparable schools that have offered a differentiated curriculum. Others can then study these schools and decide if they agree that schools with a common curriculum are better off. Or, you might argue that only a common curriculum is consistent with democratic ideals. Others can then study this argument and decide if they agree with it.

We may represent the rational core of resolution as a process of considering relevant evidence and arguments. From this point of view, those judgments are soundest that are the best informed or most considered. Qualitatively, this means that deliberators have considered the most important arguments and evidence. Quantitatively, it means that they have considered the greatest number and widest range of relevant arguments and evidence. If, after due consideration (a complex judgment), one course of action seems better, on balance, than another (a complex judgment), then the better must be compared against the next candidate until at last the best course of action is determined.

Resolutions of practical problems reached by deliberation are seldom final or definitive. The reasoning employed in deliberation is plausible inference, not formal logic, mathematical proof, statistical inference, or scientific verification. These rigorous forms of substantiation are not achievable in practical curriculum disputes, not even in principle. In particular, the final weighting of the relative force of various arguments for and against proposed alternatives can never be demonstrated to be superior to other weightings. It is appropriate, though, to ask whether the resolutions reached fit with the available evidence, formal and informal. And it is appropriate to ask that the resolution settled on be supported by the available evidence and argument better than any other course of action that the group proposed and considered.

But the best that we can expect from deliberation is a resolution relative to a limited set of considerations and relative to the abilities, values, priorities, and perspectives of the deliberating body. What may seem at the time a final resolution, always turns out to be a temporary one sustained by the shared limitations of a particular view that happened to prevail at the time. When circumstances or advances in knowledge change the prevailing view, the resolution stands revealed as only a partially valid resolution, and calls are heard for new reforms to bring practice in line with newly emerging views.

Although resolution by design adds additional flexibility and power to the possibility of an abstract resolution of curriculum problems, resolutions by design remain subject to the limitations inherent in all practical problems. Resolutions, whether expressed in a design or verbally, are still relative to the judgment of the deliberating body, and therefore different deliberators may reach different resolutions. Any resolution may be upset by the discovery of an alternative course of action not previously considered or by a previously unknown line of argument. Any resolution requires weighing incommensurable considerations, and a new weighting may result in a different resolution.

When is Deliberation Worth the Effort?

Because it does not lead to definitive resolutions, should we take practical reasoning seriously, then? Will we be squandering our limited time and energy in deliberation when no resolution can ever be shown definitively to be best? If resolutions are mere matters of opinion, why not just express the opinions in the first place and avoid the hassle of deliberation? In considering these important questions we must be careful to avoid polarizing all possibilities for the status of resolutions into two extreme opposites: truth and opinion. In such a dualism all answers to curriculum problems fall into the realm of opinion, and so all effort at rationality seems futile. Even if we cannot reach the perfect solution possible in theoretical problems, we can still aspire to make better decisions than we would have if we had simply acted on our first impressions. Whether the benefits of deliberation are worth the effort depends on the situation and on how well it is done. Decisions can be over-considered as well as under-considered, as the great English lexicographer and wit, Samuel Johnson, pointed out so eloquently more than 200 years ago when he said:

> Life is not long, and too much of it must not pass in idle deliberation how it shall be spent; deliberation, which those who begin it by prudence, and continue it with subtility, must, after long expense of thought, conclude by chance. To prefer one future mode of life to another, upon just reasons, requires faculties which it has not pleased our Creator to give us (Boswell, 1766, p. 368).

Whereas theoretical problems generally have only one solution, and that one perfect, practical problems generally have many imperfect ones. Infinitely fine gradations of resolution are possible. The quality of resolutions will in general depend upon the situation. A course of action may be better than all known alternatives for urban schools, but not rural ones, for large schools but not small ones, for academically talented students but not for average ones, for communities where children have few other opportunities but not for communities with a surfeit of juvenile options, and so on indefinitely. A course of action may be better than all known alternatives in the judgment of educational psychologists but not of professional educators in the field, in the judgment of educators but not the lay community, in the judgment of the better educated but not the less well-educated, in the judgment of progressives but not traditionalists, and so on indefinitely. The more the judgments differ, the more nearly a resolution seems to be a matter of mere opinion; the more they converge, the more nearly resolutions seem to be solidly grounded in something approaching truth. But the territory between these two extremes is the domain of the practical and it is there, where rationality guides but does not dictate, that most curriculum decisions fall.

From a humane perspective, the fact of being unable in general to reach universally acceptable, completely adequate resolutions to practical problems is an asset as much as a liability. It leaves us with a rich diversity of defensible actions. Who, after all, would want to live in a world where rationality dictated our every move? When, after due consideration, several courses of action seem defensible, then we have scope for freedom, self-expression, invention, assertion of will, even playfulness. Surely the world is a better place when scope for human choice can coexist with rationality.

Good deliberation is the main strategy for reaching better curriculum decisions, but deliberation is not a panacea. To do it well is an art that demands much study and long practice and entails much trouble and expense. The best-considered decision can lead to poor results because of human ignorance or unforeseeable events. Yet all hopes for rationality in human affairs rest on the assumption that better considered choices will turn out better, on the average and over the long run, than less well-considered choices. The alternative is to assume that our minds are impotent and our actions beyond our understanding. Even good deliberation can go awry and cause harm, the harm of wasted resources and delay if not more serious harm. As for poor deliberation, even the most inveterate and unexamined reliance on theory can be no worse than deliberation done poorly.

Using Practical Reason in Curriculum Improvement

Good deliberation is an art that demands study and practice and takes some trouble. Good deliberation should lead to informed, well-considered decisions, but even the best-considered decisions will not always lead to good results because of unforeseeable events or mistakes in implementing decisions. Furthermore, deliberation takes time and resources. As for poor deliberation, even the most inveterate and unexamined reliance on theory can be no worse than deliberation done poorly. Yet all hopes for rationality in human affairs rest on the assumption that better-considered choices will turn out better, on the average over the long run, than less well-considered choices. The alternative is to believe that our actions beyond our understanding.

A major purpose of the remaining chapters is to show how curriculum practice can be strengthened and improved through the adoption of a practical perspective and mastery of the associated practical arts. In this section we look at ways teachers, school leaders, and other curriculum practitioners can use the arts of the practical to improve curriculum practice.

Analyze Deliberations

The discussions of curriculum planning groups are typically freeform and hard to follow or summarize. A speaker often tucks a point into a convenient lull in the conversation even though it applies to an old issue or raises a new one. The unprepared listener can come away from an hour or more of deliberations with little more than a vague impression that the group seems to agree about most points but are divided on a few. Unraveling the tangled points and taking notes that make sense is much easier when you listen with the structure of deliberation in mind.

The basic structure of deliberation is to propose a course of action that someone thinks may resolve the practical problem and then to argue the pros and cons of that action in relation to others in order to pick the most promising action. The things to listen for in deliberations are therefore:

- the problem or problems the discussants intend to solve
- the courses of action they consider
- the arguments they give for and against each course of action
- the principles that they appeal to in order to give these arguments force
- the evidence that they use to substantiate these arguments.

In taking notes of deliberations, I use a format like that in Fig. 7.1. I start a fresh sheet for each problem I hear mentioned. Making a horizontal line about one quarter of the way down the sheet, I use the top section to record anything I hear people say about the problem, recording their exact words whenever I can. The larger bottom section I divide in

Problem	
Action 1	Argument 1.1
	Argument 1.2
	Argument 1.3
	Argument 1.4
	Argument 1.5
Action 2	Argument 2.1
	Argument 2.2
	Argument 2.3
	Argument 2.4
	Argument 2.5

FIG. 7.1. *Format for taking notes on deliberations.*

half vertically. The left-hand side I use to record the courses of action proposed, leaving much space between actions on the list. The right-hand side I use to record arguments I hear about any course of action. I mark arguments for the action with a '+' and arguments against it with a '−.' I also note principles they state in this column, marking them with a "P" and evidence, noted with an "E." Later, I can use these notes to restate the arguments clearly, completely, and coherently.

Following philosopher Stephen Toulmin's analysis of practical reasoning in *The Uses of Argument* (1958) we can express the basic form of practical arguments in the following sentence-patterns, one stated positively and one negatively.

[Positive] Since we are committed to principle P, we must favor action A because it would uphold value V and bring the favorable consequences F.

[Negative] Since we are committed to principle P, we must rule out action A. To do otherwise would commit the wrong W, and would risk the negative consequences N.

Some curricular arguments we encountered in the science curriculum development deliberations can readily be cast in this form. For example, consider the following paraphrases:

1. Since "students should learn to think as scientists do, which among other things requires that they decide for themselves when their data are adequate" (P), we must rule out "having teachers tell them that they must measure more accurately" (A). To do otherwise would "give them the wrong impression of scientific work" (W) and invite "formation of inappropriate authoritarian, unscientific attitudes" (N).

2. Since "students should not learn incorrect or misleading scientific principles" (P), we must rule out "allowing them to conclude erroneously that the period of a pendulum varies with its amplitude or mass" (A). To do otherwise would "teach falsehoods" (W) and invite "criticism from scientists, parents, and educators" (N).

Suppose we now adopt a skeptical attitude toward such arguments and ask: "How do you know that this principle rules out that course of action?" In responding to such a challenge we would give another argument that support the principle we used in the previous argument. This argument would refer to some evidence in the form of facts or data that we believe support our claim. We call this type of argument a justification.

In the first of the two arguments parsed above, a team member might ask another to justify the principle that "students should . . . decide for themselves when their data are adequate." Possible justifications might be:

• Good scientists decide for themselves when their data are adequate.
• Various respected science education authorities have gone on record urging that students should judge the adequacy of their data for themselves.
• Students who can't decide the adequacy of their data for themselves will not score well on statewide examinations.
• They have no choice; there are no experts in the classroom who would be better able to judge the adequacy of data than the students.

And so on. . . .

Someone could ask for evidence to support each of these justifications. How do we know that good scientists judge the adequacy of their data for themselves? When and where did those authorities express their support for this principle? I don't think that there are any items on the state tests that ask students to judge the adequacy of data. Don't teachers have more expertise than students? Wouldn't a junior scientist in a lab ask a senior supervisor to verify the adequacy of the data? Ultimately justifications convince the participants or they don't and build support for the action or undermine it.

The science curriculum developers frequently used evidence from observations they had made in classrooms that used the pendulum activity. They observed that students did not see the need for careful measurement even when the teacher gave them various hints. They observed that students' measurements of the pendulum's swing were not accurate enough to determine that the amount of weight on the pendulum does not affect its rate of swing. They observed that many students drew erroneous and misleading conclusions about motion from the activity. These data played a pivotal role in the deliberations. The team only discovered the problems when they saw students' reactions to the preliminary versions of the activities. The team members' extensive experience in teaching science to children enabled them to make many informed guesses about how students would respond, but in this case the students' reactions surprised them. For this reason we would be justified in calling these deliberations data-driven.

Not all curricular arguments are data-driven. Presumably, at an earlier point in their deliberations, when the team decided to undertake an activity such as this one, an activity that involved studies of the variables influencing a system, an activity that would demonstrate the value of careful measurement, they employed mainly theory-driven arguments. In theory-driven arguments, the key elements are general statements about education, science, science education, society's needs, children's needs, and the like, and the data are provided by the ordinary experiences of students and teachers.

Some such justification as this lies behind each argument given for adopting a course of action or ruling one out. The grand or ultimate conclusion that "We should do A" rests on many arguments for and against many potential courses of action, and each of these arguments implies data, warrants, and qualifications. It is this entire web or network of practical argumentation that forms the basis for and justifies the ultimate conclusion.

This discussion enables us to gain further insight into the relationship of theory to practical reasoning. Curriculum theory focuses our attention on the principles and values in which such arguments are grounded, to the neglect of the data, of the specifics of the courses of action, and of the qualifying conditions. Theory plays an indispensable part in deliberation by supplying and clarifying terminology, principles, and lines of argument and by drawing out hidden implications, pointing out needs for additional data, and the like. But the attempt to decide what should be the purpose, content, and organizing principles of an educational program by the use of theory alone (or primarily or first before practical considerations are taken up) sacrifices the intimate interplay of data, warrants, qualifications, and conclusions. Achieving a productive interplay of principles and data in making the many judgments and decisions that must go into any curriculum is the goal toward which we must strive.

No objection can be sustained, however, against the use of theory as a resource of mind for identifying, discussing, and resolving practical problems. Theories of various kinds can provide the concepts needed for posing and discussing problems, the substantive principles upon which to base arguments showing that one course of action is better than another, and even the criteria by which a resolution may be judged. We can now see how it is possible to resolve curriculum problems rationally without fulfilling the impossible requirement to build a comprehensive theory to answer all the questions that arise in curriculum practice.

Pose Problems More Insightfully

When given an opportunity to work on a curriculum problem, those who know about practical reasoning will examine the statement of the problem and look for ways to improve it. The accepted, conventional understanding of a problem is seldom adequate to guide curriculum improvement. "Everyone knows" that American youth have a "drug problem," but the developers of a school program to prevent teenage drug abuse would need a deeper understanding of the problem. Do these youngsters lack information about the harmful consequences of drugs? Do they lack alternative outlets for adolescent rebellion? Are they vulnerable to drug abuse because they suffer from poor social adjustment or low self-esteem or because they have too much time on their hands and too little sense of purpose? A curriculum improvement team would need answers to such questions in order to develop an effective program.

A curriculum leader serving on a committee to develop an improved beginning reading curriculum for a school or district might find committee members split between advocates of phonics and advocates of Look–Say methods. Presenting Itzkoff's analysis of the three stages of learning to read might enable the committee to pose the problem in a new way that avoids the polarization.

Leaders who adopt a practical perspective will look for an analysis of the problem, its origins, and its causes. What does research suggest about the incidence of the problem and variables associated with it? What does scholarship reveal about the adequacy of the various concepts people use to describe it and explain it? What has been the history of the problem? What are the views of the major contending parties and interests? What are the limiting cases of the problem, situations where it is and is not found and is more and less serious? A deep analysis would require one to compare alternative conceptualizations of the problem and alternative causal models, perhaps collecting additional evidence from library or field research and even to challenge strategic assumptions of prior investigators or recast the problem in new ways.

Groups are usually reluctant to spend time analyzing the problem. They are afraid that time spent on discussing the problem will be wasted, and they want to move quickly to considering solutions. A good leader can sometimes guide a team to discuss the problem productively, but it is not an easy task. A team that does not experience early success in such discussions will abandon them and begin exploring solutions. Analysis of the problem therefore usually falls to curriculum specialists who must do it as homework and find ways to smuggle the topic onto the group's agenda. A better strategy may be for leaders to commission an analysis of the problem before appointing the deliberating body. A leader might ask the group as their first order of business to consider the alternative ways of posing the problem explored in the analysis given them and to state the reasons for choosing the formulation that they decide to use.

Consider More Promising Alternatives

Before a group can find a solution to a curriculum problem, the solution must be among the alternatives they consider. Most curriculum improvement groups consider only a narrow range of options, most of them similar to present practice, and the rest inspired by if not taken from currently popular innovations. New and radically different possibilities, just because they are so unfamiliar, seem riskier and less likely to work. When the alternatives being considered consist of familiar activities, the likelihood is low that any of them will be markedly better than the ones in the current curriculum. Expanding their view to include currently popular innovations helps, but risks mere trendiness unless the group has a way of independently judging the educational value of the innovations.

Wise curriculum leaders stimulate curriculum improvement groups to consider at least one or two higher risk options that seem to hold great promise. Research is a promising place to look for radically new ideas that might prove quite powerful. For example, Martin E. P. Seligman in *Helplessness* (1975) presented a new theory of motivation that curriculum planners could use to help them think about how to improve students' motivation to learn. Seligman describes animal and human studies that show that when an organism experiences helplessness, that is, comes to expect that nothing it can do will change its unsatisfactory situation, it gives up responding altogether. He calls this learned helplessness.

Seligman showed that rats put into water after being subjected to prolonged helplessness by being held tightly until they ceased struggling would swim only half an hour on the average before they gave up. Rats not given the prior experience of complete helplessness swam for up to 60 *hours* before succumbing to exhaustion. In another experiment, dogs administered electric shocks that they could not avoid lapsed into complete lethargy. Even when the experimenters opened a way for them to escape, the dogs that had experienced helplessness did not move to take advantage of the new escape route. Eventually the experimenters had to drag them out several times before they finally learned that they could escape on their own.

Seligman maintains that these experiments show that helplessness—the expectation that one is powerless to change a bad situation—saps motivation, disrupts the ability to learn that one's responses can be effective, and ultimately produces depression.

Seligman's ideas provide curriculum planners with a way to think about how to motivate students to strive to learn. In dealing with students who have already experienced helplessness in learning, the lesson of learned helplessness is that these students may have to be forcefully guided to experience success before they will realize that they can learn. To prevent the development of helplessness, the curriculum maker will want to build opportunities for students to control their situation and also to build in safeguards against repeated experience of failure.

More subtly, Seligman's theory suggests that it may be important to challenge students. "To reverse classroom helplessness, it is necessary to experience some failure and to develop a way to cope with it. . . . If a young adult has no experience of coping with anxiety and frustration, if he never fails and then overcomes, he will not be able to cope with failure, boredom, or frustration when it becomes crucial" (pp. 157–158).

More adventurous curriculum leaders will be constantly on the lookout for new ideas that might be more powerful than familiar ones. They attend conferences, read journals, talk with other innovators, and try to be among the first to recognize new and promising approaches. More cautious leaders will monitor the experiences of their more adventurous colleagues and consider only those innovations that seem to succeed when tried in path breaking schools.

Choose More Judiciously

Ordinarily curriculum planning groups rely entirely on their own judgment to evaluate the alternatives that they consider. The science developers discussing the pendulum activity were exceptional in giving so much attention to evidence from classroom tests of preliminary activities. What they learned in these classroom tryouts affected their work profoundly, illustrating how much is to be gained by supplementing the unaided judgment of team members with relevant evidence.

Conduct Field Trials in Classrooms

Trying out new curriculums in a few classrooms and having the curriculum planning group discuss what happens in detail is one simple way to improve the evaluation of alternatives in curriculum planning groups. Such discussions can be centered on reports such as the one in the science example or on examples of students' work.

Materials developed by any method are only guesses at what might foster learning in classrooms. A field test in classrooms is a way to find out if the guess was on target. Peter Dow (1975) reports a surprising discovery from the field tests of an early version of *Man: A Course of Study*, an innovative social studies curriculum project developed in the late 1960s. The developers had teachers show students films of a baboon troop in the wild in order to contrast the behavior of baboons and humans. They discovered much to their surprise that children imputed human characteristics to the baboons. The children believed, for example, that the baboons had a baboon language just as complex as human language; humans just could not yet understand baboon language. Since the developers had introduced the unit on baboons to contrast animal behavior with human behavior, this finding of the field test forced major revisions. Subsequent versions of the materials included units on lower animals as well as baboons.

The main reasons to conduct field tests of curriculum materials are to answer two basic questions:

Do the materials work as developers expect?
Do students learn what developers expect them to learn?

Questions to ask prior to the field test:
Was it clear to students what developers expected them to learn?
Was it clear to students why developers believe that this is important to learn?
Did students believe that it was important to learn?

Questions to ask during the field test:
Were students able to comprehend the instructions and the tasks?
Did teacher and students complete the activity satisfactorily?
Were students and teachers able to tailor the activity to suit them and their
    different classroom situations?
Did the activity make good use of appropriate resources?
Did the activity support and assist students at critical points where they might
    falter?
Did the activity require resources not normally present in the classroom?

Questions to ask after the field test:
Did teachers and students find using the materials to be a positive experience
    that they would like to repeat?
Did students comprehend the materials?
Did teachers believe that students learned what developers intended?
Did students believe that they learned what developers intended?
Did the quality of students' work or their performance on authentic
    performance measures indicate that they had learned what the developers
    intended?
Was the learning achieved proportional to the resources consumed?

FIG. 7.2. *Basic questions for field tests of curriculum activities.*

"Working" includes such mundane but vital matters as:

- Does what happens in the classroom resemble what the developers had in mind?
- Can teachers and students use the materials without too much difficulty?
- Do teachers and students find use of the materials rewarding enough to continue to use them spontaneously?
- Is the project realistic in its demands on time, effort, facilities, teacher and student ability, and so on?

Figure 7.2 suggests more detailed questions of this same sort. If curriculum materials do not pass such tests as these, they are not really viable and must be revised or replaced.

Consider the Negatives, Too

Another simple way to improve the evaluation of alternatives in curriculum planning groups is to make a point of considering the negative points of their most promising alternatives. Groups are so determined to find a good alternative that, having found a promising one, they dare not look at its shortcomings for fear that it, too, will fall short and they will be left with nothing. Yet every course of action has limitations and undesirable side effects, and a mature professionalism will recognize these, call teachers' attention to them, and suggest ways of coping with them.

I try always to ask how and under what circumstances a curriculum fails. Some work pretty well in the hands of poorly prepared teachers while others fail miserably. Some work well even though students have a wide range of knowledge and skill while others only work when all students have a certain base of prior learning.

Be sure when comparing curriculums to compare them at their best and at their worst, as well as typically. Guard against unfair comparisons of one curriculum at its best to another at its worst. Look for outcome data from research and evaluation to supplement everyone's judgments about how well students will learn from a curriculum. And check the demands a curriculum makes on teachers' time and energy. I've seen a wonderful high school curriculum fail after a year or two because teachers could not continue to read and comment on student writing as often as the curriculum required. When student assignments became less frequent and teachers' comments less intense, a remarkable curriculum slid into mediocrity. Looking at a curriculum's limitations and the risks it may pose may seem negative, but when it becomes standard practice and leaders ask for it, participants will soon come to see it as constructive criticism.

Balance Diverse Considerations

Curriculum problems can look simple when we leave out important considerations. If the well-being of the individual child is paramount, then a highly individualized curriculum to meet each child's needs looks like a good solution. When we also consider society's need for common knowledge and a common language, the problem becomes more challenging. Curriculum change can seem to swing back and forth like a pendulum as reformers emphasize first one and then another consideration and push others far into the background. It would take the wisdom of Solomon for any individual to balance all the competing considerations perfectly, assuming that the ideal of perfect balance is even meaningful. But professionals acquainted with the history of curriculum reforms are in a good position to judge when things may be reeling out of balance. Curriculum professionals should look at the big picture and help other participants to see it, too.

The commonplaces of curriculum discourse are a useful conceptual tool for judging balance. If reformers emphasize students, say, over teachers, subject matter, or society, the emphasis may or may not be justified. If it corrects a previous neglect of students in shaping the curriculum, a temporary over-emphasis on students may be desirable. Another safeguard against imbalance is to make sure that the voices of all interested parties are heard. If subject matter specialists do not participate in curriculum planning, then they have no opportunity to protest that interdisciplinary curriculums are slighting important concepts from the individual disciplines. Giving students and parents choices may also be a way to ensure that their voices are heard.

Helping Practical Reason Work

Deliberation only leads to improvement under certain conditions. The practical problem must be important. The group needs to have enough internal agreement, organization, skill, and resources to implement a promising course of action. The deliberating body must be empowered to act or at least be assured of having great influence over the final decision-makers. And the deliberations must be timely. In this section we focus on some curriculum improvement practices that will help curriculum workers use practical reason to make sound, substantial, and lasting improvements.

The Deliberative Ideal

Ideally, good deliberation will lead to a course of action that is better, relative to certain values and beliefs. To show this, the deliberative body must:

1. construe the problem in the most defensible way;
2. consider all the most promising alternative courses of action;
3. consider in full the merits of each alternative, taking into account all relevant knowledge and using valid arguments to examine the bearing of this knowledge on the issue;
4. include the points of view and values of all interested parties to the decision; and
5. reach a fair and balanced judgment.

To reach this ideal a deliberative body would need complete knowledge and perfect justice, and so real curriculum deliberation always falls short of this ideal. The ideal's usefulness lies in setting an absolute standard against which to compare real deliberations. All other things equal, the closer deliberation comes to this ideal, the more faith we can have in our decision.

Challenges of Deliberation

Real deliberating bodies encounter several challenges in trying to approach the deliberative ideal.

Limited Knowledge of Principles

If they understood the problem, its causes, and consequences completely, the deliberating body could know that they have construed the problem properly and considered the best courses of action. A full understanding of the problem helps in examining the merits of alternative actions, too. Real deliberating bodies must make do with the partial understanding they can construct from generally accepted beliefs, available theory and research, professional judgment, commonsense, and guesswork.

Limited Knowledge of Particulars

Deliberating bodies must choose actions suited for particular situations—a particular period in the history of a particular country, state, and community, in one or more particular schools or school systems, staffed by particular teachers, led by particular administrators, and attended by particular students. To choose wisely they need to know the particulars of the situations that they are responsible for. They must rely on available data and keen, well-placed observations of a large sample of the realities of the settings, examined from the perspectives of various stakeholders, and interpreted with the same care that skilled therapists apply to understand individuals and families.

Limited Resources

Deliberation takes time and time is money and both are in very short supply for curriculum work. A local school system may be able at best to afford to pay half a dozen teachers to spend a few weeks in the summer or a few weekends in the school year. The deliberation that happens under severe time constraints is too superficial to lead to substantial curriculum improvements.

Deliberating bodies also need material resources to carry on their deliberations. Good deliberation may require background research, advice from experts, experimental field trials, and evaluations. Few funding agencies are willing to support anything as diffuse and ephemeral as deliberation except in times of crisis or when the deliberating body seems almost certain to make a major breakthrough. Limited resources prevent most deliberating bodies from achieving a deep understanding of the problem and fully exploring all the promising possibilities.

Limited Power

Ideally, deliberative bodies have the power make curriculum decisions themselves and to order them carried out. Real deliberating bodies usually recommend actions to some official or governing body with the power to act. When deliberative bodies lack the power to decide and act, their only option is to attempt to influence those who do. All too often those who discuss curriculum issues lack any power to act and their first priority is to acquire some influence over those who do. This complicates and distorts the deliberation by introducing a different criterion for a good resolution: one that the powers-that-be will accept. Persuading those with the power to act can become an end in itself rather than the means of implementing good curriculum decisions. On the other hand, ignoring the wishes of those with the power can make the deliberation a waste of time.

Furthermore, deliberating bodies in the real world must always keep in view the goal of building or retaining a base of power in addition to resolving the practical problem at hand. Because the authority to make curriculum decisions in the American system is widely distributed and constantly shifting, most curriculum deliberations need to influence a wide audience of teachers, school leaders, and parents. This broad audience restricts the group's ability to use esoteric scholarly or technical language and reasoning or deal with potentially controversial issues.

Limited Agreement on Value Priorities

Because arguments about the merits of a course of action always appeal to some values, different values or a different priority ordering among them may lead to a different final judgment. Curriculum decisions often hinge on value questions even more than on questions of knowledge and belief. For example, members of a school–community council may agree on the value of teaching students to think like scientists, but they may disagree about whether this aim is more desirable than teaching them to respect authority. Deliberating bodies whose members are deeply divided on values may find it impossible to resolve practical problems. The widespread disagreement on educational values characteristic of American society poses a serious challenge to curriculum deliberations.

Conclusion

Strictly speaking, then, full and fair deliberation requires conditions never fully realized and seldom closely approached. The ideal remains useful, however, if we understand that real deliberations need not attain it but should approach it as closely as circumstances permit.

Managing Deliberation's Difficulties: Some Practical Arts

Recognizing that curriculum problems are fundamentally practical and that deliberation is the essential method for resolving them in a principled way merely starts us off on the right foot. Much artfulness is required if we are to reach a sound resolution. There can be no rules for doing good deliberation. It requires the artful use of many skills. In this section we will briefly survey some of the skills that help groups to do better deliberation.

Collaborate

Individual schools and teachers lack the resources to do good deliberation except when they can focus their resources on very specific topics over a long time period. Nor do schools employ a wide enough range of world-class experts such as subject matter specialists, assessment specialists, psychologists, publishers, and the like. Teachers and schools need to reach out to innovators nationwide and even globally to find the best ideas. Curriculums are common creations of a people and of humanity. The wider the representation in creating them, the better. Collaborating with others outside the school who are interested in similar curriculum problems can be a powerful way to strengthen local curriculum improvement initiatives.

Teachers can collaborate with colleagues in their school and school system. Form study groups. Share the work and discuss your experiences. Seek out fellow teachers around the state, nation, and world who are working on similar curriculum problems, form a network, and collaborate electronically. Find innovators wherever they work—in schools, universities, think tanks, government agencies. Read what they have written. Ask them to confer with you, review your work, advise you, and visit your school.

A number of organized curriculum improvement networks, collaboratives, and coalitions are already in operation. The National Writing Project (*http://writingproject.org/*), one of the first curriculum improvement networks, began as the Bay Area Writing Project centered at the University of California at Berkeley. It now has many regional sites where teachers and professors interested in improving the teaching of writing meet periodically and work and study and learn together. If a suitable group focused on your curriculum problem has already formed, join it. If not, consider forming one yourself. Officials in your local district, state Department of Education, U.S. Department of Education, and professional association should be able to guide you to resources, people, and organizations.

Build a Sound Platform Based on Research, Theory, and Experience

A deliberating body should give explicit attention to the knowledge and beliefs that they will use. Curriculum development groups typically adopt a set of shared ideas that will guide their deliberations. This set of ideas constitutes a platform that expresses their beliefs and values and guides their deliberations in the same way that a political platform can guide party members in deciding on what political initiatives to support.

Writing down a platform of key shared understandings explicitly early in the life of a deliberative body and updating the platform periodically during the group's work can be a helpful tactic. It is important that the deliberative platform include explicit models of the curriculum problems or issues the group will be concerned with. Why and how did the problem arise? Why has the problem persisted? What are its causes? What are its consequences? Where, as will often be the case, they are uncertain about answers to such questions, they should make assumptions and explicitly label them as such. Where alternative assumptions seem equally plausible, they should state the alternatives and strive to study the problem further until they can reconcile them or show that one is preferable.

Adopting a theory as the backbone of a platform simplifies the deliberating body's task. Embracing a theory unquestioningly as an all-encompassing ideology simplifies deliberation and makes the deliberating body's commitments explicit, but it hinders pursuit of the ideal of full and fair deliberation by closing their minds to other aspects of reality and other values.

Those who commission deliberation on curriculum issues might well sponsor a sort of design competition among deliberative bodies, in which each is invited to submit preliminary platform statements and plans to the commissioning group. The commissioners can then solicit comment and criticism from the public, the profession, and various kinds of experts to these proposals.

Study Examples Closely

Deliberating bodies can guard against some of the pitfalls of theory both in building platforms and in deliberation by grounding their discussions in shared experience of real phenomena. They can develop a habit of discussing issues by reference to real cases, instances, and examples. When these are not available, they can construct hypothetical ones. In considering courses of action, they need not stop with verbal descriptions. Right from the beginning, they can develop hypothetical models or sketches of proposed actions and schematic or physical models or prototypes of the most promising ones.

Precedents can be systematically studied, especially where some precedents succeeded and others failed, so that some comparative analysis of faults and causes of failure becomes possible. Good deliberators try out promising solutions early and often and discuss the results intensively.

Be Constructively Self-Critical

Good deliberating bodies are self-critical. They study their own deliberations to identify weak arguments, unexamined assumptions, and overlooked considerations. When they find a gap or contradiction in their platform, they welcome the discovery as an opportunity to extend and deepen their understanding and to reach a more satisfactory resolution of their problem.

Consult with Experts

Good deliberating bodies actively seek additional knowledge by reading, consulting appropriate experts, and even by commissioning papers. They seek out informed and able people to comment on and criticize their work, including platform statements, design prototypes, and draft materials. They open their work to scrutiny by others and welcome comment and criticism.

Make Artful Use of Knowledge Through Argumentation

Good deliberators work hard to ensure that they consider the most promising alternatives. They resist the temptation to focus on one promising alternative early in their deliberations. Good deliberators make a point of seeking out the best available evidence. Deliberating bodies can explore proposals in more depth by deputizing doubters and dissenters to explore promising alternative paths. When comprehensiveness of deliberation is particularly important, they can use checklists to guide deliberation and make maps showing issues and arguments explored so far.

Good deliberators make a point of exploring the negatives of promising proposals. The euphoria of finding a new course of action that seems more promising than the others often blinds deliberative bodies to hidden weaknesses. Many people are reluctant to argue against a promising proposal for fear of alienating its proponents, gaining a reputation as a negative person, as disloyal, or as "not a team player," or interfering with the formation of the consensus needed for action. Good deliberators also make a point of testing the limits of claims and qualifying them appropriately. The best action overall may work well for many students and teachers but still fail for some, and good deliberators note these limitations and qualifications.

Good deliberation requires a willingness to reconsider how the problem under deliberation is posed. If the problem itself is not subject to deliberation, if people are prevented from asking whether this is really the problem and the most important problem, then the deliberations are limited and the problem is to that extent being treated in a technical rather than a practical way.

Learning to conduct and support good deliberation is an important skill for curriculum professionals. Doing good curriculum work of any kind—teaching with a curriculum, school curriculum leadership, policymaking, development, implementation, or evaluation—requires fluency, power, and precision in deliberation.

Manage Conflicts of Belief and Value

The deliberations of a group that is deeply divided about fundamental beliefs and values will always be contentious, and progress, if any, will be slow and painful. Nevertheless, a public divided about fundamental beliefs and values must often decide together on a common course of action. To expect deliberation to reconcile deep differences in social values is unrealistic. Working together to decide what to teach their children can bring different groups within a community closer together, but in general differences in beliefs and values will remain, and so deliberation must often proceed in spite of these differences.

Mutual comprehension of different points of view is an essential preliminary. In principle this involves learning the images, ideas, and judgments that constitute the others' point of view, learning what it emphasizes, what it leaves out, and what it depends upon, and appreciating the value commitments that support it. In practice, it means not only a great deal of talking and listening but also attentive monitoring of one another's decisions and actions with reference to cases, real and hypothetical. Comprehending others' different points of view is difficult work intellectually and emotionally, and it can take a long time. People need strong reasons to undertake it.

Those bent on particular reforms will resent time spent understanding other points of view. Some may feel threatened when it becomes apparent, as it usually does, that the other view has much to be said for it. Those responsible for the deliberations must make a delicate judgment as to whether the potential benefits of attempts to reconcile conflicting points of view outweigh the costs.

If so, a good beginning is to search for regions of validity for each position, those cases or situations that each view seems to handle best. Anatol Rappoport argues convincingly in *Fights, Games, and Debates* (1960) that until the parties acknowledge the validity of one another's views in their most favorable cases, they have no basis for further dialogue. When the parties are able to acknowledge at least some region of validity for the others' views then remaining disputes can be approached more constructively.

It often happens in curriculum issues that all views rest on a limited base of experience. The clash of opposing views offers an opportunity to reach out for new experiences that will inform everybody's views. Visits to schools, interviews with teachers, consultations with experts, and similar shared experiences that expand the base of common experience can often help to soften hardened views.

Those responsible for deliberations can increase the incentives for divided deliberative bodies to reach a commonly acceptable decision. For example, funds might be made available for implementing proposals on the condition that all parties endorse them. To increase the incentives for toleration and openness to other points of view, deliberation could be conducted in public, where intolerance would create an unfavorable impression on the uncommitted and thus penalize partisan dogmatism.

Those responsible for the deliberation must take care to see that weaker parties are not unduly coerced into participating in deliberations on unfavorable terms. Dominant groups can arrange deliberation so that weaker groups are forced to agree to conditions they would not freely accept. Views of minorities or less powerful subgroups within the deliberative body that are unacceptable to the majority or dominant subgroups may simply be ignored and the views of the dominant ones adopted as the group's joint view. All deliberation is somewhat coercive, but there are moral and legal limits.

The path of least resistance when faced with fundamental differences of belief and value among deliberating body is to let the contending parties go their separate ways without attempting to resolve conflicts. Those unhappy with a look–say reading program may be invited to enroll their children in another classroom or school that uses a phonics approach.

This tactic of curriculum differentiation can be constructive, but its usefulness is limited. When it frees representatives of different points of view to develop their own resolutions based on their separate values, it enriches everyone's options. But it costs more to maintain several alternatives and, since no society can ever afford to provide every curricular option anyone might want, the necessity for making hard choices still remains for some. Administration of curricula with multiple alternatives is more complicated. Families must invest more time and effort in studying the merits of the alternatives and making a choice. Curricular differentiation promotes social fragmentation and undermines social unity, as different economic, social, ethnic, or economic groups enroll in different curricula.

The best possibility of all would be to develop curricular alternatives that are clearly superior to the other options for all parties. Some authorities maintain that the techniques for mathematics teaching used in Japan and China produce results for all students that are superior to techniques used by American teachers. Others hold out the promise that the learning sciences or brain research are leading to the development of new teaching strategies that are markedly more effective for all students.

Consider Alternative Points of View

Good deliberation looks at problems from the points of view of all the interested parties and seeks whenever possible resolutions that are superior from every point of view. People bring an integrated point of view to deliberation, not just a collection of ideas. An individual's ideas about a particular curriculum question are an integral part of a larger fabric or framework of more or less consistent ideas that form that person's educational point of view. Adding or changing one idea can create tensions, and people naturally resist adopting any new idea until they can reconcile it with their point of view.

When most people or the dominant group share a particular worldview, we speak of it as the dominant view or the prevailing view. Most curriculum problems encountered in the daily work of educators come posed in terms of the prevailing view among educators. Most people hold the prevailing point of view in a state of tacit, unquestioned acceptance. Seriously considering an alternative view requires them to question the prevailing view, a view that they and everyone they know holds. Continuing to hold the prevailing view after questioning it requires a choice, a new commitment, and an assumption of true responsibility for the consequences of this view in light of their new awareness that there are alternative views with different consequences.

Considering alternative points of view is risky socially and politically as well as intellectually. Except for those who love lost causes, it only makes sense to undertake the risk when there is reasonable support in the school community for an alternative point of view. Even then, persuading members of a deliberative body to consider another point of view is a very high and difficult art.

Consider Context

Good deliberation respects the conditions set by the social and institutional context. That context has a powerful influence on deliberation whether anyone wishes it to or not. Institutions typically determine membership of the deliberative body, its charge, its authority, and the resources at its command. Good deliberations also take context into account in their reasoning.

Much consideration of context happens tacitly. Members of the deliberating body who have lived and worked within the context use the rich images they have formed of it in their personal experience. They remember people, events, stories, sayings, artifacts, and conversations, and these images affect "gut feelings" about issues. Tacit images surround and suffuse articulate, formal thought and discourse. Each person will have a unique set of images, but they will overlap to some degree with the images of others who experienced the same context. They will rely on these images in many ways during deliberation. Their memories of teaching activities may inspire ideas for new ones, or they may perform thought experiments to predict how the people in their school might respond to a proposed course of action.

The problem for those who seek better deliberation is to extend, deepen, and sometimes change outdated or inappropriate images individuals bring with them to deliberation and to reconcile conflicts among them to achieve a sufficiently common basis for judgment and action. Good deliberating bodies arrange to experience the context at first hand whenever possible by observing classrooms and schools, examining student work, touring communities, visiting homes and businesses, and interviewing stakeholders and inviting input from them. A member of the team may shadow an individual (student, teacher, school official, etc.) through all the events of one day or week. Studies, such as opinion polls and demographic projections, can often provide more valid and extensive knowledge of the context than is accessible to personal experience.

Gaining common experience with the context is especially important in schools and communities that are changing rapidly. To imagine how their context might be different, they might visit other schools and communities with similar characteristics that have successfully addressed the problem they are trying to solve.

Taking context into consideration in curriculum deliberations requires difficult and delicate judgments. The rights of individuals and role groups are affected. Resolving curriculum problems requires actions in specific classrooms and schools staffed by particular people whose identity is a matter of public record. When a deliberative body decides on a course of action that a teacher or a principal will be responsible for carrying out, they need to know about those individuals. But learning about them may intrude on their privacy, perhaps upon their professional autonomy, and might well put them in the position of having the quality of their prior work evaluated. When the curriculum problem involves a number of sites, the threat to individuals is less immediate, but the threat to role groups remains strong. Situations so crucial to the welfare of those concerned must be handled in ways that respect the legal and moral rights of those affected.

Representation of affected individuals and groups on the deliberating body is basic in ensuring that they and their rights will be fairly and accurately represented in the deliberations. Deliberative bodies must also be careful in deciding which matters to consider publicly and which to handle privately. Determining which authorities have jurisdiction over various matters and giving them appropriate roles in the process is also important, as are negotiating roles for the parties involved and procedures for assigning individuals to those roles, and arranging for appropriate places, times, and auspices for meetings.

To go much further on the topic of the role of context requires us to consider deliberation in specific kinds of contexts. The chapters that follow will treat considerations that deliberating bodies should attend to in two primary contexts for curriculum work: classrooms and schools.

Limitations of Deliberation in Curriculum

Appointing a committee to conduct deliberations is not the appropriate response to every curriculum problem. In fact, full face-to-face deliberation by representatives of the major interested parties to a decision is a relatively specialized technique that requires some rather unusual conditions. Figure 7.3 lists some of these conditions. Situations where all these conditions are met seldom arise spontaneously in curriculum planning.

Deliberation is primarily helpful when:

- The community that sponsors and supports the deliberations agrees to resolve the problem by rational search for a common, defensible course of action, in preference to such other methods of resolving the problem as power politics, voting, leaving decisions to be made in a market, or violence.
- The parties to the deliberations are in genuine doubt about which course of action is best, as contrasted with a situation in which all of the parties are convinced in advance that one course of action is best and enter deliberations to convince the others.
- The deliberating body agrees on fundamental commitments, or failing that, when all contending parties have a strong desire to reach a common resolution, and when institutional arrangements have been established for resolving conflicts definitively on the basis of rational arguments.
- The deliberating body is empowered to make the final decision, or, failing that, when the resolution recommended as a result of the deliberations will carry more weight with the actual decision-makers than other recommendations.
- The problem is important enough to justify the trouble and expense of deliberation.
- Enough knowledge exists to give a sound rational basis to the discussions, ensuring that it is not just a clash of insupportable opinions.
- The deliberating body has or can get the knowledge, expertise, resources, and time needed to resolve the problem.
- The social and institutional context leaves the deliberating body free to consider all points of view.

FIG. 7.3. *Conditions necessary for effective deliberation.*

- Precedent, custom, routine, tradition
- Unconstrained choice by individuals
- Politics (voting, organizing, activism, etc.)
- Choices of buyers and sellers in a market
- Raw power (threats, violence, domination)
- Formal negotiation (bargaining)
- Delegation to an expert

FIG. 7.4. *Alternatives to deliberation for resolving curriculum problems.*

Figure 7.4 lists some alternatives to deliberation for resolving curriculum problems. Each of these has its limitations, too. Presumably the exercise of raw power is a last resort on both moral and practical grounds, though it is an important last resort for those whose other actions go unheeded. Tradition in its various forms is most convenient, effective, and economical until circumstances change or new alternatives become available. Delegation to an expert merely displaces the responsibility for deliberation from the authorized body to the expert, a desirable displacement in fact-driven decisions where specialized knowledge or intricate calculations are appropriate. Reliance on unconstrained choices by individual teachers, students, or parents limits the need for official decisions, but does not eliminate it since someone must still decide which options to offer. In a true market system even this decision is left to sellers. Formal negotiation seems appropriate only when attempts to secure agreement through deliberation have failed.

Several of these seem to be promising alternatives to deliberation for the general case of making major curriculum decisions. Individual choice either from official options or from those provided by a market, formal negotiation, and some sort of voting seem to me to hold the most promise. Student choice seems to work reasonably well in colleges and universities. Voucher systems now being tried experimentally in some states would create a market in schools from which students and parents could freely choose, and schools would probably respond by adjusting their offerings to suit customer preferences, thus creating a market in courses and programs as well.

The chief contrasts between market mechanisms and deliberation is that deliberation is inherently and fundamentally public and verbal, whereas markets operate privately by direct actions of buyers and sellers. The highly verbal, public processes of formal deliberation may not always be the most suitable way of making curriculum decisions. Nathan Rosenberg and L. E. Birdzell, Jr., express this point well when they contrast political decisionmaking ('the verbal method') with economic decision-making via the market.

> The verbal method of decision making allows extended debate, further experiment, a weighing of costs and benefits, conflicts of expert opinion, successive resort to different political jurisdictions each with the authority to obstruct change, pleas for reconsideration, and other familiar exercises in decision making and law. . . . The use of verbal decision making . . . implies . . . that the benefits of the innovation are sufficiently understood and predictable that they can be persuasively verbalized in advance of its adoption (Rosenberg & Birdzell, 1986, p. 310).

Because of its verbal nature, deliberative decisionmaking tends to favor those who are articulate in public debate, which means well-educated, economically advantaged groups are favored, along with professionals trained in the use of specialized language.

That deliberation is a public performance favors conventional ideas. Less familiar ones are more likely to seem strange and thus threatening or laughable, and so may not be taken seriously in the heavy atmosphere of public decisionmaking. Extremely unpopular ideas also stand little chance of gaining a fair hearing in such a setting.

There is a whole universe of considerations that are of great personal importance but that are taboo in serious public decisions in our culture—sentimental or emotional attachments, feelings, beliefs close to the core of one's personality, or family values and traditions. Individuals making their own decisions about what to study, by contrast, are free to consider whatever they please in complete privacy. Reliance on individual decisions made in private, on the other hand, sacrifices the possibility that truth may emerge from a dialogue, though some form of dialogue still emerges as people comment on one another's choices in public.

These contrasting characteristics of deliberation and market choices suggest that they may complement one another and that it might be desirable to allow both to come into play in some way in curriculum decisionmaking.

In general, then, individual choice and market mechanisms seem to provide useful alternatives to deliberation as methods for resolving curriculum problems. Which is better will depend on the situation.

Raw power seems to be the least desirable option, but in reality it often comes into play. Those responsible for curriculum decisions can do a great deal to check the arbitrary exercise of power. They can learn to recognize partisan manipulation of deliberation and expose it. Deliberation can be subverted all too easily with such tactics as hand-picked committees stacked in favor of one alternative, obfuscation and mystification through the use of jargon, unrealistic limits of time and resources, grandstanding, bandwagoning, sloganeering, even intimidation and coercion. By establishing conditions that make it necessary for the powerful to employ such tactics openly, political opposition can often be aroused to check their power. Administratively, deliberation is subject to subversion by bureaucracy, red tape, and unreasonable formalism, ills that alert, and vigorous leadership can forestall.

Leaders can encourage deliberating bodies to resolve conflict in principled ways, to maintain an open mind, and to consider other points of view. The best ways to encourage such tendencies are by example, by maintaining open, representative institutional procedures, and by heaping public honors on those responsible for conspicuous instances.

Deliberation, along with all other methods of curriculum decisionmaking, is subject to the limitations of the culture it operates within and the limitations of the human situation. Curriculum planners cannot step outside the culture, no matter how hard they try. One of the most important arts of deliberation, then, is to know when deliberation is justifiable and when an alternative would be better.

Practical Approaches to Curriculum Improvement

Approaching curriculum improvement from the perspective of the practical can add dimensions not apparent in common sense approaches or theory-based approaches. Practical approaches can be guided by the latest and best theory and research yet not blinded by them to important common sense considerations. Practical reasoning offers a way to be thoughtful and rigorous about curriculum decisions without being pedantic or doctrinaire. It offers a way toward a better curriculum that allows for diversity of values and views. It has much to recommend it.

Questions and Projects

1. Observe a class or a videotape of a class in which an able, experienced teacher teaches a subject you know well. Find the points when the teacher adjusts the curriculum to the students.
2. Read about an historically important curriculum project. Identify its sponsors and find out how the founders negotiated a charter with the sponsors. If possible, examine materials created by the project. In what ways are they consistent and inconsistent with the project's charter?
3. Write a briefing paper to the new executive director of a foundation who wants to improve the curriculum in a particular subject. Assume that she is knowledgeable about the subject but not about curriculum development. Explain what can and cannot be accomplished by curriculum materials development projects. Explain what is involved in sponsoring a curriculum materials development project.
4. Find a curriculum development group at work in your area, and ask to sit in on their meetings. Record and study their deliberations. Write out the main ideas in their platform. Watch how they rely on ideas from their platform in making decisions. See if you can locate weaknesses in the platform by studying instances where the team is unable to resolve questions or where controversies persist.
5. Read a book or article from psychology, philosophy, or a social science that you think might provide the same kind of platform support as Hughes' or Seligman's works. Abstract the main ideas that you believe would be useful for a curriculum development platform. Apply those ideas to existing materials in some school subject and suggest how the materials should be revised to be consistent with these ideas.
6. Write a critical assessment of the comparative merits of two or three competing ideas as alternative platform elements. For example, Seligman's learned helplessness and Bandura's social modeling theory.
7. One of the weaknesses of curriculum development projects is that perspectives of the clients and users of the materials (teachers and students especially) sometimes get lost. Suggest how this weakness might be mitigated.
8. Choose a particular educational problem that you feel familiar with, such as teaching science or foreign language to elementary school children. Identify two or three educational programs designed to resolve this problem. Critically and comparatively assess these two programs on the criteria suggested in this chapter. Suggest design features that would make the programs more effective curriculum improvement initiatives.
9. Analyze existing curriculum materials in an area you are familiar with. Ask questions such as those included in Fig. 7.2 about these materials. Does the entertaining of these questions generate ideas for improving the materials?
10. Choose an educational activity that you find intrinsically interesting for whatever reason. Analyze this activity and identify its basic schema. Develop a theory that explains how the activity promotes learning. Assess the strengths and limitations of the activity for various educational uses. Find a better activity or, if you cannot, find the next best alternative activity.
11. Observe teachers using curriculum materials. Note the kinds and degrees of adaptation and variation they make as they use the materials. Comment on whether you think these adaptations strengthen or weaken the learning intended by the project and the overall learning students do as a result of using the materials.

12. Choose a unit from a curriculum development project, preferably a real one but possibly a hypothetical one. Prepare an evaluation plan for it. Make up a set of questions specific to your project that would help determine if the curriculum worked and how it can be improved. Outline observations, interview questions, and test instruments that would provide the best evidence on each of the questions you raise. List what you consider to be the three most serious threats to the validity of the answers you would get from the data you mentioned earlier. Suggest low-cost methods for controlling for them or accounting for their contribution to the results.
13. Find or develop measures for a given outcome of some sophistication. Criticize the measures that you find and suggest ways to improve them.

Further Study

The seminal work on the topic of this chapter is Joseph Schwab's *The Practical: A Language for Curriculum* (1970). It is powerfully but tightly argued and elegantly but densely written, and this makes it demanding reading, but it amply rewards close study and many careful readings. His subsequent papers on the practical (Schwab, 1971, 1973) are more difficult and address narrower questions but are still of great value. William Reid's *Curriculum as Institution and Practice* (1999) contains useful ideas on the application of practical reason to curriculum. Robert Ennis's chapter in the *Eightieth Yearbook of the National Society for the Study of Education*, "Rational Thinking and Educational Practice" (1981) is a very careful and thorough analysis of the concept of rational thinking in educational practice that can be usefully applied to curriculum decisions. Sir Geofrey Vickers seems to me to be the most eloquent contemporary spokesman for practical reason as the preferred method for making public decisions in a democracy. *Value Systems and Social Process* (1968) is the most relevant to the concerns of this chapter. *Making Institutions Work* (1973) is also pertinent.

The primary sources on the nature of practical reasoning are accessible to the general reader. Aristotle's *Politics* is still a useful beginning. David Gauthier's spare volume, *Practical Reasoning* (1963) is a sparklingly clear philosophical introduction. Stephen Toulmin's *The Uses of Argument* (1958) meanders about several themes, but the parts on construing practical arguments are still the best elementary treatment of the logic of practical reasoning. Brian Barry's *Political Argument* (1965) suggests many useful parallels with those types of curricular argument that occur most often in debates over policy issues. Oliver Stutchbury's *The Use of Principle* (1973) covers much the same territory as Schwab and Toulmin and reaches similar conclusions on the logic of practical discourse, but poses them in a manner more sympathetic to theory, treating the practical as application of theory to particular cases.

A number of investigators have studied curriculum deliberations in detail. My own investigations of several curriculum projects (Walker, 1970, 1971a, 1971b, 1971c; Walker & Reid, 1975) provide analyzed examples of real curriculum deliberations. Judith Riley (1984a, 1984b, 1984c) has studied the course development processes of the Open University and characterized those deliberations.

CHAPTER EIGHT

Improving Classroom Curriculum

The landscape of teaching, learning, and teacher education is changing. Once, teachers majored in elementary or secondary education. Today, most states require that all teachers, elementary and secondary alike, major in an academic subject. Once, mastery of basic skills was considered sufficient education for most students . . . Today, we expect all students to complete high school and most high school graduates enroll in postsecondary education. Furthermore, students are expected to develop more sophisticated understandings of subject matter to prepare themselves for a changing and increasingly technological society.

— Pamela Grossman and Susan Stodolsky, American Educators, 1995

Questions

- What challenges do teachers face in making major changes in the curriculum of their classroom?
- How can curriculum specialists help teachers make major changes in the curriculum of their classrooms?

Changing the Classroom Curriculum: The Hardest Curriculum Problem?

Achieving substantial, lasting improvements in the curriculums of large numbers of classrooms may be the greatest curriculum challenge. It is probably not impossible, although Americans have not achieved it in this century. The dozens of massive curriculum reform movements Americans have seen since World War II, including the standards-based reforms currently underway, have all failed to change the curriculums of most American classrooms. Few progressive reforms can be found in American classrooms today. The post-Sputnik reforms did not transform the teaching of science and mathematics. The Great Society reforms did not substantially reduce the gap in educational achievement between privileged and disadvantaged children. Let us see what makes this problem so hard.

Conventional Classrooms

Conventional classroom instruction, directed by teachers, centered on a textbook, using traditional didactic methods, has been out of favor with educational leaders and teacher educators for at least a century. Nearly every scholar who looks at teaching concludes that more adventurous methods that place students in more active roles, individualize instruction, and present more challenging and authentic content would be more effective. Yet conventional classrooms endure. Year after year in school after school most teaching follows these routines. Even those teachers who want to break out of conventional classroom routines find it difficult to do so.

Over the past 3 or 4 decades, curriculum scholars have studied the persistence of the conventional classroom in the face of so many determined efforts to change it (Cohen, 1988; Cuban, 1993). They point to four main causes for the continuing success of conventional classrooms: confining frames, old-fashioned public expectations, ingrained teacher habits and beliefs, and the usefulness of conventional teaching strategies for teachers.

Confining Frames

Frames that can severely limit teachers' flexibility in changing classroom routines include:

- **Types of classes offered**—officially determined categories such as grade levels (K–12) and school subjects
- **Time allotments**—the amount and distribution of time in the school schedule allocated to a class
- **Space allotments**—the size of room allocated to a class, provision for use of other rooms
- **Teacher characteristics**—characteristics of the teacher assigned to the class, such as subject-matter competence
- **Students, number, and characteristics**—the number and characteristics of the students assigned to the class, especially age, academic ability, and prior achievement
- **Materials and facilities**—type of teaching/learning materials and facilities supplied for use in the class.

A classroom assigned a large number of students and little space will be so crowded that any movement or noise by students would disrupt classroom activities, so a teacher faced with such a situation would be forced to institute strict rules to control noise and movement. Similarly, a teacher given too little time and inadequate teaching materials may find that lectures and seatwork are the most effective ways to cover the prescribed material. On the other hand, a high school that offers courses such as inventing, the minority experience, designing computer games, and home and family living invites teachers try innovative teaching methods.

The curriculum materials available in a classroom powerfully influence the content presented to students. Students learn from them directly, of course, but materials also influence what teachers present. Various studies suggest that from 30% to more than 90% of all classroom instruction is based directly on textbooks and other published curriculum materials (Komoski, 1976; McCutcheon, 1980). McCutcheon (1980), for instance, studied 12 elementary teachers and reported that they all relied on the textbook as the major source of their classroom activities.

From 85–95% of reading and mathematics activities in these twelve classrooms was based on suggestions in the teacher's guide (p. 8).

For teachers to cover any content that is not included in the standard curriculum materials provided to each student requires additional work from teachers. They have to present the materials to students themselves orally or find materials or create them and provide them to students. Also, teachers must assume full responsibility for materials they introduce into their classroom, whereas the authority of the institution protects teachers when they use the officially provided materials.

Public Expectations

Public expectations put pressure on teachers to keep a certain kind of order and atmosphere in their classroom and to achieve certain kinds of results. We saw in Chapter 6 one formulation of the expectations placed upon teachers and students (Westbury, 1978):

Coverage—presenting certain topics, content, or material to students
Mastery—acquiring certain levels of achievement, demonstrating certain qualities of performance
Affect—maintaining constructive feelings and attitudes in the classroom
Order—maintaining good conduct, discipline, and order in the classroom

According to Abrahamson, the public expects teachers to maintain acceptable overall levels of performance in all four of these areas. Meeting one, two, or three of these expectations is a great deal easier than meeting all four. A teacher who increases demands for coverage and mastery may find that affect or order or both suffer.

The official curriculum is the most visible way that the public expresses its expectations for coverage. Tests are the most visible way it expresses mastery expectations. Published standards of conduct reinforced by observations by the principal and other officials express expectations for affect and order. In addition to these public, official expressions, word of mouth among informal social networks also expresses informal social expectations.

Ingrained Habits and Ideas

Conventional teaching reflects and reinforces commonly held ideas about teaching and learning. George Hillocks (1999) studied 19 teachers of writing in a large urban community college system for 2 years. He found that frontal teaching, teacher-directed lecture or recitation occupied nearly three-fourths of class time. Small group work, independent work, and individual conferences occupied between 10 and 15% of class time. Hillocks identifies several of beliefs that supported teachers in using conventional methods. One is what he calls an "objectivist epistemological stance": "These teachers appear to believe that teaching is objective, that what is to be learned may be laid out, and that learners can listen and learn, as though the knowledge is directly absorbable into the mind, without transformation" (Hillocks, 1999, p. 93). Hillocks contrasts this belief with what he calls a constructivist stance, a belief that students must take active roles in their own learning, transforming what they encounter into their own personal forms of understanding. Hillocks concludes that changing conventional teaching will be more difficult than anyone expected because it requires the teacher to change fundamental beliefs and adopt a new professional identity.

In addition to ingrained beliefs, teachers in conventional classrooms have also developed ingrained habits. Teachers have overlearned the patterns and rituals of conventional teaching to such an extent that teaching conventionally seems natural and effortless, whereas other ways of teaching require effort and practice. Changing ingrained habits is always an enormous challenge.

Teachers are not the only ones whose ingrained habits and beliefs sustain conventional teaching. During the century that conventional classrooms prevailed in American elementary and secondary schools, generations of students have experienced years of conventional instruction. Students, teachers, and the public hold images of good teaching that are so strongly colored by everyone's experiences with conventional teaching that any other pattern seems strange. Innovators who advocate new classroom patterns face a skeptical public firmly attached to familiar patterns.

Usefulness to Teachers

An important reason why these traditional patterns are so pervasive and persistent, despite so much opposition, is that they permit teachers to cope with some rather difficult constraints of classrooms. Conditions prevailing in classrooms make many demands on teachers and place strict limits on the resources available for meeting them. Conventional teaching helps teachers to meet the demands within all the imposed limits.

The public expects teachers to maintain acceptable overall levels of performance in coverage, mastery, affect, and order in an environment that is in some respects quite limited. It is limited in space to one room, which must accommodate 20 to 40 students. It is limited to one teacher with just so much talent and preparation, to those students who happen to be assigned or elect to attend, to a few textbooks per pupil, and to a fixed number of hours per day and days per year. These limitations do a great deal to determine what sort of social interactions will be successful in classrooms. Because mastery is expected of students, evaluation of students is necessarily a prominent feature of classrooms. Since classrooms are crowded, evaluation, along with everything else that happens, is necessarily public. Under these circumstances, competition is almost inevitable. Because the ratio of children to adults is so large, and because space is so limited, interactions between children are likely to be frequent and, unless the children are exceptionally well-socialized, many of these interactions will be noisy, violent, or otherwise disruptive. Maintaining enough order so that demands for coverage, mastery, and affect can be met requires a great deal of attention and effort from the teacher. Under these conditions, a focus on strict discipline is almost inevitable.

The conventional classroom interaction pattern, competently implemented, enables teachers to cope with these rather restrictive demands and limitations. A good teacher running a conventional classroom establishes rules and routines early in the year which limit students' movement, actions and noise, and thus fulfill the demand for order while simplifying what would otherwise be an excessively distracting environment.

By dealing with the class as a whole in a single set of classroom activities, the teacher simplifies the situation even further. The teacher plans activities to suit as many students as possible, and paces activities to ensure adequate coverage of the content assigned to the course. The textbook presents content to be learned, offers exercises for practice, and problems to test mastery. By questioning pupils and giving homework and tests, the teacher discovers what they have and have not learned. Intermittent questions and continual supervision help the teacher keep students' attention.

Teachers who strive to achieve ambitious learning goals such as deep conceptual understanding, problem-solving, or expressive fluency and power often experience extra tensions. The learning they seek cannot be packaged neatly in textbooks, worksheets, or tests. Students, parents, colleagues, and superiors may be skeptical of its value. They may question teachers' judgments about the quality of student work. An adventurous teacher must respond to unique works students create and this is more demanding than responding to students' answers to set questions. Many teachers understandably prefer to avoid these tensions. One way to avoid them is to adopt conventional practices.

Critics of conventional teaching refer to this as "teaching defensively." Teachers ask little of students. They eliminate difficult content and goals and anything ambiguous or open to multiple interpretations. They distill complex subjects into neat lists and stories for students to remember. They set a high priority on covering prescribed topics. They present the content in packaged forms as lists of items to be recalled for passing tests.

Linda McNeil in *Contradictions of Control: School Structure and School Knowledge* (1986) traces the cause of defensive teaching to efforts by the school organization to control teachers. "When the school's organization becomes centered on managing and controlling, teachers and students take school less seriously.... They fall into a ritual of teaching and learning that tends toward minimal standards and minimal effort. This sets off a vicious cycle. As students disengage from enthusiastic involvement in the learning process, administrators often see the disengagement as a control problem. They then increase their attention to managing students and teachers rather than supporting their instructional purpose" (McNeil, 1986, xviii).

Conventional teaching is not necessarily defensive. Good conventional teaching will have none of these characteristics of defensive teaching. But the forces that make conventional teaching easier and safer than more adventurous teaching, harnessed by school leaders bent on control, can produce the pathology of defensive teaching.

The secret of the conventional classroom's success is that the conventional formula does many things reasonably well in varied circumstances while economizing on limited resources. In conventional classrooms teachers can carry out simultaneously the functions of custodial care, socialization, and academic training. Conventional classrooms require only one adult with a college education and little specialized training to supervise 30 or more children. They economize on the teacher's time, energy, and expertise. They require little capital or technology. Schools can set conventional classrooms in operation in an almost identical form in any location. They can be adjusted easily for age ranges from kindergarten to graduate school and for virtually any subject, academic or otherwise. They are familiar and unlikely to arouse controversy.

Compared to individualized instruction, for example, the conventional classroom achieves test results that are at least comparable and often superior (Miller, 1976; Schoen, 1976) while placing less severe demands on the teacher's resources of time, skill, knowledge, attentiveness, imagination, and energy. Individualized instruction requires a greater variety of more carefully designed and expensive self-instructional curriculum materials. It requires specialized teacher training in managing a more complex classroom organization and record system. If we adopted a smaller pupil–teacher ratio and invested more capital in self-instructional materials and educational technology, individualized instruction might become the dominant formula for classrooms. But schools would then be more expensive.

Similarly, teachers could be trained to operate classrooms with more varied and complex social interactions—including, say, students helping one another and flexible use of a variety of media by small groups of students. But such classrooms would require teachers with much more specific training than conventional classrooms require. The more specialized alternative would have to offer definite benefits to offset this greater cost and vulnerability to failure.

Why Conventional Classrooms Persist

The conventional classroom is a limited and limiting form. It makes very inefficient use of students' time, energy, and talents. Time is wasted in waiting for the teacher—since nothing can happen without the teacher—and for the entire class to get ready for the next lockstep move. Some students expend frantic efforts to keep up with a pace that's too fast for them, while others waste it studying things they already know because most of the class needs to learn them. All students waste weeks of their lives every school year simply sitting and listening because that's all they're permitted to do when they could learn more by using and testing more actively what they are learning. The conventional classroom is not effective for teaching manual skills, eye–hand coordination, performing, or other forms of nonverbal learning. Social interactions among peers and between adults and children are so restricted by classroom interaction patterns that social learning is hampered.

The conventional classroom organization persists not because it is effective, but because it is cheap, familiar, robust, and versatile. All that it requires are a very small room with adequate lighting and ventilation, a chalkboard, some chairs, a teacher, and a set of textbooks. Even teachers with limited knowledge of the subject matter and little training in teaching methods can make a conventional classroom work well enough to satisfy the public under almost all conditions. Basically, the same classroom pattern can be used to teach kindergartners their letters and high school seniors Shakespeare. Competing forms of classroom organization that are more effective—produce higher test scores, are better rated by experts or students, or conform better to prevailing theory—will need to be as cheap, robust, and versatile if they are to challenge the dominance of the conventional classroom in American schooling.

Not all classrooms conform strictly to the conventional pattern. Many classrooms are home to some student-centered practices such as student-initiated projects or portfolios of student work. But it takes more effort and expertise for teachers to sustain such practices. Classrooms are not neutral stages on which any sort of curriculum can be enacted, but social settings so constrained by expectations and limitations that only a few kinds of activities can easily happen there. The classroom curriculum is so thoroughly fused with these patterns that it, too, is highly constrained. To determine whether a proposed new curriculum can take root in classrooms and maintain itself without special attention requires a close analysis of its demands on teachers and students and its compatibility with curriculum materials and frames.

What It Takes to Change the Classroom Curriculum

Teachers realize the curriculum in their classrooms, and teachers must change it. All others who want to bring about change in the classroom curriculum must find ways to influence teachers to make the necessary changes. Figure 8.1 lists eight needs teachers have in order to make a major change in their classroom curricula. These needs are not just desirable; they are essential if lasting classroom curriculum change is to be achieved. Let us consider why each is essential and some of the ways each can be accomplished.

Opportunity to Study the Change Proposal

Teachers need to understand the key features of a proposed curriculum change, why each feature of the change is important, and the implications of each for classroom practice. Teachers who do not fully understand the proposed change are unlikely to implement it faithfully. I recall visiting a high school chemistry class in the late 1960s where the teacher was purportedly using an innovative inquiry-oriented curriculum. The teacher read from the textbook, pausing every now and then to ask the class a question. Afterward the graduate student for whom I was observing asked the teacher how he liked using this inquiry-oriented curriculum. He replied with evident enthusiasm that he liked it very much. He found the new book to be much more interesting than the one he had used before because it explained how chemical knowledge was discovered. No, he did not use the recommended laboratory

1. An opportunity to study the change and its implications for classroom practice.
2. A voice in the deliberations leading to a decision to undertake the change.
3. Incentives to undertake the change effort in their classrooms.
4. An opportunity to learn what students will be expected to learn.
5. An opportunity to master the new teaching skills required by the change.
6. Access to resources, temporary access to the resources required for making the transition, and continuing access to the resources required by the new practice.
7. Ways to check the quality of their realization of the new pattern.
8. Continuing support to work out bugs in the new pattern and to resolve conflicts between the new pattern and what remains of the former one.

FIG. 8.1. *What teachers need to change the classroom curriculum.*

experiments because they took too much time. The class would not be able to finish the whole book if he took time out for the laboratories. This teacher thought he was implementing the curriculum as its developers intended, just making a few minor adjustments for greater efficiency. In this case, superficial understanding of a curriculum change led to a classroom curriculum that bore little resemblance to the curriculum the textbook writers wrote or the curriculum the school district adopted.

For some teachers and some changes reading the teachers manual, hearing a single speech, or reading a brief article may be enough to bring adequate understanding of a proposed change. In most cases, though, teachers need an opportunity to discuss the change with their peers in order to bring to light features of the change and aspects of the rationale and its implications that are not immediately obvious upon first hearing or reading about it. Possible negative features of a change are seldom mentioned in the professional literature, and thorough consideration of pros and cons is essential for a considered professional decision to make the change. Discussions among disinterested colleagues, discussions that include opponents as well as advocates of the change, will promote more informed decisions. Advice from disinterested experts would surely deepen teachers' knowledge even further.

In addition to listening, reading, and discussing, teachers generally find it extremely useful to visit a school or classroom where the proposed change is in operation. They get a great deal more information from a visit than they could from listening or reading about it. On the other hand, richness of information can be confusing or misleading, so a combination of observation, explanation of key features, and discussion has much greater potential for fostering understanding than any one used alone. Video presentations offer the possibility of artfully combining all these ingredients in a medium that can be used flexibly. When practical, teachers should try the change out on a small scale; often, however, a new practice is too complex to be tried without considerable preparation and expense.

A Voice in the Adoption Deliberations

Any pretense of professionalism requires that the professional be the judge the value of new practices. Teachers therefore have a professional right and responsibility to study the change, form sound professional judgments, and communicate these to their clients and the public. If teachers are to be more than bureaucratic functionaries then they must have the freedom to make independent judgments of the merits of proposed changes and make their judgments known both within the school and in public.

No principle presently stands in the way of teachers making their views known to their employers or the public. As individuals, they can write letters or request an audience with responsible officials. As members of local teacher organizations, they can appoint study groups, develop position papers, and negotiate formally with the school district. And as members of national professional organizations, they can see that their representatives act on their behalf in reference to a particular curriculum change. There may be several reasons why teachers have not been more active in making their views known on curriculum issues in their schools. They may feel that their views are adequately considered already. They may fear to challenge local authorities. They may put a low priority on influencing local curriculum changes. In a well-run school, teachers may be content if the principal or sponsoring district officials offer them a chance to speak publicly or privately about a proposed change. They may then be willing to trust the decision to the professional judgment of school officials.

Typically, school administrators assess the extent and quality of teacher support for any change in a variety of informal settings before they commit themselves to a local change effort. A public show of hands may be sought at some point to confirm teacher support. A secret ballot would be even more convincing. A requirement that a secret ballot of teachers be taken on every major curricular initiative and publicly reported to the board before it votes would greatly strengthen teachers' voice in adoption decisions without infringing on the power of the public and its appointed school officials to make decisions.

Incentives to Undertake the Change Effort

Over-commitment plagues teachers as it does other busy professionals. Most teachers believe that they are working hard and doing a good job now. Every teacher can see ways to improve further, but unless the incentives to change what they are doing are strong enough to overcome the extra effort, cost, and risks of changing, most find it easier to continue what they are now doing. Whether the incentives are intrinsic to the task or extrinsically provided, teachers need to perceive a favorable ratio of benefits to costs for them before the effort to make the change will seem worthwhile.

The most satisfactory incentives are those intrinsic to the task. When teachers believe in the value of the change for students and for the society, they can see their effort on its behalf as a personal contribution to human betterment, and many teachers find this a major satisfaction of their work. A teacher who loves a subject and loves to teach it to young people may be thrilled at the thought of undertaking an arduous effort on behalf of an inspiring curriculum innovation, even if there are no tangible rewards. Also, sometimes teachers find the process of change itself rewarding, because it brings relief from routines, contacts with different people, chances to go to new places and undertake novel personal and professional challenges. On the other hand, many teachers value their routines and resent intrusions on them.

Sometimes teachers receive tangible rewards for helping to change the curriculum in their classroom. Students, parents, colleagues, or superiors may show their appreciation by awarding gifts or public honors. The teacher's reputation may rise in the community, the school, the profession, or all three. (On the other hand, if the change proves unpopular, the teacher runs a risk of a damaged reputation.) Through their efforts in curriculum work teachers may bring themselves to the attention of persons in a position to employ them or to recommend them for professional advancement. Sometimes teachers are able to earn additional income by working on a curriculum change project during summers or on their free time. Sometimes the expertise teachers acquire bring opportunities for earning further income, as when a teacher learns a great deal about the language and culture of another country and then finds summer work as a tour guide. If teachers are to continue to work on behalf of changes, they must feel that the effort they will have to expend on the change effort and the costs and risks they are likely to incur are probably going to be outweighed by benefits they find personally and professionally rewarding.

Opportunity to Learn the New Content

Teachers need to know what they are going to teach and know it very well. When teachers only know a few major items of knowledge in a field or when their knowledge is superficial, they can only present the subject to students as they learned it. To improvise as they teach or to respond to students' questions opens such teachers to the frightening possibility of revealing personal ignorance of a subject they are supposed to know well enough to teach. So, teachers whose knowledge of a topic is too limited can only implement a curriculum in a rigid way (Carlsen, 1988).

Major changes in the content students are expected to study and learn generally call for substantial periods of formal study by teachers. At best teachers learn only a few basic concepts from the typical one or two day in-service workshops provided by schools. They cannot learn expository writing, the Constitution, set theory, computer programming, or plate tectonics. Teachers with the best general education will have the best preparation for continuing to learn on their own, but there comes a time in every teacher's life when further progress demands sustained study. Most colleges offer courses for teachers over the summer and in evenings, but most teachers need this time for their families or need the money they can get from working. Self-study from video, audio, or print sources is more convenient, requires less time for commuting, and permits more flexibility in scheduling, but it still takes a major time commitment and it places greater demands on teachers for self-direction and self-discipline. Collaborative study groups combined with self-study can provide additional support and maintain higher participation rates. Participation in curriculum development can motivate teachers to learn more about a topic and provide an occasion for learning that enhances professional dignity and self-respect. However it happens, teachers must somehow learn, and learn well, whatever content they will be expected to teach.

Opportunity to Master New Teaching Skills

Teaching can be thought of as requiring a combination of teaching skills in several areas including classroom management, planning, presentation, and evaluation of student learning. Most teachers master a limited set of teaching skills so well that they can adapt them to teach most any teaching situation. Their personal teaching style is then built around a few focal skills. Nearly all teachers learn the teaching skills required to give a lecture, to conduct a discussion, to supervise students during seatwork, to administer tests, and to review the results of a test with the class. Some subjects have distinctive types of lessons. In mathematics, teachers often have students work problems at the chalkboard; in science students do experiments; in reading students may read aloud; and so on.

When teachers try a teaching skill they have not fully mastered, classes do not go as smoothly and teachers are likely to be dissatisfied with the results. A science teacher who tries to use guided discovery, for example, or to teach writing as part of science classes, or to use cooperative learning groups in the classroom, or to use computers feels nearly as awkward as in learning to teach in the first place. Teacher who can keep a question-and-answer session moving quickly along preset paths toward the correct answers must do a lot of learning in order to guide students to formulate hypotheses, to work out their consequences, and to compare the results with available data in a guided discovery lesson. New teaching skills of this order are not learned in a day.

To master a complex teaching skill teachers generally require a variety of learning experiences, including:

- thorough description and demonstration of the skill
- opportunity to plan and rehearse with expert advice
- repeated practice with feedback from a master
- ongoing coaching until they achieve mastery
- continuing forum for sharing problems and discoveries with knowledgeable others.

Unfortunately, in typical curriculum change efforts, teachers must do without these forms of assistance.

Mostly teachers develop their teaching skills in the early years of their career by imitating other teachers. Later, a teacher may read a journal article or book about some new teaching technique that they heard about at a conference or from a colleague. The teacher may rehearse alone or with a close friend and try out techniques in the classroom a little bit at a time. When something does not go well, the teacher will drop it or modify it, adapting the technique until it feels comfortable. Sometimes such informal self-teaching of teaching technique works beautifully. And when it works the teacher gains a precious independence. But it has its limitations. The self-taught teacher, like the self-taught artist or ball player, often ingrains habits that work initially but limit future performance. Also, a self-taught teacher who is not persistent and thorough will tend to jettison the most innovative features of a new teaching technique. The newer and stranger the technique, the more likely it is to misfire the first time a teacher tries it, and teachers who do not persist and adjust intelligently will conclude prematurely that the technique does not work for them.

Not every teacher absolutely requires all of these experiences for learning every new teaching technique, but good teaching produces results that are generally superior to self-instruction for teachers as well as for school children.

Access to Resources

The realization of any curriculum change benefits from, when it does not actually require, teachers and students to have access to resources such as materials and time. Teachers need materials that students can use to study individually or in small groups, materials that they use with the entire class, materials to assist them in planning, and an allocation of time in the classroom free from other demands. Teachers sometimes acquire their own materials and make their own adjustments in the classroom schedule, but most teachers would consider this to be service above and beyond the call of duty and would only do it for changes they believed in deeply.

When someone other than the teacher seeks to initiate classroom curriculum change, the sponsors and champions of the change must provide whatever resources teachers need if they expect teachers to make the change. Occasionally, a curriculum change requires modification of the physical environment of the classroom such as providing running water, storage space, or additional electrical outlets. In addition, the process of change itself requires resources, especially additional time for teachers to plan new lessons and materials to inform teachers about the change and to assist them in making it.

Ways to Check the Quality of Classroom Realization

Teachers must decide whether what they are trying is a good and faithful version of the change. This is the most neglected phase of classroom curriculum change. Teachers who have participated in developing a particular change often comprehend it fully and they should have little trouble determining how faithfully their classroom curriculum realizes the plans they themselves helped to make. On the other hand, if the plans were developed by someone else, if the change is complicated, and especially if the teacher's only exposure to the change has been a brief workshop, teachers will not be competent to judge how well they have realized the planned change.

Teachers should be able to present a sample of their teaching that they consider a good example of the change to a knowledgeable person or group and to receive and discuss the judgments of these persons about the quality of the realization and its congruence with plans. Those who make these judgments should serve as consultants to teachers, the consultation should be confidential, and the consultant should not be able to affect the teacher's career prospects. Their purpose would be strictly to help the teacher to compare their classroom curriculum to the plans and ideals the teacher is striving to attain. The possibility of videotaping classroom sessions for later viewing by others makes such a proposal feasible.

The practice of studying videotapes of teaching with colleagues is becoming an accepted strategy for improving teaching. The National Board for Professional Teaching Standards (1991) requires that teachers applying for board certification submit a teaching portfolio in which they write reflective papers that use students' works, videotapes, and other types of documentation. This strategy seems particularly appropriate when teachers are trying new curriculums in their classroom.

Continuing Support

The learning of any complex skill takes place in stages over an extended period of time. Only when teachers achieve a basic minimum level of competence will they put their skill to use, develop fluency and flexibility, and assimilate the newly learned techniques fully into their teaching repertoire. Teachers who need support at all will need continuing support throughout the months, perhaps, during which they are continuing to learn and assimilate new knowledge and techniques.

As teachers learn more about the change, they will find ways to improve it. The change set in motion can thus continue to be revised and adapted for years. The ability of teachers to take the change into their own hands and make continuing refinements and developments over a period of years is a valuable benefit gained through thorough implementation efforts.

District supervisors traditionally have been assigned responsibility for providing continuing support, but their small numbers in relation to the number of schools and teachers to be served make effectiveness in this role nearly impossible in most districts. Some schools have regular staff meetings to discuss the changes being implemented. These may be called quality circles or simply faculty meetings, but in them teachers are encouraged to report on their successes and problems and to call issues to the attention of colleagues, authorities, and the sponsors and champions of the change. When necessary, outside experts may be consulted.

Bottom Line: Extra Time, Effort, and Resources

Clearly, teachers who undertake to make any substantial change in the curriculum of their classroom must expect to spend extra time and work on the effort and to assume significant professional risks. Those who want to see particular changes take place in classrooms must find ways to incite teachers to undertake these efforts and endure these risks on behalf of the change they advocate. It has taken 3 decades of disappointing results from major reform efforts to show how daunting a challenge this is.

- Local adoption of new curriculum materials
- Development of local curriculum guides
- Local curriculum development projects
- In-service workshops for teachers
- Team planning by teachers
- National curriculum reform movements

FIG. 8.2. *Common approaches to fostering classroom curriculum change.*

Approaches to Improving Classroom Curriculum

Common Approaches to Improving Classroom Curriculum

The many persons and organizations who seek to influence the curriculum of K–12 education in the nation have tried hundreds of ways to affect teachers and classrooms. Figure 8.2 shows some of the approaches most commonly employed.

Adequacy of Common Approaches

Consider how many of the eight needs identified earlier each of these strategies meets. For instance, local adoption of new curriculum materials—typically textbooks and accompanying workbooks—simply confronts teachers with a new frame that they must somehow incorporate into their planning. New materials that are very different from those already in use disrupt more of teachers' previous plans and therefore require teachers to revise more of their classroom curriculum plans.

Unless other approaches are also used, materials adoption leaves teachers with only the teachers' edition of the textbook to help them learn new content and pedagogical skills. Materials adoption leaves teachers with no way to check the quality of their initial efforts to try the new curriculum and to make continuing improvements. Able, dedicated teachers can accomplish these other tasks on their own, especially if the changes demanded are not extensive or radical, but only with efforts that go beyond their contractual obligations to the school.

None of these common approaches offers a comprehensive strategy for supporting classroom curriculum change. Most of them do not even involve teachers in discussions of what should happen in their classrooms. They bring the teacher into contact with some material or activity and then hope that the teacher will take appropriate action behind the classroom door. No wonder that getting curriculum innovations through the classroom door has proven so difficult. Those who think that rapid, substantial, coordinated changes in the curriculums of many classrooms should be possible as a matter of routine underestimate the difficulties teachers face in maintaining and changing their classroom curriculum.

In order to make lasting and substantial changes in their classroom curriculum teachers need all of the eight items in Fig. 8.1. But meeting all these needs for all teachers with separate efforts would be impossibly expensive. If possible, we would like to find ways to meet multiple needs with simple, inexpensive actions. When this is not possible, perhaps we can find ways to meet just enough of the needs for enough teachers in strategic situations so as to set in motion a process that will eventually lead to meeting all the needs for all teachers. We can imagine ways that this might be done.

Teachers as Curriculum Makers

When teachers try to change the curriculum in their own classroom, they avoid the highest hurdle facing other change agents: gaining the teacher's cooperation. Still, teachers trying to change curriculum in their own classrooms must overcome a number of obstacles. The most serious obstacles fall under three broad headings: resources, expertise and authority. The most indispensable resources for curriculum change are the time for teachers to plan and access to curriculum materials. Teachers usually have one class period per day to plan daily lessons; grade homework and tests; keep records; meet with students, parents, and colleagues; as well as plan curriculum changes. To plan a new unit that will take, say, 3 weeks' class time, teachers need at least a week of this planning time. Unless teachers devote evenings and weekends to curriculum planning, all the available time comes in brief snippets of an hour or less.

The activities a teacher plans often require printed materials, audio or video recordings, or apparatus of some kind. Unless the teacher proposes to tell students everything they need to know, or unless the information is readily available in the textbook, students need additional materials that present what they are to learn. Teachers often make these materials or scrounge for them, both of which add to the demands on their time. Teachers often buy materials with their own funds to avoid the delay and red tape needed to buy them through the school.

Planning curriculum changes can require several kinds of expertise. All teachers presumably gain expertise in lesson planning during their professional training, and this is presumably enough to make minor curriculum changes. Planning a substantial change, on the other hand, typically requires expertise of several kinds not routinely provided by teacher training.

If teachers must introduce substantially new content, such as mathematical proof, inequalities, or number systems in bases other than base 10, then teachers will need to acquire expertise in the new content. If teachers must prepare new curriculum materials for students to use, they will need at least amateur competence as a writer, applied psychologist, graphic designer, and evaluator. When a curriculum change calls for new patterns of classroom interaction, teachers may need to learn new teaching skills in order to enlarge their repertoire of teaching styles. For example, a teacher would be foolhardy to use peer teaching or small group learning without at least reading about these techniques and rehearsing them. Formal training under the supervision of someone who has mastered these teaching styles would be advisable.

Teachers seldom attempt changes that require expertise they do not already have. Teachers who have developed a talent for writing word exercises for language instruction may spend considerable time preparing such materials, but other teachers will not. Teachers whose repertoire of teaching techniques already includes cooperative work groups will develop lessons that call for cooperative work groups, but other teachers will not.

Too often curriculum changes teachers make on their own seem to experts to be timid, merely incremental adjustments made in the interest of a narrow practicality, or one-sided, reflecting the teacher's hobby horse. When teachers must make do with their own preexisting competence, they can only responsibly attempt changes that use their competence. Greater access to a wider range of deeper expertise would strengthen most teacher-initiated curriculum change efforts. On the other hand, one can be confident that teacher-initiated curriculum changes can be made to work under realistic classroom conditions, which cannot always be said about externally initiated curriculum changes.

Making major changes in the classroom curriculum on their own initiative is not a normal job requirement for teachers. A teacher who initiates a major curriculum change makes a public statement that may be seen as implying dissatisfaction with the officially adopted curriculum, an indirect criticism of superiors and colleagues. Thus, even if teachers had full authority to shape their own classroom curriculum, they would still need to worry about possible opposition to the change from colleagues and superiors, as well as students and parents, all of whom can make life difficult for teachers if they try.

As things are, though, school administrators, school boards, and the public do not acknowledge the right of teachers to plan their own classroom curriculum. They do acknowledge teachers' right and duty to adapt official plans and materials to the specifics of their individual classroom. The line between planning and adaptation is vague and different schools draw it differently, but the unwritten rule in many schools is "Don't make waves." If a curriculum change becomes controversial, the school system will be forced to assert its authority and either pronounce the teacher's initiative to be official school policy or reject it. Either way, committees will need to consider the change using officially prescribed procedures for curriculum planning in the schools of that community, usually a time-consuming, bureaucratic process.

In schools where controversy arises frequently over curriculum matters, teachers are well advised to seek approval for their initiative from the department chair, principal, and perhaps also central office personnel in advance. In less conflicted contexts, teachers may be encouraged to try even substantial changes with only a requirement to report what they did and how it worked.

In some schools controversy is so rare that teachers are effectively ceded broad discretionary authority over their classroom curriculum. Such freedom in curricular matters is reported to be one of the attractions of private school teaching. But teachers' autonomy in regard to their classroom curriculum is also limited by the need for coordination among teachers and among curricular components such as tests, textbooks, and curriculum guides. Because students stay with teachers for only a year and, after the first few grades, for only a small part of each day, the work of one classroom must be coordinated with that of others if students' school programs are to retain any coherence. Therefore, substantial changes in any one curriculum will require adjustments in all those subsequent or concurrent curriculums that depend upon it. This dependency is greatest in the skill subjects of mathematics, reading, writing, and foreign languages, but it is evident to some degree in all subjects. Also, curriculum changes have implications for tests, textbooks, and curriculum materials that may impact other parts of the school. In short, the curriculum, even the classroom curriculum, is a public matter given in trust to schools and delegated by them to varying degrees to teachers. Legally, teachers and school officials are public servants in regard to curriculum matters, not professional experts. And the classroom curriculum is not, therefore, the teacher's private preserve or professional prerogative.

In general, making minor changes in the classroom curriculum presents teachers mainly with the problem of finding the time and resources and enduring the (usually small) risk of controversy. For teachers who enjoy curriculum work, these problems are minor annoyances and the satisfactions of planning far outweigh them. For many others, curriculum work of this sort is an unpleasant chore.

But teachers making major changes in the classroom curriculum on their own initiative is a different matter altogether. The more a proposed curriculum change disrupts established classroom routines, the riskier and more difficult it becomes. The planning will require more time and expertise. The teacher will run into more difficulties in trying to implement the change. Students will notice the change and may react negatively. The change will be more visible within the school and community, and the risk of controversy will be greater.

Teachers who successfully initiate major curriculum changes in their classroom gain the respect of colleagues and superiors for their work. They may become local experts on curriculum matters and assume leadership positions in official curriculum change efforts of the school or school system. They may also develop curriculum materials for publication. In effect, teachers who succeed at changing their own classroom curriculum carve out an uncertified professional specialty in curriculum planning.

Planning Innovative Classroom Activities

To change a classroom curriculum is to make different classroom activities happen there, ones that present different content, ones intended to achieve different purposes, ones structured in different ways. Planning new classroom activities is therefore one of the most fundamental steps in bringing about classroom curriculum change. Usually teachers find ideas for new classroom activities in professional publications such as teachers' guides, teachers' editions of textbooks, or books or articles about teaching and adapt them for their personal use. This customizing process is an interesting one that deserves more study than it has received, but it is a special case of the development of a new activity from scratch.

Activity development is a form of teaching expertise that all teachers possess in some measure, but the development of new activities is not a necessary part of classroom curriculum change for all teachers. One can be quite a good teacher simply by relying upon activities developed by others. Skill at devising classroom activities seems to require experience as a classroom teacher. In this section we will examine how teachers, beginning with a teaching problem or challenge, can get ideas for activities and develop these ideas into complete activities they can use in their classroom.

The Complex Nature of Educational Activities

Every human activity has the possibility to exhibit structure, meaning, and purpose on several levels simultaneously. The raising of one hand above the head is a simple action that can be described physiologically and anatomically in terms of muscles and joints, but it may also be described as a stretch, a salute, or a bid to be recognized. Each of these actions, in turn, may be described in terms of the person's motives: to answer a question, to show off, or to conform to classroom norms. The structure of an activity is a matter of its form, of relations between its parts. The meaning of an activity is a matter of relations between the activity itself and other things outside the activity. The structure of a classroom activity on *Macbeth* might consist of assigning parts and reading the play aloud in class, with pauses at intervals for discussion. The meanings of the *Macbeth* activity depend upon the substance of those discussions. They might have to do with such matters as loyalty, ambition, and evil; or such matters as plot, metaphor, and literary form; or such matters as getting a good grade, impressing the teacher, and getting into college.

Every activity intended to be educational has the potential for at least three types of structure and therefore four levels of meaning: as a task in itself, as a symbolic representation, as a level of meaning, and as a form of social interaction. Educators may not always attend to all four levels, but they are there as resources to be used for education anyway. Furthermore, the educational outcomes of interest in general education are always complex. Typically we expect students to come away from any educational activity with

1. achievement (learned ability to perform)
2. retention (indefinitely continued)
3. transfer to new situations (both similar to the learning situation (near transfer) and quite different (far transfer))
4. understanding (ability to provide a correct explanation and to relate to other learning)
5. motivation (continuing interest and willingness to pursue the matter further)

These complex expectations for outcomes and these levels of meaning and structure apply to nearly all activities designed for inclusion in the curriculum of general education. To ignore this multidimensional complexity of activities and treat whatever happens in classrooms as purely, simply, and definitely one thing and one thing only, reduces its meaning and impoverishes classroom life.

The Essential Starting Point: What the Student Does

The most important principle of classroom activity design is that *the student's actions determine what will be learned.* Curriculum materials can present information, but students only learn when they bring their attention and their abilities to bear on what is presented. Curriculum materials can influence students' actions, but they are only one influence and seldom the strongest. Ultimately, curriculum materials have an effect on students, if at all, by encouraging, directing, and assisting their own efforts to learn. The kernel of an educational activity, then, is what the student is to do.

A teacher's chief resource for generating tentative suggestions for activities is a set of *activity schemata* that are either tacitly held in memory or explicitly included in the platform. A schema is a kind of script for creating an activity, a general form whose blanks when filled in describe a particular activity of a certain type. Everyone would be able to fill in the blanks in the lecture activity schema to create a specific lecture. What the student does in a lecture is listen, take notes, try to understand, and ask questions if puzzled. The lecturer selects appropriate and important ideas, organizes them convincingly, memorably, and entertainingly, and delivers them clearly. Lectures may vary in content, length, purpose (to inform, to entertain, to persuade, etc.), and style. Someone from another culture would have to learn this schema, but it is so common in western civilization that everyone can be assumed to be familiar with it, though not necessarily to be able to perform well as either a lecturer or auditor. Other activity schemata likely to be familiar to teachers include:

Class discussion
Reading groups (circles)
Going over homework
Seatwork
Testing
Field trips

Teachers with a more progressive orientation are likely to be familiar with such activity schemata as these:

Teacher–pupil planning
Class projects
Individual student projects
Games
Independent study

Some school subjects include specialized activity schemata, such as:

Laboratory (science)
Rehearsal (music)
Calisthenics (physical education).

And new activity schemata are invented (sometimes reinvented or rediscovered) continually.

To employ more than a handful of fundamentally different activity types within a single course or unit puts stress on teachers and students. Teachers must become fluent with many types of activities, which is not an easy task. Students must learn to play their proper part in the orderly realization of an activity and, as generations of teachers and a few recent researchers will testify, they, too, must learn how to participate productively in a new type of activity. The time needed to learn and become fluent with a new activity type is an additional cost of employing varied activity types. For these reasons most teachers rely upon a small number of basic activity types, which they repeat with variations. The teacher's first response to the task of designing a new activity is therefore typically to ask which familiar type of activity is best suited to the present purpose. In some cases, a plausible activity of a familiar type springs readily to mind, but when one does not, an activity can be developed by using a kind of heuristic reasoning.

One form of heuristic begins by determining what students should do either during or at the conclusion of this activity. A plausible educational activity can be designed from this beginning by using the following line of heuristic reasoning.

Here's something we would like students to be able to do. Call it T, for target activity. Suppose we just show them T or tell them about it and then have them do it. (If this works as a learning activity for students then use it. If not, we proceed as follows.)

Supposing that just showing the target activity or telling about it will not work because of certain specific barriers, call them B_1, B_2, and B_3, can we find or devise an activity that is nearly equivalent to T but that does not present these barriers?

Usually the target activity comes from some field of human endeavor to which students are being introduced. For example, "read a novel" is an activity that originates in literature as a living tradition and has a hallowed place in the English curriculum of secondary schools. Why not just select a novel and ask students to read it? Well, our students may not be able to read fluently enough (B1), they may not know how to extract any meaning from a novel except the plot (B2), and they may be uninterested and unwilling to give novel reading a serious try (B3). Can we then find an alternative activity that is nearly equivalent to reading a novel, but does not have these shortcomings?

We can easily devise several plausible candidates. For instance, in response to the first barrier, we can find a novel that makes relatively light demands on reading skill. Or we can write one, commission one, or adapt one. We can even create a comic book version of an existing novel. Taking a different tack, we can permit students to listen to a recording of someone reading the novel while they read along. Or, we might decide to enlist parents or volunteers as aides to help individual students with their reading. If the contortions required are too great, we might simply postpone or cancel the attempt to teach this particular target activity. Each of these courses of action has its costs and risks as well as its advantages. Depending on the situation, we might have good reason to prefer any one to the others.

Adapting real-world activities to educative purposes in this way is a staple heuristic for generating possible curriculum activities, especially in secondary schools and in higher education. Science experiments, mathematics problems, foreign language dialogues, community surveys, vocational education projects, musical performances, and art projects are common examples that present opportunities for using real-world activities in very nearly their mature, fully developed forms.

For younger children it is often necessary to produce a simplified version of the target activity. Instead of novels, we offer stories written especially for children. We offer simple scientific observations and experiments, simple arithmetic problems, and other miniature, child-sized versions of adult activities. Activities adapted from serious adult endeavors for the education of children are most educative if they retain all the essential values of the original. In particular, the objects and operations of the adapted activity should ideally be genuine instances, however simplified, of the developed activity. Children's mathematics should still be recognizable as mathematics by mathematicians, children's literature still recognizable as literature by literati, and so on. The best examples of the adapted activity should stand comparison in some meaningful sense with the great exemplars of the developed activity. The adapted activity should be capable of evoking similar kinds of responses in children to those that the developed activity evokes in adults. The thought processes required to deal appropriately with the adapted activity ought to be useful when applied to real-world problems in the related adult domain. Adapting serious adult activities for use by children is a difficult challenge to our understanding of both children and subject, and requires a gifted creative imagination.

A second type of heuristic we can follow for generating activities is to create new, artificial tasks to serve as exercises for the development or training of some ability or aptitude. This exercise heuristic works something like this:

- Search for small activities that are constituents of many important larger activities, or that develop abilities required in many such activities.
- Practice these in steadily increasing doses so that we build gradually improved performance on the exercises.
- Practice on the target activities may be carried on simultaneously or it may be introduced when students become capable of a sufficiently high level of performance on the exercises.

The physical exercises known as calisthenics are a clear example of using this strategy. The motions have no effect on the world and they don't mean anything. Their only purpose is to develop strength, flexibility, and endurance for use in other physical activities. Phonics drills on meaningless letter–sound correspondences are designed to help children to learn a meaningful and useful activity—reading. Musical scales and arpeggios, multiplication table drills, flash cards, sentence diagramming, filling in blanks, connecting dots to make letters, science and foreign language vocabulary lists, and history names and dates are other familiar products of the exercise heuristic. Currently, new types of exercises modeled on intelligence test items are being recommended as a way to teach thinking skills.

Exercises are a staple activity type in all subjects and grades, but they are generally regarded as a necessary evil. Many people have painful childhood memories of working away at exercises when they would rather have been doing something else. (On the other hand, many children find great satisfaction in mastery of arbitrary but difficult tasks.) Educators with progressive leanings strive to eliminate mere exercises in favor of meaningful and intrinsically satisfying activities.

Perhaps the greatest danger of using exercises is that they will acquire a life of their own and come to be considered useful or meaningful or both, in their own right. Spelling exercises, once an aid to writing, have grown into a school subject. We have spelling books, spelling tests, and spelling bees. In many elementary schools, children receive a grade in spelling. Performance on exercises is easily measured and so people tend to compare one another on the basis of performance on exercises. Consider the Olympic Games (or, for that matter, the Olympics of the Mind). Test items are a kind of exercise, and so testing tends to promote exercises in the school curriculum.

Exercises also appeal to us as orderly rule-bound actions and therefore lend themselves to ritualization. The military dress parade and the drills of marching bands at sporting events are exercises that have become rituals valued for their intrinsic order and precision. Exercises can clearly be carried too far, acquire an inflated importance, and become detached from their educative purpose. Nevertheless, the heuristic strategy of looking for exercises can generate valuable educational activities.

Educational activities can also be generated from children's own spontaneous activities—play and games. Children spontaneously engage in make-believe, pretending they are

Mommy, Daddy, the doctor, the firefighter, the police officer, and so on. An educational activity schema—role-playing—has been patterned on this intrinsically satisfying child activity. Also, children in many cultures play games with tokens, a practice that in our culture has evolved into board games of various kinds, which serve as the inspiration for any number of educational games. The activities children do in kindergarten have nearly all been designed with this play heuristic, which might be expressed this way:

1. Make a game that models the key features of what you want to teach.
2. Let children play the game until they grasp the teaching intuitively and incorporate it into their actions.
3. Then, and only then, and only if necessary, teach about it formally.

There are surely many more activity-generating heuristics. We have not yet considered the simplest and most common one of all: **telling**.

Tell students about it.

Any school textbook, workbook or teachers' methods book will show dozens of others.

When an activity kernel has been developed that shows promise of working, it can be shaped, revised, and enriched to make it more educationally valuable, by considering in detail various features that might be incorporated into it. This is not necessarily a process of adding on other bits of activities, making the original more complicated, but is rather a consideration of various versions of the basic activity with different emphases and orientations. The result of this reconsideration of the activity can as easily be a simplification of the original activity kernel as a complication of it.

The heuristic reasoning employed here is deliberative—strengths and weaknesses are considered and ways are found to capitalize on the one and to compensate for the other. The essential method of reasoning is to isolate first one feature and then another of the kernel activity and to ask of each feature whether an alternative to the present one can be found that improves the activity. An unlimited number of features may be isolated from any activity. The teacher's educational ideas and commitments suggest which features are likely to be most central to the operation and success of the activity.

Teachers must rely on their judgment to decide whether a prototype activity can be improved, to set priorities on possible improvements, and to make the improvements. For example, suppose a teacher had decided to teach *Macbeth* by assigning students to read different parts and interrupting the reading at intervals to discuss the play. This is what we have called the prototype activity. The teacher would need to consider what features of this activity might need to be modified. Perhaps the teacher would judge that students were likely to find Shakespeare's vocabulary and grammar so difficult that the reading would be unclear, would absorb nearly all of students' attention, and might even be embarrassing.

Having reached this judgment, the teacher might consider various modifications of the prototype activity. The teacher could prepare a sheet of notes on difficult passages and assign students to study these and rehearse their parts as homework. Alternatively, the teacher might divide the class into small groups and assign each small group the task of understanding both the literal meaning and possible connotations and allusions of one character's speeches. The teacher would then review each group's analysis prior to the reading for the whole class.

The teacher would certainly need to give further thought to the discussions to be held at intervals in the reading of the play. When should the reading be interrupted? Which of many possible purposes should be pursued in these discussions (clarifying the dramatist's meaning, analyzing language, examining characters' motivations, discovering how the dramatist achieved his effects, or exploring students' personal associations, for example)?

What questions should be posed? How long should the discussion be permitted to go on? How closely should the teacher guide the discussion? What criteria should the teacher use to judge the quality of individual contributions or of the discussion as a whole?

By considering such questions as these the teacher finds and exploits opportunities to improve the activity. The original activity design is modified, sometimes by adding features, sometimes by eliminating them, sometimes by reorganizing. Depending on what questions teachers ask at this point and how they answer them, the prototype activity could take on completely different complexions in the teacher's planbook. And depending upon the skill and judgment with which the teacher carried out these plans, the developed activity could take on completely different complexions when realized in the classroom. It is this dependence of the classroom curriculum on so many judgments, some made in advance and some necessarily made on the spur of the moment, that makes the realization of plans made outside the classroom so problematic. This is also the reason why the individual teacher plays the pivotal role in shaping the classroom curriculum.

Shaping Classroom Activities

The examples presented in Chapter 5 of ideas about arithmetic, reading, and motivation based on research show how ideas can suggest classroom activities. Developing exciting, powerful activities is an art or at least a craft, certainly not a science or technology. Much of the skill is subject-specific and age-specific. Nearly everyone who becomes adept at it begins as a teacher and develops the knack by planning activities for their own classroom.

Developers starting a project already have in mind a large repertoire of ordinary teaching and learning activities that people have used for teaching and learning this and similar things in other times and places. Repurposing these activities could make an interesting and valuable curriculum project, but the innovative contribution would be small. If the developers want new activities that are more effective and exciting than the ones already available, they will have to invent them. No one can give a formula for inventing good, original activities, but much can be learned from studying how experts do it.

For postadolescent students, activities from important enterprises in the world outside school offer productive starting points for devising learning activities. Riley (1984a, 1984b, 1984c) found that course developers at the Open University in England started developing materials for college distance education courses by collecting sources: original and secondary. They located sources by examining published writing on the subject of the course, corresponding with appropriate authorities, and through personal contacts. Developers would ask students to use these sources in activities that were versions of the activities that experts would do with them. In a literature course, students might write critical essays about the works they read. In an environmental science course, students might read scientific research papers and prepare a position paper for a political leader.

Adapting real-world activities into good learning activities for younger children is more problematic. Children often lack the interest, patience, skill, and prior knowledge to do adult activities. Games and play offer models of activities that children find intrinsically interesting. Most developers of materials for children include game-like and playful activities. Activities from traditional folk cultures are also often useful sources or models of learning activities for children. Traditional stories, songs, dances, and crafts usually appeal to people of all ages. Having children teach other children in peer tutoring or reciprocal teaching has been shown to be a powerful way for fostering academic learning (Palincsar & Brown, 1986).

Sequences of activities form curriculum units and several units make up the curriculum for a year. Finding a good sequence for activities can be as important as inventing good individual activities. In sequencing the topics in their courses, the Open University course developers that Riley studied faced a fundamental choice: to cover the ground, i.e., present all important material, or to select and arrange source materials to support an argument or thesis. A decision to cover the ground commits the developer to a search for a sequence that covers all the content. A decision to build the course around an argument commits the developer to using the argument as a focus and its key steps as organizing principles.

Elementary and secondary course developers probably use a greater variety of starting points and strategies, but they, too, must select an organizing focus and organizing principles for their units. Posner and Strike (1976) present a useful categorization of principles developers may follow in sequencing activities within a course or unit. They distinguish several sequencing principles:

- **world-related** (structures based on realities in the world as we perceive it, such as ordering a geography course by continents, or a chemistry course by the periodic table),
- **concept-related** (structures based on ideas, such as ordering a biology unit around natural selection),
- **inquiry-related** (structures based on the method or process which produces knowledge, such as ordering a geometry course around the idea of proof or a history unit around interpreting historical evidence),
- **learning-related** (structures based on how students learn the material, such as ordering a unit to begin with simple, familiar topics and proceed to more complex and novel ones), and
- **utilization-related** (structures based on how one may use what is learned, such as ordering a physical science course around familiar devices and situations to which physical principles can be applied).

Another important part of designing activities is to choose a teaching strategy. Teacher-centered strategies such as lectures, discussions, films or videos, seatwork, answering questions at the chalkboard, and so on are safe because nearly all teachers know how to conduct such activities. Still, innovative curriculums may demand new and unfamiliar kinds of lectures or discussions. If so, the materials need to help teachers learn to conduct these familiar activities in new ways. Many student-centered strategies are also familiar to most teachers—field trips, small projects, and the like. But more adventurous teaching strategies involve greater risk. Many teachers find inquiry-oriented teaching particularly challenging. Organizing students into cooperative teams can be a challenge for teachers who have never used this strategy. Figure 8.3 lists some of the major decisions involved in designing a unit.

The Crafts of Curriculum Development

Designing good curriculum materials requires mastery of a number of crafts. If materials are printed, the quality of the writing and the graphic design will be critical. Each medium—audio, video, computers, etc.—has its own associated crafts and standards of quality. The design of activities demands its own skills such as guiding children in a learning setting. If we add these skill demands to those of working with the content itself, it becomes easy to understand why a team nearly always designs curriculum materials.

Curriculum materials design is, finally, the creation of intricate layers of order—program, course, unit, activity; content, purpose, structure, approach—in order to facilitate teaching and learning. The many hundreds of decisions embodied in each layer are each subject to many disparate considerations. The materials that result are woven from these simpler decisions as a tapestry is woven from single-colored threads. In curriculum materials as in

Preliminary Considerations

Consider the educational problem
Consider your approach
Describe key ideas and methods to be used
Consider the frames
    Student frames
    Teacher frames
    Time frames
    Facility & equipment frames

Elements of a Unit Design

Purpose
    List the most important aims to be pursued
    Indicate relative emphasis among them
    Describe broad categories of student accomplishments
    Write essays on important aims (as needed)
Content
    List the main items of content to be included. Indicate relative emphasis
       among them
    Essays on main items of content as needed
Structure
    Organizing focus (theme)
    Organizing principles
    Schedule (relations of unit parts in time)
Teaching strategy
    Learning setting
    Social climate
    Teaching style
    Mode and medium of presentation
    Main activity types
    Rationale for the above
    Essays on teaching as needed

FIG. 8.3.   *Considerations in designing a curriculum unit.*

tapestries, the quality of the final product depends on the total configuration of decisions and upon how well they are carried out in creating the actual materials. The only way to learn to recognize good orchestration, let alone to do it, is to study examples. The more examples, the better the examples, the more intensively they are studied, and the more they are discussed with others of varied backgrounds—the more you will learn.

Work with Reforms

When others try to initiate changes in the classroom curriculum, they must rely on teachers to realize their plans. The obvious and natural strategy for an outsider intent on initiating change in the classroom curriculum is therefore to try to get teachers to treat the initiative as if it were their own. Experienced hands speak of "ownership" of the change by teachers, by which they mean getting teachers to regard it as their own initiative. When this happens, implementing externally initiated changes in classrooms reduces to the problem of helping teachers to bring about their own changes in the classroom curriculum. If external agents can also provide additional time for teachers to plan, curriculum materials or funds to acquire them, appropriate expertise, and the backing of school authorities, then the obstacles to classroom curriculum change are minimized.

There are no formulas for winning over the hearts and minds of teachers to a proposed curriculum change. Approaches range from advertising and public relations to inspiration, co-optation, intimidation, and education. Traditionally, curriculum reformers play to teachers' idealism and try to persuade teachers that implementing their reform will help their students or contribute to a better society or both. They also try to get a bandwagon rolling, to create the impression that teachers who implement their reform will be in the vanguard setting the direction other schools will later follow. Local school officials often attempt to co-opt teachers by involving them in planning the details of reforms to be adopted. School systems also sponsor speakers who lecture about curriculum problems and solutions, sponsor training sessions, buy books for the teacher's lounge, and even reimburse teachers for college courses, in an effort to win them over by education.

Sometimes authorities avoid the problem of winning over teachers by simply mandating reforms. Simple mandates have a miserable record of effectiveness. Every state has laws on its books requiring that something be done in classrooms—teach the evils of alcohol, drugs, and tobacco in every class every year or offer 15 minutes of vigorous physical activity every day. Unless school officials enforce these in some way, they are largely ignored. Enforcement by direct observation of classrooms is impractical, though tests seem to be an effective enforcement tool. In general, though, teachers have such broad discretion in managing their classrooms that willing initiative is much more likely to be effective than grudging compliance. Still, grudging compliance may be preferable to noncompliance from the point of view of legislators or educational authorities.

Outsiders may also hope to influence the classroom curriculum indirectly by changing curriculum materials, classroom frames, or even by influencing what students do. Change agents may hope that changes in these will bring pressures to bear on teachers and cause them to change or that such changes will bring about curriculum change directly, even when the teacher does not change. The situation in which teachers are presented with an externally developed program in the form of written plans and materials has been extensively studied. It is clear that teachers are usually influenced by the plans and materials to change what they do in their classrooms, but it is also clear that teachers transform the prepared program. What happens in the classroom is neither what was happening before the external program was adopted nor exactly what the program's developers propose, but some sort of compromise. This is mutual adaptation again.

The net effect of mutual adaptation is to ward off, redirect, or blunt attempts to control the curriculum from outside the classroom. Experienced teachers whose schools have adopted many of the national educational reforms produced during the last quarter century have become adept at meeting official guidelines while retaining their professional integrity and continuing to exercise their professional judgment. Those who thought they had revamped the school's mathematics curriculum by winning the school board's endorsement of checkbook balancing in the mathematics curriculum will be disappointed to discover that they have only made a marginal change. But they will have made some change, which is more than the teachers who opposed it would have liked. The art of negotiating changes in classrooms with teachers lies at the heart of facilitating curriculum change. We will consider it in detail in a later chapter.

In the case of a distant reform adopted by state or district officials but not supported by local school administrators, no one is present in the local school to bargain with teachers, and so those who do not prefer the reform do not implement it in their classroom. If all the curriculum reformer has to bring to the negotiating table—which also happens to be the teacher's desk—are written documents exhorting teachers to change, the result is a foregone conclusion. On the other hand, if proponents of the curriculum change have even one person who is an experienced, respected member of the local school staff and who acts as a champion of the reform, chances for implementation of the reform are much better. And if, in addition, a strong administrator is willing to bargain hard, using up political capital in the process, then it may be possible to persuade teachers to go along with an unpopular change.

Changing classroom frames is in some respects easier and in others much more difficult than other ways of influencing the classroom curriculum. It is much easier for a local school official to create a new course or special program in the school, recruit teachers committed to the change to staff it, buy new curriculum materials, and so on, than it is to try to change the hearts, minds, and classroom actions of dozens of established teachers in their conventional classrooms. The administrator controls most of these decisions directly, few teachers' routines are disrupted, and no teacher need be coerced into adopting a curriculum change. On the other hand, changes in frames often have budget implications and require personnel changes and changes in teacher and student assignment that must be approved by others.

In principle, it is possible for external agents to try to influence classrooms by working with students, though only a few gestures are ever made in this direction. Measures that increased students' active efforts to learn, for example, or redirected them in more productive channels could certainly result in greater coverage and mastery and improve classroom order and affect. Students' efforts could be co-opted as are teachers', by involving them in planning changes in the classroom curriculum. Students could even be trained to help maintain a different classroom pattern. For example, students could be trained in peer tutoring and cooperative group learning in order to make it easier for teachers to implement such reforms in classrooms. Even just explaining the rationale for the change and asking for students' help in bringing it about would be likely to facilitate change in the classroom curriculum.

The most prominent curriculum reforms of this century have demanded extensive changes in classroom routines. Progressive education called for nothing less than a complete transformation of the classroom. The new math demanded not only the teaching of new content unfamiliar to most teachers, but also teaching young children to prove mathematical relationships, to solve unfamiliar and difficult problems, and to explore and discover mathematics on their own. It called for the use of blocks, balances, beads, geoboards, and a host of other apparatus. The teaching of writing across the curriculum demands major adjustments from secondary school teachers who had never before considered this part of their responsibility. The use of computers in science, math, or English classrooms will require major adjustments. Such changes as these require enormous amounts of time and effort from teachers sustained over years. They are almost equivalent to learning to teach again in a new way. This can be done with several hours of work per week sustained over several years and appropriate opportunities for practice, feedback, discussion, and psychological support. But in most cases teachers were expected to make these changes after at most a single college course in the evening or over a summer.

Even changes that preserve conventional classroom patterns and call for only incremental changes usually require extensive adjustments in several aspects of classroom routines. Just substituting one unit of content for another within an existing course requires changes in the curriculum materials, tests, and teacher's plans, and may possibly also require that teachers learn new content, revise their understanding of the subject, or learn new teaching skills or strategies. Teaching is seldom divided into units so independent that one can be changed without affecting others. Even the incremental curriculum changes typically attempted in schools, such as adopting a new method of reading instruction, increasing emphasis on writing in the upper elementary grades, making mathematics more or less practical, or updating science content, require far reaching adjustments throughout the curriculum.

Every curriculum change demands a change from teachers. At a minimum, teachers must revise their plans to include the changes in content, purpose, or form, and revise their class activities to realize these changes in plans. They may also need to learn new content. They may need to reconsider their conception of the subject, the student, teaching, education, or society and to reconcile new ideas and values with familiar ones. They may need to learn new teaching skills and strategies. The more difficult and extensive the changes demanded of teachers, the more difficult it will be to implement that curriculum change in the classroom.

Teachers need incentives to make the changes required to modify the classroom curriculum. They must envision possible benefits from making the change that exceed their costs and risks. These may be material incentives such as extra pay. They may be intangible incentives such as professional pride and recognition. As we have seen, teachers feel rewarded by their contacts with students and by being able to help them. Making a curriculum change that they believe truly benefits students substantially may therefore be so inherently rewarding that it requires no extrinsic rewards of any kind. Teachers can readily see, though, that few teachers achieved rewards other than intrinsic ones for their efforts in implementing earlier curriculum reforms. Champions of one reform movement may have become heroes for a time, but they eventually endured criticism when reactions came or obscurity when the next wave of reform crested. Teachers found themselves criticized as causes of the current problems by each successive band of reformers. Newspaper headlines never trumpeted their success. By contrast, in the progressive era teachers who labored to realize the new student centered, activity-oriented reforms were hailed as heroes helping to usher in an enlightened modern era, to create a fuller democracy, and to realize the potential inherent in each child.

Promising New Approaches

Teach Collaboratively

Teachers can work together to plan a sequence of lessons that use a challenging unconventional teaching strategy and then share their experiences in teaching the lessons. George Hillocks (1999) describes one such collaborative teaching scheme that he calls a teaching workshop.

> The workshop involves four to five teachers in the planning, teaching, and evaluation of teaching in a single class. This is . . . collaborative teaching in which all teachers participate in planning and evaluating each day's activities over a period of four to five weeks. Only one teacher teaches in a given class hour, but over the course of several weeks, all teachers participate equally in the teaching (Hillocks, 1999, p. 135).

Whenever possible, collaborative teaching teams should have an expert mentor who is knowledgeable and experienced with the teaching style they are trying. A mentor provides technical assistance, research support, help when the team gets stuck, and confidence.

Jacob Adams (2000) studied a network of teachers in California attempting to implement a complex new course in high school mathematics called "Math A." Adams found that teacher networks facilitated change by providing a common time for teachers to attend to making the change, organizing resources at all levels that might support teachers in making the change, and fostering discourse leading to a common practice. This successful network featured a common purpose based on a strong policy context, frequent interaction, immediate and common experiences, and a person to link teachers to resources (Adams, 2000, p. 169).

Discuss Student Work

In the past decade in-service educators and school curriculum leaders in many forward-looking schools have instituted the practice of teachers discussing student work. This practice began as a method for setting standards for assessing students' work, but the depth and quality of the discussions convinced many of those who participated in them that they had potentially great value for teacher development. Teachers bring to meetings examples of work their students have done in class, typical work, extremely good work, or extremely poor work depending on the specific purpose of the meeting. They discuss how they would grade the work and develop rubrics for assessing the quality of work of that type. A rubric is a scoring scheme that describes the characteristics a student work product should have to meet various levels of a standard.

Discussions of student work can go in several directions. Teachers can discuss the rubrics they will use to grade students' work. They can discuss the specific learning difficulties responsible for unsatisfactory work and ways to help them overcome those. Or, they can focus on the assignment that led to the work and discuss other types of assignments that might challenge students more, help them develop deeper understanding, or be better suited to the students in some other way.

The main benefits of discussing student work in comparison with other topics teachers might discuss are the focus on classroom activity, the specificity and detail it makes possible, and the focus on students' learning. Discussing student work can be a more productive way for teachers to discuss teaching practices than a more direct focus would be since discussion of student work treats teaching as a means to the end of student learning rather than as an end in themselves. The specificity that student work brings enables teachers to engage in productive discussions of curriculum issues that might otherwise be too general to be helpful.

Having studied samples of students' work and identified tentative sources of students' difficulties, teachers can look for more successful learning and teaching strategies and ways to help less successful students use them.

Select Activities in a Principled Way

In some cases the classroom activities that most teachers use for teaching a topic or skill lead to results that fall far short of everyone's expectations year after year. In these cases teachers and curriculum leaders can undertake a more systematic and rigorous search for more educationally powerful activities. Figure 8.4 outlines steps of a process for selecting activities in a principled way. Clearly this process is too time-consuming, effortful, and expensive to use with all classroom activities, but it would be appropriate for especially critical topics and goals that many students fail to master.

Field Test New Curriculum Plans and Materials

Materials developed by any method are only guesses at what might foster learning in classrooms. A field test is a way to find out if the guess was on target. The main reasons to conduct field tests of curriculum materials are to answer three basic questions:

1. Select a topic and form a study team.

   Identify a crucial topic that students have trouble learning. Choose a modest, manageable topic; initial reading is too big. Take this as your topic for the year. Form a study team with teaching colleagues. Enlist a researcher from a nearby college or university to advise you. Ask your colleagues, principal, or a district official to help you locate expert advisers.

2. Collect your own thoughts on the problem.

   Why do you think this topic is more difficult to learn than others are? Do all students have trouble or only some? Do you recall any notable success in which a student had a sudden insight or improved markedly? How do you think the topic should be taught?

3. Find out what the experts say.

   Look for published writing on the teaching of your topic. Consult books by well-known authors on teaching whose opinion you value. Ask your expert advisors to recommend other books and authors. Search reference books such as the *Encyclopedia of Educational Research*, the *Handbook of Research on Teaching*, the *Handbook of Research on Curriculum*, or a handbook of teaching in your subject. Look in recent textbooks on the teaching of your subject. You should find at least a few pages that mention your topic. If it's a big well-known problem, you may find several books about it. Normally, you'll find one or a few relevant articles or chapters. If it has been little studied you may need to do a computerized search to locate specific studies.

4. Look for innovative curriculum projects.

   Government agencies such as the Department of Education and the National Science Foundation as well as private foundations fund innovators to create new curriculum plans and materials. Search for projects that cover your topic and see how they teach it.

5. Select the most promising teaching approaches.

   Critically review the literature and innovative projects. Were you able to find strong evidence for the effectiveness of any of the teaching approaches? How convincing is the evidence? Comparing all the approaches given what you know, in your judgment which approaches are the most promising?

6. Develop or adapt principled teaching plans implementing a promising alternative approach.

   Plan a sequence of classroom activities that should work if the explanation of the difficulty is right. Draw on the teaching strategies that experts say show promise for improving the learning of the topic.

7. Develop an assessment procedure.

   Consider including several indicators of students' learning, such as teacher judgment, student self-assessments, peer ratings, portfolios of student work, performance on authentic tasks, and tests. Develop pre-measures of students' prior knowledge and performance.

8. Carry out a teaching experiment.

   Try out your teaching plans. Compare the traditional method against one or two alternative approaches. Randomly decide which classes receive which kind of teaching. Assess their prior knowledge and performance. Assess their performance at the end of the unit and after several additional weeks have passed.

9. Report your findings to professional colleagues.

   Write a brief report and submit it to ERIC. Make a presentation to your department or a regional professional meeting.

FIG. 8.4. *A process for principled activity selection.*

1. Do the materials work as developers expect?
2. Do students learn what developers expect them to learn?
3. How can the materials be improved?

"Working" includes such mundane but vital matters as:

- Does what happens in the classroom resemble what the developers had in mind?
- Can teachers and students use the materials without too much difficulty?
- Do teachers and students find use of the materials rewarding enough to continue to use them spontaneously
- Is the project realistic in its demands on time, effort, facilities, teacher and student ability, and so on?

Figure 8.5 suggests more detailed questions of this same sort. If curriculum materials do not pass such tests as these, they are not really viable and must be revised or replaced.

Peter Dow's (1975) field tests of an early version of *Man: A Course of Study*, mentioned in Chapter 6, show how helpful field tests of curriculum materials can be. Recall that the developers showed students films of a baboon troop in the wild. They were planning to contrast the behavior of baboons with that of humans. The field tests showed much to their surprise that students imputed human characteristics to the baboons. They believed, for instance, that baboons had a language so complex that humans could not yet understand it. Because the developers had introduced the unit on baboons to contrast animal

---

Questions to ask prior to the field test:
    Was it clear to students what developers expected them to learn?
    Was it clear to students why developers believe that this is important to learn?
    Did students believe that it was important to learn?

Questions to ask during the field test:
    Were students able to comprehend the instructions and the tasks?
    Did teacher and students complete the activity satisfactorily?
    Were students and teachers able to tailor the activity to suit them and their
        different classroom situations?
    Did the activity make good use of appropriate resources?
    Did the activity support and assist students at critical points where they might
        falter?
    Did the activity require resources not normally present in the classroom?

Questions to ask after the field test:
    Did teachers and students find using the materials a positive experience that
        they would like to repeat?
    Did students comprehend the materials?
    Did teachers believe that students learned what developers intended?
    Did students believe that they learned what developers intended?
    Did the quality of students' work or their performance on authentic
        performance measures indicate that they had learned what the developers
        intended?
    Was the learning achieved proportional to the resources consumed?

FIG. 8.5. *Basic questions for field tests of curriculum activities.*

behavior with human behavior, this finding of the field test forced major revisions. Subsequent versions of the materials included units on lower animals as well as baboons.

Conducting field tests in a way that allows developers to answer these simple questions is not so simple. Developers must decide what to observe, what questions to ask of students and teachers, and how to assess learning. They must infer from data collected in the field whether the materials are working, producing learning, and can be improved. These inferences are generally hazardous. Two observers of the same field trial might well reach differentconclusions on whether the materials worked and what revisions were most needed. Worse, it often happens that neither observer can conclude anything with confidence, both coming away confused and uncertain about the significance of what they have seen.

So much will be going on in the classroom where materials are being tried out that there will be no hope of noticing everything, let alone recording it. Developers need more than observations; they need data—observations selected and organized to speak to a question. The most common and easiest form of data collection is informal observation—you simply look and listen. As a precaution, you might get a disinterested observer to look and listen and report to you. Another common, easy source of data is interviews with teacher and students. Both interview and observation can be strengthened in some respects by using structured lists of things to look for and questions to ask and standardized methods of recording and analyzing data.

Often developers create some sort of evaluation instrument that poses appropriate problem and records students' responses. In this way they can introduce some types of tasks that they know have special relevance to what they are attempting to teach; they don't have to wait for them to occur naturally. Developers can simply present students with an appropriate problem and ask them to think aloud or give an oral or written response in their own words. In fact, if the topic is not especially verbal, developers can simply watch and see if they do it and how. At the other extreme, developers can select published, standardized tests of achievement.

These three types of data—observations, interviews, and test instruments—are the mainstays of field-testing. They are versatile enough that developers can probably get useful evidence on just about any question they might want to ask by using them.

Questions and Projects

1. When should students' learning difficulties cause teachers to consider changing the curriculum? Think about your own experience and discuss the matter with other teachers. Describe briefly some cases where curriculum change seems clearly appropriate, others where it seems clearly inappropriate, and the remainder where appropriateness is in doubt. Examine your descriptions and identify some major considerations, pro and con, for changing the curriculum under these circumstances. What additional kinds of information would enable a teacher to reach a firm conclusion about the merits of a curriculum change when students have difficulties?

2. What other circumstances besides students' learning difficulties might lead a responsible person to question whether a curriculum is appropriate for a group of students? Repeat the steps of the previous activity with each of these other circumstances.

3. Interview curriculum specialists about cases they have encountered when a curriculum seemed inappropriate for some students. Ask for background information and

ask what actions were taken. Write up the case. Show it to others—teachers, parents, principals, or curriculum professionals. Do you find a clear consensus that changing the curriculum was a good or bad idea in this case, or do you find differing opinions?

4. Reflect on your own teaching. Recall the first few days of one of your classes. Describe how you introduced the curriculum of that class to your students. Are you happy now with what you did then? How would you change it?

5. Conduct a case study of how one or more experienced teachers introduce their curriculum to students in the first few days of class. Observe the class and interview the teacher. Compare with what student teachers do and what they say about it.

6. Examine some textbooks. How do they introduce the subject? Can you suggest ways to improve them?

7. Identify the frames in a typical elementary class, a typical secondary class, and a typical undergraduate class. How are they alike and how do they differ? How might the differences affect teachers' planning at the three levels?

8. Examine two or more unit plans. Assess their strengths and limitations and suggest ways they might be improved.

9. Some observers maintain that teachers are powerless pawns in curriculum reform, while others maintain that teachers are the most powerful shapers of the actual curriculum students receive. Can you shed any light on this dispute using the ideas presented in this chapter?

10. Find one or more teachers who have recently been expected to adopt a curriculum reform that required them to make a substantial change in their classroom curriculum. Interview the teachers about their attempts, the support they received, how they felt about the process, and what happened as a result of it.

11. Choose one of the activity schema mentioned in the chapter or identify an additional one. On a single sheet of paper list the "slots" or blanks that need to be filled in when creating a specific activity of that type.

12. Develop an educational activity by beginning with some out-of-school activities that are not usually taken as sources of educative activities. For example, try: job-hunting, chanting, shopping, telling jokes, writing graffiti, gossiping, and travelling.

Further Study

A great deal has been written on the topic of teacher professional development as the key to improving the classroom curriculum. *Teaching as the Learning Profession: Handbook of Policy and Practice* edited by Linda Darling-Hammond and Gary Sykes is an excellent compendium. Ann Lieberman and Lynne Miller in *Teachers—Transforming Their World and Their Work* (1999) is an eloquent and inspiring call to action on behalf of this agenda. Michael Connelly and Jean Clandinin have been making this case for decades. Their latest volume, *Shaping a Professional Identity: Stories of Educational Practice* (1999), is a valuable addition that focuses on the curriculum as reflecting a teacher's professional identity. George Hillocks' *Ways of Thinking, Ways of Teaching* (1999) is an engaging synthesis of cognition and practical knowledge. His concept of a teaching workshop sounds like a viable practical approach to supporting teachers in making deep changes in their practices.

Quite a lot has been written about whole school reform under the assumption that changing the whole school will thereby change the curriculum. Ann Lieberman's *School Reform Behind the Scenes* (1999) is a good example of this line of thought. The volume

Teaching for Understanding (1993) edited by Cohen, McLaughlin, and Talbert presents the same arguments but seems more aware of the scope and depth of the difficulties in changing teachers' teaching by reforming schools.

Eleanor Duckworth has been a passionate and thoughtful proponent of the view that improvement in teaching and learning comes from teachers studying and reflecting on students' learning and on teaching. Her *Tell Me More: Listening to Learners Explain* (2001) and *Teacher to Teacher* (1997) are worthy successors to her path-breaking *The Having of Wonderful Ideas & Other Essays on Teaching & Learning* (1996). The edited volume by Cobb, Yackel, and McClain entitled *Symbolizing and Communicating in Mathematics Classrooms* (2000) shows examples of intensive studies of teachers trying constructivist approaches in mathematics classrooms. Magdalene Lampert and Deborah Ball have also pioneered in this line of study. Their book, *Teaching, Multimedia, and Mathematics: Investigations of Real Practice* (1998), sets the standard for this kind of work.

The best introduction to the topic of teacher networks as a curriculum improvement strategy is Jacob Adams, Jr.'s *Taking Charge of Curriculum: Teacher Networks and Curriculum Implementation* (2000). I find it to be an extremely thoughtful case study informed by a careful reading of the literature on teacher networks. Christenson, Johnston, and Norris in their edited volume *Teaching Together: School/University Collaboration to Improve Social Studies Education* (2001) provide a helpful introduction to this important form of collaboration.

On the whole, the recent literature on improving the classroom curriculum began as a promising approach to the hardest curriculum problem but has now become an over-reaction to the failures of the imposed curriculum development projects of the previous decades. Whereas some of these earlier projects may have attempted to be teacher-proof, contemporary approaches often seem to be curriculum-proof in that they assume that the need for curriculum work will disappear when we have truly professional teachers working in reformed schools. Readers who have read the earlier chapters of this book will not find this a plausible position. The pendulum will swing back.

CHAPTER NINE

Improving School Curriculum

To change the curriculum of the school...means bringing about changes in people—in their desires, beliefs, and attitudes, in their knowledge and skill.
—Alice Miel, *Changing the Curriculum: A Social Process*, 1946

Questions

- What work must be done to improve a school curriculum? Who participates in this work? How is this work carried out, coordinated, and evaluated?
- What problems arise when school officials and teachers try to improve school curriculums and what can be done to overcome them?
- What strategies do school leaders commonly use in their efforts to improve their school's curriculum?
- What other strategies hold promise?

Common Approaches to School Curriculum Improvement

For a curriculum innovation to take root in a school many conditions must be met. Principals must support the innovation. Teachers must discuss it and adapt it to their styles and circumstances. The central office must provide critical personnel, resources, and expertise when they are needed to support the innovation. Otherwise, school curriculum improvement is virtually impossible.

Schools parcel out the work of curriculum improvement among principals, lead teachers, department chairs, curriculum coordinators, and other school and district officials in various ways, but for our present purposes we do not need to know exactly who does what. For simplicity's sake I will refer to those who do school curriculum improvement as "school curriculum leaders."

Also, schools and districts divide curricular responsibilities differently. Sometimes local school leaders are dominant. Elmore et al. (1996) quote one school principal on the way she handles district administrators:

> District administrators for the most part have no idea what's going on in the better schools, no idea what to do if they did know, and no idea how their jobs relate to what goes on in schools. On top of that, they are very easily threatened, so you have to spend a lot of time mollifying them, or you just don't tell them what you're doing [said by a principal in an innovative school] (Elmore et al., 1996).

This chapter is not the place to discuss how best to administer schools, so I gloss over all these questions. This chapter simply assumes competent administration and leadership at the school and school system. Similarly, it assumes that sound democratic school governance arrangements are in place.

Most of the curriculum work that local school personnel do is necessarily devoted to keeping the curriculum they already have in working order. The additional work of improving the school curriculum can be analyzed into six main functions: reviewing the school curriculum; considering curriculum changes; instituting changes; helping teachers to change their classroom curriculums; monitoring curriculum change efforts; and long-term planning. In practice these are blended together with one another and with the many other tasks required to run a school. In this chapter we have the luxury of studying each separately.

Most experienced teachers want to control the curriculum of their classroom. They see the curriculum of their classroom as rightfully their professional responsibility. Teachers do not even want fellow teachers to control their curriculum. They want freedom from all organizational authority in matters that concern the classroom curriculum. Lortie summarized the results of a survey of teachers in Dade County, Florida, asking about their preferences for different types of organizational control in these terms: "These teachers want to loosen organizational claims in favor of teacher decision-making in the classroom" (Lortie, 1975, p. 164). Beginning teachers, by contrast, often welcome guidance from official curriculum documents, provided they have the freedom to deviate from them when they think best.

Control of curriculum is often a source of conflict between teachers and school administrators. School administrators see the curriculum as one of the few means they have for influencing what happens behind the classroom door. In particular, implementing school-wide reforms often requires changes in the classroom curriculums of an entire school. Because school administrators generally carry the responsibility for implementing school-wide reforms, they need the power to influence the classroom curriculum. The idea implicit in the phrase "implementing a reform" is that teachers should faithfully follow the new curriculum. Thus, the school administrator's ideal of teachers as implementers of school curriculum stands in direct opposition to the teachers' ideal of autonomy.

In practice, the classroom curriculum emerges from a process of mutual adaptation between the official curriculum and the curriculum a teacher wants (Berman & McLaughlin, 1975). When teachers face an official curriculum that they disagree with, they try to find ways to satisfy both the external demands and their own professional judgment, conscience, and style. For example, district policy may dictate that children be taught to balance checkbooks in math class. That policy would conflict with some teachers' deeply held beliefs about the importance of teaching mathematical concepts and problem solving. Teachers can ease the tension of this conflict in several ways, such as by:

- completing the checkbook balancing lessons ahead of schedule, leaving time for other goals;
- devising problems with significant mathematical content within the format of checkbook balancing;
- creating materials to teach checkbook balancing as homework and seatwork so that maximum class time can be devoted to other topics.

None of these expedients is as good in teachers' eyes as being able to follow their own mathematics curriculum, but all meet the letter of the law and yet preserve a measure of professional integrity.

Teachers may find themselves in an ethically untenable position if the official curriculum contravenes a deeply held personal belief. For instance, teachers who believe that education requires a genuine human interaction with students about matters of real concern to them will be unable to maintain their professional integrity if required to follow a curriculum that calls for prescribed units planned in advance to achieve specific behavioral objectives. An English teacher who is personally committed to maintaining traditional standards of good English usage may have trouble accepting nonstandard English as equally worthy of respect, even if the official curriculum guide says that they should. For teachers to follow a curriculum that conflicts with their beliefs and values means that they must work constantly with divided minds and divided loyalties. No wonder, then, that teachers crave the power to control their curriculum, to teach what they see fit, as they see fit, using or not using at their discretion any curricular guidance authorities offer.

Figure 9.1 lists some conditions that enable schools to improve their curriculum. These conditions can be met through many specific institutional procedures that can be adapted to suit local conditions. In practice, local curriculum improvement efforts often do not meet some of these conditions or meet them only marginally, and these shortcomings rather than problems with the innovation or implementation strategy account for many implementation failures. In this chapter we will consider ways in which these requirements can be met at each stage of the process: reviewing the quality of the existing curriculum, considering curriculum changes, instituting curriculum change efforts, and facilitating curriculum change in classrooms.

- A working consensus in support of the change among:
    parents and community
    teachers
    school leaders, formal and informal, lay and professional
- Able and eager students who understand and support the change
- Consistency of the change with given frames, including
    economic constraints
    policies of higher authorities
    other relatively fixed local realities
- Local champions with leadership and organizational ability
- Deep, clear understanding of the change, including
    central features that must be present
    appropriate variations
- Ideas (theories, rationales) supporting the change
- Training and support for teachers, including
    explanations and demonstrations
    opportunity for practice with feedback
    continuing support to overcome difficulties
    incentives for the extra effort of change
- Material and administrative support for the change effort, including
    provision of curriculum materials
    adjustment of routines to accommodate the change
    assistance in handling unanticipated problems
    provision for revising the plan to adapt it to local circumstances
    provision for monitoring change efforts and evaluating their effects

---

FIG. 9.1. *Conditions enabling curriculum improvement in local schools.*

Reviewing the Quality of a School Curriculum

In a sense the curriculum is under constant review. Teachers discuss it in the teachers' lounge and at department meetings. School officials discuss it at their meetings and in informal contacts with community members. Leaders keep their ear to the ground, listening for expressions of discontent and judging how serious and widespread they are. School officials field complaints from parents. They monitor disciplinary actions against students for the possibility that a curriculum problem may be partly to blame. They compare notes with their colleagues in other schools. They attend conferences and read professional journals and books about educational scandals and reforms, and they compare their own curriculum to the others they learn about.

If these informal reviews suggest a potential problem, they may arrange to visit some classes and to speak with some teachers to see if they spot further signs. They might meet with a department and discuss needs for curriculum revision or devote part of a faculty meeting to such a discussion. If consultations with teachers, parents, possibly students, and community members suggest that a problem exists, school officials may appoint a committee to look into it.

On rare occasions the curriculum receives more intense scrutiny. A formal investigation may be launched. These investigations go by many names—studies, reports, surveys, evaluations, assessments, needs assessments, . . . —but they are all curriculum reviews. Curriculum reviews are described in Chapter 2, Traditions of Curriculum Practice. Reviews are costly and time-consuming. They are such major undertakings that decisionmakers must strongly suspect that a major problem exists in order to justify the effort and expense of a formal review.

In this section we will use the term "review" for any systematic effort to collect information for the purpose of making a judgment about the quality of an educational program. Curriculum reviews may be planned, regularly recurring reviews, as in annual reports, periodic accreditation studies, or cyclic revisions of curriculum guidelines and selection of textbooks. Or, they may be unexpected reviews precipitated by some crisis, demanded by an outside authority, or required as part of a grant proposal the school wishes to make. Reviews may be comprehensive, dealing with all aspects of the entire school program, or they may be focused on a particular problem. A review may involve dozens of people from the public and profession or it may consist of a study by a single individual. Reviewers may be empowered with nearly prosecutorial investigative authority and the funds to go with it, or constrained to use only publicly available information. Reviews may operate in the full glare of public meetings covered by the media or in private sessions with confidential reporting to officials only.

Explicit formal reviews of a school curriculum can serve many purposes. They can be used to disturb the complacency of school staffs and spur them to greater ambition. They can be used to explore and discover the nature and seriousness of possible problems. Reviews that focus on a particular problem can be used to send a message that school leaders are determined to deal with that problem. Reviews offer a possibility of capitalizing on unique historical opportunities for curriculum improvement by creating local concern about issues when political and economic support is momentarily strong. Reviews can help to find an appropriate school response to changes in the community, and they can provide an occasion for a stable community to consider whether the curriculum still meets their needs.

Several types of arrangements are commonly made for conducting curricular reviews. Most reviews are in fact self-studies, conducted by the same people who are responsible for the curriculum under review. The stimulus for the review may come from outside this circle, outsiders may participate in the review, and the results of the review may be communicated to outsiders. Outsiders may even impose conditions on how it should be conducted. But the carrying out of the review is usually the responsibility of the school staff. Almost the only exceptions to this are reviews of a school's curriculum carried out by staff from the district office.

The most common external audiences for reviews of school programs are the superintendent and school board. Accreditation committees become a significant audience when a school is undergoing accreditation. Schools occasionally conduct voluntary reviews and needs assessments for a state or federal agency from which they seek funds or recognition. In normal times, the audience for reviews consists largely of professional educators and school leaders familiar with the school. In times of crisis, however, the general public and others with no previous knowledge of the school and no special expertise in dealing with educational issues, such as citizen groups, legislators, or judges, become important members of the audience.

Comprehensive Program Reviews

Labeling a review "comprehensive" simply signals an intention to include in the review in some way any relevant matter proposed by any participant. A truly complete review would require a study beyond the means of the wealthiest school and beyond the technical capability of the most advanced research. Selection is unavoidable. Most of the matters considered in any review would receive only cursory attention. Still, the striving toward comprehensiveness is important politically and organizationally.

Consider by way of illustration the case of the Schenley High School Teacher Center, which the Pittsburgh Public Schools created in 1981 on the recommendation of Superintendent Richard C. Wallace, Jr. When Wallace was asked how he persuaded the board of education to approve such a project, he replied as follows:

> ... it grew out of a comprehensive needs assessment. Probably the smartest thing I ever did when I arrived in Pittsburgh in September of 1980 was to get Bill Cooley and Bill Bickel [of the University of Pittsburgh] to work with me.... We conducted a very broad-based needs assessment, surveying samples of public school and private school parents, community leaders, and every level of employee in the district ... (Brandt, 1987).

He explained that the board members were able to use the needs assessment to focus attention on a few achievable priorities from among their diverse concerns and to unify the board on behalf of some important projects.

In their book, *Decision-Oriented Educational Research*, Cooley and Bickel (1986) report 11 case histories they did to help identify strengths and weaknesses of the educational program of the Pittsburgh public schools. One of the case histories recounts a districtwide needs assessment that they did at the request of the newly appointed superintendent, a fairly common occasion for program reviews of all types. The purpose of the review was to determine the extent to which the Pittsburgh public schools were meeting the needs of children enrolled in them and to identify priorities for program improvement. The review used data from two sources: surveys of stakeholders' perceptions and existing school records. The superintendent appointed a 30-member task force to assist with the design of the study. Half of the task force members were community leaders and the rest were teachers, principals, and other employee groups.

The technical staff composed the items for the survey instruments and field tested them, designed a sampling plan, and settled the practical details of distributing, collecting, and analyzing the data. The planning and instrument development occupied between 2 and 3 months, data were collected in less than 1 month, analyzed in less than 1 month, and reviewed by the board of education in less than 5 months from the first meeting with the superintendent. The study collected data relevant to questions that the superintendent, task force, and technical staff considered important, including percentages enrolled in remedial programs, enrollment trends, suspension rates, and costs per pupil in various schools.

Based on these data, the needs assessment identified five pressing needs: improving student achievement in basic skills, better procedures for personnel evaluation, attracting and holding students, managing enrollment decline, and improving individual schools. For each need, the study was able to deliver fairly detailed documentation of the extent and nature of the problem. For instance, they were able to discover that several supposedly distinct remedial programs offered by the district were in fact quite similar, and that the coordination between what was taught in these remedial programs and what was taught in regular classrooms was lax. Study personnel presented the results of the assessment in a series of slide shows over a period of 3 months for different audiences, including the superintendent, the board president, the entire board, the central office staff, building administrators and supervisors, teachers, task force members, and the press.

On the Monday following the first presentation of results to the superintendent and school board at a weekend retreat, the superintendent announced publicly his intention to develop an "action plan" to address two major areas: school improvement and cost-effective management. At its next meeting the board endorsed these initiatives and authorized funds to begin the planning.

This example is typical of needs assessments in several respects. It was initiated by a newly appointed superintendent. It was jointly planned by technically trained staff, the superintendent, and a representative steering group. No facet of the school system's operation was excluded from consideration in the study. The study used numerical data already available in district files as well as results of surveys of a representative sample of various stakeholders.

The study is exemplary in several other respects. It was completed very quickly, in less than one academic year. The data were analyzed with particular care and astuteness. The results were disseminated with special thoroughness. And the relation of the review to actions based upon its results were particularly close. This is an example of a district-level needs assessment, rather than a school-level program review, but in the most important respects the two are similar. Needs assessments are more often done for a school district rather than an individual school, though newly appointed principals may also conduct needs assessments for their schools. Accreditation reviews are the most common types of comprehensive reviews of school programs. They, too, include all aspects of school operation, including the educational program but also including finance, personnel, administration, and even buildings and grounds. Accreditation reviews take place on a fairly regular schedule, typically every 5 years or so for a school where few problems are identified, though as often as every year or two in the case of a school with serious problems.

Just how effective are comprehensive reviews? Are they worth the money? As the case of Pittsburgh showed, comprehensive reviews can be powerfully effective in calling attention to problems, in gaining consensus on priorities, and in precipitating action on the problems identified. But they will only repay their cost when there is a reasonable chance of doing something about the problems discovered.

Focused Selective Reviews

Comprehensive formal reviews are major undertakings. The costs and risks associated with them must be carefully weighed against their benefits in any given situation. Intentionally selective reviews are preferable in many situations. A frankly targeted review is preferable when the existence of a problem with a particular aspect of the curriculum is not in question, but it is necessary to define the problem better, to document its extent and seriousness, or to identify its causes. Sometimes it may be clear to school leaders that complacency has set in with some component of the curriculum and a focused review may call the situation to everyone's attention. Sometimes it is important to look into rumors or charges being circulated in order to confirm or dispel them. When a change is under consideration, a focused review of the present situation may help in planning the development and implementation of improvements.

A focused selective review should begin with a statement of the reasons for undertaking a review of this part of the curriculum at this time. It should describe the current program, what is known about its outcomes, and the initial questions to be answered by the review. All participants should understand that there is likely to be disagreement on these matters and alternative positions should be welcomed as helping to guide the review. Also, everyone should understand that the chief outcome of the review is likely to be a different appreciation of the situation and therefore a redefinition of the problem and a restatement of the questions of most importance. For this reason, focused selective reviews should have fluid, flexible designs.

Collect data that are easy and cheap to collect as early as possible and use these data to check assumptions about the program and its problems. Make plans for the next phase of the study after discussing these results with the governing body. As understanding develops from the review, it is likely that questions will multiply. It will probably be necessary to spin off substudies to pursue different questions. The entire review should be organized in such a way that substantial progress can be made in a matter of a few weeks and the entire study redesigned in progress, with staff re-deployed, expanded, or reduced as necessary. For such an organization to work, communication lines must be short, because there is no time for results to filter through to a wide, distant audience. The governing body must be trustworthy, because an unscrupulous person or group could leak emerging conclusions early for their own advantage. And the technical staff must be tolerant of compromises with professional standards of disciplined inquiry.

Mixed Reviews

A mixed strategy is often appropriate. The initial phase of a review might include a broad and necessarily superficial look at the entire program. Two or three levels of intensity of review might be distinguished in this first phase, greatest attention going to those components that are believed to need most attention. Since some resources will be directed toward all major components, the review would be comprehensive, but it would also be focused right from the start on some areas more than others. In later phases, the review could focus only on those areas where those involved judge that studies are most likely to reveal something of importance.

Figure 9.2 lists some questions that might guide a comprehensive review. Initial questions undergo continued refinement and development as the review proceeds, but in the meantime they guide planning. The review must answer the questions considered most important by the steering group and not the questions easiest to answer with available data. Investigators can usually find some evidence useful in answering any question, but on some questions of paramount importance the evidence gained from the kinds of studies that are practical may be of little help, yet an equal effort in studying another question only slightly less important might yield penetrating insights. So decisions about the best questions to ask need to be informed by technical considerations but not controlled by them.

Data Collection and Analysis

To answer questions such as those in Fig. 9.2 and to acquire the data listed in Fig. 9.3, a review must generally use data beyond that available in school records. Surveys may need

1. How are our graduates performing in important domains by relevant standards after they leave our school?

   (Important domains might include academic, personal vocational, and civic. Possibly relevant standards include their own, their families', their community's, the school's, the state's, the nation's, and international standards.)

2. How well are our students meeting relevant expectations at various stages of their schooling?

   (Possibly relevant expectations include participation and involvement in school activities (especially attendance), mastery of curricular content and objectives, satisfactory development in nonacademic domains (personal, civic, vocational, . . .), curricular electives chosen, . . .)

3. Do the curriculums students actually receive meet appropriate standards?

   (Do content, goals, and school and classroom climate meet appropriate standards?)

4. Is the school program functioning smoothly?

   (Are students attending, participating, engaged with school activities?)

5. What resources are devoted to the school program?

6. Is there a clear positive relationship between the pattern of curricular inputs and the students' achievements?

7. How are these resources distributed among students? Is this distribution equitable?

FIG. 9.2. *Possible questions for curriculum reviews.*

to be made of parents, graduates, employers, admissions officers of schools that graduates attend, and others outside the school. In addition, the following kinds of rough indicators of public perceptions of school quality can be solicited: reputation of the school, ease of recruiting and retaining staff, extent to which quality of schools is a factor in local real estate transactions, and ratings of the school by college admissions offices. Additional test data or other student performance data may be useful.

Finding sound data that faithfully represent such complex matters as these and yet can be collected economically is the greatest technical challenge facing designers of reviews. The intellectual compromises involved in using, say, a student's reading score on a standardized test as a measure of what the student has learned in elementary school are enormous. But the compromises involved in choosing other indicators, such as grades on teacher-made tests or grades in middle school English, are at least as great. Multiple measures can compensate for the limitations of any one, but only at additional cost. Such tradeoffs haunt designers of reviews.

We have few adequate measures for the global processes and outcomes of schooling. We have relatively good tests of many important specific outcomes, such as mastery of arithmetic or reading comprehension, but tests of overall mathematics achievement are problematic for two fundamental reasons. First, there is no consensus on the weight that should be given to different kinds of mathematics learning or to different content. As a result, different tests give different results. Second, valid interpretation of the scores on such a test depends on knowledge about the curriculum that the student experienced. Students who missed an item covering knowledge they never studied must be distinguished from those who missed

Inputs

Offerings
Programs
Time allotments
Teacher characteristics
Student characteristics
Home community characteristics
Curriculum materials
Courses of study
Tests
Statements of purpose and philosophy
History, tradition

Processes

Teacher assignment
Services provided to teachers
Engaged time
Attendance
Course completion (drop outs)
Critical incidents (discipline, failures, complaints)

Outcomes

Reputation
Visits from other schools to study programs
Honors and recognition for curricular excellence
Frequency of complaints
Tests
   Teacher
   District
Standardized (e.g., Scholastic Aptitude Test (SAT))
Grades
Student achievements
Student honors won

Consequences

Admission to selective schools
Performance in later schooling
Jobs
Recognition, honors, awards
Achievements (e.g., patents, publications, etc.)
Perceptions of graduates

FIG. 9.3. *Potentially important data for curriculum reviews.*

it despite encountering the knowledge in their school program. Otherwise reviewers may draw wrong conclusions about the program's strengths and weaknesses.

So, designers of the data collection for a curriculum review must carefully balance the competing demands of validity, relevance, coverage, and cost in selecting data to include in the review. Emphasizing low cost and validity at the expense of relevance and coverage, for example, yields a tough-minded, hard-nosed, quantitative review focused on those matters most readily captured by current educational measurement methods: attendance, enrollments, grades, and test scores. Reversing the priorities by emphasizing relevance and wide coverage at the expense of economy and validity, yields a tender-minded, subjective, qualitative review. Needless to say, the results of two such different reviews will not necessarily agree. Therefore, the design of data collection for a curriculum review should never be left in the hands of technically trained people only. The governing body for the review should make major design decisions after consulting with technically trained staff.

Generally, planning and carrying out the data collection requires expertise in research methods not normally found in school staffs. These experts are usually trained in psychological methods of testing, measurement and evaluation, and they tend to recommend review procedures that call for collection of numerical data in objective forms obtained under controlled conditions. In recent decades, qualitative methods have been developed to the point where they can claim evidence as sound as that of quantitative methods. An intensive ethnographic study of schools, classrooms, or community settings may yield more helpful data less expensively and with more credibility than quantitative studies that count incidence of particular occurrences in these same settings, for example.

Analyzing the data in a way that leads to valid, defensible conclusions about the questions actually of interest in the review is another major technical challenge. Hundreds of thousands of individual items of data must be reduced to comprehensible patterns. The numerical data must be reduced to summary statistics, a few numbers that represent the key information in all the data. The qualitative data must be reduced to an executive summary or abstract. Decisions about data analysis are generally best left in the hands of the chief technical person on the staff of the review, but this person should be given a clear set of questions to be answered and must be involved in the planning. When the plan of the review is complete, the data analyst should be able to say which questions will be answerable with these data and with what range of uncertainty.

Considering Curriculum Changes

Jon Schaffarzick (1975) coined the term "curriculum change consideration" to identify the process by which local curriculum leaders consider whether to undertake a proposed curriculum change. It can be as brief and informal as a hallway conversation or as imposing as a formal inquiry by a school–community task force. The change consideration process is important because most proposed innovations do not proceed beyond this stage. At any one time there are dozens, perhaps hundreds, of innovations being urged upon schools. In any particular school, several, perhaps dozens, of these will find local champions who will propose them in some way for adoption in that school. Curriculum change consideration is the varied and often little structured process by which this proposal either fails and drops from active consideration or succeeds and becomes an official curriculum improvement project. It is the death knell for most innovation proposals, and a major step toward realization for the survivors.

A proposal survives the change consideration process when the school leadership launches an effort to make the proposed curriculum improvements. This decision, in turn, rests upon leaders' assumptions that support for the change would eventually be widespread

- Origination
    Some person or group comes to believe that a curriculum change of some sort is needed and suggests that a change be made.
- Preliminary Consideration
    Some person or group (usually different from #1) is authorized by legitimate authorities to consider whether change is needed, if so, to propose what type of change and how it should be further considered.
- Full Consideration and Preparation
    The main difference between preliminary and full consideration is the investment of resources required to carry them out. Preliminary consideration is quick and cheap. When it provides an insufficient basis for the commitment required by an official decision, further consideration becomes necessary. Some authorized person or group collects additional information, defines the proposal more fully, and prepares the background for the adoption decision.
- Official Decision
    Some person or group decides to adopt or reject the suggested change and, if adopted, how it is to be implemented. It is easy enough to list the kinds of questions that should be asked in considering whether to undertake a particular curriculum change. Figure 9.5 includes some of them. The hard decision is how much to invest in the effort to answer each one.

FIG. 9.4. *Typical stages in curriculum change consideration.*

enough to permit it to be implemented. This means the test that the change consideration process imposes on proposals is fundamentally political: those it will affect must appreciate the merits of the change proposal.

In many schools the process of change consideration is visible only to top school leadership, and completely hidden from the sight of casual participants, such as parents or outside observers, and largely hidden from those teachers who seldom participate in school affairs. On the other hand, some schools have an open, public change consideration process. In any event, the process must become visible when, as must happen eventually, those in control of the process seek the collaboration of teachers and the approval of the public. Figure 9.4 describes some stages typical of such an open, explicit curriculum change consideration process. Figure 9.5 lists some pivotal questions officials should ask about curriculum proposals.

Schaffarzick (1975) surveyed a stratified random sample of 188 schools in 34 school districts in six northern California counties in 1976. He found that in most cases curriculum change consideration took place in obscurity. When an issue became controversial, the change consideration process became more political but it also became more public, more rational, and open to wider participation. When controversy burst out, contending parties demanded the right to state their case and to influence the decision. These opposing pressures on decisionmakers mobilized rational procedures—hearings, studies, and the like—as a protective measure, if for no other reason. Thoroughgoing institutionalized rationality, giving full and systematic consideration to an issue, was rare in his sample and was associated with having a clear, simple, open set of procedures in place.

Schools varied considerably in the quality of their curriculum change consideration processes. Large, wealthy districts with well-qualified staffs entertained more options, proceeded more rationally, and experienced more conflicts than others. Schools in communities with higher socioeconomic status and education, higher community educational aspirations,

1. Is the proposal good in its own terms?
   What evidence of its quality do we have?
   How credible is this evidence?
   If necessary, how could more credible evidence be gotten? Should we try?
2. Is it better than competing alternatives?
   What are the closest competitors?
   Why is this proposal preferable to the others?
3. What would it displace?
   What are its advantages compared to the program in use now?
      Disadvantages?
4. Is it in the long-term interest of all parties?
   School officials, community, students, teachers, and leaders? If not,
      whose views are most important to consider in this case?
5. Among those with a vital interest in the issue, whose views are well and
      whose poorly represented in the change consideration process?
6. Who are the proposal's supporters and champions?
   What is their power base?
   Will the proposal advance their self-interest at the expense of others'?
7. Who offers resistance, opposition?
   What are their power bases?
   Will defeat of the proposal advance their self-interest at the expense of
      others'?
8. Is the proposal relevant to this school's situation now?
   Its agenda; morale; history; staffing; budget, community relations,
      relations with district, etc.
9. How will it affect what happens in classrooms?
   What changes will be required of students and teachers?
   What are costs and benefits for students and teachers
10. How will it affect what happens in the school?
    Forces tending to maintain present situation
    Forces supporting change
    Cost/benefit for principal
    Cost/benefit for community
11. How will it affect school–community relations?
12. Is it worth the costs and risks of implementation?
13. Can we afford it? (money, time, opportunity cost)
14. Are the risks of undertaking the improvement effort tolerable?
    (conflict, implementation failure, unanticipated negative consequences?)
15. What are the costs and risks of rejecting it?

FIG. 9.5. *Pivotal questions about curriculum proposals.*

more open politics, and less social diversity had better change consideration. Schools that had a positive attitude toward change, offered incentives for innovation, and that had a history of successful innovation were more likely to have better change consideration procedures.

On the whole, however, these districts' change consideration procedures were not impressive. "Valid, reliable, objective, comprehensive evidence of the effectiveness of the programs being considered was infrequently sought, rarely obtained, and rarely utilized in the cases I studied" (Schaffarzick, p. 164). Of 112 cases on which he had data, 19% used no evidence at all in considering the change, while an additional 35% considered only the materials to be used in the proposed program. In 22% of cases, evidence from observations of pilot programs was considered. Test scores and results of program evaluations were considered in only 4% of cases and available research results in only 3% (p. 167). Even so, Schaffarzick concluded that

> The participants in the cases of curriculum change consideration that I studied were better about searching for alternative solutions to problems than they were about defining and verifying the problems to be solved (p. 162).

An official decision to terminate the change consideration process was not always made; often it just dwindled away or moved smoothly into implementation without any clear, official decision. When official decisions were made, boards of education made them most often (40%) and after them miscellaneous agencies, committees, and advisory groups (32%). Unilateral decisions by principals were common in small decisions, but when official institutional action was required the board or some group delegated responsibility by the board or superintendent were most often the final authority.

Teachers were nearly always involved in the curriculum change consideration process, but they seldom played central roles. Schaffarzick noted that

> The changes that teachers initiate are relatively small in scale. . . . The . . . activities that teachers frequently carry out . . . are often delimited by earlier . . . decisions. And, although teachers are included in more planning and review committees, the major decisions are still dominated by administrators and Board members (p. 117).

Members of the lay community participated in some way in 38% of cases (p. 139) and Schaffarzick commented that "Laymen can be influential when they genuinely care" (p. 143).

Lay groups were among the winning factions on 14 of 19 cases that were disputed between opposing factions, and among losers in only 6 of the 19. And in three of the loser cases the groups involved had developed reputations as opposing almost everything about the schools (pp. 143–144). On the other hand, lay advisory committees frequently did little more than "rubber stamp" professionals' plans. And professionals sometimes subverted proposals and decisions made by laypeople (pp. 117–118).

Instituting Curriculum Change Efforts

Assume now that school leaders have made a commitment to bring about a certain kind of change in the curriculum of a school. The change itself has been defined in some detail, perhaps in the form of a set of curriculum plans and materials. And school curriculum leaders have determined from the change consideration process that the change has sufficient support from interested parties in the school and community. Now those responsible for the school must make the commitment a reality by introducing the change into the school.

The typical school curriculum change effort is a rather casual, almost off-hand affair, more personal than institutional. An influential person—the principal, a superintendent, or an influential teacher, say—champions an innovation. Their proposal runs a gauntlet of approval processes as part of the change consideration process and emerges with an OK. A champion is appointed to a committee charged to bring about the change. The committee meets, some individual members work hard between meetings, the principal, if he or she is not the key figure, keeps up to date on developments and provides necessary institutional support. The rest is individual work.

When the individuals are talented and respected, a low-key, informal approach to institutional change may be all that is needed to bring about lasting and substantial change in the school curriculum. But a more serious effort at institutional change will needed in many cases. Many curriculum innovations never go beyond the classrooms of the teachers who champion them because the institution takes them too lightly. The school provides too few resources, too little visibility, and too few occasions for teachers to discuss the innovation.

To counter this tendency to slight local curriculum change efforts, I will discuss "curriculum change projects," by which I mean an identifiable effort that has the status of a temporary unit within the school, its own personnel assignments, budget, goals, deadlines, and a place within the formal organization. When school leadership expects a teacher to play a major role in a curriculum reform project, they should assign that teacher to work some fraction of time on the project and count the salary as a cost of the project. That way, project participants, supporters, and advocates can know what is required in order to implement their proposals, and responsible officials can estimate the benefits, costs, and risks of incorporating the experiment into the fabric of the school program.

School leaders must arrange the support necessary to establish the change project and make it work. Typically, the school leadership creates a project team, which may or may not include the principal but which, if it does not, will report to the principal. The school leadership must also arrange for staffing the change effort, scheduling it, and supplying it with the material support necessary to carry out its task. The project staff must negotiate its charge, which normally includes some targets and a timeline. School leaders must negotiate with project staff about arrangements to monitor the progress of the project.

The overwhelming number of local curriculum change efforts do not require such a curriculum change project because they fall into one of the standard types of curriculum changes for which schools have built-in provisions: curriculum materials selection, course approval, course of study development, and teacher in-service education. Schools are prepared for these standard kinds of curriculum changes. Steps have been agreed upon in advance by interested parties. The expenses have been included in the budget and the necessary tasks written into job descriptions. Everyone knows what to expect. They will not disrupt established routines because they have themselves already been routinized. No wonder, then, that a school leadership's first, automatic response to any proposed curriculum change is typically to ask how it can be accomplished through the curriculum revision procedures already in place.

These built-in standard forms of local curriculum change provide an opportunity for committee members to negotiate mutually satisfactory resolutions of the major types of recurring, planned school or district curriculum decisions. As such, they are an important form of participation by teachers in decisions about the conditions of their work, and a vital step in the process of negotiated design that establishes the legitimacy of the school curriculum. They may also perform other useful functions, such as adapting commercial materials to local conditions, enabling teachers to share ideas about their craft, or securing more cooperation from teachers in making the changes decided upon. But they are seldom effective vehicles for bringing about significant curriculum changes.

For instance, what schools call curriculum development rarely involves the development of original plans and materials for teachers and students to use. A typical first step in what is conventionally called local curriculum development is a search for commercially published materials and for ones created by other school systems. If anything even remotely suitable is found, committees of local teachers adapt it to local needs. Actual development by local schools of curriculum materials used by students and teachers is rare, as Schaffarzick discovered and numerous others have also reported.

In only 10 of the 112 cases studied (9%) did people in the schools and districts actually develop program materials themselves. In all other cases, already available programs, including commercial programs and programs developed by other schools and districts, were suggested for adoption or adaptation. This low rate of actual development coincides with the observations of several interviewees, who pointed out that people in schools and districts rarely have the time, money, or expertise required for actual development (Schaffarzick, 1975, p. 102).

The curriculum changes recommended in the course of these standard procedures are all relatively minor incremental adjustments. They may seem large to those who have to do the work to bring them to life, but when measured against the range of curriculum change proposals discussed in the professional press and in public policy debates, or against historical changes in what is taught in schools, they are small. Only if they cumulate over decades and across subjects and grades will these incremental changes become significant for public education policy.

The standard procedures are fine for new textbooks and teaching methods, but they don't work well with major, radical change proposals. For instance, proposals that require interdisciplinary cooperation fit poorly into standard curriculum change procedures—writing across the curriculum, environmental studies, career education and integrated science and mathematics, come to mind as examples. Standard procedures treat all subjects in the same way they treat academic curriculums. For instance, standard procedures result in curriculums that treat health-related topics such as weight control, stress reduction, or avoidance of tobacco, alcohol, and drugs in the same way they treat reading and mathematics. The standard procedures are notoriously ineffective in dealing with proposals that call for new pedagogical approaches, such as direct instruction, cooperative group learning, inquiry-oriented teaching, or computer-based instruction.

Substantial curriculum changes require substantial change projects, more than a few person-months, expertise beyond that possessed by the local school staff, methods for influencing teachers stronger than a written guide or a 2-day workshop, and procedures that include all the major stakeholders.

Changing Schools Does Not Necessarily Improve Teaching

Elmore, Peterson, and McCarthey (1996) studied the changes in teaching made by teachers in three restructured schools. Two of the three schools had changed such core features as the self-contained classroom, how they grouped students, and the subject organization of their day in the hope that these structural changes would free teachers to teach for understanding rather than for superficial coverage of facts and skills. The third, Northeastern, had begun with a commitment to change teaching and then had restructured their school to support the changes in teaching. The investigators found that "Northeastern teachers as a group were more sophisticated and concrete in their ability to articulate ideas about good practice, and more consistent in applying these ideas in the classroom" (p. 227). The investigators attribute this difference to the fact that Northeastern chose a structure that would support their shared beliefs, values, and practices about what should happen in classrooms (p. 212). Teachers in the other two schools also implemented changes in teaching that they thought realized the vision of teaching for understanding, but as the researchers saw it, they made only superficial changes in teaching. "New and complex ideas of teaching practice seemed to be filtered through the teachers' existing practices, with idiosyncratic and confused results" (p. 71).

From their close analyses of teaching in these three schools, the researchers concluded that "the relationship between changes in formal structure and changes in teaching practice is necessarily weak, problematic, and indirect; attention to structural change often distracts from the more fundamental problem of changing teaching practice" (p. 237, emphasis in original). "The transformation of teaching practice is fundamentally a problem of enhancing individual knowledge and skill, not a problem of organizational structure" (p. 240, emphasis in original). Northeastern's greater success is due, in their view, to the teachers' greater knowledge both of content and of ways of teaching for understanding. Northeastern's teachers gained the knowledge they needed through individual teachers' independent studies augmented by teacher networks. The school community set very high knowledge expectations for entering teachers and maintained a norm that teachers should have a continuing intellectual interest (p. 232).

Facilitating Curriculum Change in Classrooms

Policymakers and administrators control what happens in the central office, but they have to find ways to influence what happens in classrooms. It is easier for school leaders to create a highly visible new program than to change what happens in hundreds of ongoing classrooms. A new course that leaders institute with fanfare will yield few benefits if teachers are reluctant or unprepared to teach it. So curriculum changes initiated by school officials often have more symbolic importance than real. Titles and descriptions change, but not practice or results. Many other attempted curriculum reforms result in trivialized classroom implementations of subtle or complex educational innovations. Teachers implement the obvious, surface features but not the complete innovation. Students mess about with apparatus in the name of inquiry methods or sit and talk in groups around tables in the name of cooperative group learning.

In order to make deep and lasting changes in the curriculum that students undergo, school leaders must influence what teachers do behind their classroom doors. The typical school organization does not provide its leaders with powerful means of influencing teachers' classroom behavior. And because of their working conditions and professional traditions, teachers have very considerable capacity for resisting unwanted influences on what they do in their classrooms.

School leaders need active cooperation from teachers in order to change the school curriculum. Finding ways to evoke active efforts from teachers on behalf of a particular curriculum change is usually the greatest challenge school leaders face in implementing it.

Involving Teachers in Curriculum Change

The most frequently used strategy for facilitating classroom curriculum change is to get teachers involved in the process. School officials hope that if they involve teachers in the process of curriculum change, teachers will embrace the new curriculum as their own. They often speak of getting teachers to "buy-in" to the new curriculum. Teachers welcome the opportunity to participate in curriculum change efforts for several reasons. They like having a say in something that affects their work so much. Being involved in curriculum decisions affirms teachers' image of themselves as professionals. They get a better chance to have a curriculum that they believe in and like. Some teachers welcome the change of pace that comes from occasional work outside the classroom.

Usually, reading about the innovation or listening to speakers talk about it does not create the kind of personal meaning teachers need. In general, teachers need to work with the innovation, adapt it to their personal style, and discuss their personal and philosophical reactions to it with others whose opinions they value and whom they trust. This is especially so for teachers who are indifferent to a particular innovation or skeptical of its value. In the process of adaptation and discussion, teachers may discover ways to use it and reasons to use it that are consistent with their personal teaching styles and developed repertoire of professional skills. As a result of "trying on" the innovation in this way, some teachers may find ways to interpret the innovation so that it seems part of them, and thus come to embrace it enthusiastically. Local curriculum planning sessions in which teachers adapt curriculum plans and materials to their own classrooms amount to a negotiation of meaning, in which teachers assimilate some features of the innovation into their personal teaching styles and modify or reject others.

For example, suppose school curriculum leaders ask the faculty of an elementary school whose student body includes an increasing proportion of children of Mexican immigrants to revise the social studies curriculum to teach more about the history and culture of Mexican-Americans. Some teachers may see this as a long overdue response to changing community demographics. Others may see it as an opportunity to reduce the parochial ethnocentrism of the traditional social studies curriculum. Still others may view it as an unwanted intrusion of community politics into the school curriculum. Some may fear that it will interfere with the assimilation of Mexican-Americans into mainstream American culture. Each teacher's willingness to work on behalf of the proposed curriculum revision will depend on how that teacher interprets it.

As each teacher considers how to incorporate the spirit of the revision into his or her classroom teaching, different approaches will prove attractive to different teachers. Some may prefer to add a unit here and there focusing a bit more attention on events in Mexico as part of the study of American history. They may add units on Spanish colonial history and the Spanish-American War. Others may prefer to focus extra attention on Mexico as part of the study of world geography. Still others may advocate study of contemporary Mexican and Mexican–American life—food, dances, art, and holidays. If teachers followed their individual preferences, the social studies curriculum in the school would lose its coherence. Requiring teachers to agree on a common curriculum, with permissible variations, insures the necessary coherence, and also provides an opportunity for teachers to discuss their differences and to negotiate acceptable resolutions of them. An effective implementation plan will find ways to involve faculty members in discussions with advocates of the innovation about these meanings as they plan for their classrooms.

Teachers' Benefit/Cost Ratios

The easy assumption that when some teachers participate in planning an innovation all teachers therefore will implement it is naive. While involvement of teachers in curriculum planning is indispensable, it will generally not suffice to produce lasting and substantial changes in the curriculum of classrooms throughout a school. Other barriers to teachers' adoption of an innovation must also be overcome. Students of recent social and educational reforms have come to a more Machiavellian conclusion. Their studies suggest that an innovation's success in the classroom depends on teachers' perceptions of the ratio of its benefits for them to its costs for them.

Teachers must expend time and effort to make changes in their classroom curriculum and go to the trouble of reexamining their personal teaching styles. These changes inevitably interfere with routines that have made life in the classroom easier for the teacher, and they run risks of disrupting classroom operations, spoiling classroom climate, and making sacrifices in mastery, coverage, order, or affect in their classroom. Serious efforts to make substantial and lasting changes in the classroom curriculum are therefore major events in the professional lives of teachers. Unless teachers receive benefits commensurate with the costs and risks, they will experience a disincentive to implement the innovation.

Benefits	Costs and Risks
Temporary excitement, enthusiasm of doing something new	Trouble of rearranging routines to fit the changes
Team membership, participation in a team effort	Greater time and effort required
Enhanced self-esteem from being a pioneer	Risk of dissension among colleagues
Opportunity for wider social and professional contacts	Diversion of attention from ongoing social and professional activities and relationships
Opportunity to make a difference in the school	Risk of failure, loss of face
Greater self-esteem, pride, and status from successful change	Loss of self-esteem and status from failed change effort
Improved prospects for career advancement	Greater risk of revealing ignorance, incompetence
Better days in class if students like it and do well	Worse days in class if students dislike it and fail
Less teacher time and effort may be required	More teacher time and effort may be required
Classroom coverage, mastery, affect, and order may be improved	Classroom coverage, mastery, affect, or order may be reduced

FIG. 9.6. *Benefits and costs of curriculum change for teachers.*

Figure 9.6 lists some of the potential benefits teachers may receive from a classroom curriculum change and some of the costs they may incur. These are classified as temporary, when they only occur while making the change, and permanent, when they continue after the change has been made.

Teams charged with implementing a school curriculum change should assess its benefits and costs for teachers, as they perceive them. Simple discussion among teachers usually suffices to reveal what they perceive as benefits and costs. Different teachers may perceive these matters differently, of course, so the team should be prepared for considerable variation. Where benefit/cost ratios are seen as unfavorable, the project team can take actions designed to influence them. Figure 9.7 lists some examples of ways school leaders might attempt to influence teachers' perceptions. Artful orchestration of such measures may transform how teachers see the change. On the other hand, clumsy efforts to fool teachers into taking actions not fundamentally in their interest are certain to backfire sooner or later.

Teachers are sometimes portrayed as wanting a packaged curriculum that tells them step-by-step exactly what to do. This is the premise behind the detailed teachers' editions provided by publishers and behind the detailed courses of study provided by many districts. Yet teachers also frequently complain that these documents conflict with their teaching

1. Provide additional benefits
    (e.g., pay participating teachers a bonus; promote teachers who pioneered; provide additional supplies to project classrooms)
2. Increase perceived value of existing benefits
    (e.g., arrange for prestigious advocates to extol the benefits of the innovation; recognize, honor teachers for success; play up the excitement of doing something new; emphasize psychic value of material benefits)
3. Decrease expectations for receiving benefits
    (e.g., appeal to altruism, call for sacrifice; emphasize need for belt-tightening; label current performance unsatisfactory; insist on more results for less reward)
4. Reduce costs
    (e.g., assist teachers to change routines; release teachers from other duties to make time, energy available for changing)
5. Reduce perceptions of costliness
    (e.g., make teacher joint planning sessions fun; make changes gradually, phase them in)
6. Reduce risks
    (e.g., provide training, coaching in new techniques; redesign the innovation to take less time, effort)
7. Reduce perceptions of risk
    (e.g., arrange for contacts with teachers who have successfully made the change)
8. Increase willingness to incur costs or risks
    (e.g., reward risk-taking; encourage teachers to invest in their professional growth)

FIG. 9.7. *Some ways project leaders may attempt to influence teachers' perceptions of benefits and costs of curriculum changes.*

style and constrain them too much. This ambivalence reflects one of the teacher's main dilemmas in attempting curriculum change.

Developing a new set of classroom routines is hard work, so teachers naturally look for the path of least effort. If they can find existing routines and advice on how to institute and maintain them, their burdens are considerably eased. On the other hand, teachers hate having to follow uncongenial routines. The trick for those who want to foster classroom curriculum change is to find ways to permit teachers to find congenial routines that achieve the goals of the innovation.

Teachers' assessments of benefits, costs, and risks change as the project proceeds. Early disappointments may dissipate initial enthusiasm, or early successes may overcome initial resistance by promising teachers greater rewards from less effort than they imagined they might need to make. In the absence of first-hand information, teachers who do not participate in a change project form their impressions of the project mainly on the basis of reports they receive from others. New projects are a common topic of casual conversation among teachers, and rumors about them spread easily. The project team can defend against potentially damaging rumors by supplying plenty of timely, accurate information before rumors have a chance to spread. If the project team includes persons adept at monitoring and influencing messages flowing in teachers' informal communication networks, their efforts on behalf of the project can be valuable in attracting more teachers to participate.

In addition to involvement in local curriculum planning and attending to benefit/cost ratios, school leaders can employ many other strategies for influencing teachers to change their classroom curriculum. In the following sections are brief descriptions of some promising ones.

Continue Recruitment

To promote wider participation by teachers, curriculum leaders can design projects to offer frequent participation opportunities on a recurring basis in small and large ways. For example, invite all teachers to attend meetings about the project, not just those who have joined the project, and circulate requests for volunteers to all teachers. Seek the opinions of all teachers about the developing project periodically. Seek ways to involve all teachers in the project in some meaningful way, however small. Project participants should maintain personal contacts with nonparticipants and guard against attitudes that imply superiority over those not currently involved. Sometimes other teachers perceive project staff members' pride in their achievements as arrogance.

Tailor Project Efforts to Individual Teachers

Local change projects can be tailored to individual teachers. Beginning teachers may be concerned about how to maintain discipline when using the unfamiliar classroom activities, while experienced teachers may be more concerned about slower rates of progress through the material. The project team could devote effort to both sets of concerns, perhaps by forming subgroups to develop techniques in collaboration with individual teachers concerned about each aspect of the innovation.

Continue Interventions

Hall and Hord (1987) found that the number of day-to-day interventions by principals with teachers on behalf of the innovation was a major predictor of implementation success. For one thing, continuing efforts demonstrate continuing commitment to making the change. For another, they respond to the changing array of difficulties that arise for teachers as they work the innovation into their routines. Making a curriculum change that calls for extensive changes in classrooms requires continuing efforts over several years, at least. Lasting and substantial change is a result of continued, cumulative efforts.

Monitor Levels of Use

Hall and Loucks (1977) developed a scale to describe levels of use of an innovation by teachers.

- Nonuse (no knowledge, no use, and no involvement)
- Orientation (some knowledge, exploration)
- Preparation (preparing for first use)
- Mechanical use (short-term, day-to day, unreflective)
- Routine use (ongoing use with few changes or improvements)

- Refinement (varied use to improve effects)
- Integration (combining innovation with other efforts of self and colleagues)
- Renewal (major modifications or alternatives, new goals and strategies)

School leaders or the project team should monitor the extent and level of use of the proposed curriculum improvement periodically and redirect their efforts to respond to whatever obstacles they discover.

Presently, school systems invest nearly all of their scarce resources for curriculum improvement in a few standard procedures: curriculum materials selection, course of study writing, course approval, and in-service workshops for teachers. A careful study of just how well these standard procedures are working to foster change in classroom curricula will usually reveal better ways to spend some of the money. We have very little firm evidence on the impact of teachers' guides on the classroom curriculum, for example, but every bit of evidence we do have indicates that they have little impact on what actually happens in classrooms. What little effect they have depends on how well they are enforced by supervisors and principals, not on the intrinsic quality of the documents. Because teachers make them, they are supposed to engender a sense of ownership and support on the part of teachers. Yet teachers who do not participate in local development may feel left out, just as much as they feel left out of the publication of the textbook.

School leaders intend service on the committees that produce these guides to be an honor, a reward, and an opportunity for renewal and growth; but not all teachers welcome this opportunity. In many cases it would be better if schools defined their curriculum policies in briefer statements of purpose, content, and structure and then relied on a variety of other strategies for realizing them in classrooms. When extensive changes in pedagogy are proposed, printed materials will never suffice. Videotapes, live presentations, and ongoing support for individual teachers will be essential.

The study mentioned earlier in this chapter by Elmore, Peterson, and McCarthey (1996) of changes in teaching made by teachers in three restructured schools showed the importance of tackling teaching change directly rather than hoping that structural changes will also change teaching. Two of the three schools changed structural features such as the self-contained classroom, how they grouped students, and the subject organization of their day in the hope that these structural changes would free teachers to teach for understanding rather than for superficial coverage of facts and skills. This did not happen. To change teaching, teachers must focus on changing teaching.

Discussing Student Work

Many recent school curriculum leaders have had good results by having teachers discuss samples of students' work as part of implementing curriculum changes. Looking at the papers and projects that students create stimulates more concrete, pointed discussions that hold teachers' interest better. When teachers compare the performance of students in colleagues' classes with their own students' performances, it feels natural to ask "How did you get your students to do so well in this way?" Some teachers may raise their sights when they see what other students are able to accomplish. For many reasons and in many ways discussions among teachers around students' work are often more productive. Some principals make discussion of student work a regular part of every teacher meeting at the school.

Video of teachers teaching has great potential benefits for prompting productive discussions of curriculum changes, but video is much more difficult to get and more threatening to teachers. Discussion of student work is an easier first step.

Imperatives for School Curriculum Improvement

School curriculum improvement poses several kinds of challenges to all who attempt it, including the challenge to

- sustain a unified community with common purposes
- reach sound decisions that keep the big picture in mind
- manage scarce resources
- work with and through other organizations
- coordinate curriculum in many venues

In this section we will look in some detail at six key things that curriculum leaders need to accomplish in order to meet these and other challenges of school curriculum improvement:

- Achieving working agreement
- Making principled decisions
- Working constructively with teachers
- Seeking substantial, lasting improvements
- Facing conflict constructively
- Combining curriculum work with other initiatives.

The curriculum leader who can consistently accomplish these things should be successful at school curriculum improvement.

Achieving Working Agreement

The Need for Working Agreement

The public and its authorized representatives control curriculum, and the public are rarely of one mind. To serve a divided constituency, institutions must achieve a working agreement in which most people support most of the institution's actions and, when they do not, go along anyway while working within the system to get actions they can support. Of course, complete consensus would be the best result, but without at least a working agreement an institution in a free society cannot act.

Working agreement on actions is essential. Agreement on philosophy, values, or theory is helpful, but not essential. People with utterly different philosophies of education can agree to support the same action. You may support multicultural education because it redresses historical wrongs done to indigenous people while your neighbor supports it because it prepares students to succeed in a competitive global economy. Both may be part of a working agreement to adopt a strong multicultural curriculum in our schools.

Professionals charged with getting curriculum work done often have no assurance of a working agreement. Without one they will almost surely fail, and they may even stir up a hornet's nest of controversy that could cost them their reputation or their job and disrupt social relationships in the school and community for years to come. So it is imperative that curriculum leaders size up the support and opposition for any proposed curriculum action.

If support is too weak or opposition too strong, a leader can abandon the effort or try to build toward a working agreement. The only way to know for certain whether a working agreement exists is to risk action and gauge the response. The need to act in order to know, the inherent risks of action, and the thrill of success in the face of uncertainty are among the main attractions of curriculum leadership for many.

Deliberation, Dialogue, and Negotiation

As we saw in Chapter 7, deliberation to be successful requires shared beliefs and values. Therefore, deliberation has limited value in seeking working agreement. Once agreement has been achieved, deliberation can help a group to agree on actions that reflect and express their shared beliefs and values. The form of discourse that may help to achieve agreement is dialogue.

Dialogue is a form of conversation in which people try to understand one another's viewpoints, regardless of whether they agree or disagree. Each person tries to see the world through the others' eyes and think as they think about it, abandoning temporarily their own viewpoint and ways of thinking. Dialogue requires genuine openness to the other person's concerns.

The classic work on dialogue is philosopher and theologian Martin Buber's book, *I and Thou* (originally published in 1923, translated by Kaufman, 1996). Buber sees authentic dialogue as a way of building relationships, bonding, and recognizing our common humanity. Daniel Yankelovich in *The Magic of Dialogue* (1999) describes the potential benefits of dialogue this way:

> Long-standing stereotypes dissolved, mistrust overcome, mutual understanding achieved, visions shaped and grounded in shared purpose, people previously at odds with one another aligned . . . , new common ground discovered, new perspectives and insights gained, new levels of creativity stimulated, and bonds of community strengthened (p. 16).

The give-and-take of dialogue shapes shared visions. People are included in the shaping of the vision and they feel a sense of ownership for the vision that emerges. Even if it includes elements that they would not have chosen, they understand how deeply others feel about these elements and they willingly sacrifice on what is for them a small matter to achieve a shared vision that they and others can freely embrace.

The spirit of dialogue is poles apart from the spirit of debate. In dialogue there is no effort to win and defeat an opponent, no critiquing of others' positions, and no defending of one's own positions. Instead, there is collaboration, listening with empathy, and seeking common ground. Also, dialogue is not a method of decisionmaking. The time for dialogue is before hard decisions must be made. Deliberation is the process for decisionmaking.

Curriculum leaders can foster dialogue on curriculum issues by sponsoring informal discussions. Ask a parent to invite friends over for coffee to talk about the school curriculum (not about the controversial issue looming). Devote a teacher's meeting to "the state of the curriculum." Create an occasion for mixed groups of teachers and parents to talk about curriculum. Curriculum leaders would be well advised to include people who disagree, but build an atmosphere of trust before they delve too deeply into divisive issues.

The really tough case for achieving a working agreement is when parties who do not share common beliefs and values are divided on what action must be taken and yet must reach a working agreement. This happens often in connection with the school curriculum because of the diversity of stakeholders' interests and the need for a single curriculum or at most a few optional programs. If the parties involved have discussed the matter and cannot reach agreement, negotiation may be necessary.

In negotiation the parties state the actions they favor and identify areas of disagreement. Each indicates what actions they are willing to take on behalf of the measures they favor, and they look for the least unsatisfactory course of action. The ultimate threat in negotiation is a refusal to go along with the action–in effect, a strike. The carrot is a course of action that, although not ideal, is more acceptable than the other alternatives that all parties will support. In the context of the American public school, the most familiar form of negotiation takes place between the local teachers' organization and school officials.

Building Working Agreement

To build working agreement on a proposal a curriculum leader must first find out how people feel about the proposal. The better a leader is at sizing up the support and opposition for curriculum proposals, the higher their odds of success. Collect stories about local successes and failures and how they happened. Compare new proposals with these stories. Do they fit better with the successes or the failures? Judgments based on past experience are always dubious, however, because circumstances change. The best source of intelligence about support and opposition for a proposal is what people say. Strike up conversations with opinion leaders in ways that let them say what they think about a proposal. Have as many of these conversations as possible before the proposal comes up officially. Discover who are its champions and advocates and who are its opponents. How deeply do they feel and for what reasons? Compare notes with others in the school and profession. What are they hearing?

A curriculum leader's intelligence gathering may show one of four things: strong support with weak opposition, weak support with strong opposition, a standoff, or an unstable, ambiguous situation. With strong support and little opposition a working agreement already exists, so leaders can move ahead with the proposal with good odds of success. But they still face challenges. If leaders believe the proposal is a good one, their challenge is to keep support strong and to keep opponents on board. If they believe that the proposal would be bad for the school, they face the challenge of defeating a popular proposal. If they've collected stories, they will find some stories that apply to each of these situations. These stories can suggest actions they might take.

Weak support with strong opposition makes the odds of success very low. A wise action would be to abandon the proposal or put it on the back burner while leaders try to strengthen support and weaken opposition. Pushing ahead with the proposal under these circumstances makes it "your baby." A success here would impress everyone with the leader's leadership ability, but here leaders put their reputations on the line in a situation where the odds are stacked against them.

Evenly balanced support and opposition poses the greatest risk of controversy and catastrophic failure. If the two sides have a history of conflict and positions have hardened, the odds of success are minimal—it would take a miracle. If the alignment is new and specific to this issue and if throwing the leader's support behind the proposal tips the balance, a leader could press ahead. If they did, their challenge would be to bring along opponents who lost after almost tasting victory and who blame the leader for their defeat. They know that if they can unseat the leader, they may win after all. If leaders decline to support the action, on the other hand, they may alienate its supporters. If leaders are not careful, supporters may lump them with the opponents and consider the leaders their enemy. Just surviving an evenly divided situation takes diplomacy and tact. If leaders also manage to achieve a working agreement that permits concerted action, they should consider themselves very lucky.

Ambiguous, unstable situations present the greatest possibility for leaders to influence the outcome. Leaders can use their personal qualities and the resources of their position to get people to view the proposal the way they want them to view it. They can use their influence to persuade people to support or oppose it. Of course, others will also be busy trying to put their spin on the situation, too.

The process of building and maintaining a working agreement on behalf of a curriculum change proposal is a form of political leadership and it can be sordid, but it need not be. You will hear stories of scheming, maneuvering, and Machiavellian machinations as people struggle for what they think is the best curriculum. You will also hear stories of courage and uprightness. You can choose to act ethically and reasonably hope to succeed. Two pillars of ethical action when building working agreement among people who are divided are dialogue and negotiation.

Making Principled Decisions

Most commonly curriculum decisions rest on custom and intuition. "We've done it that way for a long time and it has worked just fine." "It feels right to me." "It fits the way we do things here." "The best schools are doing it." These reasons are all relevant, but they are weak. Stronger reasons would rest on a broader base of experience, be more objective, and bear more directly on the benefits of the decision. It may have worked fine for your school, but the decision would be better grounded if you could show that it worked well for many other schools. It felt right to you, but harder, more objective evidence would make a more convincing reason. That other schools are using it only speaks indirectly to its value. Evidence about students' learning or performance after the curriculum would be a more direct, and therefore stronger, indication of the value of the curriculum.

Theories, research, and experience give us the strongest basis for our curriculum decisions. We speak of decisions justified by appeal to theory, research, or experience as principled decisions. Noddings' (1992) ideas about caring can give us principled reasons for advocating a broader curriculum than a strictly academic one. Gardner's (1999) ideas about multiple abilities can give us principled reasons for emphasizing visual and spatial abilities on a more equal footing with words and numbers.

But theories have some fundamental shortcomings as sources of ideas for informing curriculum actions, as we saw in the discussion of practical reasoning in Chapter 7. Curriculum issues are too many-sided for any single theory to cover. No single theory can unite ideas about students (their previous knowledge, needs, abilities, interests), teachers (their beliefs, knowledge, skill, experience), the subject (key ideas, structure), and the society (its needs, etc.) into one all-encompassing set of ideas, so theories usually concentrate on a few of these topics and leave the rest out, something curriculum decisionmakers cannot responsibly do.

Also, theories never completely capture all the relevant features of the individual case that we must consider when we make wise curriculum decisions. Curriculum problems happen to specific, unique, living, three-dimensional people and communities and a good curriculum decision must be right for this case.

Finally, theories that deal with curriculum are always contested. As Schwab noted "There is not one theory of groups, but several. There is not one theory of learning but half a dozen. All the social and behavioral sciences are marked by 'schools'" (Schwab, 1970, p. 21). This is certainly true of curriculum theories.

Research and experience compensate for some of these limitations of theory. The best case is when researchers have done studies of school situations very similar to the ones we face in our decisions. If studies are lacking, it may be that teachers and school leaders from schools that have faced similar problems have practical experience to offer. Even with principled justifications, decisions can still misfire, but a principled decision is the best assurance one can have of a favorable outcome. Holding out for principled decisions when all about you are ready to move ahead on shared intuition takes courage, but the habit of expecting principled justifications for major decisions is worth the risk.

Working Constructively with Teachers

Teachers have deeply ambivalent attitudes toward the curriculum they work with. Some see curriculum matters as extremely important parts of their work while others have little interest in it. Some are grateful for official curriculum guidance and rely on it while others struggle to be free of institutional control. This ambivalence affects teachers' curriculum practice profoundly.

It seems that most teachers are less concerned with curriculum matters than with the interpersonal aspects of their job. Teachers are people-oriented and derive their greatest job satisfactions from their contacts with young people. Lortie (1975) reports from an extensive survey of teachers that the high point in teaching for most teachers is "having a good day" in the classroom with their students. Working on the curriculum requires teachers to deal with plans, documents, colleagues, meetings, and the like, and these bring them less certain, more meager, and delayed satisfactions. Philip Jackson in *Life in Classrooms* (1968) characterizes teachers as valuing immediacy, informality, and individuality. Curriculum planning, though, calls for a certain emotional distance, for systematic analysis, and for moving students' individual identities to the background of attention. These values do not lead most teachers to want to do curriculum work. Most teachers are content to follow the official curriculum so long as it is basically consistent with their own philosophy and values. Only a minority of teachers want to spend time developing a curriculum plan for their school or district.

Curriculum work also confronts teachers with attempts by outsiders to control their teaching. The officially prescribed school curriculum is one of the main avenues through which others seek to control what happens in the classroom. Textbooks, tests, mandates, rules and regulations bring influences from outside into the classroom, and teachers are then forced to deal with them. As we have seen, the curriculum enters into virtually every nook and cranny of the teacher's work. To relinquish control over the curriculum seems very nearly tantamount to relinquishing control over teaching. Teachers without control over curriculum become mere performers following a script or score, not autonomous professionals.

Ultimately, succeeding at curriculum work means getting teachers to change their classroom curriculums. Reformers have tried to do this impersonally by writing and speaking eloquently and inspirationally, creating appealing curriculum plans and materials, and enacting forceful laws, but with limited success. Reforms need local champions to serve as models and help other teachers make the change. Some teachers who are attracted to the role of pioneer will follow distant calls for reform and change their curriculum through their own creative efforts. But most teachers will not make the effort and take the risk to try a new curriculum without help.

For curriculum change to succeed, some person must be able to influence teachers to consider trying a new curriculum. A position of official authority carries some weight, but teachers see themselves as the ultimate authority over what happens in their classroom. Would-be curriculum leaders can use their personal qualities to influence teachers, their winning personality, social graces, warmth, wit, and charm. Personal magnetism is surely an asset, but it only opens the door. It may not be enough to persuade teachers to invest a lot of work in changing their curriculum and risk failure in doing so.

Teachers are most likely to follow the advice of other teachers they trust and respect who can demonstrate convincingly that a new curriculum works in their classroom. Former teachers with excellent reputations may also be credible, but some teachers will discount their advice because "They don't know what teaching's like today." If you are responsible for supporting teachers in making curriculum changes, you must either have their professional trust and respect or ally yourself with teachers who do. Over time, you can earn teachers' trust and respect by repeatedly demonstrating that you can help them succeed in changing their classroom curriculum in ways that they ultimately prize.

Curriculum leaders who want to retain influence with teachers will be wise to demonstrate their excellence quietly and modestly. Ideally teachers will feel that the change was their idea that they made to work with your help, not that they participated in your reform. Think not only about succeeding at this curriculum change, but also about building lasting relationships with teachers that will earn you influence with them in the future.

In working with teachers, curriculum leaders are certain to meet individuals who hold the full range of educational ideals and traditions. If you want their respect, you must respect their traditions and ideals. No matter whether you are a progressive with radical tendencies or a traditionalist committed to academic excellence, respect others' views. If teachers believe you are using your influence to promote your own ideals at the expense of theirs, they will distrust your advice and actions. Those who share your ideals may applaud you and follow you, but you will have divided the faculty, strengthened opposition to the changes you sought, and lost the trust of some of the teachers you sought to influence. On some occasions you may want to take a frankly partisan stand. You can do this in a way that retains the respect of those who disagree with you on this issue, and they will still listen to you and follow you on other issues.

Teachers may try something because they respect the person proposing it, but in the long run teachers will only incorporate the innovation into their teaching if it makes their lives better, and if they feel better about themselves and their work. The wise leader will look for innovations that make most teachers feel better about themselves and their work.

Seeking Substantial, Lasting Improvements

Sensible curriculum leaders want their successes to last, to spread, and to contribute to even more momentous change. They don't want them to go down the drain, swept away by a backlash or the bow wave of the next reform movement. While no one can foretell the future, leaders can make more informed guesses if they try to see the big picture and take the long view. How is what's happening at your school related to what's going on in other schools throughout the district, state, nation, and world? How is your local situation related to what's going on with powerful education interest groups, to developments in politics, the economy, and society, and to new ideas and scientific discoveries? Put things in historical perspective. Surely something like this has happened before in the United States or abroad. What can you learn from this earlier experience?

Align your efforts with larger forces. Figure out a way to use the current reform movement to promote related curriculum changes at your school. If you think the national reform is just right for your school, become a local champion or help the local champions. If the national reform is not exactly right for your school, work with teachers and school leaders to adapt the reform to make it better for your school. If you think the current reform would move your school in the wrong direction, focus your attention on other less well-known reforms. Or, ally yourself with those who oppose it and work with them to develop a better way to achieve the goals that attract many to the reform. Respond constructively to curriculum reforms. Use them to your school's advantage.

Sometimes local interests do not align with larger ones. The local economy may depend on old-fashioned heavy manufacturing while manufacturing elsewhere is rapidly automating. In that case leaders must decide whether it is more important to meet strictly local needs or to prepare students for a wider world.

A look back at the history of the curriculum of American schools shows schools and teachers trying hundreds of innovations every year. Most of these innovations leave little trace after 10 years. Some innovations, by contrast, become important parts of the standard curriculum and last a century or more. Maria Montessori's approach to the education of young children remains influential after nearly a century. Today's high school curriculum is still organized along lines laid down in reports of the Committee of Ten almost a hundred years ago. Vocational education, introduced in the early decades of the twentieth century, has declined in recent decades but had a long run and may be morphing into new directions such as career education and design and technology education. Those who want to make lasting and substantial improvements to the school curriculum want to work on projects like these and avoid fashionable initiatives that briefly thrive and quickly die.

How can you identify initiatives that are likely to last and remain important? No one has a crystal ball, but there are some likely signs. Tyack and Cuban (1995) identified four characteristics of reforms that lasted.

- Structural add-ons that fit within the standard curriculum framework
- Reforms that were not controversial to lay community
- Reforms with influential constituencies committed to their continuation, especially employees
- Reforms required by law and easily monitored (p. 57).

In addition, major lasting initiatives respond to deep and important trends, especially demographic, economic, and social trends. At the present time I judge that curriculum improvements that respond to globalization, multiculturalism, and an increasingly complex world of work stand a better chance of playing a major, lasting curriculum role than ones that respond to, say, student behavior problems, self-esteem, public service projects, and postmodernism. Although the latter initiatives are admirable in many ways, I don't think that they respond to trends that are as fundamental.

Initiatives that cost more are poor bets. Funds for education are scarce and competition for them is keen. In particular, the unmet demand for increases in teacher salaries alone could easily consume the entire budget for curriculum improvement. Initiatives that call for lower class size or expensive equipment and materials face a bigger challenge than ones do that can be done within the existing per-pupil expenditure. Initiatives that save money have a significant advantage.

Low odds of ultimate success is not by itself sufficient reason to abandon a worthy curriculum improvement initiative, but when you have a choice among many worthy initiatives, lend your efforts to those that have a greater chance of ultimate success.

Facing Conflict Constructively

Some curriculum leaders try to avoid conflict. They act as if consensus exists when even a working agreement is missing, deceiving themselves or hoping that wishing will make it so. As we've seen throughout this book, people feel strongly about curriculum matters and they are willing to fight when they feel that their vital interests are threatened. So it will eventually be necessary to confront the opposition in any event. Ignoring them only frightens and insults them.

Conflict is inevitable in curriculum matters, but controversy can usually be avoided. The existence of deep differences of opinion and value among the interested parties to a curriculum need not create a contentious, acrimonious atmosphere. Ignoring the opposition and hoping that they won't notice as you quietly install a curriculum that they oppose is certain to draw an angry response eventually. Treating opponents as if they are evil or their views silly or contemptible is certain to generate hostility. Treating them as you would like to be treated in similar circumstances will usually avoid a blowup.

Wise curriculum leaders engage the opposition in dialogue and try to understand how they think, what they value, and why they favor some actions and oppose others. They do not treat them as heathens to be converted to the true religion, but as believers in a different faith.

Leaders can set a constructive tone by listening honestly and respectfully to all views and acknowledging what's good and true in them. Even the deepest educational disagreements are differences of priority among goods rather than good versus evil. Honestly disagreeing in a civil way will seldom generate hostility. In a contested situation, curriculum leaders should take special pains to keep lines of communication open, to make all meetings and decisions open to everyone, and to maintain trust. If necessary, set up committees representing the contending parties to monitor the process. If all efforts at finding a common curriculum fail, allow choice so that no one is forced to send their children to a curriculum that they despise.

Combining Curriculum Work with Other Initiatives

We have seen throughout this book how intimately curriculum is linked with everything else that happens in schools and classrooms. Significant curriculum improvements will affect materials selection, teaching, testing, budget, and perhaps school organization and parent–school or community–school relations. And changes in these other aspects of school will also affect the curriculum. As we saw in Chapter 6, the time and resources available for curriculum improvement in schools and classrooms are extremely limited. Under these circumstances combining curriculum improvement efforts with other initiatives to improve teachers, classrooms, and schools makes good sense. Districts who synchronize curriculum updates with their textbook replacement cycle recognize the value of this strategy. Coordinating in-service workshops for teachers with curriculum improvement initiatives is another common example.

Anyone interested in curriculum improvement should ask the following questions. What other initiatives are underway or under discussion? How can we work on these in a way that also facilitates desirable curriculum changes? Perhaps a group of teachers are constructing a common semester examination. Could this be an occasion for identifying parts of the present curriculum that the group considers less important now or new elements that they would like to consider or new emphases, such as applying ideas to complex, authentic problems?

Suppose that a new principal is looking for ways to make teachers' meetings more relevant and dynamic. How about having teachers look at examples of students' work? How about bringing in personnel officers of companies that hire high school graduates or admissions officers of a nearby college for a conversation about standards? Perhaps several teachers in the school are engaged in a study team or gearing up for certification by the National Board for Professional Teaching Standards. Has the new superintendent authorized a needs assessment for the district? Is the school–community council asking for proposals for local grants? All these could be opportunities for curriculum improvement.

Today, many schools find themselves considering how to achieve national and state standards and prepare for external examinations. This can be a marvelous, if not always welcome, opportunity to consider curriculum improvements.

Local Curriculum Improvement Projects

Mounting Local Projects

To mount a curriculum improvement project in a local school is, first and foremost, to recruit time, talent, and energy from a school staff that is already over-committed. Those who have the most talent and energy are usually the most over-committed. And, except in very large schools, expertise vital to the project's success may exist in only one or two individuals. Failing to recruit them to participate dooms the project.

The local project team must include individuals with a deep understanding of the reform, of its central defining features and its optional variable ones, and of the rationale that supports these features. Without such knowledge and the authority to use it, the project can become a blank screen onto which participants project any image they wish. Many reforms are trivialized or distorted for lack of such deep authoritative understanding. In any given school, only a handful of individuals will have this deep understanding on any given topic, so the fate of the reform in this school hinges on recruiting these individuals to join the project.

The charge given to the local project team may be as narrow as to develop a plan for a new course, or as broad as to redesign the entire curriculum to foster deep understanding of important concepts. We will consider the case where the project team has a broad mandate. The team needs to have a clear idea of what kinds of changes in the school curriculum are needed. They need to determine what would have to change about the school in order to bring about these changes and, especially, who would have to change. And they need to consider what combination of actions on their part and on the part of school leadership would facilitate those changes.

In considering the types of curriculum changes needed, the team will of course be guided by work done earlier in review and change consideration. When they inherit from earlier phases a clear and complete specification of the purposes of the reform, they can proceed to implement it. Usually, however, they inherit only a vague and general indication of rough directions and boundaries. In this case, the conventional advice is to begin by formulating objectives for students: What should students be able to do? This is sound advice if the team knows exactly what it wants students to be able to do. Typically, they do not. They may be able to state a few specific objectives, but they generally will not be sure that their initial aims and objectives are sound, complete, or exact enough to form a secure basis for further work. And so, they will generally need to reflect further on their intentions and those of the other interested parties they represent. This can be done in many ways.

With purposes clearly expressed, the project team then needs to consider options for incorporating the change into the school program. Figures 9.8 and 9.9 show some of the more common options, arranged roughly in order of likely disruptiveness and therefore difficulty of making the change. Fitting a change of most of these types into the school program entails major changes in school routines, such as finding a place in the master schedule or reassigning teaching staff. Such changes always require approval of the principal and often district, community, or board review. The project team would have to recommend to school leaders the best options for the particular situation and create further plans in accordance with the decisions made.

When they have a clear idea of the curriculum change to be sought, the project team should then consider what and who would have to change in order for this plan to be realized. A teacher would typically handle an effort to revise a single high school course, consulting with a principal or department chair. A single teacher might possibly develop a new course without needing to change what any other teacher does (though the new course would siphon off enrollment from others and might therefore affect other teachers). Instituting a new course taught by a single handpicked individual is one of the quickest, most direct and most powerful ways school leaders can make a big difference in a small part of the curriculum. Changes that call for the entire school to change are especially challenging. Changes that require that many teachers change their classroom routines radically are especially difficult for school leaders to bring about and control, yet these are the types of changes reformers most commonly call for.

- Change the organizational framework of the entire school curriculum
    (e.g., flexible modular scheduling; from subjects to a house system with seminars)
- Institute a change across the curriculum
    (e.g., teachers as counselors; writing across the curriculum; daily silent reading period)
- Offer a new program of study
    (e.g., school within a school; community service internship program)
- Offer a new course sequence in a subject
    (e.g., aeronautics (in a vocational program); computer programming; economics I, II; accelerated mathematics sequence)
- Offer a new course
    (e.g., Japanese language; music composition; ecology, human biology)
- Substantially revise an existing program or course sequence
    (e.g., to English I–IV from multiple electives; to discipline-based art from studio courses)
- Revise a course
    (e.g., physics, to rely less on math; English 9, to include more grammar, writing; typing, to teach keyboarding, word processing)

FIG. 9.8.   *Options for fitting a curriculum change into a high school program.*

- Change the organizational framework of the entire curriculum
    (e.g., to team teaching from self-contained classrooms, nongraded school students stay with same teacher several years)
- Initiate a schoolwide change affecting all grades and subjects
    (e.g., schoolwide testing, computer center)
- Offer a new program of study for some or all students
    (e.g., accelerated program for disadvantaged students, prekindergarten program)
- Include a new subject over several grades
    (e.g., computer programming with Logo, music taught by specialist teacher, K–6)
- Introduce a new subject in one grade
    (e.g., conflict resolution in grade 4, keyboarding in grade 3)
- Substantially revise an existing program or subject
    (e.g., the K–6 reading or math program, conceptual understanding in K–6 mathematics; hands-on science in grades 3–6)
- Revise the teaching of one subject in a grade
    (e.g., heterogeneous small groups in grade 5)

FIG. 9.9.   *Options for fitting a curriculum change into an elementary school program.*

- Materials used by students,
    (e.g., textbooks, workbooks, activity sheets, video, software)
- Materials used by teachers,
    (e.g., teachers' guides, audiotapes, videotapes for teachers)
- Classroom environment,
    (e.g., equipment, supplies, facilities; i.e., computers, TV)
- Personnel
    (e.g., aides, volunteers)
- School organization,
    (e.g., team teaching instead of self-contained classroom; collegial evaluation
    of teachers by teachers; parent participation in classrooms)
- Classroom frames,
    (e.g., principal, supervisor expectations, standards)
- Teachers' beliefs and attitudes,
    (e.g., by talks, workshops, quality circles, discussion groups)
- Teachers' skills and knowledge,
    (e.g., by talks, workshops, demonstrations, videotapes)

FIG. 9.10. *Avenues by which a local project team might influence classroom curriculums.*

As the needed changes become clear, the project team must consider whether they are feasible. Can the individuals be persuaded to change their behavior? Can the money be found to buy new materials? Can other interested parties, particularly school leaders, teachers, students, and the community, be persuaded to accept the needed changes? If, as often happens, a project requires substantial changes in the classroom curriculum, the team needs to consider what are the avenues through which they might influence what happens in classrooms. Some of the likely prospects are listed in Fig. 9.10.

Consider the following strategies to strengthen local curriculum change projects.

Broaden the Base of Expertise

Schools can hire scholars, scientists, artists, or local citizens with appropriate expertise as subject matter specialists to review the content of a K–12 program in their field or recruit them as volunteers to work with a curriculum planning team. Collaboration with faculty in a nearby college or university in a joint project may be possible. Collaboration might be arranged with teacher preparation institutions to offer courses and degrees that meet common needs of many schools. Recently many curriculum projects have encouraged participation by schools and teachers in a regional or national network. Joining such a network gives schools easy access to greater expertise than any school could possibly afford otherwise.

Schools might join in and even initiate joint ventures in curriculum development with many types of outside agencies—federal and state education authorities; professional associations, charitable foundations, and other nonprofit organizations; publishers of educational material and other profitmaking firms, as well as other schools, even schools in other states and national or even international networks of schools. Local schools might supply some of the funding, perhaps in the form of support for their staff members to have released time for work on the project. Additional support, in money and in expertise, would come from the outside agencies, which might contribute funds and expertise in exchange for rights to the joint products (curriculum plans and materials, tests, videotapes, etc.) and for access to schools as field sites. One organization, Educational Research Corporation of America, already solicits joint participation of a number of districts in developing curriculum materials along lines the districts support. ERCA works with staff of the local schools to develop, field test, and revise curriculum materials, which it then seeks to market through contracts with commercial textbook publishers. Many local and regional philanthropic foundations might be delighted to support joint projects of interest to a number of schools in a city, state, or region even though they may resist funding projects that benefit only a single school system.

Local schools could also put out curriculum reform projects for competitive bidding. Requests for proposals could be prepared specifying what kinds of curriculum work the school needed, when, and how much they would pay for the work. Local school employees, or possibly also private organizations (which might include teachers supplementing their regular employment), would be invited to submit proposals. Relevant expertise could be specified as a criterion for accepting proposals.

Of course, all use of outside expertise entails costs and carries risks, chiefly the risk of incompatibility between local thinking and the expert's. These will have to be weighed against the benefits in each particular case. Unfortunately, local interest groups contest local school budgets so heavily that spending funds on personnel not regularly employed by the school system is interpreted as a vote of no confidence in local staff and thus becomes a political act.

Overcoming the Domination of Commercially Published Materials

The chief attractions of published materials are relatively low cost, convenience for the teacher, and high production values. If locally developed materials are to compete, they must equal or exceed these advantages or offer other compensating ones. The latter strategy seems most promising, though the former should not be neglected. One of the inherent advantages local development holds is the possibility of widespread participation by teachers in development activities and materials. Suppose, for example, that the project team only produced sample lessons and that all teachers in the school or school system were invited to submit their own lessons for inclusion in a steadily expanding teachers' guide. This would presumably act as an incentive for teachers to develop their own lessons and yet the project would retain editorial control over the teachers' guide. High school departments or elementary grade level teams of teachers could be responsible for jointly planning those lessons in which the differences were greatest between the commercial materials and the project's plans. That way teachers could support one another in "deviating" from the textbook.

Materials created by the project team for use by teachers should be as convenient and attractive as possible. Suppose the project team actually wrote alternative textbook chapters and sections of a teachers' guide. Or, suppose they created a package of supplementary materials for teachers to duplicate and use, materials more closely tailored to local conditions. Many such variations on the theme of producing a teachers' guide can be found which will encourage and support teachers in their efforts to tailor their classroom curriculum to the characteristics and needs of their students and communities.

Even more radically, suppose teachers submitted syllabi for the board to approve, and that, after approval, teachers were permitted to select their own curriculum materials within a given budget. The project team could assist the board by developing guidelines concerning content, purpose, and structure of particular courses and programs, but the preparation of syllabi for board approval would be the responsibility of individual teachers or teacher teams.

Increasing the Impact on Teachers' Classroom Behavior

Measures that make the products of local curriculum development more useful and attractive to teachers would increase their influence on the classroom curriculum, of course. Beyond that, suppose teachers received clearer instruction in exactly how to incorporate them into their teaching and continuing advice and support in trying out the new patterns. For example, suppose that videotapes were produced of the classrooms of teachers who were well-versed in teaching according to the new plans. Suppose these videotapes were viewed and discussed at teacher in-service meetings. Suppose teachers were given time to meet once a week to report on their experiences in attempting to make changes in their classrooms, to discuss their successes and problems in a safe collegial context, and to bring issues as a group to the project team for discussion. Substantial curriculum changes amount to a professional remodeling job for teachers, and it is difficult to see how they can be expected to make them without sustained involvement with the change and with others about the professional problems of making the change.

A Variety of Approaches

Schools might well institute several of types of projects, ranging from a multiple-year project involving a substantial fraction of the school staff to a lightning strike effort over spring break to develop plans and materials for a specific problem in one subject or grade. It might be possible to arrange for students in one class to work more independently and free that teacher to develop teaching/learning materials to facilitate more independent work in other classes less prepared for it initially. Joint projects might be launched with museums, youth organizations, or city government. School systems can be conceived as marshalling the entire resources of the community for education, not just the full-time professional staff. Videotapes show promise as a means of communicating curricular innovations, demonstrating their practicality, and as a training device to help teachers master new classroom techniques. It is always difficult to convey a skill, particularly an interpersonal skill, in print. Also, video can be shown at the viewer's convenience rather than at a single time and place. No school needs to be limited to the pattern of teacher committees meeting after school or over vacations and writing courses of study and teachers' guides.

An obvious limitation of all these improvements in local curriculum development procedures is that they cost more, either in real budget dollars or in time and energy diverted from other school activities. If standard practices are producing effective curriculum change in the schools and classrooms of a particular school system, then these improvements are not needed. But the evidence is strong that most local curriculum development is ineffective, so that the resources currently devoted to it are not being well utilized. Slight additional investment combined with substantial reforms in the local curriculum development process may yield much greater effectiveness. Alternatively, school systems that cannot afford the funds to make local curriculum development really effective may find that it would be wiser for them to limit their attempts to a single project and make a really serious effort there. Also, by joining in leagues of cooperating schools, local systems may be able to spread the costs of local development more widely.

Using Ideas from Theory and Research

We saw in Chapter 7, Improving Curriculum, how ideas from theory and research can guide development of innovative curriculum plans and materials. Ideas such as Itzkoff's

(1986) on reading, Hughes' (1986) on early mathematics, Seligman's (1975) on learned helplessness, Noddings' (1992) on caring, or Gardner's (1999) on multiple intelligences can make the difference between a truly innovative and powerful curriculum and one that is only marginally different or superficially different.

The accepted, conventional understanding of a problem is seldom adequate to guide the developers' efforts. "Everyone knows" that American youth have a "drug problem," but the developers of a project to prevent teenage drug abuse would need a deeper understanding of the problem. Do youngsters lack information about the harmful consequences of drugs? Do they lack alternative outlets for adolescent rebellion? Are they vulnerable to drug abuse because they suffer from poor social adjustment or low self-esteem or because they have too much time on their hands and too little sense of purpose? Developers need answers to such questions in order to develop effective materials and activities. Developers look to ideas in their platform to help them articulate and explain the problem.

What does research suggest about the incidence of the problem, the adequacy of the various concepts people use to describe it, and plausible causes? What has been the history of the problem? What are the views of the major contending parties and interests? What are the limiting cases of the problem, situations where it is and is not found and is more and less serious? A deep analysis would require the developers to compare alternative conceptualizations of the problem and alternative causal models, perhaps collecting additional evidence from library or field research. They may want to challenge strategic assumptions of prior investigators or recast the problem in new ways.

Developers express the ideas that will guide their work in the proposal for funding. Proposals usually include an analysis of the problem that prompts the project, its origins, causes, and possible cures through the use of curriculum materials. Proposals state the fundamental curriculum ideas and values that they hope to embody in the curriculum they propose to develop. They show or describe some models or exemplars of the kinds of things that they might design, and of the process they will use. The ideas in the project's platform provide the terms that the group will use in its deliberations to define issues, describe alternatives, and frame arguments. The platform also expresses shared beliefs that unite the team and form its identity. Members who dissent from the platform usually leave the team. To the outside world, the team's platform is an emblem signifying its commitments. Onlookers who share the team's commitments can support the project, while those who oppose them can criticize it. Platforms thus serve important technical, political, and social functions and, in so doing, they are essential ingredients of deliberative design.

The ideas in a project's platform usually undergo some development during the course of the project, but the basic concepts and principles seldom change. Much of the thinking that shapes a curriculum development project is thus done before the project officially begins.

Affiliating with National Reform Consortiums

As we saw in Chapter 8, a number of national reforms have organized coalitions and networks of schools to share information and support one another in school improvement. Four prominent examples are the Basic School Network, built around the ideas of Ernest Boyer (1995); the Essential Schools Project, built on the ideas of Theodore Sizer (1992, 1996); the Comer School Development Program, built on the ideas of James Comer et al. (1996, 1999); and the Accelerated Schools Project, built on the ideas of Henry Levin (Finnan et al., 1996, Hopfenberg et al., 1993).

Each of these is a comprehensive school reform project that functions like a local franchise of a national retail chain. Local schools pay a fee to belong and commit to a philosophy and to following a certain reform process. In exchange, they get a tested school program that integrates changes in teaching, staffing, teacher development, curriculum and other school procedures. The program is based on research and theory. Schools can read about it before they decide to join. They also gain access to other schools in the network for sharing experiences and information.

Long-Range Planning for Curriculum Improvement

The case for long-range planning in curriculum is easy to make. Implementing a curriculum change takes years. The results stay with children for a lifetime. To realize cumulative, long-term curriculum improvements demands long-term planning. Although the figures are somewhat arbitrary, I suggest that schools make curriculum plans for 2, 5, and 10 years ahead. (Planning for next year happens anyway and need not concern us here.)

Elaborate methods of strategic planning are generally out of place in schools, but a valuable form of advance planning can be carried out within the frames most schools face. The three critical types of information a school needs for long range curriculum planning are (1) where are we now, (2) where do we want to be, and (3) what resources will we have. Chapter 3 on the curriculum in schools tells how to describe a school's current curriculum. Adapting those ideas to the challenge of collecting data to describe a school's curriculum is relatively straightforward.

How best to determine where a school and community want to go is not so clear. A properly designed set of surveys will help to find what the community or staff wants, but surveys can't capture people's dreams. Interviews may be an improvement, if done imaginatively. Even the best imaginable process assumes that the people interviewed know what they want.

Ideally, people would be asked to express preferences for things that have real meaning and significance to them. For example, parents of a youngster in the primary grades can easily be drawn into thinking about what they want their children to study and learn over the next 10 years. Teachers clearly have a long-term interest in curriculum planning. Even students are interested in what they will study and learn later on, and graduates are usually eager to tell what they wish they had done in school.

Schools' long-term curriculum plans will generally be affected by conditions in several important areas of community and cultural life including:

demographics (e.g., number of students, aging)
politics (e.g., votes for schools, priorities among aims)
economics (e.g., funding levels, career aspirations)
religion (e.g., treatment of sensitive issues)
social mores (e.g., family structure, social mobility)
ideas in wide currency (e.g., ecology, information)
technology (e.g., electronic communication, biotechnology).

Widespread or large changes in any of these areas will almost certainly affect either what kinds of curriculum changes are desirable or what kinds are possible or both. Explicit guesses about possible and likely changes in such characteristics should support any long-term curriculum plan.

The most fundamental assumptions are those that pertain to factors that affect priorities among content and purpose: what students need to know. Also important are factors that affect critical elements in the educational situation, such as students' willingness to learn different topics, teachers' ability to teach them, and so on.

It is generally helpful to develop alternative scenarios reflecting critical uncertainties in assumptions and to develop contingency plans for coping with all likely scenarios. Get students involved in developing these scenarios. Discuss them with stakeholders, leaders. Maintain a dialogue. Relate current problems to long-term trends. Address currently unmet high-priority needs.

Concluding Note on the Importance of Leadership

The very characteristics that make the curriculum so resilient in the face of change, conflict, and severe resource constraints, also make it resistant to reforms. Reform-minded leaders have an enormous task in getting those involved to question seriously the content, purpose, and organizing framework of the educational programs they participate in and thus to give new ideas a fighting chance. Yet, in view of the masses of people affected and the comprehensiveness and intimacy of the changes they are required to make, it is probably fortunate that making lasting and substantial curriculum changes is so difficult. Learning to consider such changes deeply and carefully is therefore all the more important.

School curriculum work is fundamental to bringing about lasting and substantial curriculum improvement. The curriculum comes to life in the classroom, but the most direct and powerful influences on the classroom are found in the school. Achieving substantial lasting improvement in the curriculum of a school is a professional and civic accomplishment of the same high order as fielding a good transit system, community center, theater, or sports team. In all these cases, many individuals and groups must work together. In all these cases, the work bears fruit only when primary performers achieve a high level of excellence. And in all these cases, leadership is critical to success.

So many shifting, conflicting purposes must be reconciled and coordinated. Such consistent attention must be lavished on the work through periods of years, even decades, as individuals assume and relinquish roles in the institution. The resources provided are so constrained and variable. The obstacles to change are so many and so deep-seated. Only with good leadership can a school hope to maintain the quality of its curriculum. Figure 9.11 lists some of the many ways school leadership contributes to school curriculum improvement.

Questions and Projects

1. Recall a curriculum improvement effort that you have experienced. If you've known many, recall one of the most successful. Write a brief account (500 words or less) for a colleague describing what the effort consisted of, what it was intended to accomplish, and what happened. In your judgment, did this effort lead to lasting, substantial curriculum improvement? Say why you think it did or did not.
2. Ask to see the latest accreditation report for a school you know well. Spend an hour scanning the report. Does it identify the needs for curriculum improvement in the school? How strong is the justification given for those being the most important priorities for improvement?

1. Find or create and express vividly educational visions and goals so that they become widely shared.
2. Encourage people to work hard for the shared visions and goals.
3. Act resourcefully in pursuit of shared visions and goals; reward resourcefulness in others.
4. Inspire feelings of competence; make people feel strong, effective, and able to influence their fate; stimulate them to strong, prompt action.
5. Build relationships of trust among those whose interests and perspectives differ but whose lives and fates are intertwined; express strong, unwavering faith in people.
6. Encourage people to work together for common goals.
7. Allocate resources appropriate to achieving shared goals; know when and when not to cut corners.
8. Confront and resolve conflicts and difficulties, not deny them.
9. Demonstrate personal competence by such steps as: planning personal goals and steps to reach them, assessing personal weaknesses and taking steps to improve.
10. Deal effectively with interests and individuals powerful enough to defeat or deflect your purpose; build coalitions, balance conflicting interests, resolve conflicts that threaten important goals.

FIG. 9.11. *Things leaders do that promote curriculum improvement.*

3. A colleague says "If they'd just leave us alone, the teachers in this school could create in this school the best curriculum in the state, maybe in the country. It's the constant meddling of administrators, parents, and government people that screws everything up." If you agree, find the weakest points in the statement. If you disagree, find as much of a grain of truth in the statement as you can.
4. Discuss the following propositions. "What's truly hard about curriculum improvement is that
   A. there's no money to support it."
   B. there's no time to do it."
   C. it's nobody's primary responsibility."
   D. nobody really cares about it."
   E. everything depends on the teacher anyway."
5. Interview an experienced school curriculum leader about curriculum improvement efforts they have seen. Ask what are the features or characteristics of efforts that achieve lasting, substantial improvements. Compare these answers to those in the chapter.
6. Interview an experienced teacher about school curriculum improvement. What reform efforts does the teacher think have made the most lasting and substantial improvements? How does she think the public and school leaders should improve the school curriculum?
7. Find a retired school curriculum leader and ask about which reforms have lasted and why.
8. Talk to a parent whose child's school is making a major effort at reform. How much does the parent know about the reform effort? What are the parent's attitudes and

feelings about it? If many parents feel as this one does, what do you think that indicates about the fate of the reform.
9. Read about one of the franchised school reforms on their Web site. Think of a school you know well. Identify the three respects in which this reform is well suited to this school and three respects in which it is not well suited.
10. Find a partner and debate the merits of franchised school reform models as a strategy for achieving lasting, substantial curriculum improvements.

Further Study

School reform has been a hot topic during the past decade or so. A great deal has been published and the work has advanced the discussion considerably. Elmore and associates (1990) and Elmore, Peterson, and McCarthey (1996) are the best comprehensive and critical guides to this work. Most authorities now accept the general picture they paint of the difficulties of sustaining major changes in the school curriculum and are looking for strategies to achieve lasting reform at last.

One group of school reformers looks toward accountability, mandates, standards, and parental choice as the Holy Grail. Another looks toward packaged franchised reforms that do a lot of the work for schools and prescribe a process for reform. A third approach looks toward teacher professionalism and teacher empowerment as the answer. The same sources that are cited in Chapter 8 on teacher professionalism are relevant here.

On school curriculum improvement generally, I find Fullan's *The New Meaning of Educational Change* (2000) to be the most useful single reference. The curriculum is the main subject of Chapter 11, and readers particularly interested in this subject will find additional references there. I still find Good and Brophy's (1986) comprehensive review of the research literature on the effects of various kinds of school-level school improvement projects useful as well as Joyce's *The Structure of School Improvement* (1983) and *Improving America's Schools* (1986). Both are deeply informed by practical experience in innovative projects as well as theory and research. Joyce is especially strong on the role of staff development in school improvement. Hall and Loucks (1977) remains the standard reference on the implementation of innovations.

The traditional literature on curriculum reviews is that on needs assessment, now largely ignored. Cooley and Brickell (1986) offer an excellent example of what I have here called a focused comprehensive review. Careful, in-depth studies of how reviews are actually done would be useful, as would more evaluations of proposed methods for carrying out reviews.

On curriculum change consideration, Schaffarzick (1975) remains the only direct reference, though Fullan (2000) has incorporated many of the general insights. I do not understand why more investigators have not followed his pioneering effort.

The traditional literature on instituting curriculum innovations is ably synthesized by Fullan (2000), who reviews the research on the roles of the various people involved and the tactics they employ.

Hall and Hord (1987) give a comprehensive set of recommendations for facilitating classroom curriculum change based on the implementation research carried out mostly in the last decade. Joyce (1988) is the standard reference on staff development.

On achieving working agreement, Anatol Rappoport's *Fights, Games, and Debates* (1960) is a lively treatment of the topic of resolving disputes from the standpoints of sociology and game theory. Daniel Yankelovich's *The Magic of Dialogue* (1999) is full of practical tips for starting and sustaining effective dialogue.

The best information on the franchised reform movements is to be found on their Web sites:

Basic School Network *http://www.jmu.edu/basicschool/*
(Also see Boyer, 1995.)
Accelerated Schools Project
http://www.sp.uconn.edu/~wwwasp/main_gen.htm
Comer School Development Program
http://info.med.yale.edu/comer/
Coalition of Essential Schools
http://www.essentialschools.org/aboutus/aboutus.html

References

Adams, J. E., Jr. (2000). *Taking charge of curriculum: Teacher networks and curriculum implementation*. New York: Teachers College Press.

Akker, J. J. H. Vanden. (1999). *Design approaches and tools in education and training*. Boston: Kluwer Academic Publishers.

American Federation of Teachers. (1997). *Building on the best, learning from what works*: ERIC ED445315.

Apple, M. W. (1979). *Ideology and curriculum*. London: Routledge and Kegan Paul.

Arizona Art Education Association. Art in elementary education: What the law requires. In *In Perspective, The Journal of the Arizona Art Education Association*, *1*, 6–24, Fall 1982.

Bagley, W. C. (1926). Supplementary statement. In *Foundations of curriculum-making: The Twenty-Sixth Yearbook of the National Society for the Study of Education, Part II* (pp. 29–40). Bloomington, IL: Public School Publishing Company.

Bantock, G. H. (1968). *Culture, industrialisation and education*. London: Routledge and Kegan Paul.

Bantock, G. H. (1980). *Dilemmas of the curriculum*. New York: Wiley.

Barker, R., & Gump, P. (1964). *Big school, small school*. Stanford, CA: Stanford University Press.

Barone, T. (1987). Research out of the shadows. *Curriculum Inquiry*, *17*(4), 453–459.

Barr, R. (1986). Classroom interaction and curricular content. In D. Bloome (Ed.), *Literacy, language, and schooling*. Norwood, NJ: Ablex.

Barr, R., & Dreeben, R. (1977). Instruction in classrooms. In L. S. Shulman (Ed.), *Review of research in education 5*. Itasca, IL: F. E. Peacock.

Barry, B. (1990). *Political argument*. New York: Humanities Press.

Barzun, J., & Graff, H. F. (1992). *The modern researcher* (5th ed.). Boston: Houghton Mifflin Co.

Beard, C. A. (1936). The scholar in an age of conflicts, *School and Society*, *43*, 278–279.

Becker, H. (1961). *Boys in white*. Chicago: University of Chicago Press.

Bell, H. M. (1938). *Youth tell their story*. Washington, DC: American Council on Education.

Bellack, A., Kliebard, H. M., Hyman, R. T., & Smith, F. L., Jr. (1966). *The language of the classroom*. New York: Teachers College Press.

Ben-Peretz, M. (1975). ·The concept of curriculum potential. *Curriculum Theory Network*, *5*, 151–159.

Ben-Peretz, M., Bromme, R., & Halkes, R. (1986). *Advances of research on teacher thinking*. Berwyn, IL: Swets North America.

Bereiter, C., & Scardamalia, M. (1993). *Surpassing ourselves: An inquiry into the nature and implications of expertise*. Chicago: Open Court.

Berliner, D. C. (1987). Simple views of effective teaching and a simple theory of classroom instruction. In D. C. Berliner, & B. Rosenshine, *Talks to teachers* (pp. 93–110). New York: Random House.

Berliner, D., & Calfee, R. (1996). *Handbook of educational psychology*. New York: Macmillan Library Reference.

Berman, P., & McLaughlin, M. (1975). *Federal programs supporting educational change: Volume III: Implementing and sustaining innovations*. Santa Monica, CA: The RAND Corporation.

Bestor, A. E. (1953). *Educational wastelands: The retreat from learning in our public schools*. Urbana: University of Illinois Press.

Beyer, L., & Apple, M. (1998). *The curriculum: Problems, politics, and possibilities*. Albany: State University of New York Press.

Bloom, B., Hastings, J., & Madaus, G. (1971). *Handbook of formative and summative evaluation of student learning*. New York: McGraw-Hill.

Blumberg, A. (1985). *The school superintendent*. New York: Teachers College Press.

Boaler, J. (1997). *Experiencing school mathematics: Teaching styles, sex, and setting*. Philadelphia: Open University Press.

Bobbitt, F. (1918). *The curriculum*. Boston: Houghton Mifflin.

Bobbit, F. (1924). *How to make a curriculum*. Boston: Houghton Mifflin.

Bode, B. H. (1927). *Modern educational theories*. New York: Macmillan.

Boswell, J. (1776). *Life of Johnson*. London: Oxford University Press, 1952 edition, (originally published, 1766).

Boyd, W. L. (1978). The changing politics of curriculum policy making for American schools. In *Review of Educational Research*, 48, 577–628, Fall 1978. (Also appeared in Schaffarzick & Sykes (Ed.), *Value conflicts and curriculum issues* (pp. 73–138). Berkeley, CA: McCutchan, 1979).

Boyer, E. L. (1983). *High school: A report on secondary education in America*. New York: Harper and Row.

Boyer, E. L. (1995). *The basic school: A community for learning*. Princeton, NJ: Carnegie Foundation for the Advancement of Teaching.

Brandt, R. (1987). On school improvement in Pittsburgh. *Educational Leadership*, 44(8):39–43.

Bransford, J. D., Brown, A. L., & Cocking, R. R. (Eds.). (1999). Committee on Developments in the Science of Learning, Commission on Behavioral and Social Sciences and Education, National Research Council. *How people learn: Brain, mind, experience, and school*. Washington, DC: National Academy of Sciences.

Bridges, E. M. (1986). *The incompetent teacher*. Philadelphia: Falmer Press.

Bruner, J. (1960). *The process of education*. Cambridge, MA: Harvard University Press, 1960. (Quotations from the Vintage Edition, 1963.)

Buber, M. (1923). *I and thou*. (W. Kaufman, Trans.). New York: Touchstone.

Carlsen, W. (1988). *The effects of science teacher subject-matter knowledge on teacher questioning and classroom discourse*. Unpublished Ph.D. dissertation, School of Education, Stanford University.

Carr, W., & Kemmis, S. (1986). *Becoming critical: Education, knowledge and action research*. London: Falmer.

Christenson, M., Johnston, M., & Norris, J. (Eds.). (2001). *Teaching together: School/university collaboration to improve social studies education*. New York: Teachers College Press.

Clark, C., & Yinger, R. J. (1987). Teacher planning. In Berliner & Rosenshine. *Talks to Teachers* (pp. 342–365). New York: Random House.

Clune, W. H. (1993). Systemic educational policy: A conceptual framework. In S. Fuhrman (Ed.), *Designing coherent educational policy*. San Francisco: Jossey-Bass.

Cobb, P., Yackel, E., & McClain, K. (Eds.). (2000). *Symbolizing and communicating in mathematics classrooms: Perspectives on discourse tools, and instructional design*. Mahwah, NJ: Lawrence Erlbaum Associates.

Cohen, D. (1988). Teaching practice: Plus Que Ca Change. In P. W. Jackson (Ed.), *Contributing to educational change: Perspectives on research and practice* (pp. 27–84). Berkeley, CA: McCutchan.

Cohen, D., McLaughlin, M., & Talbert, J. (1993). *Teaching for understanding*. San Francisco: Jossey-Bass.

Cohen, S. (1974). *American education: A documentary history* (5 vols.). New York: Random House.

Collings, E. (1923). *An Experiment with a project curriculum*. New York: Macmillan.

Comer, J. P. (1999). *Child by child: The comer process for change in education*. New York: Teachers College Press.

Committee on the Reorganization of Secondary Education. (1918). *Cardinal principles of secondary education*. Washington, DC: U.S. Bureau of Education, Bulletin No. 35.

Connelly, F. M., & Clandinin, D. J. (1988). *Teachers as curriculum planners: Narratives of experience*. New York: Teachers College Press.

Connelly, F. M., & Clandinin, D. J. (1999). *Shaping a professional identity: Stories of educational practice*. New York: Teachers College Press.

Cooley, W., & Brickell, W. (1986). *Decision-oriented educational research*. Boston: Kluwer-Nijhof.

Cooper, H., & Hedges, L. V. (Eds.). (1994). *The handbook of research synthesis*. New York: Russell Sage Foundation.

Corcoran, T. B. (1988). *Working in urban schools*. Washington, DC: Institute for Educational Leadership.

Counts, G. S. (1932). *Dare the school build a new social order?* New York: The John Day Co.

Cremin, L. A. (1961). *The Transformation of the School: Progressivism in American Education, 1876–1957*. New York: Knopf.

Cremin, L. A. (1970). *American education: The colonial experience, 1607–1783*. New York: Harper and Row.

Cremin, L. A. (1980). *American education: The national experience, 1783–1876*. New York: Harper and Row.

Cremin, L. A. (1988). *American education: The metropolitan experience, 1876–1980*. New York: Harper and Row.

Cronbach, L. J. (1982). *Designing evaluations of educational and social programs*. San Francisco: Jossey-Bass.

Cronbach, L. J., & associates. (1980). *Toward reform of program evaluation: aims, methods, and institutional arrangements*. San Francisco: Jossey-Bass.

Crosbie, L. M. (1924). *The Phillips Exeter Academy: A history*. Exeter, NH: The Academy.

Cuban, L. (1986). *Teachers and machines: The classroom use of technology since 1920*. New York: Teachers College Press.

Cuban, L. (1993). *How teachers taught: Constancy and change in American classrooms 1890–1980*. New York: Longmans.

Cubberley, E. P. (Ed.). (1934). *Readings in public education in the United States*. Boston: Houghton Mifflin.

Cusick, P. A. (1973). *Inside high school*. New York: Holt, Rinehart, and Winston.

Cusick, P. A. (1983). *The egalitarian ideal and the American high school*. New York: Longmans.

Darling-Hammond, L., & Sykes, G. (Eds.). (1999). *Teaching as the learning profession: Handbook of policy and practice*. San Francisco: Jossey-Bass.

Davis, B. (1995). Thinking otherwise and hearing differently. Enactivism and school mathematics. Reprinted in W. F. Pinar (Ed.). (1999). *Contemporary curriculum discourses*. New York: Peter Long, pp. 325–345.

Davis, R. B., & McKnight, C. (1976). Conceptual, heuristic, and algorithmic approaches in mathematics teaching. *Journal of Children's Mathematical Behavior, 1*, 271–286.

De Charms, R., & Moeller, G. H. (1962). Values expressed in American children's readers, 1800–1950. *Journal of Abnormal and Social Psychology, 64*(2), 136–142.

Dewey, J. (1897). *My pedagogic creed*. Washington, DC: Progressive Education Association.

Dewey, J. (1902). *The child and the curriculum*. Chicago: University of Chicago Press.

Dewey, J. (1916). *Democracy and education*. New York: Macmillan.

Dewey, J. (1938). *Experience and education*. New York: Macmillan.

Dodd, M. A. (2000). *Like letters in running water*. Mahwah, NJ: Lawrence Erlbaum.

Dow, P. (1975). MACOS: *The study of human behavior as one road to survival*. Phi Delta Kappan, 57(2): 79–81.

Doyle, W. (1977). The practicality ethic in teacher decision-making. *Interchange, 8*, 1–12.

Doyle, W., & Carter, K. (1984). Academic tasks in classrooms. *Curriculum Inquiry, 14*(2), 129–149.

Doyle, W., & Ponder, G. (1977). The practicality ethic in teacher decision-making. *Interchange, 8*, 1–12.

Duckworth, E. (1996). *The having of wonderful ideas & other essays on teaching & learning*. New York: Teachers College Press.

Duckworth, E. (1997). *Teacher to teacher*. New York: Teachers College Press.

Duckworth, E. (2001). *Tell me more: Listening to learners explain*. New York: Teachers College Press.

Duncan, D., & Frymier, J. (1967). Exploration in the systematic study of curriculum. *Theory Into Practice VI*, 4.

Easton, D. (1965). *A systems analysis of political life*. New York: Wiley.

Education Commission of the States. (1997). *A policymakers' guide to education reform*. Denver, CO: Author.

Education Commission of the States. (1998). *Catalog of school reform models: First edition*, prepared by the Northwest Regional Educational Laboratory (*http://www.ecs.org/ecs/ecsweb.nsf/*) checked October 2001.

Education Policies Commission. (1947). The imperative needs of youth of secondary school age. *Bulletin of the National Association of Secondary School Principals, 31*(145), March.

Eisner, E. W. (1994). *The educational imagination* (3rd. ed.). New York: Macmillan.

Elbaz, F. (1983). *Teacher thinking: A study of practical knowledge*. New York: Nichols.

Elmore, R. F. (1982). Backward mapping: Implementation research and policy decisions. In W. Williams, *et al. Studying implementation* (pp. 18–25). Chatham, NJ: Chatham House Publishers.

Elmore, R. (1990). *Restructuring schools*. San Francisco: Jossey-Bass.

Elmore, R. F., Peterson, P. L., & McCarthey, S. J. (1996). *Restructuring in the classroom: Teaching, learning, and school organization.* San Francisco: Jossey-Bass.

Elson, R. M. (1964). *Guardians of tradition, American school books of the nineteenth century.* Lincoln: University of Nebraska Press.

Ennis, R. H. (1969). *Logic in Teaching.* Englewood Cliffs, NJ: Prentice-Hall.

Ennis, R. (1981). Rational thinking and educational practice. In J. S. Soltis (Ed.), *Philosophy and education. Eightieth yearbook of the national society for the study of education.* Chicago: University of Chicago Press.

Erickson, F., & Shultz, J. (1992). Students' experience of the curriculum. In P. W. Jackson, *Handbook of research on curriculum* (pp. 465–485). New York: Macmillan.

Feldman, A. (2000). *Network science, a decade later: The internet and classroom learning.* Mahwah, NJ: Lawrence Erlbaum.

Fisman, C. (1996). *Accelerated schools in action: Lessons from the field.* Thousand Oaks, CA: Corwin Press.

Flagg, B. (1990). *Formative evaluation of educational technologies.* Mahwah, NJ: Lawrence Erlbaum.

Floden, R. E., Porter, A., Schmidt, W., Freeman, D., & Schwille, J. (1981). Responses to curriculum pressure: A policy-capturing study of teacher decisions about content. *Journal of Educational Psychology, 73,* 129–141.

Freire, P. (1970). *Pedagogy of the oppressed.* New York: Herder and Herder.

Fuhrman, S. J., & Malen B. (Eds.). (1991). *The politics of curriculum and testing.* London: Falmer Press.

Fullan, M. (2000). *The new meaning of educational change.* New York: Teachers College Press.

Gardner, H. (1993). *Frames of mind:* New York: Basic Books.

Gardner, H. (1999). *The disciplined mind: What all students should understand.* New York: Simon & Schuster.

Gauthier, D. (1963). *Practical reasoning.* Oxford: Clarendon Press.

Glaser, B. G., & Strauss, A. (1967). *The discovery of grounded theory: Strategies for qualitative research.* Chicago: Aldine.

Goldsmith, J. A., Komlos, J., & Schine Gold, P. (2001). *The Chicago guide to your academic career: A portable mentor for scholars from graduate school through tenure.* Chicago: University of Chicago Press.

Good, T. L., & Brophy, J. (1986). School effects. In M. Wittrock (Ed.), *Handbook of Research on Teaching* (3rd ed.). New York: Macmillan.

Goodlad, J. I. (1984). *A place called school.* New York: McGraw-Hill.

Goodlad, J. I. (1994). *Educational renewal: Better teachers, better schools.* San Francisco: Jossey-Bass.

Goodlad, J., & Klein, F. (1970). *Behind the classroom door.* Worthington, OH: Jones.

Goodman, P. (1963). Why go to school? The New Republic. reprinted in P. C. Sexton (Ed.). (1967). Readings on the school in society. Englewood Cliffs, NJ: Prentice Hall.

Goodman, P. (1964). *Compulsory miseducation.* New York: Vintage Books.

Gray, J., & Caldwell, K. (1980). The Bay Area Writing Project. *Journal of Staff Development, 1*(1), 31–39.

Greene, M. (1995). *Releasing the imagination: Essays on education, the arts, and social change.* San Francisco: Jossey-Bass.

Grobman, H. (1968). *Evaluation activities of curriculum projects.* Chicago: Rand MsNally.

Grobman, H. (1970). *Developmental curriculum projects: Decision points and processes.* Chicago: F. E. Peacock.

Gross, N. (1958). *Who runs our schools?* New York: Wiley.

Grossman, P., & Stodolsky, S. (1995). Content as context: The role of school subjects in secondary school teaching. *Educational Researcher, 24*(8): 5–11.

Grossman, P., & Winefury, S. (Eds.). (2000). *Interdisciplinary curriculum: Challenges to implementation.* New York: Teachers College Press.

Hall, G. E., & Hord, S. M. (1987). *Change in schools: Facilitating the process.* Albany, NY: State University of New York Press.

Hall, G. E., & Loucks, S. F. (1977). A developmental model for determining whether the treatment is actually implemented. *American Educational Research Journal, 14,* 263–276.

Harrington, M. (1962). *The other America: Poverty in the United States.* New York: Macmillan.

Harris, W. T. (1885). *Compulsory education in relation to crime and social morals.* Washington, DC: U.S. Office of Education.

Hawridge, D. (1981). The telesis of educational technology. *British Journal of Educational Technology, 12,* 4–18.

Hessler, J. (1977). *The content of arguments in individualization of instruction.* Unpublished Ph.D. dissertation, Stanford University.

Hill, P. T. (1997). *Reinventing public education.* Chicago: University of Chicago Press.

Hill, P. T. (1998). *Fixing urban schools.* Washington, DC: Brookings Institution Press.

Hillocks, G., Jr. (1999). *Ways of thinking, ways of teaching.* New York: Teachers College Press.

Hirsch, E. D., Jr. (1987). *Cultural literacy: What every American needs to know.* Boston: Houghton Mifflin.

Hirsch, E. D., Jr. (1996). *The schools we need and why we don't here them.* New York: Doubleday.

Hopfenberg, W. S. (1993). *The accelerated schools resource guide.* San Francisco: Jossey-Bass.

Hord, S., & Hall, G. (1987). Three images: What principals do in curriculum implementation. *Curriculum Inquiry, 17*(1), pp. 55–89.

Hughes, M. (1986). *Children and number.* London: Basil Blackwell.

Iannaccone, L., & Lutz, F. W. (1970). *Politics, power, and policy: The governing of local school districts.* New York: Teachers College Press.

Itzkoff, S. (1986). *How we learn to read.* Ashfield, MA: Paideia Press.

Jackson, P. W. (1968). *Life in classrooms.* New York: Holt, Rinehart, and Winston.

Jackson, P. W. (1992). *Handbook of research on curriculum.* New York: Macmillan.

Joyce, B. R. (1988). *Student achievement through staff development.* New York: Longman.

Kandel, I. L. (1926). *Twenty-five years of American education.* New York: MacMillan.

Kandel, I. L. (1934). Mobilizing the teacher. *Teachers College Record, 35,* 476–478.

Kaplan, A. (1964). *The conduct of inquiry.* San Francisco: Chandler.

Kilpatrick, W. H. (1932). *Education and the social crisis: A proposed program.* New York: Liveright.

Kimbrough, R. B., & Burkett, C. W. (1990). *The principalship: Concepts and practices.* Englewood Cliffs, NJ: Prentice Hall.

Kirst, M., & Walker, D. F. (1971). An analysis of curriculum policy-making. *Review of Educational Research, 41,* 538–568.

Kliebard, H. M. (1970). The Tyler rationale. *School Review, 78,* 259–272.

Kliebard, H. M. (1986). *The struggle for the American curriculum.* 1893–1958. Boston: Routledge and Kegan Paul.

Kliebard, H. (1992). Constructing a history of the American curriculum. In P. W. Jackson (Ed.), *Handbook of Research on Curriculum* (pp. 157–184). New York: Macmillan.

Komoski, K. (1976). Educational Products Information Exchange. *EPIEgram, 5,* 1.

Krathwohl, D. R. (1998). *Methods of educational & social science research: An integrated approach.* New York: Harlow.

Kremer, L., & Ben-Peretz, M. (1980). Teachers' characteristics and their reflections in curriculum implementation. *Studies in Educational Evaluation, 6,* 73–82.

Krug, E. (1964). The shaping of the American high school (Vol. I). New York: Harper and Row.

Krug, E. (1972). *The shaping of the American high school* (Vol. II). Madison: University of Wisconsin Press.

Labaree, D. F. (1982). Politics, markets, and the compromised curriculum. *Harvard Educational Review, 57,* 483–494.

Lampert, M., & Loewenberg Ball, D. (1998). *Teaching, multimedia, and mathematics: Investigations of real practice.* New York: Teachers College Press.

Lampert, M., & Blunk, M. L. (Eds.). (1998). *Talking mathematics in school: Studies of teaching and learning.* Cambridge: Cambridge University Press.

Learned, W. S., & Wood, B. D. (1938). *The Student and His Knowledge.* New York: Carnegie Foundation.

Leonard, J. P., & Eurich, A. C. (Eds.). (1942). *An evaluation of modern education.* New York: Appleton-Century.

Levinson, L., & Stonehill, R. (1997). *Tried and true: Tested ideas for teaching and learning from the regional educational laboratories.* Washington, DC: U.S. Department of Education, Office of Educational Research and Improvement.

Lieberman, A. (1999). *School reform behind the scenes.* New York: Teachers College Press.

Lieberman, A., & Miller, L. (1999). *Teachers—Transforming their world and their work*. New York: Teachers College Press.

Lightfoot, S. L. (1983). *The good high school: Portraits of character and culture*. New York: Basic Books.

Lortie, D. C. (1975). *Schoolteacher*. Chicago: University of Chicago Press.

Mann, D. S. (Ed.). (1978). *Making change happen?* New York: Teachers College Press.

Martin, J. R. (1994). *Changing the educational landscape: Philosophy, women, and curriculum*. New York: Routledge.

McCutcheon, G. (1980). How do elementary teachers plan? The nature of planning and influences on it. *Elementary School Journal, 81*, 4–23.

McGuffey, W. H. (1879). *McGuffey's Second Eclectic Reader*. Cincinnati: Wilson, Hinkel & Co.

McLaughlin, M. W. (1978). Implementation as mutual adaptation: Change in classroom organization. In D. S. Mann (Ed.), *Making change happen?* (pp. 19–31). New York: Teachers College Press.

McLaughlin, M. W. (1978). Implementation of ESEA Title I: A problem of compliance. In D. S. Mann (Ed.), *Making change happen?* New York: Teachers College Press.

McLaughlin, M. W., & Oberman, I. (Eds.). (1996). *Teacher learning: New policies, new practices*. New York: Teachers College Press.

McLaughlin, M. W., & Talbert, J. (2001). *Professional communities and the work of high school teaching*. Chicago: University of Chicago Press.

McNeil, L. (1986). *Contradictions of control: School structure and school knowledge*. New York: Routledge.

McNeil, L. M. (2000). *Contradictions of school reform: Educational costs of standardized testing*. New York: Routledge.

McPherson, G. (1972). *Small town teacher*. Cambridge, MA: Harvard University Press.

Mertens, D. M. (1998). *Research methods in education and psychology: Integrating diversity with quantitative & qualitative approaches*. Thousand Oaks, CA: Sage Publications.

Miel, A. (1946). *Changing the curriculum, a social process*. New York: Appleton-Century Company.

Miles, M. B. (Ed.). (1964). *Innovation in education*. New York: Teachers College Press.

Miller, R. L. (1976). Individualized instruction in mathematics: A review of the research. *Mathematics Teacher, 69*, 345–351.

Moe, T., & Chubb, J. E. (1990). *Politics, markets, and America's schools*. Washington, DC: Brookings Institution.

Morgan-Fleming, B. (1997). Children's interpretations of curriculum events. *Teaching and Teacher Education, 13*(5), 499–511.

Musgrave, P. W. (1968). *The school as an organisation*. London: Macmillan.

National Assessment of Educational Progress. (1999). *National Assessment of Educational Progress*. Washington, DC: U.S. Dept. of Education, Office of Educational Research and Improvement, National Center for Education Statistics.

National Board for Professional Teaching Standards. (1991). *Toward high and rigorous standards for the teaching profession*. Washington, DC: Author.

National Commission on Excellence in Education. (1983). *A nation at risk: The imperative for education reform*. Washington, DC: U.S. Government Printing Office.

National Education Association. (1918). *Cardinal principles of secondary education*. Washington, DC: Author.

National Society for the Promotion of Industrial Education. (1907). Constitution. *NSPIE Bulletin, 1*, 10.

Neustadt, R. E., & May, E. R. (1986). *Thinking in time, the uses of history for decision-makers*. New York: The Free Press.

Noddings, N. (1992). *The challenge to care in schools*. New York: Teachers College Press.

Oakes, J. (1985). *Keeping track: How schools structure inequality*. New Haven: Yale University Press.

Oakes, J., & Sorotnik, K. A. (1986). *Critical perspectives on the organization and improvement of schooling*. Boston: Kluwer-Nijhoff.

Ogbu, J. (1974). *The next generation: An ethnography of education in an urban neighborhood*. New York: Academic Press.

Ong, W. (1971). *Rhetoric, romance, and technology*. Ithaca, NY: Cornell University Press.

Page, R. N. (1991). *Lower-track classrooms: A curricular and cultural perspective*. New York: Teachers College Press.

Palincsar, A. S., & Brown, A. L. (1986). Interactive teaching to promote independent learning from text. *Reading Teacher, 39*(8): 771–777.

Parker, F. W. (1891). *Notes of talks on teaching.* New York.

Pellegrino, J., Chudowsky, N., & Glaser, R. (Eds.). (2000). *Knowing What Students Know: The Science and Design of Educational Assessment.* Washington, DC: National Research Council.

Peshkin, A. (1978). *Growing up American: Schooling and the survival of community.* Chicago: University of Chicago Press.

Peshkin, A. (1982). *The imperfect union.* Chicago: University of Chicago Press.

Peshkin, A. (1986). *God's choice: The total world of a fundamentalist Christian school.* Chicago: University of Chicago Press.

Peshkin, A. (1991). *The color of strangers, the color of friends: The play of ethnicity in school and community.* Chicago: University of Chicago Press.

Peshkin, A. (1997). *Places of memory: Whiteman's schools and Native American communities.* Chicago: University of Chicago Press.

Peshkin, A. (2001). *Permissible advantage?: The moral consequences of elite schooling.* Chicago: University of Chicago Press.

Peterson, P., Marx, R. W., & Clark, C. (1978). Teacher planning, teacher behavior, and student achievement. *American Educational Research Journal, 15,* 417–432.

Piaget, J. (1977). *The essential Piaget.* H. E. Gruber, & J. J. Voneche (Eds.). New York: Basic Books.

Pinar, W. (1994). *Autobiography, politics, and sexuality: Essays in curriculum theory 1972–1992.* New York: P. Lang.

Pinar, W. F. (Ed.). (1999). *Contemporary curriculum discourses.* New York: Peter Lang.

Pinar, W. F., Reynolds, W. M., Slattery, P., & Taubman, P. M. (1995). *Understanding curriculum: An introduction to the study of historical and contemporary curriculum discourses:* New York: Peter Lang.

Popkewitz, T. S. (Ed.). (1987). *The formation of school subjects: The struggle for creating an American institution.* New York: Falmer.

Porter, A., Archbald, D., & Tyree, A., Jr. (1991). In S. J. Fuhrman, & B. Malen (Eds.). (1991). *The politics of curriculum and testing* (pp. 11–36). London: Falmer Press.

Porter, A., and associates. (1994). *Reform of high school science and opportunity to learn.* New Brunswik, NJ: Consortium for Policy Research in Education.

Posner, G. J., & Strike, K. A. (1976). A categorization scheme for principles of sequencing content. *Review of Educational Research, 46,* 665–690.

Powell, A. G., Farrar, E., & Cohen, D. K. (1985). *The shopping mall high school.* Boston: Houghton Mifflin.

Purpel, J., & Shapiro, D. (1995). *Beyond liberation and excellence: Reconstructing the public discourse on education.* Westport, CN: Bergin & Garvey.

Rappoport, A. (1960). *Fights, games, and debates.* Ann Arbor: University of Michigan Press.

Ravitch, D. (1985). *The schools we deserve.* New York: Basic Books.

Ravitch, D. (1983). *The troubled crusade: American education, 1945–1980.* New York: Basic Books.

Ravitch, D. (2000). *Left back: A century of failed school reforms.* New York: Simon and Schuster.

Reagan, T. G. (2000). *Non-western educational traditions: Alternative approaches to educational thought and practice* (2nd ed.). Mahwah, NJ: Lawrence Erlbaum Associates.

Reid, W. A. (1999). *Curriculum as institution and practice: Essays in the deliberative tradition.* Mahwah, NJ: Lawrence Erlbaum Associates.

Resnick, L. (1987). *Education and learning to think.* Washington, DC: National Academy Press.

Rice, J. M. (1897). The futility of the spelling grind *The Forum, 23,* 163–172.

Rickover, H. G. (1959). *Education and Freedom.* New York: Dutton.

Riley, J. (1984a). The problems of drafting distance education materials. *British Journal of Educational Technology, 15,* 192–204.

Riley, J. (1984b). The problems of revising drafts of distance education materials. *British Journal of Educational Technology, 15,* 205–226.

Riley, J. (1984c). An explanation of drafting behaviors in the production of distance education materials. *British Journal of Educational Technology, 15,* 226–238.

Rosenberg, N., & Birdzell, L. E., Jr. (1986). *How the West grew rich. The economic transformation of the industrial world.* New York: Basic Books.

Rudolph, F. (1977). *Curriculum: A history of the American undergraduate course of study since 1636*. San Francisco: Jossey-Bass.

Rugg, H. (1927). *National society for the study of education. Foundations of curriculum making. Twenty-sixth yearbook*. Bloomington, IL: Public School Publishing Company.

Rugg, H. O. (1941). *That men may understand*. New York: Doubleday, Duran and Company.

Rugg, H., & Counts, G. S. (1927). A critical appraisal of current methods of curriculum-making. In Harold Rugg (Ed.), *Foundations and technique of curriculum-making. Twenty-sixth yearbook*. Chicago: National Society for the Study of Education.

Rugg, H., & Shumaker, A. (1928). *The child-centered school*. New York: World Book Company.

Runyon, Laura L. (1900). A Day with the new education. *Chautaquan, XXX*, 590–591.

Salisbury, R. H. (1980). *Citzen participation in the public schools*. Lexington, MA: Lexington Books.

Sarason, S. (1982). *The culture of the school and the problem of change*. Boston: Allyn and Bacon.

Saxe, R. (1975). *School–community interaction*. Berkeley: McCutchan.

Saylor, G., & Alexander, W. (1954). *Curriculum planning for better teaching and learning*. New York: Holt, Rinehart, and Winston.

Schaffarzick, J. (1975). *The consideration of curriculum change at the local level*. Unpublished Ph.D. dissertation, Stanford University.

Schein, E. H. (1987). *The clinical perspective in field work*. Newbury Park, CA: Sage Publications.

Schlesinger, A. (1990). When ethnic studies are un-American. *Wall Street Journal*, April 23.

Schmidt, W. H., McKnight, C., Houang, R., Wang, H.-C., Wiley, D. E., Cogan, L., & Wolfe, R. (2001). *Why schools matter: A cross-national comparison of curriculum and learning*. San Francisco, CA: Jossey-Bass.

Schoen, H. L. (1976). Self-paced mathematics instruction: How effective has it been in secondary and post-secondary schools? *Mathematics Teacher, 69*, 352–357.

Schubert, W. (1980). *Curriculum books: The first eighty years*. Lanham, MD: University Press of America.

Schwab, J. (1969). *College curriculum and student protest*. Chicago: University of Chicago Press.

Schwab, J. (1970). *The practical: A language for curriculum*. Washington, DC: National Education Association.

Schwab, J. (1971). The practical: Arts of eclectic. *School Review, 80*, 493–542.

Schwab, J. (1973). The practical 3: Translation into curriculum. *School Review, 81*, 501–522.

Schwille, J., Porter, A., Belli, G., Floden, R., Freeman, D., Knappen, L., Kuhs, T., & Schmidt, W. (1983). Teachers as policy brokers in the content of elementary school mathematics. In L. S. Shulman & G. Sykes (Eds.), *Handbook of Teaching Policy*. New York: Longman.

Seguel, M. L. (1966). *The curriculum field: Its formative Years*. New York: Teachers College Press.

Seligman, M. E. P. (1975). *Helplessness*. San Francisco: W. H. Freeman.

Seybolt, R. F. (1925). Source studies in American colonial education: The private school. Bulletin no. 28. Urbana, IL: University of Illinois Bureau of Educational Research.

Shaver, J., & Berlak, H. (1968). *Democracy, pluralism, and the social studies*. Boston: Houghton-Mifflin.

Shockley, B., Michalove, B., & Allen, J. (1995). *Engaging families: Connecting home and school literacy communities*. Portsmouth, NH: Heinemann.

Silberman, C. (1971). *Crisis in the classroom: The remaking of American education*. New York: Vintage Books.

Sizer, T. R. (1984, reissued in 1992). *Horace's compromise: The dilemma of the American high school*. Boston: Houghton Mifflin.

Sizer, T. R. (1996). *Horace's hope: What works for the American high school*. Boston: Houghton Mifflin.

Skinner, B. F. (Burrhus Frederic). (1974). *About behaviorism*. New York: A. A. Knopf.

Slattery, P. (1995). *Curriculum development in the postmodern era*. New York: Garland.

Slavin, R. E., & Fashola, O. S. (1998). *Show me the evidence! Proven and promising programs for America's schools*. Thousand Oaks, CA: Corwin Press.

Smith, B. O., & Orlovsky, D. (1978). *Curriculum development*. Chicago: Rand McNally.

Smith, E. R., Tyler, R. W. and the evaluation staff. (1942). *Appraising and recording student progress*. New York: Harper and Brothers.

Smith, M., & O'Day, J. (1990). Systemic school reform. In *Politics of Education Association Yearbook* (pp. 233–267). New York: Falmer Press.

Spencer, H. (1878). What knowledge is most worth? In Education: Intellectual, moral, and Physical (ch. 1). London: Watts.

Spring, J. (2001). *Deculturalization and the struggle for equality: A brief history of the education of dominated cultures in the United States.* Boston: McGraw-Hill.

Sternberg, R. J. (1997). *Successful intelligence.* New York: Plume.

Stevenson, H. W., & Stigler, J. W. (1992). *The learning gap: Why our schools are failing and what we can learn from Japanese and Chinese education.* New York: Simon & Schuster.

Stodolsky, S. (1988). *The subject matters: Classroom activity in math and social studies.* Chicago: University of Chicago Press.

Stratemeyer, F. B., Forkner, H. L., & McKim, M. G. (1947). *Developing a curriculum for modern living.* New York: Teachers College Bureau of Publications.

Stutchbury, O. (1973). *The use of principle.* London: The Boydell Press.

Sykes, G. (1990). Fostering teacher professionalism in schools. In R. Elmore, and Associates (Eds.), *Restructuring Schools* (pp. 59–96). San Francisco: Jossey-Bass.

Taba, H. (1962). *Curriculum development, theory and practice.* New York: Harcourt Brace.

Tanner, D., & Tanner, L. N. (1970). *Curriculum development.* New York: Macmillan.

Thayer, V. T. (1928). *The passing of the recitation.* New York: Heath.

Thorndike, E. L. (1924). Mental discipline in high school studies. *Journal of Educational Psychology, 15,* 1–22, 83–98.

Toulmin, S. (1958). *The uses of argument.* Cambridge: Cambridge University Press.

Tournier, M. (1972). *The ogre.* (Barbara Bray, Trans.). Garden City, NY: Doubleday.

Tucker, H., & Zeigler, H. (1980). *Professionals versus the public: Attitudes, communication, and response in school districts.* New York: Longman.

Tyack, D., & Cuban, L. (1995). *Tinkering toward utopia.* Cambridge, MA: Harvard University Press.

Tyler, R. W. (1949). *Basic principles of curriculum and instruction.* Chicago: University of Chicago Press.

Ulich, R. (1947). Three thousand years of educational wisdom. Cambridge, MA: Harvard University Press.

U.S. Department of Education, Office of Educational Research and Improvement. (1997). *Tested ideas for teaching and learning from the regional educational laboratories.* Washington, DC: Author.

Vickers, G. (1968). *Value systems and social process.* New York: Basic Books.

Vickers, G. (1973). *Making institutions work.* New York: Wiley.

Walker, D. F. (1970). Toward more effective curriculum projects in art. *Studies in Art Education, 11,* 3–13.

Walker, D. F. (1971a). A study of deliberation in three curriculum projects. *Curriculum Theory Network, 7,* 118–134.

Walker, D. F. (1971b). *Strategies of deliberation in three curriculum development projects.* Unpublished Ph.D. dissertation, Stanford University.

Walker, D. (1971c). A naturalistic model for curriculum development. *School Review, 80,* 51–65.

Walker, D. F. (1975). Curriculum development in an art project. In W. A. Reid & D. F. Walker (Eds.), *Case studies in curriculum change: Great Britain and the United States.* London: Routledge and Kegan Paul.

Walker, D. (1992). Methodological issues in curriculum research. In Philip Jackson (Ed.), *Handbook of research on curriculum.* New York: Macmillan.

Walker, D. F., & Schaffarzick, Jon (1972). Comparing curricula. *Review of Educational Research, 44,* 83–112.

Wang, M. C., Haertel, G. D., & Walberg, H. J. (1998). *Achieving student success: A handbook of widely implemented, research-based reform models.* Publication Series No. 12. Philadelphia, PA: Mid-Atlantic Laboratory for Student Success.

Webster, N. (1789). *An American selection of lessons in reading and speaking.* Boston, printed by Isaiah Thomas and Ebenezer T. Andrews.

Webster, N. (1831). *The American spelling book.* New York, George F. Cooledge.

Weigand, V. K. (1970). A study of subordinate skills in science problem solving. In Robert M. Gagne (Ed.), *Basic studies of learning hierarchies in school subjects.* Berkeley, CA: University of California.

Welch, W. W. (1979). Twenty years of science curriculum development: A look back. In David C. Berliner (Ed.), *Review of Research in Education 7* (pp. 282–306). Washington, DC: American Educational Research Association.

Welch, W. W., & Walberg, H. J. (1972). A national experiment in curriculum evaluation. *American Educational Research Journal, 9,* 373–383.

Westbury, I. (1978). Research into classroom processes: A review of ten years' work. *Journal of Curriculum Studies, 10,* 283–308, p. 288.

Wilson, J. W., Cahen, L. S., & Begle, E. G. (1968–72). *NLSMA Reports* (Vol. 1–25). Stanford University: The Board of Trustees of Leland Stanford Junior University.

Wirt, F., & Kirst, M. W. (1997). *The political dynamics of American education.* Berkeley, CA: McCutchan.

Wright, H. K. (2000). Nailing Jell-o to the wall: Pinpointing aspects of state-of-the-art curriculum theorizing. *Educational Researcher, 29*(5), 4–13.

Yankelovich, D. (1999). *The magic of dialogue: Transforming conflict into cooperation.* New York: Simon and Schuster.

Yinger, R. (1977). *A study of teacher planning.* Unpublished doctoral dissertation, East Lansing: Michigan State University.

Zahorik, M. (1975). Teachers' planning models. *Educational Leadership, 33,* 34–159.

Index